D0874040

LAW, INSTITUTIONS, AND THE GLOBAL ENVIRONMENT

LAW, INSTITUTIONS, AND THE GLOBAL ENVIRONMENT

PAPERS AND ANALYSIS OF THE PROCEEDINGS

of the Conference on

Legal and Institutional Responses to

Problems of the Global Environment

jointly sponsored by

The American Society of International Law

and

The Carnegie Endowment for International Peace

edited by

JOHN LAWRENCE HARGROVE

OCEANA PUBLICATIONS, INC.—DOBBS FERRY, N.Y.
A. W. SIJTHOFF—LEIDEN
1972

Library of Congress Cataloging in Publication Data

Conference on Legal and Institutional Responses to
  Problems of the Global Environment, Arden House, 1971.
  Law, institutions, and the global environment.

    The conference, held in Sept. 1971, was sponsored by
the American Society of International Law and the Carnegie
Endowment for International Peace.
    1. Environmental law. 2. Environmental policy.
3. International agencies. I. Hargrove, John Lawrence,
ed. II. American Society of International Law.
III. Carnegie Endowment for International Peace.
IV. Title.
Law   301.31   72-1153
ISBN 0-379-00024-5   (Oceana)
ISBN 90-286-0142-2   (Sijthoff)

Manufactured in the United States of America.

PREFACE

This volume comprises, for the most part, papers prepared for the Conference on Legal and Institutional Responses to Problems of the Global Environment, jointly sponsored by the Carnegie Endowment for International Peace and the American Society of International Law, and held at Arden House, Harriman, New York, September, 1971. A smaller portion of the book consists of the brief essays which introduce three of its four main parts, and which contain analysis distilled by the editor from the five days of discussion sessions of the conference. The conference was made possible through a grant to the Society from the National Science Foundation, supplemented by funds from the Council on Environmental Quality, and the sponsors are deeply grateful for this support.

Participants in the conference (of whom a full list appears at page ix) consisted of legal advisers and other officials of international organizations with special interests in problems of the environment, certain government officials, and members of the academic community. The meeting was the fifth in the series of conferences of official legal advisers convened by the American Society of International Law, and the first in which the Society has had the good fortune to be joined in cosponsorship by the Carnegie Endowment for International Peace.

The conference papers reproduced here speak for themselves, although a word about their arrangement is in order. The editor has chosen to introduce the volume with Abram Chayes' "International Institutions for the Environment", in the belief that the questions dealt with by all the succeeding material are best examined within a framework of practical issues upon which fairly early action within the international community might be contemplated. Professor Chayes' paper on "institutional" issues serves this purpose, even for much of those succeeding portions of the book which deal with more purely "legal" matters; for many questions about both the content and the method of international lawmaking for the environment are found to be closely bound up with preliminary questions about new or existing institutions.

It should be noted that a number of papers and other documentation, largely descriptive of the work of international organizations in the environmental field, were submitted to the conference, in some cases having been specially prepared for it by representatives of those international organizations. The conference greatly profited from this material. It has not been included in the present volume, because of necessary limitations of space and because of the belief that its reproduction here would in some measure duplicate material now available among the documentation prepared for the United Nations Conference on the Human Environment or elsewhere. The single exception is Thomas

Mensah's "The IMCO Experience", which it seemed especially useful to include because of the backdrop it supplies for the considerable discussion of IMCO conventions which appears elsewhere in the book.

The authors of papers reproduced in this volume, except for Mr. Serwer and Mr. Mensah, are members of the Society's Panel on International Law and the Global Environment or that on The Law of the Sea. These Panels are chaired, respectively, by Stuart Udall and Professor Milton Katz.

The essays at the opening of parts II, III, and IV of the volume, labelled "Editorial Analysis," require some explanation. As indicated, they have been drawn by the editor from major points made in the conference's informal discussion sessions. The reasoning behind this approach was that a distillation and systematization would enable the reader to benefit from the discussions, without imposing upon him the formidable burden of assimilating the entire verbatim transcript of the proceedings. For such a benefit, however, the reader pays a price: what is presented to him is highly selective; it contains many of the editor's own extrapolations and inferences; and it doubtless is overlaid with the editor's own prejudices. The reader might have preferred to be left to do his own distilling and extrapolating, feeling that he could have done a better job, and the editor would be the last to challenge him on this point.

The essays are intended for the most part to be complementary to the papers, rather than introductions to them, and the editor has undertaken to avoid duplications of substance. They serve more to identify issues, and major positions on those issues, than to provide exhaustive analyses. The omission of one or two of the more lawyerly topics within the field of international environmental protection — e.g., the question of machinery for dispute-settlement — may be surprising for a meeting consisting predominantly of lawyers. These omissions are explained simply by the fact that time did not permit thorough treatment of everything embraced within the conference agenda.

Finally, it should be understood that while the essays were drawn from the conference discussions, in the manner just described, they do not amount to a "report" of the conference, and none of the views which they express can properly be imputed to any individual participant or be regarded as necessarily having commanded general support by the conference. At the same time, the editor claims no credit for any useful insight the essays might be found to contain. The credit for making them possible must obviously go to the conference participants, including in no small measure Oscar Schachter, Deputy Executive Director of UNITAR, whose sage, witty and ironfisted chairmanship contributed greatly to the worthwhileness of the meeting. The editor himself assumes full responsibility for any errors of fact or judgment or infelicities of text.

Special thanks are due to Misses Jan Schneider, Katherine Schwering,

vi

and Becky Ford, for their invaluable assistance in readying the conference papers for publication. Similar thanks go to Mrs. Barbara Phillips, Mrs. Dorothea Bodison, and Mrs. Audrey Goba of the Society staff for their diligent work on the preparation of the manuscript.

John Lawrence Hargrove
Washington, January 1972.

CONFERENCE ON INTERNATIONAL LEGAL AND
INSTITUTIONAL RESPONSES TO PROBLEMS OF THE
GLOBAL ENVIRONMENT

Timothy Atkeson, Esq., General Counsel, Council on Environmental
Quality

J.Alan Beesley, Esq., Legal Adviser, Department of External Affairs of
Canada

Professor Richard B. Bilder, University of Wisconsin Law School

Dr. Hans Blix, Counselor, Swedish Foreign Office

Professor Abram Chayes, Harvard Law School

Paolo Contini, Esq., Legal Counsel, Food & Agriculture Organization

Alden Lowell Doud, Esq., Assistant Legal Adviser for Environmental
Affairs, Department of State

Professor Rene Jean Dupuy, Professor of International Law, University
of Nice and Secretary-General of the Hague Academy of International Law

Arthur Z. Gardiner, Jr., Esq., General Counsel, Agency for International Development

Professor Richard N. Gardner, Columbia University School of Law

Professor L.F.E. Goldie, Director of International Legal Studies, Syracuse University College of Law

Dr. H. Golsong, Director of Legal Affairs, Council of Europe

Mr. Frank Gutteridge, Legal Adviser, World Health Organization

M. Heenan, Esq., Deputy Director, General Legal Division, United Nations

John Lawrence Hargrove, Esq., Director of Studies, American Society
of International Law

Mr. John Haskins, Agency for International Development

Mr. Arthur Heyman, Organization of American States

Mr. David Kay, Visiting Research Scholar, Carnegie Endowment for
International Peace

Robert McManus, Environmental Protection Agency

Thomas Mensah, Esq., Head of the Legal Division, Intergovernmental
Maritime Consultative Organization

Mr. R.L. Munteanu, Chief, Administrative and Common Services Division, World Meteorological Organization

TABLE OF CONTENTS

PART THREE. TOWARD AN INTERNATIONAL LAW OF ENVIRONMENTAL PROTECTION

PART FOUR. DEVELOPING INSTITUTIONAL PROCESSES AND STRUCTURES

PART ONE

A FRAMEWORK OF POLICY ISSUES

PART I.
A FRAMEWORK OF POLICY ISSUES

INTERNATIONAL INSTITUTIONS FOR THE ENVIRONMENT

by *Abram Chayes**

I.

General Assembly resolution 2398 (XXIII) convened a United Nations Conference on the Human Environment, which is to be held in Stockholm in June, 1972. The purpose of the Conference is:

> to provide a framework for comprehensive consideration within the United Nations of the problems of the human environment in order to focus the attention of Governments and public opinion on the importance and urgency of this question and also to identify those aspects of it that can only or best be solved through international cooperation and agreement.[1]

The action of the General Assembly is only one index of the prominence of the environmental issue in world political and public attention. Another measure is a recent estimate that expenditures on environmental programs in fiscal 1972 by government agencies in the United States, federal, state and local, will aggregate $6 billion. Other nations, particularly in the northern hemisphere, if they do not see the issues with quite the same urgency as the United States, have turned increasing attention to problems of environmental pollution. It was the initiative of Sweden, itself deeply concerned about pollution of its atmosphere possibly emanating from transnational sources, that resulted in the decision to convene the Stockholm Conference.

The Conference is described as "action oriented." In practice, only a very few significant international actions can be taken in completed form at Stockholm, and these will, in effect, have been negotiated in advance.

For the most part, "action" at Stockholm means decisions "which would set forth the elements of the basic work program in the international field for the post-Conference period."[2] This so-called Level II (or action-plan level) program would consist of 20 to 30 items.

---

*The author, formerly the Legal Adviser, Department of State, is Professor of Law at the Harvard Law School.

1

Item VI on the Conference agenda is "The International Organizational Implications of Action Proposals." Since so much of the work of the Conference will consist of a program to be carried into effect in the months and years to follow, the success of the Conference as a whole is likely to hinge crucially on success in dealing with this agenda item.

From this point of view, the question of institutional arrangements is *the* international environmental issue.

II.

Institutional design for international environmental affairs depends on the basic conception of the environmental problem. For many, it appears as a threat of impending catastrophe. There is a fear that large-scale changes resulting from burgeoning human activity will, in the realtively near future, alter fundamentally the terms of human existence and may even affect the possibilities for human survival.

This is, by and large, the guise in which environmental issues have moved toward the center of the political stage in recent years. The apocalyptic note echoes, for example, in U Thant's celebrated Texas speech on "Human Environment and World Order".[3]

A conception of the environmental problem as a series of imminent threats suggests a need for drastic, even emergency action. The threatening substances or activities must be identified and strict limitations on permissible levels must be adopted and enforced. This in turn has certain rather straightforward institutional implications. It calls for a legislative body capable of establishing binding standards or norms and an enforcement authority with power to make conclusive determinations as to complicance. Logically enough, the Secretary General proposed just such an array of international decision-making institutions.

It requires very little acquaintance with the international system as presently constituted to realize that it would be unable to meet this institutional prescription. The resources both for legislation and enforcement at the international level are painfully slender, and they are not likely to be increased in the immediate future. If the environmental problem really does take the form of an imminent threat of irreversible catastrophe, there is little basis for hope that the international community can respond in time with the necessary action.

Fortunately, scientific investigation of environmental phenomena over the past several years, has made it increasingly difficult to substantiate this view of impending environmental crisis. Almost every responsible scientific study has produced a consensus not on imminent threat, but on uncertainty, risk and the need for further research and study.

Moreover, although it is easy to recognize the many insults to local or regional environments caused by industrial activity, inadequate waste

2

disposal, improper agricultural practices and the like, it has been difficult to identify more than a handful of activities that raise even a possible short-term threat to the integrity of the biosphere. For example, the 1970 MIT summer study, *Man's Impact on the Global Environment*, focussing on "environmental problems whose cumulative effects on ecological systems are so large and prevalent that they have worldwide significance" was able to identify less than ten processes and substances requiring careful surveillance on this account.[4]

This is not to say that there is no ground for concern. If it has been impossible to demonstrate imminent peril, it has been equally difficult to dispel the worry that some of these processes or substances might pose a near term threat. On one or two items, such as ocean dumping or oil pollution of the seas, an international consensus, technical and political, seems to be reaching the point where it will provide a basis for rather stringent international regulatory action.

But the central conception of the global environmental issue is shifting. The sense of immediate threat has receded, but it has become increasingly clear that present trends in population, energy production and industrial activity cannot be extrapolated indefinitely without reaching the limits of the capacity of the earth to sustain them. If the crisis point in this sense is not at hand, neither is it geologically remote; and the lead times for corrective action are very long.

For example, Dr. Thomas Malone is inclined to believe that under present conditions the maximum limit on global energy production will be reached in 100 to 150 years. He suggests that it would take ten years of intensive scientific research to establish whether there is such a limit, and if so what it is. He estimates that the reversal of existing practices relating to demand for and production of energy might take another 30 years. But the establishment of the political institutions that can take and carry into effect the decisions necessary to reverse those practices — and these decisions must be essentially global in scope — involves, absent catastrophe, a period of slow growth and maturation extending over decades.

The fundamental message of the environment is that mankind inhabits a finite planet with finite resources. If the human race is to survive under conditions that make life worthwhile, it must devise ways of maximizing the productivity of this finite stock of resources and of sharing the product in some rational and equitable way.

If this conception is correct, the environmental issue does not consist primarily of a discrete set of problems each with a finite technical/legal solution. And what is required from political agencies is not a series of clearly identifiable "environmental decisions" matching up problems and solutions. This kind of response will be needed in some cases, notably where serious existing degradation must be repaired or imminent hazard averted. But it would be profoundly wrong to think that once these

3

actions have been taken, the problem of the environment will have been settled, and we can all go about our business.

The most important and most difficult political requirement is to ensure that environmental considerations are systematically and explicity taken into account across the whole spectrum of legislative and administrative action. This will involve pervasive adaptation of existing decision-making institutions at every level. Moreover, the new awareness of environmental constraints implies a political process extending indefinitely in time. Its characteristic instruments will not be policing and regulation of environmental insults, but planning and management of environmental resources.

For such a planning process to succeed it must have much better access to and understanding of scientific and technical information about the environment. But it is a mistake to think that the issues are susceptible of scientific resolution. Pollution is most often a by-product of other and highly valued human activities — driving automobiles, killing anopheles mosquitoes, generating power, making steel, building houses, and the like. The problem is to conduct these approved activities in such a way and perhaps at such a level as to avoid the harmful side effects. This in turn means that those activities must be carried out at higher real cost. For the underdeveloped countries higher costs may mean slower development. In some cases, ecological values themselves may come into conflict, as in birth control, where adverse health side effects must be weighed against the efficacy of the pill in keeping down birth rates.

Environmental goals will therefore often confront competing considerations — economic efficiency, income distribution, various social objectives, even national security. The weight that is given these competing considerations and the choice among them, if that becomes necessary, reflect the fundamental values of a society, registered through its political processes and institutions. It is apparent that these weights and choices will by no means be uniform at different places around the globe or at different times in history.

III.

The institutional implications of this view of the environmental problem are a good deal more complex and equivocal than the imperatives that would derive from imminent threat.

Mr. George Kennan has proposed that international action on the environment should be carried forward in a new organization, established outside the United Nations by the major industrial and polluting states of the northern hemisphere.[5] Such a proposal simply misconceives the problem.

Both the bulk of the earth's resources and the bulk of the people who

4

must share them live not in the northern countries with a common culture and heritage and a long tradition of international intercourse. They are concentrated in the new countries organized in still unstable societies, striving for a share of the goods of life.

The developing countries make their contribution to many of the most serious current threats to the global environment: DDT and oil in the oceans, particulate matter in the atmosphere, the explosive concentration of urban populations.

Already, some of the practices of the developing countries for the exploitation of their own resources of agricultural land, forests, water and minerals may be needlessly depleting the common stock. It would be to the interest of all to induce and assist the new countries now to adopt better resource management practices without sacrifice of the goal of rapid development.

Today, more than 25 percent of the basic raw materials for United States industry comes from abroad, mostly from the developing countries. The figures for other industrial countries must be comparable, or even larger. This is a crude measure of the current dependence of the industrial north on the goodwill and cooperation of the developing countries in resource management. It is bound to grow at an increasing rate as man's needs press more insistently against the finitude of his resources. As the new countries gain in economic strength and political coherence, it will be increasingly difficult to exact cooperation by northern military and economic power.

To quote U Thant:

The developing countries are intimately concerned in these problems, which are crucial both to their own future and to the future of the environment. Their voices must be heard, and listened to, even if at the outset their technical contribution may be relatively small. Their confidence and their cooperation, as representing the largest part of the world's population, are vital. Otherwise we shall once again increase the gap between advanced and developing nations which is already one of the major sources of tension in the world.[6]

The need to implicate the developing countries both in the process of identifying and combating current threats and in the long-term planning and management of resources cannot be met in the setting of a rich man's club. For this purpose, there is no alternative to the U.N. The developing countries would simply not countenance an effort to bypass the international forum that they regard as peculiarly their own.

Moreover, if the major powers were deliberately to reject the United Nations as a central focus for international cooperation on a matter of this magnitude, one wonders what the effect of such a vote of no confidence would be on the international organization itself.

This is not to say that international environmental problems require global solutions uniformly applicable. On the contrary, as has been noted, most of the problems, or at least the solutions, are national or regional in scope. In particular, with regard to air and water pollution from industrial activity with which Mr. Kennan seems to have been primarily concerned, action in a regional forum comprised of highly industrialized nations would be wholly appropriate. If the problem is seen as one in pollution abatement, remedial action can be pursued through ECE, where East-West cooperation is thought to be decisive; otherwise through NATO's Committee on Challenges to Modern Society. If the problem is to moderate the impact of domestic pollution control programs on the economic position of domestic industry in foreign trade, the countries involved are again the highly industrialized nations that compete in the international market place. They are organized for the discussion of economic and trade matters in the OECD and GATT. These organizations have already begun to consider the economic and trade impacts of the domestic pollution control programs of their members.

One of the important specifications for any global machinery is that it be able to accommodate, and indeed to stimulate this kind of regional or multinational activity.

IV.

A second approach to international environmental institutions is exemplified by U Thant's call for "global authority" within the framework of the U.N. "with the authority to insure that the agreed measures are the right ones and that they are actually carried out... able, if necessary to police and enforce its decisions." U Thant recognized that such an authority would be "something new," and would "depart radically from the hitherto sacred paths of national sovereignty."[7] Though he did not flesh out the details of this proposal, it sounded as though he had in mind a new specialized agency, some said a "super-agency."

Some academic commentators, including the present author, concurred at least in general with the Secretary General's prescription. But not a single government of any importance has endorsed it, and one must assume that, as a practical matter it is dead.

It is no secret that there is little enthusiasm for the U.N. specialized agencies among governments, particularly the few that supply the great bulk of the funds. This may account for some of the reluctance to embark on another such venture. But there is also a sound insight that the specialized agency format is not well adapted as a focal point for environmental concerns at the global level.

In the first place, a policy-making organ having as members all or substantially all of the governments of the world seems unnecessary. There will be few occasions in the immediate future for the elaboration of uniform standards or regulations binding on governments worldwide. As suggested above, immediate needs for standard-setting can be met in a regional context or by ad hoc conferences on specific threats as they come ripe for global action. And for policy planning, co-ordination and review, the hundred-member assembly of the typical specialized agency is too unwieldy an instrument.

Secondly, more than a score of U.N. organs or agencies are already engaged in environmental programs and activities. Some of these are of very great scope and importance. A partial list of only the most significant would include WMO's World Weather Watch, WHO's work on fresh water supplies and sewage disposal, FAO's broad concerns with resource management, ILO's regulation of the environment of the workplace, UNESCO's Intergovernmental Oceanographic Commission and Man and the Biosphere Program, IMCO's sponsorship of conventions on marine pollution, ICAO's work on air and noise pollution connected with civil air transport, and IAEA's surveillance of radio-nuclides in the environment.

Nor can even a truncated list end with these. ECOSOC has responsibility under the U.N. Charter for international cooperation in the economic and social spheres, and it has been active on urban environmental problems and in the population field. UNDP, with its mission of coordinating the development support activities of the U.N. must constantly face the problem of introducing environmental considerations into development planning. So does the World Bank group. So do the regional economic commissions and the newer organizations like UNCTAD and UNIDO.

It is apparent that environmental activities are badly fragmented throughout the U.N. system, and this is one of the problems to be solved. But the solution is not to divest the existing organs and agencies of their environmental concerns to bring them together in a new operating agency. If something may be lacking in the execution of these programs, there can be no doubt that in most cases they are closely related to the agency's main-line responsibilities. For this reason, it would make no administrative sense, as a general rule, to remove the environmental programs from their existing locations and vest them in a single new agency. For the specialized agencies proper, there is the further consideration that the programs have been undertaken by appropriate action of their governing bodies under their charter powers.

On the bureaucratic side, a new agency would find it difficult to escape existing staffing patterns, regulations and practices. These would impose undesirable rigidities and might interfere with what both U Thant and George Kennan agree is necessary: a staff of "experts, scientists and scholars who will be true international servants, bound by no national or political mandate, by nothing in fact, other than dedication to the work in hand."[8]

Finally, a new specialized agency would be one among many. The others are older. They have longer traditions and well established relations with constituencies and within national and international bureaucracies. The new agency would not be well placed to exercise a leadership or co-ordinating function.

V.

A third possibility would be to use the U.N. system in its present form, simply expanding the work of the specialized agencies and other existing organs as needed to carry the new load of environmental affairs. Many of the papers submitted by the agencies in preparation for the Stockholm Conference seem, at least tacitly, to adopt this approach.

Even if all the organizations in the bewildering array listed above were efficient, effective and well managed, they would provide a setting that is far too fragmented for the conduct of international environmental affairs. Environmental policy cuts across the traditional functional specialties of agriculture, health, labor, transport, industrial development and the like. Some central point for the development, coordination and evaluation of policy and programs is needed. Most of the agency reports and certainly most outside commentators recognize this need.

No existing agency has, or can achieve this necessary overall perspective. In this respect, the international organizational problem is not unlike that which confronts national governments internally, and which in the United States resulted in the establishment of the Council on Environmental Quality. The problem with the specialized agencies, like their functional counterparts in national governments, is precisely that they are specialized.

Moreover, the organizations and agencies in the existing U.N. system are not uniformly effective, efficient and business-like. The Jackson Report[9] has documented in great detail the overlapping, duplication, bureaucratic infighting and jurisdictional quarrels that impair the capacity of the system to carry out U.N. development policy and programs. There seems little doubt that similar deficiencies would disqualify the system, in its present form, as a vehicle for developing and carrying out global environmental policies and programs — especially so, since much of the operational side would be related to development activities. Some of the changes suggested by the Jackson Report are being undertaken. But the process will be slow at best, and faces inherent difficulties in the fundamentally decentralized character of the U.N. system.

One suggestion for dealing with the problem of lack of coordination has been to designate a "lead agency" for each aspect of the environment requiring international attention. WMO would be the lead agency on matters concerning the atmosphere, WHO on fresh water supply, FAO on land management, and so on. The designated lead agency would have responsibility for developing a coordinated plan using fully the existing resources and skills of the entire U.N. system for an attack on the particular problem.

The question of which agency should take the lead in a particular area is not always free from doubt. Ocean pollution is a good example. And to raise the question in this form does not seem the best way to minimize bureaucratic jealousies and jurisdictional controversies. Moreover, the approach does not avoid the fatal defect of trying to divide "the environment" into sectoral pigeonholes, without providing any single focus for articulation of overall policy.

۰ ۰ ۰ ۰ ۰ ۰

Neither a new organization outside the U.N. nor a new agency within it, nor the system as it presently stands can effectively meet the organizational requirements for international environmental affairs. What seems to be needed, at a minimum, is some form of high level policy planning, coordination and review unit within the U.N. proper. This is the conclusion to which most thoughtful students of the problem are coming. It has the double merit of being, in broad outline, politically feasible as well as substantively appropriate for the present stage of international environmental action. Properly established and operated, such an organization would have the capacity to grow and develop, so as to be able to accept new functions and responsibilities as they emerge.

Before examining the functions and structure of this unit, in somewhat further detail, it is useful to consider a second major element of an institutional system for effective international cooperation in environmental affairs — the scientific component.

VI.

In the last analysis, decisions on environmental policy, like all government decisions, are political acts registering choices among essentially incommensurable values. But increasingly in modern time, these value choices have to be made in a context heavily colored by scientific knowledge (or uncertainty), and with an awareness of available technical possibilities and their benefits and burdens.

This is especially true for environmental affairs. In fact, the emergence of environmental issues to the forefront of public and political attention has been a function of increasing scientific understanding of the facts, or at least the risks of the present course of events.

There can be no monopoly, of course, on scientific advice to political leaders. Scientific work on problems of the environment has been conducted in ordinary course by the world scientific community for thousands of years — back at least to the hydraulic engineers of Egypt and Babylon. In one sense, perhaps the most essential, the understanding of humankind itself, has been the major goal of the whole scientific enterprise.

In the future, as in the past, the great bulk of environmental research will be carried forward by hundreds of individual scientists working in a great variety of institutional settings — universities, scientific institutes public and private, government agencies national and international, and the like.

There is no reason to believe that this pluralistic attack — under the scientific ethic of freedom of research in pursuit of truth — will fail to produce the major results in this field that it has elsewhere in scientific endeavor. Quite the contrary, efforts to impose an excessive tidiness on the organic growth of science are foredoomed.

Moreover, there is a special reason for reliance on widely dispersed scientific and technical activity on environmental matters: Most of the pressing environmental problems are not global in extent but are rooted in and qualified by the unique characteristics of a particular geographical or ecological region. To a large extent they must be studied on the spot, and this is increasingly true the more the focus is on the elements of a technical solution. For this purpose, the values, the economics and the cultural characteristics of the region involved may be crucial.

Without denying or detracting form these conclusions, both scientists and political leaders have voiced a need for some further concentration of scientific responsibility and research activity on global environmental problems.

The International Council of Scientific Unions, the organized expression of the international scientific community, has for a number of years given heavy emphasis to environmental questions. It recently established a Scientific Committee on the Protection of the Environment (SCOPE). At the request of the Secretary General, SCOPE has actively participated in the preparatory work for the Stockholm Conference.

In discussions between American and Russian scientists in the Dartmouth Conference at Kiev in early July the subject of a world environment research institute or institutes was explored. Although no decision was reached, the Soviet response was favorable and the communique stated that the question should be pursued.

The United States Senate has considered a resolution calling for a world environmental research institute.

These and other expressions suggest that there is a need for informed, unbiased and credible judgment on (1) the state of scientific knowledge on environmental threats or problems as they arise, (2) priority requirements for research and investigation, and (3) assessment of the technical implications of particular processes or policies.

It should be recognized that on many such questions it will not be possible to achieve unamimity or even broad consensus. More fundamentally, it may be granted that on issues of such political sensitivity there is no such thing as "pure" scientific fact, uncolored by preconceptions and assumptions, perhaps unconscious, carrying policy overtones. Government leaders and the general public must come to understand better these inherent charactersitics and limitations of scientific opinion. Nevertheless, it is important to have a source of scientific and technical judgment that is insulated as fully as possible from these distortions, and in which the discipline of professional standards and the appraisal of professional colleagues will have the widest purchase.

The functions thus far described are primarily advisory. They could be carried out by a high level council of scientific advisers to the U.N. environmental unit. The council could work through a system of panels, ad hoc advisory committees, study groups and the like, on the model of a national academy of sciences or the President's Science Advisory Committee in the United States. A case can be made that it is desirable to go further and vest this advisory group with one or more internationally funded operating research facilities:

All of the organizational endorsers of a world environmental institute cited above have assumed that it would include a research component. Their judgment is entitled to considerable weight.

On the merits, there is arguably a special international responsibility for scientific research in the more than 70 percent of the biosphere that lies outside national jurisdictions. It is not surprising that many of the most important global environmental problems manifest themselves in these places — the high seas and the atmosphere above them.

It would be desirable, also, to be able to undertake internationally sponsored research where urgent priorities had been identified that could not be adequately met elsewhere.

There is an acknowledged need for some kind of central data storage and retrieval system for environmental information. This facility could not displace existing national and specialized data banks and repositiories. It would supplement them and provide a central link among them. It seems appropriate that such a central facility should be internationally owned and operated.

Finally, the creation of a high quality global research institution, really the first of its kind, would symbolize the commitment of the international community to the development and application of scientific knowledge to help solve the problems of the environment.

For all these reasons, it seems likely that Stockholm may be asked to give its endorsement, in some form, not merely to a science advisory group to support U.N. activities on environmental affairs, but to a full fledged international research institute.

* * * * * *

11

We can expect, then, proposals for two major new institutions for international cooperation on environmental problems that might be put in place at Stockholm: on the political side, a high level policy planning and coordinating office; on the scientific side, a world institute for scientific advice and research on the environment. It becomes appropriate to examine in somewhat more detail the organizational and to some extent legal problems that might be involved in establishing these two institutions.

VII.

The principal functions to be performed by the U.N. environmental unit would be policy planning and review. It would maintain a continuous inventory of the activities of national governments, international organizations and private bodies, identifying needed programs and actions and stimulating the appropriate entities to carry them into effect. It would also have responsibilities for education and information exchange on international environmental matters.

A number of tools would be available to the unit and its head to perform this basic function:

(1) It could provide a forum for periodic meetings of governments to consider and debate the broad range of international environmental problems. It would not be surprising if Stockholm itself were to schedule another U.N. Conference on the Environment, or even to find that such a conference becomes a regular, quadrennial event. The broad overview provided by these intergovernmental debates could be deepened and fortified by annual or biennial reports prepared by the unit on the state of the world environment.

(2) In this connection, it could assemble, analyze and review reports of national governments and international organizations on their policies and activities affecting the environment, like those developed in preparation for the Stockholm Conference. Certainly it could be expected that these reports would become increasingly detailed and meaningful.

(3) It could serve as a point for the collection and dissemination of practical national experience in solving environmental problems.

(4) It could conduct on-site inspections or hearings to focus regional and world attention on particular issues.

(5) The unit and its chief could propose the convocation of international conferences on matters where international legislation seemed necessary or possible. Similarly, they would call the attention of regional organizations and national governments to matters appropriate for their action.

(6) As a central reference point within the U.N. for environmental con-

12

cerns, the unit could provide good offices for the adjustment or avoidance of international disputes growing out of national actions affecting the environment. (It seems unlikely that governments will be prepared in the near future to submit such controversies generally to third-party settlement mechanisms.)

It would appear that all of these functions, with the possible exception of the power to require periodic reports from national governments, could, as a legal matter, be exercised by the unit without express authorization. The extent to which these and similar authorities should be written into terms of reference will depend principally on tactical considerations when the enabling resolutions are being drafted.

The exact title and designation of the unit — whether Commission or Office — and its head — whether Commissioner, Director or Administrator — will depend on the intricacies of U.N. nomenclature and the contingencies of negotiation. But it seems clear that the head of the unit should be a senior U.N. official, to be appointed by the General Assembly upon the nomination of the Secretary General. He should report directly to the Secretary General, and through him to the General Assembly. Only in this way can he be given status and authority commensurate with the scope of his responsibilities.

The unit itself should be autonomous, that is, it should not be located within any of the regular departments of the Secretariat. It should be financed out of the regular U.N. budget. The staff should be small — not more than 50 professionals — but of the highest quality. The staff should have the technical capability to review and evaluate scientific research and findings and should be strong on policy analysis and assessment. It would not itself conduct operations or do scientific research, but it should have the skills needed to supervise and evaluate outside contractors.

For these purposes it would be desirable to have greater flexibility in recruitment than is afforded by current rules and practices of the Secretariat. The field of environmental policy is a new one in which the required competences and skills cannot be fully specified in advance. Moreover, there is a shortage of technically trained personnel in this field, particularly among the developing countries. Flexibility should not be at the expense of adequate geographical and political variety among staff members, however. Short-term employees, staff members seconded by governments and consultants on contract are devices that have been used, notably by IAEA, to ensure technical competence combined with geographical and political balance. The same techniques should be available to the environmental unit.

Provision must be made for political accountability of the administrative unit. The problem is to design an arrangement that satisfies the legitimate requirements for governmental oversight without unduly hampering the freedom of action of the executive officer and his staff.

The details of these political arrangements, and the exact balance to be struck would no doubt be negotiated concurrently with the appointment of the first executive head of the unit. A useful precedent exists in the relationship already established between the Preparatory Committee and the Secretariat of the Stockholm Conference.

The Committee consists of 27 nations, including the great powers, with an appropriate geographic, political and economic balance. This number seems large enough to permit an adequately representative group of governments and small enough to permit effective functioning. Members could be rotated periodically, if that seemed desirable.

The Preparatory Committee is not in permanent session, but meets at the call of the Secretary General. If the Committee were to be extended or made permanent, the practice of periodic meetings should be retained to permit the possibility of high-level representation at its meetings. The schedule should be regularized to provide for stated meetings once or perhaps twice a year. The powers of the present Committee are in form advisory, but in fact the Secretary General must secure their assent on broad matters of policy. If the Committee were to be made permanent, this arrangement would presumably extend to the budget, as well.

On the other hand, the Secretary General retains considerable independent authority. Most important are his powers to make recommendations and seek advice. Extrapolated into the setting of a permanent institutional arrangement, these would seem to imply (1) the power to make proposals and recommendations to the U.N., international organizations or governments on his own initiative and without the endorsement of the committee, and (2) the power, within the limits of available funds, to constitute and consult ad hoc panels or special groups with governmental, non-governmental or mixed membership, as appropriate to assist on particular issues, projects, studies or evaluations.

Both of these are significant powers, especially as wielded by a strong-mined and dynamic officer. But without them, it hardly seems possible that the U.N. unit would have the requisite strength to influence governmental policies or to attract energetic and effective leadership and staff. This much autonomous authority seems essential if it is intended to create anything more than another routine bureaucratic office.

Again there is a question of how far these relationships and powers would need to be spelled out in constitutive resolutions or terms of reference. In any case, the successful deployment of what are, after all, only rather tenuous sources of influence will require very great wisdom, political and diplomatic skill, energy and dedication from the head of this unit and its staff.

A final question arises on the place of any permanent committee in the broader U.N. structure. One possibility with considerable support among some commentators and governments, is to establish it as an

ECOSOC commission. Environmental affairs seem to fit comfortably within the mandate of ECOSOC as defined in the Charter.

Upon further consideration, there are a number of objections to this course, and cumulatively they seem decisive:

To place the Committee under ECOSOC is to layer environmental activities well down in the U.N. structure, thus detracting from their importance and diminishing the influence of the environmental unit. ECOSOC already has seven commissions, which would, presumptively, be on a par with the new one.

Equally important, ECOSOC has never been an effective policy-making or coodinating unit. Efforts are under way to enlarge and revive the Council; but this is envisioned as a ten-year process, even if it is successful, and environmental needs are pressing.

Staff support for ECOSOC is provided by the U.N. Department of Economic and Social Affairs. This would cut across the notion of building an independent staff for the environmental unit.

A special defect is that ECOSOC has long been regarded by the developing countries as the special preserve of the industrial states. To make it, even in its proposed enlarged form, the channel for cooperative action between developed and less developed states in environmental matters is to complicate needlessly an already difficult task.

The alternative to an ECOSOC commission seems to be a special committee of the General Assembly. Although this format has certain drawbacks, particularly in that it is rather unwieldy, they do not equal those of the ECOSOC solution.

VIII.

The scientific institute could be established by the scientific community itself with such funds as it could muster from governments and private sources. As has been said, steps are already being taken in this direction by ICSU through SCOPE. The United Nations could give its blessing to this effort in a General Assembly resolution.

It has been suggested, however, that the institute would have a much more impressive basis if it were, in effect, chartered by the U.N. This would seem especially appropriate if governments, as has been proposed, should supply the basic funding. And it would be a suitable recognition that the institute is the instrumentality to which the international community looks, not in an exclusive but in a special sense, to carry out the responsibilities for scientific advice and research outlined above.

At the same time, the institute should be organized and operated by the scientific community itself. Independent management would be necessary for the credibility of the work produced by the center; and it comports with the scientist's desire to be free of the fact or appearance of governmental influences on his results. The relationship would be not unlike that between the government and the national academy of sciences in the United States and a number of other countries.

The U.N. imprimatur could be accorded by a resolution of the General Assembly—or indeed of the Stockholm Conference—calling for the establishment of the institute, outlining its governance, embodying the broad terms of reference and providing for funding. The governing body might be a council of scientists nominated by various national academies of science or comparable bodies. The terms of reference should include the authority to conduct scientific research on environmental matters. The obligation of the governing council to provide scientific advice on environmental questions at the request of the United Nations or any of its organs or agencies should be specified. The actual establishment of the center could be planned and carried out by ICSU, perhaps acting through SCOPE, by a consortium of international scientific unions, or by a group of national academies of science or comparable bodies.

Some doubts have been expressed whether governments would be willing to accept the formula of public funding and non-governmental management. But most governments are familiar with a similar pattern on the national level in academies of science or research councils. It combines semi-official status with at least a modicum of scientific independence, and both are desirable from the government's point of view. It should be possible to dispel any hesitation by careful drafting of the terms of reference. In the end, governments need not continue to provide funds if the performance of the institute is consistently unsatisfactory to them.

The research facilities of the institute should be modest in size but unsurpassed in quality. A call to its staff would be regarded as an unusual professional honor and distinction. Each facility should have its own laboratory and computer facilities. It might begin with a complement of some 30 scholars, some permanent members and others who are in residence for a term. In this way, the institute can perform an important role in fertilizing and improving national scientific communities. The staff should include members from the whole range of sciences involved in the environment and from the social sciences, as well, for the problems of the environment are not the exclusive domain of any one discipline. But it should probably never expand in any facility beyond a size that permits personal interchange among all members of the group.

It has been estimated that the funding requirements for an institute of the type described would be of the order of magnitude of $10 million for operating costs over the first three years, allowing for reduced expenditures during the start-up period. Initial capital requirements would be of the same dimensions or perhaps somewhat larger, but capital ex-

16

penditures would begin only after several years of detailed planning.

If the suggestion of a U.N. "charter" is followed, the basic funding should be subscribed by governments on a voluntary basis, but the institute should be free to accept gifts from any source, public or private, in support of activities within its basic terms of reference. Government contributions could be channeled to the institute in one of three ways: (1) by direct grants to the institute; (2) through the administrator of the U.N. environmental unit, or (3) through national academies or research councils. Although not much turns on the choice, the first would seem preferable. The second seems to subordinate the institute to the U.N. unit or its head; the third does not sufficiently highlight the commitment of governments to the enterprise.

IX.

The scientific institute and the U.N. environmental unit will have to work closely together on many major problems. The first of these joint tasks should be the establishment of a global environmental monitoring network.

The institute, on the basis of wide consultation within the world scientific community, should identify those substances and activities as to which there is now ground for concern that the limits of global environmental tolerance may be approaching. It should specify also the research needed to clarify present uncertainties. It should draw up a plan for the monitoring required in connection with this research, including monitoring parameters, program, data collection standards and the like.

On the basis of this advice, the head of the U.N. environmental unit should promptly convene a conference of the interested parties from the scientific world, the specialized agencies and national governments with a view to getting the global net into operation at an early date. Monitoring stations would be operated by those entities, national or international, that seemed best qualified to do so. In many cases, these would be the specialized agencies. WMO's World Weather Watch already monitors many aspects of atmospheric pollution, and no doubt more could be added. IAEA has an effective capability for measuring radioactive pollution in various environments. And examples could be multiplied. In other cases national or non-governmental facilities would be used.

It would be necessary to agree on interconnections among these elements, to identify gaps in the system, to fix responsibility for filling them, and to designate sources of new funding, if necessary. It is apparent that an extensive and rather complex technical negotiation is involved. A comparable exercise, though on a smaller scale, was the negotiation between WMO and ICSU leading to the establishment of the Global Atmospheric Research Program. Valuable preliminary work for the monitoring negotiations has been done as a part of the Stockholm preparatory process by the Intergovernmental Working Group on Monitoring and the SCOPE Monitoring Commission.

Nevertheless, prompt agreement among the parties and establishment of the net will require in full measure the leadership and catalytic capacities of the head of the U.N. unit.

X.

The deficiencies of the specialized agencies, singly and in combination, as the focal point for United Nations concerns on the environment have been discussed earlier. It remains to consider what role these agencies *should* play in international cooperation on problems of the environment, and what their relationship should be to the new political and scientific organizations already discussed. A paradigm of that role and relationship may perhaps be seen in the outline just given of the design and operation of a global monitoring network.

Much has been written about the ineffectiveness and disarray of the United Nations specialized agencies. They have been accused of all manner of bureaucratic sins, of which duplication, overlapping effort and lack of coordination have headed the list A good many of these complaints are no doubt true. They have resulted in a considerable reserve on the part of major contributors to the agency budgets, a reserve that transcends usual east-west differences. And, as has been noted, efforts at reform are under way.

Some qualifications on current negative attitudes toward the agencies are in order, however.

(1) Not all of the agencies are equally infected with bad management or bureaucratic sloth. Without meaning to be invidious, it can be said that there is consensus among observers about the effective performance of, for example, WMO and IAEA in carrying out their missions.

(2) Not all the activities of the agencies have met equal criticism. On the whole, they have been quite successful in providing a forum, promoting information exchange and, to some extent, stimulating research in their areas of concern. These are the principal functions they would be called on to perform in the environmental field.

(3) Some of the agencies have important operating capabilities for environmental programs that it would be foolish not to exploit and use. Some of these, in the field of monitoring have already been touched on, but they are not confined to this field.

(4) Each of the agencies has developed its own constituency both within and outside member governments. Though these are often deployed

18

defensively to protect agency prerogatives, they also represent a resource of people and institutions that the agency can reach and influence with its programs, including environmental programs.

(5) The developing countries, as the principal clients of the agencies, have their complaints, but on the whole take a considerably less critical view than the money suppliers. This may represent simply a difference in perspective between donor and beneficiary; even so it suggests that truth is somewhere between the two.

The question of "coordination" among the agencies raises special problems. Given the constitutional independence of the agencies, it does not make sense to call for "coordination" in terms that suggest an external administrator or process with authority to allocate responsibilities among them. Moreover, some of the demands for coordination reflect a desire for order and symmetry in organizational affairs that is simply at odds with the real world. Some of it bespeaks a misconception of the nature and role of the specialized agencies.

These organizations may be viewed as analogues of national ministries in specific functional areas of policy and administration. Thus, the FAO can be thought of as the international counterpart of a Ministry of Agriculture, the WHO as the counterpart of a Ministry of Health and so on. The analogy is not exact, but it is instructive for present purposes. Each entity deals with problems within its own sphere of competence and responds to its own identifiable constituency. Indeed relations of the specialized agencies tend to run to their counterpart national ministries rather than to the foreign offices of member states.

For present purposes, a basic objective is to infuse these agencies with what might be called an environmental perspective. From this point of view, it is not necessarily a matter of concern that many of them have launched their own environmental programs. Quite the reverse: it may be a sign that they are getting the message. Nor is it necessarily evidence of duplication or overlapping, on any more than the verbal level, if two agencies — say WHO and FAO — are both running programs aimed at water pollution. The probability is that one agency is talking to doctors and public health people and the other is dealing with farmers and agricultural officials. Neither could reach the other's constituency, nor is it likely that a new international pollution control agency could be constructed to do so without an equal amount of duplication and inefficiency.

This is not to give general endorsement to the agency proposals for environmental programs that have been floated in recent years. These will continue to depend on the resources governments are willing to commit and the decisions they are prepared to take in the appropriate forums, in light of a vast array of pertinent considerations. But there is little to be gained from any extensive exercise in redrawing jurisdictional boundaries or cleaning up organizational charts. The specialized agencies should continue to concentrate their energies on the delivery of services in their respective areas of functional responsibility rather than being summoned to the arid endeavor of carving up the environment among them.

The U.N. environmental unit would have vis a vis the agencies the same powers of initiative and persuasion, backed by scientific authority, that will hopefully permit it to influence governments and other operating entities.

In addition, there is no reason why each of the agencies should not be placed under the immediate obligation of making detailed and comprehensive annual or biennial reports to the environmental unit covering the effects on the environment of the agency's programs and actions. These reports should be reviewed and analyzed by the staff of the unit, which would prepare critical comments going not only to substantive matters but also to organizational questions, such as failure to coordinate properly with other agencies. Thereafter, there might be a general conference of the heads of reporting agencies at which the reports and staff comments would be debated.

Another possibility that merits careful consideration is the adaptation of the environmental impact statement technique that has been begun in the United States. Impact statements are required by law to be filed by a government agency with respect to any new project or program having potentially significant environmental effects. As the practice works in the United States, the agency with which the document is filed cannot veto any project on the basis of anything contained in the impact statement. The statement becomes a public document, however, and may be used to energize administrative, legislative or judicial action.[10]

If the technique were extended to the UN system, impact statements might be prepared by a specialized agency before beginning any project or program substantially affecting the environment. They would be filed with the environmental unit and would become public documents, together with any comments the unit wished to make. In addition to insuring that environmental factors were adequately taken into account, the information derived from these statements would be an important management tool for the unit in its efforts to harmonize and rationalize the actions of the agencies in the environmental field.

Although the legal position is not free from doubt, it is probable that the reporting and impact statement procedures could be put into effect, as a practical matter at least, by a resolution of the General Assembly in response to a recommendation of the Stockholm Conference.

The most effective leverage that could be given the environmental unit would be some control over specialized agency resources for environmental programs.

At the extreme, if an environmental fund were to be established as

20

discussed in the next section, existing budgetary allocations for such programs could be pooled and transferred to the fund. The head of the environmental unit would then decide in accordance with agreed criteria which agency projects merited support, and would allot the pooled funds accordingly. Resources for new or expanded programs would be made available to the fund by governments upon an adequate showing of need by the unit. This approach would provide the unit with a good deal of power, but it is probably impracticable both legally and politically.

A more moderate version would be to channel new monies for international environmental programs through the fund, without changing existing agency budgets. It would perhaps be possible at Stockholm to get a resolution or recommendation endorsing this policy. Or it could be adopted informally by the chief contributors to the agency budgets. In either case, and especially the latter, it is doubtful that the policy could prevail as a legal matter against a budgetary resolution duly adopted according to the regular procedures of a specialized agency.

A still milder approach would simply have the environmental unit comment on agency proposals for programs concerning the environment. Again, various degrees of formality would be possible. The procedure could be instituted by a General Assembly resolution upon recommendation of the Conference. Such a resolution might even contain a provision calling on agency governing bodies not to adopt proposals that do not carry the endorsement of the unit. At the opposite extreme, any state wishing to do so could announce its intention to seek the advice and comment of the environmental unit on any such proposals, and to be guided in its action by such advice. It would seem desirable at a minimum to adopt some version of this advice and comment procedure.

XI.

The magnitude of the financial requirements for environmental programs, even considering only those with strong claims to international funding, will dwarf any amount that would conceivably be contributed to any international fund for these purposes over the next few years. On the other hand, there is no doubt that the powers of influence and persuasion vested in the environmental unit would be greatly magnified if it could back them up with control over significant financial resources.

In addition to its effect in strengthening the hand of this central international policy unit there are three main considerations favoring the creation of such a fund:

(1) It will symbolize the reality of the international commitment to the required cooperation on environmental problems. The institutional ar-

rangements outlined above taken together with the other actions likely to emerge from Stockholm, add up to a poor earnest of that commitment. Without such a commitment, visibly and demonstrably displayed, the whole program for international cooperation is unlikely to get very far off the ground.

(2) As mentioned above, control over financial resources is the most effective means for influencing the conduct of the specialized agencies. Even if the more far-reaching budgetary proposals in the last section prove infeasible, supplementary funds for programs of interest to the central unit will provide an incentive that can be used in influencing agency policy.

(3) Most important of all, the developing countries, whose participation in this international effort is essential, will have neither the interest nor the means to do so unless external financing is provided.

These three reasons imply also a fund of some size, although, as noted above, it cannot be expected to match the dimensions of the problem. Without meaning to suggest more than an order of magnitude, it would seem that unless the fund could reach something like $150 to $250 million for a three-year period it would be so trifling as to be worse than nothing. Contributions to the fund would be on a voluntary basis.

Assuming that there is such a fund, for what kinds of activities should it be used? If the central scientific research institute is separately financed as proposed above, the fund should be devoted primarily, if not exclusively, to the support of activities in the developing countries. The disparity in resources and priorities is so great that it would be wholly inappropriate to devote these stringently limited international monies to programs being carried out in the industrialized countries, even if the programs are primarily international in scope.

Three categories of activities suggest themselves as likely candidates for grants from the fund:

First, and most obvious are facilities located in the developing countries that are needed for global programs. The clearest example might be a monitoring station in the global net. In such a case the benefits to the host country are extremely remote in terms of its scale of priorities. Absent the requirements of the international community at large, the station would never be built. It seems only appropriate that the international community should pay for the service. It is not likely that this class of cases would account for very much of the fund.

The second object of the fund should be the support of research and development on environmental problems in the developing countries. This would serve a number of important purposes:

(1) It would heighten the awareness and understanding of environmental issues and their relation to the objectives of sound development. In this way it would help to ameliorate the naive, but still widespread feeling that environmental and development goals are in fundamen-

tal conflict.

(2) It would give developing-country scientists a stronger role in formulating research problems and methodology. It is apparent that developed-country scientists, through sheer weight of numbers and talent, have dominated this process almost to the exclusion of their colleagues in the developing countries. This has not been intentional, but it has had distorting effects, particularly on the acceptability and usefulness of the results in dealing with local problems.

(3) It would strengthen the scientific infrastructure in the developing areas, thus contributing not only to overall economic and social development, but also to an appropriate weighting of environmental factors in policy making.

(4) It would tend to produce solutions to developing country environmental problems, particularly in the field of resource management — solutions that would be effective because they accepted and reflected the cultural setting, political priorities and technological capability within which they must operate. In this connection, the fund should be available to assist pilot projects embodying innovative approaches to pollution control or resource management adapted to the requirements of developing countries.

Grants might be made to support individual research projects. An alternative policy would be to concentrate on trying to bring into being regional centers of environmental research. This could be accomplished either by establishing a new institution or building on an existing one.

ICSU, through SCOPE, has stressed the importance it attaches to a network of regional research centers. These would not be hierarchically subordinated to the global institute, but would stand in some kind of special relationship to it.

It has been suggested also that the special interdisciplinary requirements for good environmental work cannot be achieved in existing research establishments or university faculties, organized along traditional disciplinary lines. Moreover, there may be a need for an authoritative source of scientific advice on environmental issues and research priorities at the regional as at the global level.

On the other hand, it is very hard to create good institutes. And there is already a tendency for available scientific resources to be spread very thin in the developing countries.

The answer is probably not to adopt a rigid policy but to finance research by individuals, by existing institutions or by new centers, as seems appropriate.

It seems likely that most of the grants from the fund would be for projects in this category.

The third, and most difficult, question is the extent to which new international resources should be available to finance the extra cost of environmental protection elements in development projects. A somewhat closer analysis helps to resolve some of these difficulties.

For some projects, and there is reason to suppose they may be a fairly large proportion of the total, the short run out of pocket savings attributable to environmental protection measures will outweigh the costs. Here the problem is simply to get a more sophisticated cost-benefit analysis that will bring these facts to light. There is no basis for a claim on international resources to finance such measures, though some technical assistance with the analysis is perhaps in order.

A more difficult case occurs where environmental expenditures will pay out over the long run, but will sharply reduce net short-term benefits. Development assistance officials state that it has thus far been possible to reach mutual agreement with borrowers on projects in this category, at least as to protection against first order environmental effects. Additional costs have averaged from one to three per cent of total project costs, and have so far been covered by increasing the amount of the loan at regular interest rates.

Despite the success of the project-by-project approach, there is ground for concern about the additional costs on an aggregate basis, especially for countries with heavy overall debt burdens. On balance, however, it does not seem proper to defray these extra costs out of a special international environmental fund. It would be appropriate to study these issues in a development assistance forum, for example, UNCTAD, DAC or IBRD.

This leaves a class of cases in which the environmental benefits to the country involved are small in comparison with those of other states or the international community at large. If the impact is on one of two neighboring states, as might be the case with an international river system, the donor should not proceed with financing the project without mutual agreement among the states involved as to the apportionment of benefits and burdens.

Where the international values are more general, as for example in the case of the protection of a wildlife reserve, there is a strong argument for paying the cost of protective measures out of international resources. This class of cases is similar to those discussed in connection with the suggested World Heritage Trust. In any case, they would be proper candidates for grants from the fund here proposed.

It should be stressed that although the World Bank and other development assistance agencies are including environmental factors in their analysis and appraisal of development projects, they have not established any rigid criteria or standards that a project must meet to qualify for approval. This is the proper approach. To insist upon compliance with fixed environmental standards as a condition of development assistance would raise the same resistance and opposition as other "strings" on aid, and properly so.

If an environmental fund is established, it should be administered by the head of the U.N. environmental unit. He would act with the advice of the scientific council, especially as to grants for research and development, but he should not be bound by it. The general criteria for grants and the division of the fund as between broad categories of projects should be reviewed and approved by any committee of governments set up to work with the unit. But the approval of this committee should not be required on a project-by-project basis.

XII.

The institutional design discussed in this paper remits the *execution* of international environmental policy primarily to national governments. The power of the U.N. environmental unit vis a vis governments would be essentially the power to persuade, backed by detailed knowledge of the scientific and other elements of the problem. That is as it must be in a world still constituted of sovereign and independent states.

Most often governments will act on their own. But there will be a growing number of issues on which they will find it desirable to act in concert, more or less formalized, with one or more other governments sharing a common problem, or through a regional or multilateral agency.

It seems likely that there will be increasing opportunities for institutional innovation and growth in the conduct of environmental action programs at the regional and subregional level. But it would be a mistake to establish or designate any chosen regional instruments for cooperation on environmental affairs. The problems are too varied in scope and impact to fit into any fixed regional matrix.

It would also be wrong to try to subject this institutional growth to tight central direction. Regional institutions and programs should essentially be expressions of locally felt needs, purposes and priorities. There will be room for the wise use of the leadership and catalytic resources of the U.N. environmental unit. U.N. specialized agencies, bilateral technical assistance programs and the resources of non-governmental agencies should be appropriately deployed in support. But for the rest, responsibility for attacking problems of local and regional environments should be left with the governments and peoples whose environment it is.

It is a virtue of the kind of system here proposed that it can accommodate without strain a variety of regional initiatives such as those of the European organizations mentioned earlier. Similarly, it will be able to accept, and hopefully to stimulate, new agencies and groupings for handling new problems as they arise.

For example, the Intergovernmental Working Group on Marine Pollution is trying to develop a convention on ocean dumping for adoption at Stockholm. IMCO has called a conference on oil pollution for 1973. In that year also there will be a U.N. Conference on the Law of the Sea. These international actions might give birth to one or more new agencies with responsibilities affecting the marine environment. Any such newcomer could be fitted readily into the institutional pattern here considered.

This is as it should be. For the process of environmental management is one that will stretch forward indefinitely in time. The organizational arrangements for international environmental cooperation must be flexible and responsive enough to shape and support this ongoing process as it unfolds in technical, political, and economic circumstances that are now only dimly foreseeable, if at all. In fact, the requirement for Stockholm is not so much to establish an organizational *structure* as to set up a parallel *process* of institutional development, capable of growth and renewal and of promoting and accommodating the specific organizational modes needed to deal with the infinite variety of new and unforeseen problems of environmental planning and management, protection and enhancement, as they arise.

NOTES

[1]U.N.G.A. Res. 2398, XXIII (December 3, 1968).

[2]*Report of the Preparatory Committee for the U.N. Conference on the Human Environment*, U.N. Doc. A/Conf. 48/PC.9 (1970), at 7.

[3]U Thant, "Human Environment and World Order," Address at the University of Texas, Austin, Texas, May 14, 1970, U.N. Press release SG/SM/1259 (1970).

[4]Study of Critical Environmental Problems (SCEP), *Man's Impact on the Global Environment: Assessment and Recommendations for Action* (1970).

[5]Kennan, "To Prevent a World Wasteland: A Proposal," 48 *Foreign Affairs* 401 (1970).

[6]*Supra* note 3.

[7]*Ibid.*

[8]*Ibid.*

[9]*A Study of the Capacity of the United Nations Development System* (2 vols.) U.N. Doc. DP/5 (1969).

[10]National Environmental Policy Act of 1969, 102, 42 U.S.C. 4321 (1969).

COMMENTS ON PROFESSOR CHAYES' PAPER

by *Eugene B. Skolnikoff**

It is difficult to comment extensively on the paper by Professor Chayes because I find myself in essential agreement with his arguments and conclusions. This is not too surprising since we have often talked of these issues in a variety of forums, including the classroom. His technical assessment of the environmental "crisis" as long-term rather than immediate I believe is basically correct, though inaction could hasten the time of crisis. The importance of political decision now is also clear, in particular because of the time required to allow new institutional mechanisms and functions to grow and mature into effective tools for action.

I agree as well with the organizational recommendations that oppose a new U.N. Specialized Agency, but suggest instead a policy planning, coordination and review unit within the U.N. Secretariat. The recommendations with regard to the scientific community also seem to me to be essentially sound, for that community must be brought directly into the battle for the environment, both to provide technical information and solutions, and as a necessary component of wise political action.

Having recorded this agreement, however, I will attempt briefly to do two things: first, make some comments about the Chayes recommendations that are in effect elaborations in the arguments, or in some cases slight changes in emphasis; and second, pose some broader questions that are particularly relevant for this assembly to consider.

I.

Quite appropriately, Professor Chayes makes no attempt in his paper to define the scope of the "environment." Very few of the recent outpouring of papers, official and unofficial, dealing with the international environmental "crisis" have defined the term either. The reason is a good one: the environment has no simple bounds. In effect, we must be concerned with the enormous array of issues affecting civilization, from disposal of wastes to population growth, production of food, transfer and control of technology, wise use of resources, among others. Thus, we are here concerned not with one new and different problem, but with many of the central problems of society.

---

*The author is Professor of Political Science at Massachusetts Institute of Technology.

27

Recognition of this fact serves to emphasize several points. One is that the "environment" cannot be separated from existing concerns and programs of governmental agencies, both national and international. More importantly, it underlines the fact that as we design new political institutions to deal with environmental questions, we are designing institutions that will in time be involved in many issues touching on major political, economic and social matters. In this sense, concern for the "environment" becomes a surrogate for concern for the preservation, amelioration and improvement of man's condition.

Cast in those terms, one is quickly aware of both the importance and the difficulty of the task. Conflicts of values must necessarily be confronted, and acceptable means for agreeing on the allocation of values will eventually be derived. Regulatory, allocation, enforcement, and adjudicatory functions will have to be performed in the international arena in time, if not immediately, and to a degree going far beyond presently accepted international practice. Much of this is in Professor Chayes' paper and proposals, but I believe it deserves greater emphasis; it is too easy to minimize the ultimate magnitude of the task when making the technical assessment that the environmental crisis does not pose imminent catastrophe.

We do also need to recognize that we are not starting with a *tabula rasa*, even when considering functions on the international scene of substantial political significance. International organizations today perform a wide variety of regulatory functions, some are engaged in allocation of resources, some even engaged in inspection and enforcement of agreed international rules. Nations have already delegated considerable sovereignty to international bodies — more than most realize — (in addition to watching the erosion of their sovereignty in a multitude of other ways through the rapidly growing unavoidable interdependence of national societies). Thus, even if the judgment is correct that the present threat to the environment does not require immediate establishment of binding norms with enforcement authority, it can be argued that we are farther down that road than is generally appreciated. But the road is a very long one, and the more difficult curves and hills remain to be traversed.

As we move toward increasing devolution of authority and responsibility to international machinery (including, but not limited to, the U.N. family of organizations), the requirements for effective performance of that machinery will grow substantially. I will return to this point later, but for the moment we can note again that new organizations and altered forms of existing organizations will almost surely eventually be needed. The innovations in organization being proposed by Professor Chayes and others may be (should be) designed not to freeze patterns, but to be capable of moulding existing, and building new, institutions as the need becomes clear.

I think a high-level policy-planning and review unit without direct operating responsibilities is the right approach. But, it will not succeed if it is not of high quality *and* influential. The two requirements are, of course, partially interrelated, but of the two I fear that over the long-term influence is the necessary, though not sufficient, prerequisite for quality. It will be possible, though not automatic, to be able to attract and maintain quality in an influential office; almost certainly an office with little influence will not be able to do so. How to build in that influence with governments, with the U.N. Secretariat, with the Specialized Agencies, with the scientific community, and with the public will not be easy.

Some power over the purse within the U.N. will undoubtedly be a *sine qua non* for influence, though I am sure Professor Chayes would agree that it is not enough. Personal support from the Secretary General, and strong support from influential governments certainly would also be important. Sooner or later, if the proposed unit is successful, it will come into conflict with existing organizations or with some governments. It must be able to survive such confrontations, and reasonably often prevail, if it is to have any real meaning.

I do not, obviously, have any panaceas on this question of organizational influence, but I commend it to your discussion. It seems to me that, at the least, it points to the need for some substantial funding power for the new unit, and also some more potent political tie within the U.N. The proposal of a new General Assembly Committee is an intriguing one in this connection that I think needs to be further elaborated.

As a footnote, let me say that if the new unit is to serve in any way as a coordinator of Specialized Agency's programs, I would fervently hope that such coordination is something more than the arid process that now occurs under ECOSOC and in the ACC. In fact, I would willingly give up the traditional coordination function that has as its purpose the "avoidance of duplication" because it is so unproductive, deadening on all concerned, and wasteful of time. I seriously question which costs more: duplication or coordination. A unit focused on policy-planning represents a more positive view of the need to "integrate" rather than "coordinate" programs.

One other question with regard to the new unit that ought to be spelled out in greater depth in advance is its relation to the UNDP. The broader efforts at country planning now being instituted in the UNDP should make it possible to include environmental concerns more easily in the development process. Close working relationships with the new unit would appear to be most important.

Professor Chayes also elucidates in some detail the role he sees for the scientific community with regard to U.N. environmental activities. Little need be added to his recommendations except to note two things. One is that the new governmental unit within the U.N. *must* itself have scientific personnel of high quality if it is to be able to work effectively with the scientific community.

Second, I would want to underscore the importance I attach to the development of analytical capabilities that are accepted as largely impartial by governments and organizations. I believe that in environmental affairs, and in many other substantive areas, there will be a growing need for "expert evaluation" of highly complex technical issues that must be resolved to indicate necessary action, to underlie allocation decisions, to settle disputes, to verify compliance with regulations, or to assess claims. These capabilities exist today, but in fact as the need grows, I do not see the capabilities equally growing (on international *or* national levels). Yet, the development of such impartial institutions takes time, time to develop knowledge, to gain experience, and most important, to earn acceptance and trust.

The scientific community will necessarily play a major part here; the suggestions offered in Professor Chayes paper seem to me to be in the right direction.

II.

Having registered such general agreement with the arguments and recommendations put forward by Professor Chayes, I feel I must also note some nagging skepticism that I find hard to suppress. It is not really skepticism about the proposals, which I believe are politically feasible, and about as innovative as can be contemplated at this time. My problem is that I am not sure the proposals really go far enough, or more fundamentally, whether the U.N. system is capable of doing the job.

I noted earlier that I believe there will have to be, inevitably, substantial devolution of authority and responsibility to international machinery. Increasingly, new technologies are global in nature, or the side-effects of more intensive application of existing technology have international and global repercussions. In time, and not very far ahead, many functions with substantial economic, political, social, even security implications will have to be performed on a wide variety of subjects in an international arena: regualtion, allocation, inspection, enforcement, adjudication, and operation.

Can we visualize present U.N. organizations evolving sufficiently to be able to perform such functions in a manner that will be at least acceptable? It is, of course, not only up to the secretariats of these organizations, but much more a matter of whether governments are willing and able to oversee the necessary evolution, an evolution that necessarily will involve political risk.

The answer to the question is not at all clear. The proposals of Professor Chayes I believe could help in that evolution, but I have grave doubts that it will be enough of an innovation and change to do the job. If not, what are the alternatives?

The only other possible choice I see is to advocate the building of new institutions outside the U.N., with limited membership or with patterns of control and influence quite different from that which prevails in most U.N. bodies. INTELSAT and Intersputnik are steps in that direction.

I accept and agree with the arguments in Professor Chayes' paper against developing new institutions outside the U.N. dealing with environment. But, if the U.N. in time proves unable to carry out the responsibilities that in a physical sense will *have* to be performed somewhere, then nations will have no choice but to turn to or devise machinery that "works" even if it is undesirable for other important reasons.

Perhaps this view is overly pessimistic with regard to the U.N. family, or is looking ahead to a more demanding set of requirements than will actually have to be faced by international machinery. I am afraid it needs to be considered, however, and kept in mind in the debates over organizational changes to be made in the next few years. Certainly, I am very much in favor of proceeding along the lines of the Chayes' proposals, for in them I see some of the best prospects for seeding a substantial evolution in the present U.N. family of organizations. Is it enough?

PART TWO

*THE INTERNATIONAL INTEREST IN THE ENVIRONMENT,
AND PRELIMINARY PROBLEMS OF CRITERIA.*

THE INTERNATIONAL INTEREST IN THE ENVIRONMENT, AND PRELIMINARY PROBLEMS OF CRITERIA.

EDITORIAL ANALYSIS

A. *Preliminary criteriological tasks.*

The current fever of activity on environmental matters within the United Nations family rests on an assumption that something should be done — and done internationally — about problems of the environment. The question is: given an international interest in protecting the environment, what should be done, how, and by whom?

Those members of national and international bureaucracies who are the chief participants in this process properly distinguish between *doing* something about the environment, on the one hand, and taking all the steps which must lead up to and lay the groundwork for doing something about the environment, on the other. The former has its prototype in the conclusion of treaties setting standards of state conduct or establishing regulatory or other institutions; relatively little of the total energies of the international community presently devoted to environmental problems is being expended on this kind of activity. The latter generates that whole complex of practical issues which arise any time human beings set themselves to the task of working out practical action on an apparent problem: Is it really a problem, for us? Why do we perceive it as such, and do we really know enough about it to say that it is a problem? What, if any, is the range of techniques by which it might be effectively dealt with? What will be the costs of dealing with it, and are there reasons for *not* undertaking to deal with it at all?

In the environmental field, it is with such preliminary questions of practical conduct as these that the international community is now primarily concerned — questions multiplied in complexity many-fold by the nature of the perceived problems, the state of human knowledge about them, and the character of the intricately interlocking national and international systems within which the contemplated "actions" must in due course be taken. A great deal of what the international community is doing is thus concerned with the working out of various kinds of criteria intended to provide an intelligent basis for making future decisions about the allocation of available resources for action. These criteriological questions may not always be recognized as such, nor are there efforts underway in every case among governments or in the international bureaucracy to articulate them formally and publicly. Nevertheless, the very logic of the questions about protection of the environment which the international community has presented to itself exposes certain underlying questions of criteria, which are in some cases being explicitly addressed but which will in most cases eventually be answered willy-nilly, whether by formal decision, by accumulated practice, or by default.

A number of these question of criteria may be called "preliminary", in the sense that they need to be addressed before the point is reached where decisions are to be taken to create an institutional structure or process, assign a particular environmental job within the international community, or undertake to devise a management regime for a particular environment problem. Among these preliminary questions are the following:

(i) By what criteria are the proper environmental concerns of the international community to be determined?

(ii) By what criteria are the respective competences of existing (and future) instrumentalities to be determined?

(iii) By what standards will the most practically efficacious mode of action be determined?

We may call these three classes, respectively, criteria of *international concern*, of *competence*, and of *efficacy*.

The first kind of criteriological problem generated by an international interest in the environment has to do with getting clear as to what that interest is. Criteria of *international concern* are devised to assist in answering the full range of questions about what kinds of environmental problems it is appropriate for an international forum — at whatever level of inclusiveness — to take into formal cognizance (whether these problems are regarded as requiring "action" or not). Such questions necessarily raise certain logically prior ones, having to do with determining what kinds of injuries or threats constitute an "environmental problem", and these in turn raise questions (which will be looked at in Part IV of this volume) both of the establishment of standards for assessing the consequences of particular injurious phenomena, and of acquiring information about these phenomena sufficient to make such assessments possible. In other words — as the international community is quickly learning in its deliberations about environmental protection — putting oneself in a position to find out what the problem is with which one should be concerned, is itself a problem to be addressed in its own right. And not surprisingly, it often must be addressed first.

Nicholas Robinson's "Problems of Definition and Scope", which concludes Part II of this book, discusses a variety of criteria by which the scope and content of international concern with the environment might be determined.

Criteria of *competence* embrace questions about the allocation of responsibilities in environmental matters among the various instrumentalities that might be capable, in fact, of discharging them — leaving aside questions about the practical effectiveness of such allocations. They embrace not only questions about the constitutional or legal authority of existing or future international organizations, but also questions about the relationship between this "delegated" authority and the relatively more massive "reserved" authority of national states.

Criteria of *efficacy*, by contrast, embrace questions of the comparative practical effectiveness of alternative courses of action to deal with problems of international concern once identified as such. And they must embrace the prior question whether *any* "action", by the international community or otherwise, is called for.

The foregoing analysis is clearly only one among a large number of possible taxonomies of the kinds of questions that must be dealt with by the international community in its preliminary efforts to think clearly about its role in environmental management, so as to organize and apply its severely restricted resources with the maximum of effectiveness; and does not purport to be exhaustive.

It should be noted, moreover, that the apparent discreteness of even these rough and general categories is quite deceptive. In practice, the answer to one of these three kinds of questions may depend strongly on the answer to another. For example, questions of the proper scope of international concern are in fact strongly influenced by the relative competences, in law and in fact, of international agencies and national states, or by considerations of the legal competence of existing international agencies and the practical difficulties of altering or expanding that competence. Or again, they may take heavily into account questions of efficacy — asking, for example, whether, in view of its limited resources, the international community can afford to bring this or that perceived environmental problem within its scope of concern. To cite only one further example: decisions as to what mode of action is most efficacious may in many cases be based largely on the conclusion that we do not yet know enough about a particular problem to define the proper scope of international concern with it. The result will be a decision to set up devices for acquiring such knowledge.

Further, each of the three questions may turn out to be strongly influenced by the same kinds of perhaps extraneous considerations, rather than resting neatly on its own exclusive data-base. It is unlikely to be assumed that "political" judgments, of the sort that are made when national governments decide to commit their support to a particular course of practical action, would be altogether excluded in answering these three kinds of questions. But it might be thought that such judgments would enter in only, say, at the first stage, when political appreciation is applied to scientific data to produce a decision as to the proper scope of concern of the international community, with judgments of competence or of efficacy being left to supposed technicians to deal with later. In fact, of course, neither governments nor intergovernmental agencies operate in this way. Both the formulation of all three kinds of criteria, and their application in particular instances, may well be determined in significant measure by the kinds of extraneous judgments of value that are often lumped incongruously together under the rubric "political".

B. *Formulating and Applying Criteria: Five Guides*

There are several pervasive considerations which may serve as guides in the task of formulating and applying criteria of the three kinds discussed above. While each may bear more directly on one kind of criteriological task than on another, the boundaries separating the tasks are so fluid, as we have just seen, that we will examine these guides with respect to all three tasks together.

1. *The distinction between having criteria and formalizing them.*
The fact that a criterion might be useful to the international community for some purpose — for example, to assist in identifying those environmental threats which should fall within its scope of concern — does not, of itself, imply that it should seek to state these criteria *formally*. The question of the wisdom or utility of getting into the business of formally stating criteria — by means, for example, of a resolution by a plenipotentiary conference of states or a plenary organ of an international organization — is one which must be examined separately and on its own merits in light of a number of tactical and strategic factors.

One such factor has already been mentioned: as the international community pursues its interest in environmental problems, certain basic decisions about criteria will get made willy-nilly, as various particular practical problems are taken up and disposed of in one way or another. They may be made well in this way, or badly — it is impossible to make any general predictions as to which. It is possible, however, to identify a number of reasons that may argue in the particular case against embarking on the enterprise of formulating criteria in general statements laid down in advance.

For example, governments are sometimes willing to concede more authority to international organizations when confronted with the concrete demands of a particular case than they would have been willing to do if asked to agree to a formal statement of such authority in the abstract. The development of principles governing the competence of the United Nations in the field of peacekeeping is a case in point. When confronted with the exigencies of crisis circumstances in the Suez in 1956-57, in the Congo in 1960, or in Cyprus in 1963, governments acceded to arrangements which implicity established points of constitutional principle under the U.N. Charter of a far-reaching scope (so far-reaching in the first two cases, indeed, that the doubts or second thoughts of certain of those governments precipitated a constitutional crisis in the Organization — the so-called "Article 19" controversy). When in 1965 the United Nations began an effort, through the "Committee of Thirty-Three", to formulate principles of peacekeeping in advance, the effort proved largely unproductive. This was true despite the fact that in 1967, following the June War in the Middle East, one of the most highly controversial peacekeeping procedures — the "Uniting for Peace" procedure — was invoked (in law and fact, if not in name) by one of its traditional opponents, the Soviet Union.

In general, then, there is an understandable tendency, when governments are asked to sign on to principles stated in the abstract, to try to hedge the statement about with safeguards against all manner of actual or hypothetical undesirable consequences, with the effect that the agreed result will represent an unnecessarily timid least-common-denominator. In the environmental field, the cases in which this *caveat* is most relevant are probably those falling most clearly within the present scope of national jurisdiction or control, and carrying the heaviest emotional or political charge: the question of population control is an example. While the United Nations has taken formal cognizance of this fundamental environmental problem for some time, it is one in which the risks in pressing for overly-ambitious declarations of international concern and intention-to-act may be particularly acute — at least if the real objective is getting states to agree to increasingly concrete measures of collective action to cope with the problem.

The foregoing paragraphs deal with risks attendant upon formalizing criteria of *international concern* or of *competence*. There may be similar risks attendant upon formalizing criteria of *efficacy*. Such an argument has been made, for example, with regard to the 1970 agreement among members of the North Atlantic Treaty Organization on the elimination of deliberate oil spills at sea. It has been argued that the NATO countries account for a large portion (perhaps 80%) of the kind of oil pollution at which this step within NATO was directed, that NATO was accordingly a logical forum in which to develop measures of pollution prevention, and that it in fact took a useful step forward whatever else may be said of the importance of that step relative to the marine pollution problem as a whole. Nonetheless, it is argued, had an effort been made in advance within a United Nations forum to state criteria allocating the marine pollution problems to various existing or prospective international agencies, it is unlikely that NATO would have been asked to do the job which it in fact undertook, and in any event the negotiation of such allocative criteria would likely have consumed more time than was required in NATO to negotiate the agreement itself.

2. *The distinction between criteria of concern and criteria of action.*

In the foregoing section we discussed the fact that the usefulness of having a well-formulated criterion to assist in policy decisions does not of itself imply that it would be useful to *formalize* that criterion. Somewhat similarly, the fact that a problem is identified as properly within the scope of concern of the international community does not of itself imply very much about the most effective mode of action for dealing with it. Indeed, as already indicated, it does not imply that any "action" at all should be contemplated for the time being, even less that there should be action within or through a public intergovernmental agency. (It must be said that this distinction has been clearly taken into account in the organization of preparations for the 1972 United Nations Conference on the Human Environment, which aims at separating out matters of international concern which appear to be ripe for "action proposals" from those which do not.)

What is important is that decisions about modes of action be made without any preconceptions stemming from the fact that the problem to be acted upon is adjudged of international concern. One should avoid, for example, any uncritical assumption that once a matter has been adjudged of international concern it should, without further ado, be made the subject of international legislation establishing standards of conduct for states or creating new institutions (a point dealt with more fully in Part IV of this book). Decisions should be made in full cognizance of the wide range of other kinds of action that might be available to bring about the desired result. For example, it is conceivable that some problems, although of admitted international concern, might be deliberately left *in toto* to national governments. (Supporters of the 1970 action of the Canadian Government in asserting prerogatives with respect to environmental protection in the Arctic beyond the limits of national jurisdiction argue that that action furnishes a case in point.) It may be that there are principles of law which can best be left to develop through the processes of international arbitration or adjudication — processes which may in some cases be more effective than the international legislative process despite their slowness and episodic character. Clearly the fact of *international* concern with the problem does not necessarily dictate a *global* approach to its solution, through the United Nations or some other universal international agency. Finally, even in cases where international action is clearly required, it may be that, for various extraneous reasons, the action initially taken cannot reasonably be designed to put a stop to injurious conduct itself, but rather should aim at the less ambitious goal of promoting acceptance of eventual, stronger action among states initially inclined to be hostile toward taking action at all.

3. *The relation between data-base and mode of action.*

The question of the extent of what is known about an apparent environmental injury, and the nature of the action which that base of knowledge can be made to justify, pervades the whole range of criteriological problems we have discussed. The question often manifests itself in the form of a controversy between supposed "activists" and "conservatives".

The former argue that the risk of irreversible injury in the event of the failure to act, warrants strong and specific measures to curtail the apparently injurious conduct even in advance of fuller scientific understanding of it. The latter argue that too little is known to justify any concrete action other than the establishment or acceleration of the means of gathering and competently interpreting relevant data.

We are learning that even those phenomena widely perceived as injuries to the environment are so diverse and individually peculiar, that it is not likely to be very useful to debate questions of this sort except in reference to a particular pollutant or other injurious phenomenon. There may, however, be one or two generalizations which the facts will support. It is indeed true that our understanding of the nature of a great many polluting activities is quite inadequate, when judged by standards of adequacy which would be applied within the scientific community itself, and that those standards would dictate continuing and expanding scientific research activities regardless of the nature of any action that may be taken in the immediate future. At the same time, we are learning that in the environmental field as in many others, policymakers and scientists ask different kinds of questions and consequently provide different kinds of answers. Policymakers must deal with political processes and legal and institutional structures, and are often faced with the problem of selecting the wisest course of action in the light of admittedly inadequate information, with a view to avoiding the foreclosure of possibly desirable future options by default. Similarly, we are learning — as the recent experience of the United States with respect to the Supersonic Transport controversy and a number of other domestic environmental problems graphically illustrates — that the concept of a monolithic opinion on purely scientific questions within something called "the scientific community" is a popular myth which would never occur to scientists themselves.

It is true that those — such as certain polluting industries — having special but publicly unsavory reasons for resisting effective environmental measures may invoke the lack of scientific knowledge as a pretext. Given, however, a common commitment to effective action and a common willingness to pay the price for it, the issue between legislative activists and foot-dragging fact-finders is likely to prove a chimera when scrutinized in the context of a particular problem. When it is prudent policy, in light of all the facts, to take action notwithstanding the inadequacy of the scientific knowledge available, then the tentative and stop-gap nature of the action should be clearly recognized. When, on the other hand, prudent policy dictates forestalling action until more data is available, then this course should be regarded not as passivism but as a better-informed — and thus more effective — activism.

The world's experience in the effort to eliminate cholera may serve to illustrate the latter point. In the latter half of the last century, efforts were pressed forward which sought to eliminate cholera by dealing with the disease when it arose. This method became the subject of international regulation through conventions, and later World Health Organization regulations, which placed emphasis on vaccination, travel restrictions, certificates, and other measures of control which have proved only relatively effective. It can be argued that a better scientific assessment of the nature of this kind of global pollution problem, taken intelligently into account by policymakers, might have redirected all these energies toward the elimination of cholera at its source by proper measures of sanitation aimed at producing pure water.

4. *The "performance gap" in international organizations*

There is often a gap between the formally stated competence of organizations within the United Nations system, as reflected in their constitutional instruments or their internal legislation, and their capacity to perform. Indeed, there may often be a gap between their formal legal competence and the legal competence many constituent governments would be willing to support for them if pressed to do so. The fact is that the same governments that have recorded great visions of the future and enshrined noble objectives in the preambles of charters have only rarely been willing to commit the resources of money and political will necessary to vindicate their declared intentions. The significance of this fact goes well beyond the question of the use in environmental management of the existing Specialized Agencies of the U.N. For it is symptomatic of the attitudes of governments toward international organizations generally, a quarter-century after the end of World War II, and must be realistically taken into account in the planning of any jobs which are to be performed through multilateral agencies existing or future.

5. *The biosphere concept and international environmental action.*

The concept of the biosphere has become popularly synonymous with a view of the earth from an interplanetary vantage point, as a single, fragile and dazzlingly intricate life system. It is a concept to fire men's imagination, to wrench them from the perspective of fiscal years to that of geologic time, and to move them to great deeds for future generations.

By contrast, the foregoing "five guides" may be taken in sum effect as a hard-bitten argument for caution and realism, an expression of distrust of grand statements of great expectations that are not firmly rooted in the capacity to perform. To the extent that this is true, such a view may be said to grow out of a clear appreciation of the way the world is in fact organized politically, a cardinal feature of which is the relative weakness of supranational structures of decision-making and action. It also stems from an appreciation of the fact that "environmental concerns may yet lie very close to the periphery of the motivating interests of most states both developing and developed. There are grounds for an educated suspicion that national commitment to the economic objectives and forms of organization and activity that have generated much of the environmental problem runs much deeper than the rhetoric of public officials sometimes suggests.

The moral, however, is not that the sweeping vision of the biosphere is irrelevant. Precisely the contrary is true. A comprehensive vision of the plight of the planet as a whole furnishes us a true standard by which to judge any effort to bring the planet's fragmented and often weak systems of social and political organization, national and international, to bear upon the problem of protecting man's environment. What is needed are persons in positions of responsibility who have *both* a clear perception of the whole from the biospheric perspective, *and* a realistic appreciation of the nature and capacities of the available social and political tools.

PROBLEMS OF DEFINITION AND SCOPE

by *Nicholas A. Robinson*[*]

"Squalid poverty lives side by side with over-abundance on our Earth. We have reached the Moon but we have not yet reached each other. Many species of our co-inhabitants on the globe from the bird and animal world have forever disappeared. Many beautiful rivers have become sewers endangering the oceans. We must heed the omens. It is time for Governments to make a fresh start and to lift themselves again to the same high level, if not a higher level, of vision and determination as that of the authors of the Charter. We must give the Charter a real chance at last. We must pass from words to deeds. We must pass from rights to obligations. We must pass from self interest to mutual interest. We must pass from partial peace to total peace."

U. Thant, *On the occasion of U.N. Day*[1]
October 24, 1970

Beyond cavil, the international community has established its concern for the quality of the natural environment as it affects mankind. Prerequisite to the success of international initiatives undertaken in response to problems of the global environment is the emergence of a more particularized international consensus as to the definition and scope of environmental concerns. There must be accord as to which of the myriad problems are the proper subjects for collective action.

In short, serious attention must be given to exploring what criteria can now be identified to aid in determining the proper environmental concerns of the international community.

I. DEFINITIONAL MATRIX

Preliminarily, it will be useful to examine the framework in which the question of criteria identification is found. Such an inquiry will provide a matrix whereby definitions of scope and terms are fixed.

While the "international community" remains necessarily a fluid and open-ended concept, it perhaps can be described best in relation to environmental issues as being the collection of nation-states, regional inter-state organizations ("international persons" in their own right). What given countries or a given international agency will decide is a proper environmental issue for global attention will invariably become such.

Notwithstanding the current debate over whether the initial stimulus for global action should come from the national level, or from international organizations, or from some new environmental body, the source of concern will come from whatever element of the international community is closest to the problem. The diversity of the international

---

[*]The author is a member of the New York Bar and a member of the Legal Advisory Committee to the Council on Environmental Quality.

44

community suggests that when any constituent member perceives an environmental issue as being of high priority, it will press that concern. The response to the initiative once raised will vary depending upon such factors as how it is raised, what it is, and what forum it is placed before.

Seen from this perspective, the preference of a nation like France or the Union of Soviet Socialist Republics for placing the origin of environmental action programs with the nation-state rather than an international agency becomes an artificial and preliminary instance of political skirmishing. Like the now diminishing debate between developing and developed countries as to the propriety of governmental ecological concerns, this political issue may recede as a better understanding of global environmental needs comes to be established. The residue of these problems will remain in terms of such questions as who pays for environmental quality and how, or who may systematically raise environmental issues and before what forum.

It should be noted that although initially agreement among the national governments or in the governing councils of international organizations will be required before action on environmental issues can be taken, it is nonetheless clear that for operational responses and specific projects the active participation and agreement of regional and local governmental and private agencies will be essential. Local attitudes, regulations, enforcement, monitoring and data gathering, all will be crucial.

Truly, the recently accepted concern for the quality of the global environmental leads to embracing Judge Philip Jessup's concept of transnational concerns and law: "all the law which regulates action or events that transcend national frontiers...[it] includes both civil and criminal aspects, what we know as public and private international law, and it includes national law both public and private...Transnational situations... may involve individuals, corporation, states or other groups."[2]

The complexion and composition of this international or transnational community will necessarily vary depending upon the given environmental problems identified. Having loosely identified who may be concerned, what is a "proper" environmental concern for the community?

Clearly the definition of what is "proper" cannot be divorced form the realities of political decision-making in the international community. It will be useful, therefore, to review here what issues thus far have found sufficient consensus to secure at least entry into the centers of international decision-making. Conversely, it is crucial to examine what environmental issues *should be*, by objectively arrived at and applied criteria, the "proper" subjects for global consideration. Both classes of issues may be deemed "proper."

Nor can "proper" be determined without analysis of the capabilities of different parts of the international community. What state or agency has the expertise, funds and general capacity to treat a given environmental

45

question? Answers to such a query will involve political as well as technical and economic considerations. What may be a proper concern for one part of the international community may not be for another, and joint "proper" concerns may produce competing or even conflicting policies and programs.

In identifying or defining criteria for either class, it must be acknowledged that definitions are most often easier to state than to apply. This essay represents an attempt to give an over-view and point of departure for the Conference. The reader's task will be to critique the analysis and extract from it what may be useful to the discussion of international organization implications of the environmental concerns here reviewed.

The definitional matrix must also touch upon the scientifically assessed realities of the natural ecosystems in which international environmental problems arise. It is clear today that the natural resources and life support systems of this planet are finite. Land accounts for only some one-fourth of the earth's surface and of this only one-half is inhabitable, because the other half is desert, mountain or polar. Water, although not always present when needed, covers the balance of the globe. Indeed, of the entire global biosphere, two-thirds lies outside any single national jurisdiction and the remaining one-third is so interdependent that it often necessarily involves several jurisdictions simultaneously. Despite this acknowledged reality, the pathways of these interlocking ecosystems are not always well understood.

Within the historic and artificial national boundaries, stress on these ecosystems comes from the increasing procreation of the human species. It took man 200,000 years to grow in numbers to one billion people; a century later two billion persons comprised the earth's population. In the thrity years between 1930 and 1960, a third billion people was added, and mankind is well along toward increasing his numbers to a fourth billion in 1975.

This vast increase in population has not only placed stress on natural systems, it has taxed the fabric of socity both within each national jurisdiction and transnationally. Social services even in so-called developed and well established cities are short in supply and quality. Individual human rights are impaired and denied. Social and economic development is undercut and unemployment is rampant, in some lands exceeding what was experienced during the Great Depression.

The population increase when juxtaposed to the finite nature of earth's resources, or the mere 25 million square miles of habitable and cultivatable land, or to the as yet crudely tapped oceanic resources, or to the increasingly polluted atmosphere, gives reason for alarm.

Even if theoretically Earth has the resources to provide for the 7.5 billion human beings, estimated number of inhabitants of the planet by the year 2000, will mankind be able to create the social systems to tap those resources, to deliver and generate the support systems to supply food, education, housing, energy, transportation, recreation, and the like to this aggregation of humanity?

The largely unplanned urban blight, spreading like a necrosis over the face of most nations, suggests a negative response to this inquiry. The plight of refugees on the Indian sub-continent similarly prompts pessimism. On the other hand, never has international co-operation been greater than today, and reports from the People's Republic of China suggest that even huge masses of people in an underdeveloped country can be organized to provide for basic needs. Moreover, the successful fertility control of lands such as Japan, when coupled with the fact that scientists know how to increase the productivity and harvest for man of the biosphere, is an indication that hope and mutual interest may yet be a viable motivating force.

What the population figures teach when combined with the pronounced concerns for public health, sanitation, air and water pollution, is that the growth in numbers and the demands generated thereby are root causes of both societal disintegration and consequential pollution. If the international community treats the symptoms of population growth gradually by slowly arrived at international consensus, it may never remedy one of the underlying sources. Man's success with mortality control must now be matched with successful institution of birth control.

Man's failure to apply known engineering technology to better ameliorate or even to resolve present population problems and other environmental troubles underscores another background element of our definitional matrix. Man has imperfectly and primitively embarked on technology analysis or the study of how technology is applied, with what consequences, what options for what alternatives, what paths are foreclosed, deliberately or inadvertently. Globally it must be asked how can man assess incremental choices in diverse jurisdictions when their aggregate constitutes a major environmental problem.

Perhaps the greatest technological problem is posed by the inordinately large engineering and technical assets devoted to military pruposes. The absurdity of the arms race is plain from the threat of nuclear annihilation which daily accompanies our more prosaic concerns for clean air and water. The absurdity of the emphasis on military prowess was recently highlighted by a political unit in one of the arms race leaders: the U.S. Senate Armed Services Committee astutely commented recently that, "If the geometric cost increase for weapons systems is not sharply reversed, then even significant increases in the defense budget may not insure the force levels required for our national security."[3]

Whether because of the primitive state of technology assessment and the questionable heavy emphasis on armaments, or whether derived from other societal shortcomings, man's technology today appears to lack a responsiveness to the environmental realities sketched here. If man *can* exploit, apparently he *will* exploit without pausing to explore how, by what alternative means, or why. Only massive public outcry prompts such examination as to the United State's Alaskan oil exploitations; and the burning of jungle in Maranhao State at the edge of the Amazon in Brazil is continuing despite the disastrous effects of fire land clearing.

Briefly stated, this is our definitional matrix: a transnational community, unsure of how to direct its technological prowess, within a biosphere of limited resources, imperfectly harvested and barely supporting a human population whose needs grow at exponential rates as do its numbers.

Before examining what are presently identified as "proper" subjects of global environmental concern in light of this definitional matrix, we must examine briefly how the state of socio-economic development projects against this matrix.

II. SOCIAL AND ECONOMIC DEVELOPMENT

A. *The Developing Lands*

Much of the international community has accepted the decision that social-economic development is a global concern of the highest importance. The international organizations, developing countries and major parts of the developed community have arrived at this view. Unlike the companion paramount issue of disarmament and security where little progress is being made, the global consensus in favor of development has caused major resources to be directed to its service.

When the United Nations General Assembly decided to convene its 1972 Conference on the Human Environment, the developing lands (already distressed at the apparent unwillingness of major donor countries to increase their contributions to development) feared that the environmental concerns would be defined as merely the rich cleaning house, diverting economic and technical resources from development needs to pollution abatement.

The fears of the developing nations had crystallized sufficiently by June of 1971 to permit their examination by a panel of experts. The panel, meeting in Founex, Switzerland, under the auspices of the Secretary-General of the Conference, summarized the fears as follows: (1) fear that the developed nations will create rigorous environmental standards for products traded internationally and generate a "neo-protectionism" excluding nonconforming goods from poor lands; (2) fear that the emphasis on non-polluting technology and recycling may eliminate or reduce demand for some raw materials or agricultural products in which pesticide residues are found; (3) fear that aid for development purposes will be delayed or curtailed if the rich lands focus largely on their own environmental problems; (4) fear that developed lands will unilaterally

48

dictate environmental standards to the developing lands without considering how to relate those standards to the conditions of the developing lands; (5) fear that the developed states will saddle the developing with their own definition of what are proper global environmental concerns.[4]

All the panel of experts wisely observed that "these are legitimate fears. But they should not be exaggerated. In any case, the best strategy for developing countries is to articulate them fully and to seek opportunities to turn the environmental concern in the developed countries to their own advantage or at least neutralize its adverse implications."[5]

More specifically, the experts counselled that environmental concern globally has its salutary aspects from the point of view of a developing state: (1) "The developing countries would clearly wish to avoid, as far as feasible, the mistakes and distortions that have characterized the patterns of development of the industrialized societies."; (2) In the context of the poor countries, "development becomes essentially a cure for their major environmental problems" requiring a redefinition of the goals of the Second Development Decade "in order to attack that dire poverty which is the most important aspect of the problems which afflict the environment of the majority of mankind."; (3) Direct contributions to resolving the environmental aspects of poverty were identified as: (a) some increased use of natural fibers over synthetics made by polluting processes, (b) more careful conserving of natural resources with the necessity of renegotiating commodity agreements, (c) increasing location of industry in the less polluted developing countries where the "environmental carrying capacity" is less taxed and where environmental controls might be less urgent, (d) additional funds must be contributed to the developing lands from donor countries — preferably via a specific identifiable new fund — if the developed states realistically wish to see environmental concerns adequately treated, (e) the environmental concerns stress training of human resources and "programs in education, nutrition, public health, water supply and other social services are beginning to be regarded favorably."[6]

Thus a considered and refined analysis by experts from developing countries concludes that environmental concerns must be carefully weighed with respect to the global commitment to development and as to each country's development plans. The need for additional and new funds to service the environmental concerns is understood. The concentration on essentially domestic environmental ills reflects the overriding national policy of the poor countries in favor of their own development.[7]

B. Developed Countries

The northern tier of rich nations sparked the global concern for pollution, endangered species and land use policies. They have solved the bulk of their own environmental "poverty" problems in the course of creating their devastated landscapes and waters. They support the advanced scientific community which through the International Council of Scientific Unions (ICSU) and national academies of science and universities has been so instrumental in focusing on environmental dangers attendant on over-development.

These rich lands have identified a series of problems to which they attach great importance; such problems are both domestic and international. The level of development of the developed lands places them in a position of greater global involvement in activities having environmental impacts than is the case with developing lands. It places the rich lands in the dubious station of generating many of the world's environmental problems which transcend mere domestic impact.

Most of the environmental problems identified by the developed countries have found a place on the roster of "proper" international concerns. As such they are set forth later in this paper and need not be separately stated here. What is important to consider is how the definitional matrix imposes itself on the concerns of the developed countries. Doubtless many of the developed lands could decide among themselves to resolve some of their problems in the short run, but when they act in the international arena, they must factor in the realities of development and population.

C. *The Interdependence of Rich and Poor*

The developing lands have major voting strength in the United Nations General Assembly and at the 1972 Conference on the Human Environment. The developed lands have the money and technology to cope with development and environment. The dependence of the developed lands on the natural resources of the poorer countries gives the former an acute interest in social stability in the latter; the stability of several developing states is presently threatened by population expansion. In short, a web of interdependent or mutual concerns emerges.

Full perception of the interdependence of the rich and poor lands underscores the need for the developed states to embrace the traditional environmental concerns of the poorer regions with as much enthusiasm as they muster for pollution threats. It may no longer be sufficient to wipe out cholera in Europe and North America yet tolerate it on the fringes of the developed world; it may also be necessary as an environmental commitment to come to grips with the malnutrition or poor educational facilities which exist as "pockets of poverty" even amidst the plenty of the rich nations.

Conversely, the developing lands must recognize the compelling scientific reality that, whatever a problem's source or lack of immediate relation to a given state's domestic priorities, if it has the earmarks of a global problem, then the entire international community must support co-ordinated global action.

Implicit in these sharings of perspective, but beyond the scope of this paper, are issues such as these: the need and method to shift capital investment from the northern tier of nations to the southern tier; new land use policies; revised international economic systems to permit major investment in developing lands while not undermining trade patterns, balance of payments, and the role and control of the multi-national corporations.

It is noteworthy to observe that some environmental issues affect both developed and developing lands. Increased population has generated acute housing and urban problems in both tiers of states. A common consensus already has emerged that such problems are "proper" international environmental concerns.

Thus the elements of a comprehensive common consensus as to proper environmental concerns exist. The perception of mutuality on the part of government officials whose first mandate is the resolution of domestic ills may be slow in reaching the global arena. Whether these elements can be welded together, and if so in what subject area, are questions pending and not fully resolved. Serious doubts can be raised as to whether man has the will to restructure his perceptions and his institutions in order to forge the common consensus.

Having singled out some of the salient considerations from the definitional matrix and the perspectives of the rich and poor states, we turn to a review of what already has been designated as "proper" international environmental concerns.

III. PRESENTLY IDENTIFIED CONCERNS

During the past two decades, although most fully within the past two years, a number of environmental problems have been designated as proper international concerns. Analysis of each reveals that it falls into one or another of certain broad classes. These classifications are distinguished by different characteristics from which some conclusions may be drawn as to what are appropriate international criteria for determining "proper" environmental concerns.

Such an empirical review and inductive approach to exploring environmental criteria has its limitations. Each problem is traceable to one or another source constituency — scientists, public health officials, developing country planners, conservationists, exploiters, etc. The place any environmental concern occupies in the international arena may be determined by political factors unrelated to an objective analysis of its importance. The classification system posed here does not reflect the source constituency for the problem listed; rather it poses problems in terms of impact and the logical interface between impact and national jurisdiction.

Alternative classification systems could be framed in terms of the source constituency, or in terms of the technical resources which are required to resolve the problem, or in terms of the type of problem and how it is created. Different implications for international co-operative efforts to resolve environmental problems flow from which classification system is adopted. This paper will spell out only one possible system, both as a model and for its utility in determining how "proper" concerns are so reached. The reader may wish to consider the reordering of the problems set forth below in light of the other possible models.

What follows sets forth what is widely identified as an accepted global environment issue, regardless of how it found its way to that station. Thereafter and separately we shall turn to the propriety of such acceptance in light of other issues which perhaps should have this status also.[8]

A. *Problems of the Commons*

Clearly meriting international concern are those problems found in the portions of the globe located beyond the domestic jurisdiction of any state. These commons, enjoyed by all, include the oceans, atmosphere, polar regions, and outer space.

Environmental problems of the commons are caused directly (e.g. oil spills on the seas, dumping of radioactive waste in the oceans) or indirectly. (The U.N. Natural Resources Committee stresses that river basin countries are "the greatest contributors to ocean pollution".) The state of knowledge as to the global effects of pollution of the commons is poor; accordingly many of the proposals concerning the commons deal with gathering more knowledge regarding their environmental problems.

To be sure, exhaustion of fish through over-harvesting, oil spills, ocean dumping and ocean floor exploitation have emerged as areas where sufficient knowledge and global concern are present to prompt negotiations, decisions and draft conventions. Nonetheless, many areas remain far from any international action other than information gathering and analysis. It will be useful to examine briefly some of the issues presently proposed as requiring global attention which are illustrative of this category.

Within the atmospheric commons, any foreign substance which does not decompose or fall out during the two weeks in which time stratospheric winds circle the globe is certainly a pollutant of global impact. These pollutants include CO_2 (which is estimated to be increasing globally by some 2% per decade), SO_2, and solid particulates. Where contaminants do fall out, as in the "acid rain" or the grey-snow of Europe, they cause inter-state pollution problems which are regional rather than global although the pathway is via the commons.

Studies of the *generation* of CO_2 (fossil fuel use, deforestation) and of SO_2 (use of sulfur-rich fuel, smelting, industry) and of particulates (industrial and domestic fuel consumption, soil erosion), of the *effects* of each (CO_2 and the fabled greenhouse effect; and possible respiratory, genetic, or carcinogenic effects; particulates and reduction in local visibility, cleanliness and possible climatic impact), and of the *amounts* present and the *pathways* of each are needed.

Beyond these atmospheric contaminants, radioactivity, thermal pollution, photochemical smog, oxides of nitrogen, ozone, ice forming nuclei, condensation nuclei, lead compounds, etc., all may require global monitoring and regulation and control. Before any decision as to the dangers of these elements can be made, more information is required.

Ocean pollution raises similar issues. Study of the presence and dispersal of poly-chlorinated biphenyls (derived originally from plastic and synthetic fibre manufacture), DDT (originating as an insecticide), mercury, lead and other heavy metal compounds (industrial and agricultural sources), of how they enter biological systems and effect food chains, and of what their consequences in different circumstances may be is needed.

The long-term effects of oil spillage are unknown although the short-term effects on marine life are very serious. Although radioactivity is curbed in the atmosphere by the partial test ban treaty, the oceans continue to receive radioactive wastes as a result of monitoring and regulation.

Polar region co-operation provides one model of international understanding. Resolution of perceived environmental problems in these areas is likely to share in the spirit of co-operation which characterizes the international community's presence in the area. As to outer space, environmental issues are less well known; the nations which possess the technical ability to circle satellites or send missions beyond earth have shown an acute concern for possible contamination. What the space commons lack is agreement to use satellites, for instance, clearly for the common good rather than to serve a given nation's security interests. Telecommunications satellites present a precedent for global co-operation which needs to be extended to the environmental monitoring field.

B. *Regional Problems*

Many environmental problems extend beyond a single nation but are limited in their effect to a region. Such are the European acid rains or dirty snow mentioned above. Such also are environmental problems which have a localized impact on a region divided between different national jurisdictions; where rivers or lakes border on different countries, pollution of even small and contained ecosystems is an international issue. Examples would be the run-off of fertilizers or sanitary and industrial wastes into the North American Great Lakes from both Canada and the United States, or the oil pollution of the Caspian Sea. The downstream effect of Rhine pollution is infamous. Where existing concerns for navigation and hydrological uses of an interstate river have been well developed, such as with the Danube Commission, it is a logical and compelling extension to explore the interstate environmental problems of the same river.

Similarly, energy generation might fruitfully be explored on a regional basis. Distribution of electrical power on a grid over a broad region — used in some areas already and not unlike a transportation grid in terms of co-operation — may increasingly become necessary to economize on power and fuel and concomitant pollution.

Where several countries share a peculiar region — as Canada, the Scandinavian states, the U.S.S.R., and the U.S.A. do the arctic region — preservation of species, such as polar bear and seal and wolf, or care and conservation of tundra are all likely subjects for regional collaboration. Precedents also can be found in interstate cooperation aimed at protection of migratory wildfowl.

Thus, within this interstate regional classification the environmental problems are of international concern largely *not* because of their nature, but because of their limited impact.

C. *Local Problems with Global Implications*

Where impact is diffuse, global concern is less likely to be activated; conversely, some problems with essentially local impact carry such global implications as to qualify for international concern. The potentiality of aggregates of local problems impinging on one aspect or another of the global environment cannot be avoided.

Thus, although social and economic development is essentially a national issue, its advancement is of global concern. Similarly, population growth is increasingly the subject of international concern and co-operation. Within these broad themes of development and population are subsumed other issues to which global attention is given, such as food production and housing. Increasingly, also, more attention globally is being given to the rehabilitation of derelict and over-exploited land. If the productivity of the biosphere is to be increased to supply for the growing population, increased global attention will be focused on this problem.

Even though some areas of concern such as the generation of energy have been traditionally wholly national concerns, the presence of other trends such as depletion of petroleum reserves, increased energy production by nuclear fission and population growth all suggest that energy will move into regional and global concerns.

Existing global trade patterns will have to expand their horizons to take into account environmental concerns. Uniform environmental standards and product quality may be necessary to assure equity in trade relations. Environmental concerns on the part of any one nation should not result in economic penalties derived from a disadvantageous trade position or state of economic development. Additionally, without uniformity there is a danger of "tariff-like" trade barriers keyed into environmental standards. GATT and existing global trade concerns will necessarily have to consider such issues. Multilateral corporations such as the Nestlé complex which have experience in product quality control may have a contribution to make in providing models for controls as to environmental checks.[9] Also the emergence of liability for environmental injuries may result in new insurance arrangements stimulated by either governments or private companies and containing international standards of conduct in order to qualify for coverage.

D. *Local Problems Recurring and Shared among Different Countries*

Given the disparities in technical and economic capacities among different nations, not all lands have the same capability to respond to environmental problems. The diversity of countries also results in some nations tackling certain environmental problems sooner or with greater success than others. These aspects of international life suggest a further area of global concerns for environmental issues — that of international co-operation on local problems.

The utility of pooling the expertise and experience of different nations through international co-operation has long been clear. Examples of such recognition are the well developed concern for urbanization and housing as spread throughout different U.N. bodies. The U.N.'s twenty-seven nation Committee on Housing, Building & Planning has studied the needs of the world's urban population which will increase from 1,330 million to 3,090 million by the year 2000. The estimated influx of 90,000 people a day into urban areas creates pressures which are inadequately being met in practically every land. So great is the demand for construction to accommodate increases in population that the U.N. Center for Housing, Building & Planning estimates that the need in the last half of the twentieth century will exceed the total volume of all building throughout man's entire existence on earth.[10]

Through the U.N. Economic Commissions in Africa, Asia, Latin America and Europe, plus the U.N. Economic and Social Office in Beirut, much study and experimentation is underway to meet these housing needs. This regional work will be reviewed at the 1972 Conference on the Human Environment under the topic "The Planning and Management of Human Settlement For Environmental Quality." The check-list of agenda concerns are all essentially of local impact, but as to each item the need to understand and resolve the problem is so great that they have become subjects of international collaboration and global concern. The cities are the nerve centers of each land, and their health immediately affects the transnational community.

Further domestic environmental issues which the global community considers important include fresh water pollutants and their sources, pathways and abatement, rural land use, agricultural production and soil conservation, basic literacy and education, and local industrialization.

E. *Common Global Heritage of Man*

In the broadest sense, all the natural resources of earth are man's common heritage. By historical coincidence their management has bee parcelled out to different congregations of men located in various lands. The management function is today closely and jealously guarded as a national prerogative; there may be a time when international concern and regulation influence and guide this national management effort more than is the case today. Suggestions of a basis for global concern as to national ecomanagement can be found in at least two areas of governmental concern; this is the recognition of a common heritage for all men in life-support resources and in unique natural phenomena.

The recognition that life-support resources are a common heritage is less pronounced than that of natural wonders. Nonetheless, it is becoming increasingly clear that all mankind shares and depends upon the commons, or the outer-layer of soil and subsoil roughly 1-3 meters deep. Loss of any of the some 140 centimeters of productive top soil on which man's food supply largely depends becomes a loss for all men. Soil conservation in light of the experiences of the American Dust Bowl or of the newly cleared Soviet land in Uzbekistan and Siberia or of the overgrazing of herds in parts of Africa is a prime international concern. Each misuse diminishes a common resource of all mankind even though it be confined to the national boundaries of a given nation state.

More clearly recognized as a common heritage of all man is the task of preserving biological or physical wonders of nature. Included here is (a) protection for endangered species, such as has been accomplished by the work of the International Council for Bird Preservation or the U.S.S.R.'s polar bear preservation program; and (b) protection of special ecosystems which are unique and illustrative by their pristine condition, such as Iran's offer to set aside some of its wetlands as a world preserve; or (c) creation of national parks to assure natural regions will

56

retain their character or natural monuments will be protected, as in the Latin American parks among the Andes or Africa's Serengeti Plane or England's Royal Forest or the Grand Canyon in the United States.

In the United Nations' International Union for the Conservation of Nature registry of national parks and in the protection of endangered species by governments, some of the greatest strides have been made toward recognizing and implementing the principle that the people of each land are the guardians of their unique resources. The role of government is here properly viewed as one of stewardship for the present management of all natural resources present within its jurisdiction. This trusteeship role is the newly perceived environmental dimension of the oft-repeated principle in U.N. circles reasserting the inalienable sovereignty of each state over its natural resources.

The acceptance of this newly pressed dimension will come slowly, but a start is underway in this category of the world's common heritage. Sufficient consensus has emerged as to the second area of common heritage here discussed that adoption of the World Heritage Foundation proposal at the 1972 Conference seems most likely.

In observing that wildlife protection is now clearly established governmental policy in India, Prime Minister Indira Gandhi has observed, "No doubt we need more foreign exchange but this should not be at the cost of the life and liberty of our beautiful species ... No doubt there is some handicap in wildlife being essentially a state rather than a central government function. But we have reconstituted the national Board of Wildlife. Here again there is a need for education. The conservationists are only at the beginning of the battle. People must be reeducated to take a long-term view not only of our fauna but of the human environment."[11]

Perhaps in this global concern for special elements of nature that are clearly accepted as a heritage of all mankind is a harbinger of how all motivation for the international environment will be framed.

F. *International Technology*

Global concern for the effects of man's technological development is different from the classifications based upon impact and is still far removed from the embryonic stewardship concepts associated with the common global heritage. Technology innovation and application are nonetheless so important that they require independent attention.

The concern in this problem area is focused on how man views technological developments and in what ways he seeks to exploit the knowledge of science through specific applications. Illustrative of some of the concerns in this area is the work of the U.N. Advisory Committee on the Application of Science and Technology to Development. The interface between public health concerns and socio-economic development

57

efforts to eliminate the environmental ills of poverty reveals the kinds of specific concerns which technology use and its underlying research generate.[12]

Even where medical innovations have been established there is a continuing need to apply the known techniques. Increased use of radiology in tuberculosis case-finding or community control of yaws through penicillin use are examples of this need. In the public health area there is a need to futher develop techniques for desalination of salt water, improved food preservation and use of computers for storage and renewal of information in the operation of community health services.

At the same time, new research, additional training of experts and the creation of new institutions are needed in the control efforts of various species of insects and rodents which are vectors or reservoirs of human disease; more study is required in the control of communicable diseases such as malaria, African Trypanosomiasis (Tsetse fly vector), American Trypanosomiasis (reduviid bug vector), Schistosomiasis (snail intermediate host) and leprosy (only 18% of the some 10,786,000 cases as of 1965 received treatment).

In the health field, the need to apply known technology and to research and develop new technology is fairly well established. Such efforts have effectively almost entirely eliminated small pox as an infectious disease; endemic foci are restricted to east Africa and southeast Asia, and a heat-stable, potent, freeze-dried vaccine is now available in both regions. The very success of science and technology in these health areas prompts questions as to how any given health issue was singled out as a priority, given adequate funding and research, applied with sufficient dispersal of experts and supplies, and re-evaluated and refined with practice. Examination of alternatives, trials and tests are all built into the health research and development; the question is posed of how to transfer these analytic methods to other technology areas. How, for instance, can the refinement of small pox vaccine teach lessons to avoid improvident uses to NTA (sodium nitriloacetate) instead of phosphates in detergents?

Despite the nascent governmental and ECOSOC interest in technology assessment and despite well established practices in some fields such as health, very little concern has been given to how the decision-making systems fix priorities for research, technological application and support and review of alternatives or implications. Much decision-making has been done by elites and the results have and still do largely benefit the elites. As a panel of the U.S. National Academy of Science has observed, "For centuries, a wide range of benefits and injuries were simply ignored in the decision-making processes that influenced technological change."[13]

How best can man assess the technological applications of each country and review the decision-making element within each country? In response to this question, governments are gradually examining what Frank Fraser Darling termed in his 1969 Reith Lectures: "The sins of our forefathers now descended unto the third and fourth generations." He viewed these as "largely the consequence of ignorance. We are ignorant no longer. Science enlarges our vision, and ecology is concerned with causes and consequences on a broad front. We should be delving ecologically into the future, but in general we are not doing so."[14]

The elimination of ignorance requires some systematic attention by governments. Just as the national governments have food and drug purity agencies to test and regulate the issuance of new drugs, so man needs a global mechanism to trigger such studies in many fields, to assist local governments in undertaking such reviews and to give an overview of national assessments made. Decision-makers need to have methods for maximizing the preservation of options, in understanding trade-offs and the consequences of actions taken or not taken.

Recognition of the need for full knowledge to underlie decisions as to research and action priorities lies behind the scientific community's proposal for the creation of an International Registry of Chemical Compounds. Such a Registry would be designed to identify the synthetic chemicals being introduced into the environment, to study their pathways and possible mutagenic, carcinogenic and teratogenic effects on man. Dose-effect relationships as to the toxicity of a given substance could be determined. Before data sufficient for the decision-maker to use in deciding to permit or deny application of synthetic chemical use is available, these initial elements of identification and research are essential.

The decisions of the International Bank for Reconstruction and Development and the U.N. Development Programme to undertake analysis of the secondary impact of development projects reveals a new sensitivity to the consequences of environmental applications of technology. Both agencies seek to feed these factors into decision-making at a very early stage, prior to commencement of projects. Impact analysis is embodied in the domestic law of an increasing number of states, including several states in the U.S.A. and that nation itself through the National Environmental Policy Act of 1969.[15]

The specific arrangements or systems for technology assessment will necessarily vary depending on the need, the context and the scope. While it is clear at this point that technology assessment is of global concern, it is still in a primitive and evolving operational stage and needs expansion into all phases of man's decision-making.

G. *Overlapping Concerns*

Merely to break down these global concerns into the categories here

59

listed is to involve a degree of over-simplification. Rarely will one category exist isolated from the others. If prime responsibility is assigned for each class of concerns to one or another part of the international community, careful consideration will have to be given to the overlap of concerns, to joint operations, to mechanisms of co-operation, etc.

Consider as a hypothetical case the production of DDT and other like pesticides. These substances are produced privately in factories of developed countries in quantities the full measure of which is not known either for each producing state or for the aggregate of all producing states. The substances are exported to developing countries and may there be used strictly domestically in conjunction with both public health and agricultural programs. The secondary effects of DDT use include its entry into the oceans through different food chains with the eventual endangerment of certain species of birds, some of which are protected in nature preserves and by laws as endangered species. The DDT concentrations are presently so high in North American woodcock that game hunting of the bird has been banned in some Canadian Provinces and United States regions because the DDT levels in the bird's tissues are deemed a threat to man himself. DDT has flowed through global pathways into the fatty tissues of both penguins in the Antarctic and low income slum dwellers who consume fatty meat cuts because they are cheap and available. All the while technological alternatives are but slowly pursued, and no single governmental unit appears to have sufficient authority to effectively deal with all aspects of DDT or even have information to make the decisions needed, facts on production, use, monitored effect, technological or biological alternatives, costs, etc. being absent.

The fact that enough is known of the DDT and pesticide situation to include it as a hypothetical illustration of the intermesh of classifications here described, but that not enough is known to do the same with other problems, is a cause of concern in itself. The mercury scares following toxic consequences from mercury pollution in Japan and the United States prompted official bans on tuna and swordfish consumption before a full understanding of mercury concentrations, sources, pathways, and effects was available. Uninformed reaction either by perpetrating a *status quo* or abruptly alerting it is hardly ecologically sound decision-making.

IV. CRITIQUE OF THE PRESENT CONCERNS

The overriding aim of these concerns is environmental quality. Definition of just what "environmental quality" means must vary with the given issue, whether it is viewed from an objective scientific perspective of what is ecologically sound or whether the evaluation is made by the governments of given states or by the collegial decision-making processes of some international agency.

Environmental quality is the focus of the 1972 United Nations Conference on the Human Environment. The agenda for that meeting reflects, in lesser or greater degrees, all the above-outlined concerns. They have been filtered through an international process of selection and deletion, emphasis and mutation, a process of decision guided by a melange of political, scientific and bureaucratic factors, and expert judgment.

As transmuted in the 1972 Conference agenda,[16] one set of concerns becomes *Planning and Management of Human Settlements*, including review of population growth only as a factor affecting flows into urban areas. *The Environmental Aspects of Natural Resource Managements* turns attention to "means for incorporating environmental considerations in the comprehensive planning and management of natural resource development." *The Identification and Control of Pollutants and Nuisances of Broad International Significance* would examine the sources, effects of pollutants and co-operative measures for their control and abatement. *Development and Environment* specifically seeks the key to defining environmental aspects of development and orient it within the Second Development decade.

Broadly viewed, these agenda items are concerned with defining the environmental problems within each sphere and achieving some better understanding of each. There are three further items focused on implementing reforms or establishing new means to meet some of the needs outlined in the substantive items listed above. *Educational, Informational, Social and Cultural Aspects of Environmental Issues* includes not only exploration of how these aspects raise environmental problems themselves, but also what education and attitude formation is needed to cope with problems perceived. Indeed, to a large extent the whole of the planning for the 1972 Conference is a system of continuing education and must be viewed as only a start in that direction. Similarly, *The International Organizational Implications of Action Proposals* are designed to set the stage for operational innovations, co-operation, and co-ordination. It must be acknowledged, however, that these implications are limited by the nature, scope and consensus of the action proposals to be framed. These proposals may *not* include some of the concerns already identified above or those which objective analysis would suggest warrant concern. Close attention must be paid to the dynamics of global decision-making here.

An over-all concept of environmental quality and its prerequisites or guiding principles will emerge from these specific considerations. On the other hand, definition of the concept has already commenced with the debate regarding a *Declaration on the Human Environment* for adoption at the 1972 Conference. Global agreement on this statement may be a benchmark from which to measure all transnational attempts to identify and cope with environmental problems.

Before turning specifically to the Declaration, it will be useful to suggest more specifically than has been done above certain elements of a critique of the global environmental concerns presently identified. Five such elements will be singled out: (a) environmental quality as an aim; (b) international functions required to realize that aim; (c) environmental implications of military policies; (d) elements of concern for the global environment inadequately recognized; (e) education and development of attitudes as basic prerequisites to change.

A. *Environmental Quality*

As elusive as the term "environmental quality" may be for some, or as hackneyed for others, it remains central to the global concern for environmental issues.

How any given member of the international community defines environmental quality will determine what, for it, is the range of "proper" environmental concerns. The definition embraced will tend to structure priorities. The choice of definition need not be between a fixed and immutable definition, as between pollution problems versus health and basic housing, or between developed versus developing country needs. Rather the content of environmental quality must turn on a regional or local assessment of needs guided by the overriding concern to preserve the integrity of natural life support ecosystems. Such an assessment could take into consideration the cultural perspective and socio-economic state of development of the given land and its people. The end aim would be sound basic health and ecological integrity so that a wholesome life could be enjoyed by the citizens of the area, and the fundamental struggle to provide human rights could proceed apace.

Of course some common international priorities must be fixed for environmental issues affecting the entire earth. Global pollution of the commons must be curbed; population growth must be arrested, and the natural heritage of mankind must be preserved. There may well be a tension in defining locally or regionally the component parts of environmental quality and the global point of view which each land must help shape and adopt. When the international concerns are combined with a given local or regional definition of environmental quality, the needs are structured and the means toward providing environmental quality can be assessed.

B. *International Functions*

Given the need for local assessments of environmental quality as well as of global concerns, several functions of government emerge which may be appropriate to all or some parts of the international community. The elaboration of these functions and the organizational responses proposed are themselves a proper concern for the international community.

Among the functions which logically emerge from the foregoing review of presently identified global environment concerns are the following:

(1) The need for *information gathering* and analysis generates several more specific functions. Monitoring of environmental phenomena and conditions includes supervision of the operation of monitoring systems, whether national or international, remote sensing or by means of special impact stations; it includes gathering, centralizing and storing data received; it requires cataloguing and making available through a dispersal system the data prepared. There is a need for creating common tests and measuring methods for collection and evaluation of environmental data. Some global clearing house will be needed involving the availability of computer systems.

(2) *Analysis* of information so gathered entails research, an integrated exchange of data and hypotheses, co-ordination of studies at all levels where appropriate, full exchange of parallel and related studies wherever undertaken and an international review and synthesis of research findings from around the globe. International evaluation and assessment must be subject to independent critique at different centers around the world.

In considering what issues need research, systematic attention should be given to those issues (a) where technological solutions are clear but the domestic priorities of a given land make the best means of implementing solutions unclear, (b) where technical solutions are not clear but the need for finding solutions is evident, and (c) where new problems can be anticipated before they emerge. Examples of each would be abatement of industrial water pollutants in the first issue, synthetic fertilizers versus eutrophication side-effects in the second item, and study of possible secondary effects of biological control of pests.

In determining priorities both for information gathering and analysis, costs, urgency of the problem and a range of other factors will emerge. The time lag between commencing information gathering and securing enough data to commence research and analysis, and again between the start and finish of research, must be taken into consideration in setting priorities.

(3) In all countries there is a crucial need for experts in environmental fields. Persons already trained in some areas of limited demand must be retrained where needed. New professional and technical *training programs* are required if personnel needs are to be met for information gathering and assessment, for environmental impact analysis and regulation, for field ecologists to evaluate all capital investment projects and for the host of other tasks which attend environmental concerns.

Technological resources need to be made available equally to all regions. The need for numerical computer modelling of different systems will be both global and recurring in each region. The tools for such modelling and those skilled in their use, however, are to be found today in but a few of the most developed countries.

Even among those trained in environmental related areas such as meteorology and public health, there will be a need for continuing professional education as new environmental knowledge and skills are developed. In-service training facilities will thus be needed.

(4) Once data is gathered and environmental issues are sufficiently understood, some mechanism for *setting standards* for the conduct of human activities in relation to the end goal of environmental quality will be needed. These standards should be objectively arrived at; the question of whether to adopt them or rest satisfied with a lesser standard (or impose a higher one) is a political decision which should be divorced from the recommended standard.

At the same time as assuring the independence and insulation required for the standard setting function, there must be a system whereby the evaluated data and recommended standards are fed into the relevant decision-making centers with weight equal to that given economic or political factors. The precise method for assuring the highest consideration of the independent environmental analysis will vary with the government unit or level of decision involved.

There is a need to consider how decision-makers can be alerted to the importance of an environmental issue in light of the fact that no political constituency will probably rally behind the objective analysis.

Environmental issues often lack an informed political interest favoring environmental quality. Perhaps special government units, ombudsmen, a complaint system or other arrangement will be required. In order to assure the integrity of the data gathered and analyzed, it will be necessary to avoid putting the information collectors and assessors in the role of sponsors for a given standard lest they be swept into the political process themselves, impairing honest analysis and refinement of data which sound decision-making requires.

Some attention must be given to standardization of the standards and criteria proposed and ultimately adopted. The regulations of a variety of jurisdictions must be integrated and regularized. Regional and global co-operation to this end should be considered with methods outlined for periodic review and revision.

(5) *Planning* will be central to concerns for a healthy environment. Developing countries have plans which can be modified favorably to incorporate environmental concerns. Many of the developed countries, on the other hand, lack plans for land use, urban growth, population distribution, energy needs, industrial growth and the like. Plans must be considered and forecasts of trends and future needs be prepared.

Planning is a key element of data analysis and provides a means for synthesizing all social, economic, cultural and other factors along with the environmental. Planning too must be better integrated into the decision-making structure, injected earlier with a capacity to command greater attention.

(6) *Co-ordination* of programs and activities will be an essential function required at each level of governmental authority. Different governmental units must compare their programs, understand the impact of one upon another, resolve inconsistencies, etc. Some international overview will be needed, not only among the specialized U.N. agencies or other inter-state bodies, but among competing national and regional policies. There is a need for some system of consultation and *ad hoc* meetings mandated to explore international environmental issues put before them and requested to pose solutions to those problems. The format for such a system needs to be considered; whether it would include an on-going meeting such as GATT or a new mechanism featuring a co-ordinating committee to pick topics and convene meetings and service meetings, or would be in another form, must be examined.

(7) *Enforcement* of standards adopted eventually will become a crucial issue domestically, regionally and internationally. At the global level care must be used so as not to institute or seek enforcement of standards unilaterally. International collaboration and consensus are essential to assure that no state will be unduly penalized because of the state of its development, nature of its chief export products or capacity to meet international environmental standards. Sanctions should be carefully framed.

Registration and licensing and inspection, as mild but often effective regulation methods, ought to be explored for use both nationally and globally. Incentives such as subsidies, grants, trade or tariff concessions, credits and other compensations for overcoming any inability to meet standards once agreed upon must be explored both within and between nations.

Prohibitions as extreme regulations will have a limited but significant utility as in preserving endangered species or halting over-exploitation of an ecosystem to permit its natural rehabilitation. Total bans depend, of course, on total adherence to the ban by the relevant part or whole of the international community. Achievement of such concurrence is in itself a formidable undertaking.

Police action domestically or sanctions or reprisals internationally need to be carefully analyzed. Some innovations in policing environmental standards regionally along the lines of customs unions might be explored. Calculated and co-ordinated multilateral sanctions could be formulated. The enforcement must await the global consensus as to standards, and it should not be prematurely raised as a desirable means in itself without reference to a specific international environmental concern. Such abstract consideration turns the issue into a political debate unrelated to the merits of enforcement in connection with a specific environmental problem.

(8) Crucial to all these environmental functions will be the method whereby they are *financed*. How shall new programs be funded? Where shall the increased funds for future environmental development be found? What trade-offs will be chosen?

Given the excess pollution of the developed northern tier of nations, further polluting industrialization in that region must be questioned. A global equilibrium, both as to socio-economic development and environmentally sound development, suggests the need for a much greater flow of resources from the developed to the developing countries.

This increased flow of funds and capital investment to the developing lands would include both relocating industry there as well as increasing aid and capital investments; all development generated by this shift would necessarily be on an ecologically sound basis. The subsidies, etc., set forth in section (7) above could be included in this shift. It could include the specially earmarked international fund already proposed as a channel to aid underdeveloped lands with their environmental problems. It would include investment in the training of experts. Some meeting of the minds on establishing fully global guidelines for future industrialization and development is needed if only to begin the planning.

In both northern and southern tier lands it must be accepted that the costs for non-polluting industry or environmentally careful natural resource extraction must be costs of production. They cannot be avoided any longer at the point of their origin only to reappear as cost of governmental abatement or restoration taxed to the entire community. Not only would it be cheaper but it would cause less environmental damage for subsidies — if needed at all — to be given to check environmental insults at their origin rather than permitting neglect and subsequent reaction.

In all countries there is a need to research and evaluate the costs for past environmental excesses. Some relationship between those costs and the pro-rata contribution from all relevant sources to meet the costs needs to be proposed in each context.

(9) Eventually mechanisms for *mediation, negotiation, conciliation, arbitration, and settlement* of conflicting national and regional environmental demands must be considered. The disputes over fishing rights on the commons illustrate the nature of some of these disputes. Care must be taken to create institutions which are not so exploitation oriented that they are blinded to environmental protection, as has been charged is the case with the International Whaling Commission.

Some accommodation of conflicting claims can be accomplished in existing international agencies within their areas of expertise. Some new system or model for fact finding and issue resolving needs to be considered, whether within present agencies or in a new form. Even if disputes are to be settled on an *ad hoc* basis, patterns and guidelines will be needed. *Trail Smelter*[17] and other international precedents may have a utility in this regard. Nonetheless, extrapolation from the issues, disputes and precedents may suggest new patterns.

(10) *New governmental tasks* include especially the responsibility for environmental impact analysis. No change in the natural environment should be incurred or permitted until a study of its impact on the environment has been made and that impact has been calculated in the decisions regarding the projects to assure respect for environmental quality and integrity.

Whether the human and technical and financial resources exist to service this need is questionable even in countries such as the United States which have fully incorporated this new task into their governmental structures. Attention must be paid to how the task is to be mandated, executed and integrated into existing governmental structures.

C. *Enviromental Implications of Military Policies*

Although it is politically expedient to separate the consideration of environmental and military matters, the division can hardly pass unexamined. Not only is it crucial that the inherent destructive powers of war be curbed, but both nuclear annihilation at one extreme and the conduct of conventional warfare at another pose serious environmental threats in themselves. Additionally, it must be observed that current government military policies unduly impinge upon environmental needs in their excessive costs, appropriation of trained men and technological tools and secretive uses of data denied to environmentalists.

In preparation for nuclear war, explosions of nuclear devices in the atmosphere and within the earth's shell continue. Unless the U.S.-U.S.S.R. efforts to prevent nuclear arms proliferation bear fruit, nearly a score of nations have or can have the ability to join the nuclear club. India and Japan and certain Middle Eastern states are among those reportedly close to developing nuclear arms if the incentive for doing so emerges. Even if only a few more states develop nuclear weapons, testing of the devices can be expected, accompanied by either known atmospheric pollution or by the not entirely understood implications for the inner earth.

Conventional warfare has recently witnessed a new era of scorched-earth policies bound to last beyond a given growing season. The United States' use of synthetic chemical herbicides in Indo-China is having clearly disastrous effects on man, wildlife and acres of plant life. The American Association for the Advancement of Science's Herbicide Assessment Commission has documented the environmental and toxic effects of the U.S. policies to the extent that they can be determined at this point in time.

These effects include destruction of all vegetation when only mangrove forest trees are attacked, soil erosion, elimination of upland forest and of scrub brush, elimination of rice fields (without denying enough food to the "enemy" to justify the action in retrospect), and not entirely understood health damage to man including possibilities of congenital abnormalities. The full impact of the sprayings may not be known for some time. Despite the elimination of some 5,514,410 acres of growth in South Viet Nam alone between 1962-69, the military utility of the venture is doubted by many.

If conventional warfare connot be entirely eliminated, it can be cleaned up in the same manner as has occurred for the rights of civilians in war or the rights of prisoners of war. An environmental analogue to the Geneva Conventions and ministrations of the Red Cross is needed for the environment.

Additionally, if governments are serious about dedicating more funds for ecologically sound social and economic development, pollution abatement and maintenance of environmental quality, new priorities of fund allocation will be required. Several governments, including the U.S.S.R., have seriously felt the need for reallocation of funds; in seeking to release monies now used for armaments, these states have pressed for arms limitations and controls. Military spending is the most likely candidate for trade-offs in the quest for new funds; to those who question this assertion, the burden shifts to them to indicate how both developed and developing lands can secure additional funds for environmental and other societal needs.

Moreover, military technology has pre-empted expertise which must be placed at the service of environmental needs. Engineering for sanitation systems, pollution abatement, mass transit development, housing and like civilian needs is sorely needed. The Scientific and Technical Sub-Committee of the U.N. Committee on the Peaceful Uses of Outer Space has reviewed the Secretary-General's reports on "The Use of Earth Survey Satellites in Monitoring the Changes in the Global Environment" and on "The Role of Earth Satellites in the Global Environment."[18] Despite the utility of satellites for environmental tasks (e.g. tracing oil dumping in the oceans), the pre-emption of these devices for military uses curbed any exploration of their availability. Those nations able to exploit space must unfreeze their technological innovations and place them at the service of all mankind instead of a costly balance of terror.[19]

D. Inadequately Recognized Concerns

Evident in the categorization of issues above and in the items of the agenda for the U.N.'s Conference on the Human Environment are several issues which, when measured against an objective analysis of global need, are inadequately recognized. Different values may be weighed in varying ways to emphasize one or another of the topics identified as concerns; rather than explore such a priority system here and rather than listing all issues which might have been identified, four international global environmental concerns are explored because the lack of priority attached to them bears little relationship to the fundamental importance of each issue: (1) technology assessment; (2) population growth; (3) energy generation; (4) socio-cultural inhabitions.

The determination that these four issues are inadequately recognized grows out of the apparent belief of the international community that it can explore other environmental concerns such as set forth above *without* at the same time considering these four. The lesson of ecology and interdependence of systems which underlies much of the present global concern runs counter to this compartmentalization of issues.

(1) The needs for increased *technology assessment* have been briefly sketched in section III.F. of this paper. Although considerable scholarship exists supporting the need and proposing innovations such as governmental and inter-governmental panels to assess technological developments, most governments have done little serious restructuring or reacting to the issue.

Each application of science requires its own analysis of secondary and tertiary impact, of interaction with socio-economic systems, of alternatives and of costs and benefits. All levels of government have a need to engage in such assessment within their authority and to mesh their study with that of other governmental units. The international community has an interest in the assessment of incremental decisions at the regional and local levels as well as an interest in technological applications on the global environment, such as international transportation systems.

A good statement of the fuction which the international community needs to find a means to implement is the statement of a panel of the U.S. National Academy of Sciences:

Timely consideration must be given to the long-term sacrifices entailed by [new technologies]...use and proliferation and to potentially injurious effects upon sectors of society and the environment often quite remote from the places of production and application. For by the time such consequences have become so obvious as to generate intense political concern, we may find that the psychological and financial commitments of various individuals or groups to technological paths and institutional arrangements already selected will have made any significant change of direction very costly if not altogether impossible. Thus, we may freeze ourselves into technological pattern whose far-reaching consequences not even their originators would deliberately have chosen...[As the undesired effects of technological change] become more nearly global in scale, we may increasingly find ourselves faced with consequences that are truely irreversible — for example, profound climatic changes, or permanent alteration in ecological regimes, or irreversible social deterioration.[20]

Concern for the global envirnoment must consider technology assessment. Present decision-making needs an influx of knowledge and recommendations regarding the effects of private and public, domestic, regional and international choices. Without such information, choices will be made in the midst of ignorance. Specific international panels might analyze given fields from time to time; a means to feed findings from such review into decision-making bodies must be devised.

Moreover, developers of new technologies need to be induced to undertake their own assessments of the impact of their innovations. A new awareness of the need must be generated.

Global inquiries on differing national or international technology evaluations could synthesize findings and report on the collective diverse conclusions in different fields. Consider the proliferation of jet planes in the atmosphere and the increases in their pollutants and water vapor exhausts; no systematic evaluation of global transportation needs has appeared to influence national decision-makers. New national airlines, new air routes, new planes such as the super-sonic transport, all lack a solid evaluation. A global over-view of national air transportation studies could be redistributed to national and local decision-makers so, at least, they would have the information available to make informed and considered judgments and, perhaps, could seek regional or global co-operation rather than acting singly. A healthy pluralism of studies when analyzed might lead to an integrated and more uniform global reaction to technological and environmental needs: this model, at least as a minimum, must be considered.

(2) Also discussed above as a major concern, the nations apparently wish to divorce consideration of environmental issues (often symptoms only of over-population) from those of curbing *population* growth rates. The 1972 Conference on the Human Environment will examine a multitude of environmental issues without singling out the prevasive and crucial element which population growth plays in each.

It is simply not sufficient to say that the United Nations has designated 1974 as "World Population Year" — such years even when located halfway into the Second Development Decade are destined by precedent to do little more than accommodate philatelic interests in commemorative stamps. The August 1974 Conference on Population to be convened at U.N. headquarters will be successful only if the U.N. members turn to action proposals before that time and key those proposals to environmental programs. The 1974 Conference cannot merely explore (a) stimulating awareness of population problems; (b) promoting knowledge of population issues; (c) arriving at action projects; and (d) generating aid for population control efforts. These aims, laudable and even progressive a few years ago, are now somewhat obsolete.

Before 1974, and hopefully as a part of the 1972 Conference, the population aspects of each agenda item must be examined. The U.N. and international community should create the infrastructure to cope with global population concerns now.[21] Such initiatives need not mean a ban on population growth in states such as the U.S.S.R. which can still accommodate increased population and desire it, but exceptions in such cases need not entail a continuation of the low level of global concern for the acute population problems in some developing areas.

A variety of proposals — for increased involvement of specialized agencies like WHO in population concerns, for creation and priority support of a U.N. Commissioner for Population to oversee integration of population, development and environment programs, increased new funding for the Population Trust Fund and other meaningful multilateral commitments to population growth issues instead of symbolic gestures — all must be seriously considered by the international community. That such matters are not prime international concerns of the same magnitude as arms control is a source of concern.

(3) Man's use of *energy* underlies concerns for (a) international oil agreements, oil pollution of the seas, oil exploitation of the arctic and attendant transportation problems, ocean-floor oil drilling, oil tanker uses; for (b) nuclear waste disposal, creation of breeder reactors, thermal pollution, radioactive contamination of cooling effluents, atmospheric radiation; for (c) strip mining and exhaustion of coal reserves, air pollution by sulphur and particulates; for (d) internal combustion engines and transportation systems; for (e) power plant siting, power-line distribution, dam building; for (f) conservation of natural gas and exploitation of this resource; and (g) related issues, not the least of which is the global dependence on certain energy sources which inhibits scientific and technological shifts to other energy sources.

Increased industrialization and population growth presently generate considerable demand for additional energy. The trend will persist into the foreseeable future. Petroleum and coal reserves will be effectively exhausted within this period. The global response to such a realization has been to increase efforts to exploit these limited resources while rapidly developing nuclear power generating plants. The need to conserve pettoleum and coal resources for uses other than the generation of electricity is largely unconsidered; short-range exploitation is guiding public and private decision-making.

There is a need to examine the environmental symptoms of energy generation without influence from the vested interests of present users. Regional planning for meeting electricity needs must be hastened; rational inter-state siting of power plants and power distribution grids so as to meet energy needs and minimize environmental dangers must be explored.

For the 1972 Conference to explore many of the symptoms of the need for energy without examining the source of the ills is short-sighted and ignorant. Energy is not merely a need prompting exploitation of natural resources; it is not a concern exclusively of developed or developing lands. Its generation, use and socio-economic or environmental implications are of the first political magnitude. The international community must turn traditional disciplines, interdisciplinary analysis, technology assessment and a review of future trends and pressures toward the basic issue of how energy is to be generated to meet global needs.

(4) It is encouraging that one of the agenda items for the 1972 Conference on the Human Environment includes examination of *social* and *cultural aspects* of environmental issues. What is disheartening is the limited scope attached to this concern. The two questions posed in the agenda are: (a) social aspects addressing "The impact of environmental consideration on relations between people; demographic and behavioral aspects of societies in relation to the environment;" and (b) cultural aspects focusing on "Cultural and quality of life implications; environment in relation to human rights; development and acceptance of an environmental ethic."[22]

It will not be sufficient to examine such issues as population density and housing, aesthetics, social infrastructures, environmental ethics, or the preservation of cultural traits and expressions and human rights while also preserving environmental quality. To be sure these issues are poorly understood today and merit important consideration equal to the concern given to monitoring the physical and natural environment.

However, there is a more basic consideration involved in socio-cultural evaluations. Why is technology assessment so slow in taking hold or why is the global perspective on population or energy issues given low priority today? There is a crucial need to analyze why systems of government and industry fail to factor environmental considerations into their decision-making. An environmental ethic, declaration of principles on the human environment, or increased educational efforts could remedy this failure to some extent. All these avenues of redress by definition represent commitments of at least a generation.

The international community needs to turn its attention to the science of good governance and decision-making irrespective of political ideologies or persuasions. Social or cultural inhibitions on change must be understood in this focus. Re-examination of existing commitments to social and technical arrangements, anticipation of new needs and trends, alternative paths of action and analysis of consequences too often are thwarted by the decision-making structure or perceptions of the decision-makers.

There is the need to anticipate critical situations in the environmental area. Although time for action is limited, a lead time from early warning signals to crisis is often five to ten years on the global level. The time for research and action may be available; the real question, then, is can a society, an industry, a government ministry, etc., marshall its resources and commit itself to change within that time span as the need for change becomes apparent.

Flexible methods of change are needed to react appropriately to the effects of new technologies. Methods for dedicating major resources to research and development as soon as a problem is identified and given priority need to be explored. Action will be necessary — some of it surely at the international community level — once research has generated proposed solutions.

Neither man's inability to marshal resources sufficient to assure clean water and sanitation systems to aid in elimination of cholera, nor his sad failure to curb trade in the narcotic and drug epidemic offers a very sanguine prospect for overcoming social and cultural inhibitors. Man's present system of allocation of priorities and resources at the national and global levels is characterized by the inability to change more than responsiveness to new needs.

The international community needs a mechanism whereby any member or part of it can bring an environmental problem with transnational implications to the attention of the community. Some sure response and analysis must automatically follow. A means for establishing guidelines for treating such petitions or complaints needs to be instituted which would prevent the problem becoming lost in the interstices of the interstate system or being thwarted by social, cultural or vested interest inhibitors. Just as a system of courts and justice is intended to apply law even-handedly to rich and poor, and independently to separate good claims from bad, so the international community needs a system for so objectively treating environmental issues before they fester into global crisis situations. Just as ombudsmen are designed to break through bureaucratic fossilization or bias, so an advocate for the hitherto unrepresented natural environment must emerge in all levels of transnational decision-making.

E. *Education and Development of Attitudes: Prerequisites to Change*

The importance of education cannot be overly stressed. This concern breaks down into several parts: (1) basic education about the environment taught in formal education; (2) inculcation of environmental principles and an environmental ethic at all levels of formal and informal education; (3) training manpower for environmental needs; (4) retraining presently skilled persons for newly defined environmental needs.

More crucial in the short term will be creation of teams of field ecologists and technicians to assist in environmental impact studies and to help avert environmental damage. More experts are needed to implement and operate data gathering, monitoring and pollution abatement programs. Not one of the developed countries, let alone the underdeveloped, has sufficient human resources to supply the needs.

73

As Robert Arvill urged in 1967:

One of the most important problems facing society is that of relating its human talent to its priorities. This is particularly so in environmental planning. The intellectual requirements for planners are obviously high, and the qualities of dynamism and persuasiveness are scarce. With so few qualified planners to take on this exacting work it is essential to place them at the key places. There should be a greater concentration of professional talent at the regional level; rarely is it efficient to employ planners at the level of the existing county districts although there is a pressing need for more employment locally of design skills. The inservice training and education of the planner must be organized to enable him to keep abreast of the rapidly increasing and changing knowledge relevant to his work.[23]

What Arvill elaborates as the needs for planners can be repeated for many other disciplines concerned with environmental problems.

Even if human talent is correlated to environmental priorities and the wasteful "brain drain" and over-education processes are turned to beneficial ends, there will remain a need for education of the general public regarding basic sciences and environmental conduct principles. The programs of the Young Pioneers in the U.S.S.R. or the world scouting and guide organizations illustrate a non-academic avenue for generating environmental awareness. Educational curriculum reform is underway in several nations.

The kind of environmental policies and principles which the next generation embraces will determine the types of choices and alternative development patterns which decision-makers will select. They will, in short, become the guiding values upon which or from which society's judgments are made.

What should the international concern for the definition and scope of these values be?

V. DECLARATION OF PRINCIPLES ON THE HUMAN ENVIRONMENT

A. *Genesis of the Declaration Proposal*

Early in the preparation for the 1972 United Nations Conference on the Human Environment, the call for a statement of these values emerged. At its first session, the Preparatory Committee enunciated the call thus:

The 1972 United Nations Conference on the Human Environment should be presented with a draft declaration on the human environment ... The declaration should be a document of basic principles, calling mankind's attention to the many varied and interrelated problems of the human environment, and to draw attention to the rights and obligations of man and State and the international community in regard thereto.

The declaration would serve to stimulate public opinion and community participation for the protection and betterment of the human environment and, where appropriate, for the restoration of its primitive harmony, etc., in the interest of present and future generations. It would also provide guiding principles for governments in their formulation of policy and set objectives for future international co-operation.

In formulating the declaration on the human environment, due account has to be taken of the environmental stresses caused by the differences in social and economic development between various parts of the world.[24]

74

Although not yet finally drafted, the efforts of the Preparatory Committee to frame a first version of the Declaration are important in themselves for the insights they provide as to the tremendous difficulties present in defining the values guiding environmental concerns. Regardless of the outcome of efforts to create a declaration, it is instructive to review the work to date in detail to learn how governments' representatives in a political forum view the concerns for the global environment.

Unprepared to produce its own version of the declaration in March of 1970, the Preparatory Committee asked the Secretariat to consult with member States and make suggestions. A great deal of effort went into the Secretariat's explorations. The views of U.N. members and agencies, of non-governmental organizations and of the scientific community were sought.

It is not surprising that a great variety of opinions emerged. When the Preparatory Committee again met in February of 1971, the call for a declaration was but little refined:

The Preparatory Committee held a general discussion on the Declaration, its principal objectives and possible form and contents. There was general consensus that the Declaration should be inspirational and concise; it should be readily understandable by the general public so that it could serve as an effective instrument for education and stimulate public awareness and community participation in action for the protection of the environment ... With regard to the structure of the Declaration, it was generally agreed that it should contain a preamble of an inspirational character.[25]

Divergences did begin to appear, however, suggesting that many States had not explored the ramifications of the declaration at their first discussion. Doubt was expressed as to the propriety of directing the declaration to include "fundamental principles recommended for action by individuals, States and the international community." The degree of specificity for the declaration's guidelines was disputed. The declaration should not, and by its nature could not, formulate binding principles of law, but it could recognize "the fundamental need of the individual for a satisfactory environment which permits the enjoyment of his human rights." Nonetheless, some States wished the rights and obligations of States to be set forth in the declaration.[26]

Unsure still of their goals, the countries' representatives found it hard to envision the proper content of this goal-oriented declaration. Some States, such as Canada,[27] sought a clear statement of State's rights and responsibilities including liability. Others wished only the most general of principles.

The working-through of these divergences was entrusted by the Preparatory Committee to an Intergovernmental Working Group composed of all Preparatory Committee members and other countries' representatives wishing to participate. This large group was to consider the various drafts proposed and the views of nations and non-governmental bodies which the Secretariat had received.

75

This Working Group met in its first substantive session in May 1971. It had met earlier in the spring and limited its agenda to debate of a preamble and fundamental principles, leaving for the third meeting of the Preparatory Committee any decision whether to include guidelines for action by States or international organizations.[28] The sessions were preceded by informal consultations among members.

The text prepared for the May meetings left much to be desired. This work product, however, should be put in perspective. The delegates labored under difficult circumstances. Time for reflection and research had been brief, and members of the Working Group itself had a few months at most. Few delegates could have had any experience with the subject matter or the environmental issues which the call for the Declaration had generated. The delegates serving on the Working Group were not environmental specialists, but rather generalists with international diplomatic experience. The deliberations lacked the benefit of the years of experimentation and growth which had preceded the drafting of the Universal Declaration of Human Rights or the Declaration of the Rights of a Child.

Add to these difficulties the facts that (1) the member states had legitimate and disparate priorities regarding national development, military and security affairs, social conditions and (2) the lack of time together with the deadlines of both the 1972 conference and the Working Group meetings led many States to adopt preconceived and somewhat arbitrary positions. Some viewed the whole environmental discussion as an intrusion on national sovereignty; others saw it as a diversion of the polluted rich nations striving to clean up their own mess while probably cutting back on assistance for development efforts in the poor lands. The blunt developing country view that "we want pollution as it is a sign of successful industrialization" yielded to the more subtle expression that "we poorer lands are less polluted than the rich, and therefore our pollution tolerance is greater, so invest and industrialize us." The most obtuse preconception was Brazil's conviction that concern for the global environment was merely preservationist, narrowly "conservationist" and anti-development.

B. *The Preliminary Draft Declaration as Framed*

In short, the May meetings found it most difficult to hammer out their divergences and create the inspirational document called for. When the preamble was finally cast, it appeared as follows:

[1] Man is the nucleus of all efforts to preserve and enhance the environment;
[2] Man's life is affected by his environment which in turn is affected by his activities;
[3] The maintenance of a safe, healthy and wholesome environment is indispensable to man's well-being and to the full enjoyment of his basic human rights, including the right

76

to life itself;

[4] Serious impairment of the environment is being caused by man's activities, in particular by uncontrolled use of technology, by lack of rational planning of the use of the earth's resources, and by increased urbanization;

[5] Excessive population growth could defeat man's efforts to preserve and enhance his environment;

[6] The dependence of man on the maintenance of the ecological balance of the biosphere requires rational use of natural resources since they are limited in quantity and quality;

[7] Each state has inalienable sovereignty over its natural resources;

[8] Each state has the responsibility to exercise its sovereignty over its natural resources in a manner compatible with the need to ensure the preservation and enhancement of the human environment;

[9] Urgent efforts are being made to bring about rapid economic and social development, and these will continue;

[10] There is no fundamental conflict between economic and social development and the preservation and enhancement of the human environment, since both seek to provide and sustain increasing opportunities to all peoples for a better life;

[11] The interdependence of a growing number of environmental problems and their regional or global character require concerted efforts for their solution;

[12] International organizations have an important role and important responsibilities in the preservation and enhancement of the environment.[29]

Several reservations or observations were registered by different members of the Working Group.[90] It was suggested that in the fourth paragraph the words "increased urbanization" be replaced by "unplanned urbanization". There was dispute over the fifth paragraph on population growth; some States continued to argue that population growth is a valid goal within their own country's boundary and, therefore, viewed population issues as domestic and not properly included in the Declaration at all. The question of whether demand and consumption ought to be reduced and scrutinized in addition to population growth was not seriously explored.

The seventh and eighth paragraphs were deemed redundant and in need of consolidation since sovereignty includes the element of inalienability by definition. These criticisms have merit; while there is no doubt that sovereignty over natural resources is agreed to by many States, the purpose of the Declaration is not to merely reiterate political statements but is rather to expand upon the environmental implications and responsibilities of that sovereignty.

Some members of the Working Group balked at the "limits" or "qualifications" set on sovereignty in the eighth paragraph. Fears that sovereignty may be impaired by phrases as in this paragraph are shortsighted, as some Committee members noted, since the thrust of the entire Declaration is to define the interdependent and interlocking nature of the natural and human environment. These so-called "limitations" are no more than the explicit recognition of the environmental implications of sovereignty.

The tenth preambular paragraph made it clear that environmental problems in developing countries are part of social and economic development. While true to a large degree, the paragraph does not acknowledge that there may be ecological detrimental development which in the long run may diminish the quality of the human environment. The Committee's debate did not explore this distinction and settled on restating the developing country's point of view.

Throughout the preamble the more skeptical governments sought to replace words like "require" in the eleventh paragraph with such words as "might require" or "could emperil" in the fifth paragraph rather than "could defeat". This reluctance reflects the lack of commitment among some of the developed lands to the requirements of an environmental ethic.

Omitted from the preamble are concerns such as the need to include environmental education at all stages of curriculum, the importance of youth in preserving and enhancing environmental quality and further emphasis on social and economic development. The Committee consensus was not to go into these areas. Several governments sought to bolster the concern for development by urging the inclusion of words like "and the fruits of economic and social development" at the end of the third paragraph, or appending to the seventh paragraph the qualifier "as well as the right to freely exploit such resources".

Such worries might be alleviated by a revised tenth paragraph which adequately set forth the relationship between the needs of both the environment and social and economic development.

In considering the body of the proposed Declaration, it should be observed at the outset that no co-ordination emerges to connect the preamble and principles stated therein with what follows. Order is not well analyzed nor especially logically arrived at.

Beyond the preamble, then, seventeen "fundamental principles" are set forth. Although the principles are not especially well conceived or logically ordered, they can be roughly broken into four classes or types: (1) rights; (2) responsibilities; (3) duties; (4) permissive or voluntary recommendations. These classes go beyond the uniform expression of individual's rights and State's responsibilities as found in the Declaration of Human Rights. To the extent the draft environment Declaration defines operational mandates it may be asked whether the text goes beyond the original consensus and purpose.

(1) *Rights.* Only the first principle purports to set forth a right: "Everyone has a fundamental right to a safe, healthy and wholesome environment for the full enjoyment of his basic human rights including the right to favorable physical working conditions and to a standard of living for his health and well-being." There was considerable debate as to the scope of this basic human right. The specialized agencies sought to have the "including" phrase provide for their own mandates; thus the FAO wished expression of the right to clean food and WHO desired a right to "an environment that safeguards the health of present and future generations." A draft by non-governmental organizations stress-

ing a conservation perspective suggested that the text read "including clean air, pure water, freedom from excessive and unnecessary noise, and the right to the natural, scenic, historic and esthetic qualities thereof." ILO felt "working environment" was preferable to the narrow expression "physical working conditions".

A suggestion not adopted sought to lay a basis for growth of international law applications to environmental issues:

In addition to focusing on basic human rights, including in particular the right to life, under this approach the declaration would also concentrate on principles relating to the rights and responsibilities of States which could serve as a basis for promoting the progressive development and codification of international environmental law. The basic premise for this approach is that the fullest realization of basic rights depends upon the preservation of an unimpaired environment which can only be assured through the co-operation and orderly conduct of States guided by clearly defined principles of international law.[31]

On balance it may be seriously questioned whether this limited statement of an individual right adds very much to human rights or present international environmental concerns.

(2) *Responsibilities*. Rather than being framed in terms of the rights of individuals, the text sought to specify the responsibilities of States with some concreteness, leaving open the question of methods of implementation. Until greater consensus as to these governmental responsibilities is achieved, this particularized approach may run into difficulties, both in its acceptance and in its effectiveness. Such difficulties would be avoided by the broader statement of rights utilized by the Universal Declaration of Human Rights.

The responsibilities can be grouped as including the following principles:

2. Everyone has a responsibility to protect the environment;
3. States shall carefully husband their natural resources and shall hold in trust for present and future generations the air, water, land and plants and animals on which all life depends;
4. States shall apply modern science and technology to the use of natural resources and to the planning of human settlements in such a way as to preserve and enhance the human environment for present and succeeding generations; ...
6. Each State has the responsibility, in accordance with the Charter of the United Nations and consistent with the principles of international law, to conduct its activities so as not to cause damage to the environment of other States, or to the environment of areas beyond the limits of national jurisdiction; ...
14. State recognize that measures to preserve and enhance the environment constitute an integral part of long-term and sustained economic and social development; requiring consideration even at the earliest stages of development planning;[32]

These responsibilities are corollaries to the basic right of "everyone". They are more general than the specific duties listed below. They reflect broad areas of consensus as to proper governmental concern. Principles two and three are so closely linked that several governments urged their merger. Some, fearing encroachments on national sovereignty, urged against "unduly restrictive" intrusions on that sovereignty, urging deletion of principle three altogether.

(3) *Duties.* Although the Declaration does not distinguish between general responsibilities and specific duties, the difference is apparent on the face of the Declaration. The command of the Declaration is phrased as States "shall" do a given act. Some delegations, such as the United Kingdom's, expressed reservations about this injunction and preferred the use of "should". Somewhat arbitrarily grouped here, principles which appeared to set forth duties include the following:

5. States shall establish and strengthen appropriate institutions to plan and manage their environmental resources and to elaborate and enforce environmental quality standards; ...

7. Each State has the duty to undertake international consultations before proceeding with activities which may cause damage to the environment of another State or areas beyond the limits of national jurisdiction; ...

9. [States shall examine the possibility of concluding international agreements providing for compensation in respect of damage to the environment caused by its activities.] [Each State has the responsibility to compensate for damage to the environment caused by activities carried on within its territory.]

10. States shall, in accordance with the Charter of the United Nations, take joint and separate action, both directly and through international organizations, to preserve and enhance the human environment; ...

12. States shall examine the possibility of concluding bilateral, regional or global agreements to preserve and enhance the human environment, in particular agreements for the establishment of international standards of environmental quality;

13. States shall make available technical assistance to other interested States to enable them to preserve and enhance their environment; ...

16. [States shall, when making assistance available for development, take into account not only the limited resources of developing countries but also the additional cost of incorporating environmental safeguards into their development planning.] [To maintain and improve the ecological balance in developing countries, taking into account the limited resources at their disposal, new financial resources should be allocated for environmental purposes, in addition to the resources which are needed for development.]

17. States shall direct their activities within international organizations so as to ensure that these organizations perform and increasingly effective role in the preservation and enhancement of the human environment.[33]

As is readily apparent, these "duties" are often little more than what is already a function of participation in the international community. Many of these duties are little more than agreements to seek agreements on substantive environmental issues, and that consensus is of distinctly limited profundity. The concept of environmental quality embracing the concerns of development and pollution abatement, as discussed at the Founex meeting, is in no way suggested in this text despite paragraph ten of the preamble.

Some States in the debate over these clauses suggested strengthening clause nine by rewriting it to open "States shall seek to conclude". Others would include a strong statement holding States liable for environmental damage to others. Both the United Kingdom and the U.S.S.R. rejected clauses seven and nine as unsuitable for a declaration.

Some delegations felt that clauses ten and twelve were included prematurely or were redundant and made no new contribution to the declaration since all States are already obliged to undertake consultations and co-operation. Some suggested limiting clause thirteen by adding "as far as practicable".

Clause sixteen was given several alternative formulations. Some States espoused still a third alternative to read:

To maintain and improve the ecological balance in developing countries, taking into account the limited resources at their disposal, their own commitments to development priorities and also the cost of incorporating environmental safeguards into their development planning, additional international financial resources, mostly in the form of grants, should be made available to those countries for environmental purposes, in addition to the resources which are needed for development.

Clearly the funding issue is unresolved and evidences considerably different perspectives between donor and recipient countries, even if they agree environmental quality is a touchstone to synthesize development and environment.

Two delegations indicated opposition to clause seventeen because it reflected an unwarranted importance or emphasis on environmental issues. One State expressed the view that environmental concerns were not a part of the original mandates of international agencies and should not be engrafted onto them. Clause seventeen was opposed also as dictating policies to sovereign states.

(4) *Permissive or Voluntary Recommendations.* Although some of the principles could be made hortatory only, or even mildly suggestive, such would render worthless the exercise of writing a separate declaration. As the text stands as of this writing, only one principle is clearly a take-it-or-leave-it proposition. Principle eight reads:

A State having reason to believe that the activities of another State may cause damage to its environment or to the environment of areas beyond the limits of national jurisdiction, may request international consultations concerning the envisaged activities.[34]

As with principle seven which reads more closely as a responsibility, several States felt that this merely states the obvious and is unnecessary in the declaration.

Many of the defects of this draft appear on its face. It is neither succinct nor very inspiring. Its internal contradictions and varying degrees of fundamentality do little to distinguish it. In the short run, such failings meant that the Preparatory Committee received the draft with little enthusiasm. Perhaps a smaller working group might have prepared a better draft and provided collective leadership, but such was not the case.

When the third Preparatory Committee met on September 13, 1971, Maurice Strong observed that since the spring meetings a panel of experts had been convened at Founex, Switzerland, whose findings marked an "historic turning point in the 'development-environment' dialogue."[35] The experts determined that the quality of the human envi-

81

ronment was of great importance to developing countries and should be an "integral aspect" of the development process.

However, despite the wide distribution of the Founex report, it had not been digested to the degree necessary to assure consensus on even this aspect of the Declaration. Sweden remarked on the first day of Preparatory Committee deliberation that more work on the Declaration was necessary before it could be deemed adequately drafted.[36] France and Iran cautioned against undue haste in preparing the Declaration and the United Kingdom observed that the present draft was not satisfactory and "should be short and lucid, with literary and intellectual value." Japan urged that the declaration be "noble and farseeing" instead of a legalistic and technical document.[37]

As the general opening debate drew to a close, India urged that the basis for the Declaration "should be the idea of creating humane conditions of life on this planet. It should avoid controversies, be 'educational and inspirational' and command the greatest measure of support." Yugoslavia observed that "although progress so far could be described as modest, it should not be forgotten that this was to be 'one of the most important documents.'" Canada moved the debate into discussion of the substance of the Declaration, again urging that it set forth the duties of nations.[37]

Argentina astutely observed that the Declaration "might be the most political of the subjects to be dealt with by the Stockholm Conference. The work done by the Working Group on this subject was of a pioneer nature, ... and it was only natural for difficulties to arise."[38]

Brazil repeated its argument that the draft declaration was "anti-developmental" and merely conservationist in nature, and therefore unsatisfactory. While not directly commenting on the Founex findings, Brazil did subscribe to the conclusions of the regional seminar held in Mexico City to discuss the Founex report. The seminar concluded essentially that environmental improvement needed to be a part of national development plans.[39]

When the Preparatory Committee began to debate the proposed text specifically, the continuing divergence of views became pronounced. Several States commented that the Declaration should reflect the aims and concerns of the 1972 Conference and could not accurately do so if drafted before the Conference.[40]

During the debate, most of the hopes and fears for the Declaration were aired again.[41] After these generalized comments, specific substantive proposals were made. Czechoslovakia expressed reservations about the fifth principle's provision that population growth directly controlled environmental quality. This was criticized as too simplistic; the Czech delegate urged that habits of consumption had a greater effect on the environment than population growth alone.

Algeria, a participating observer, criticized the attitudes of the developed lands. The Algerian diplomat argued that "the 'have' countries were not prepared to repair the damage they had caused in developing economies of the 'have not' countries." Algeria urged a fuller expression in the Declaration of developing country needs. Colombia further urged that the draft should reflect the differentiations between the developed and developing lands as expressed in the Founex findings.

The chairman of the Working Group, Giovanni Migluolo of Italy, noted at the close of the Preparatory Committee debate that the Working Group's product had a preliminary character. He observed that the Group needed the advice of the technical and scientific sub-committees of the Preparatory Committee and of ECOSOC. He urged all States to review the Declaration and suggest positive improvements.[42]

C. Critique of the Draft

In Migluolo's closing remarks emerges an insight into how to improve the Declaration. Clearly the Declaration must be based upon a realistic evaluation of what the environmental problems are; it must draw on the consensus which has emerged as to proper international environmental concerns as expressed in the scientific and technical sub-committees of the Preparatory Committee, the ECOSOC and the other committees of the General Assembly. The independent consensus of international bodies such as the International Council of Scientific Unions or the International Union for the Conservation of Nature must be drawn upon as well as meetings of experts such as the Founex sessions.

Rather than determine in the abstract what basic principles are needed, an empirical examination of needs should precede choice of principles. To short-cut such an examination is, in substance, to magnify the pre-existing political, economic and social differences among nations.

The Preparatory Committee can draw on the final product of its subgroups as well as the *Report on the State of the Human Environment*, when issued, to determine what substantive analysis commands support. Using this approach, a useful draft may yet be presented in Stockholm. The final draft may well reflect the degree to which such examination occurs.

Several specific further criticisms can be cited:

(1) Central to such extrapolation from empirical analysis is the scientific fact of an interdependent and interacting series of ecosystems. It must stress the concept of environmental quality as defined by (a) scientific criteria with reference to the biological and physical well-being of natural ecosystems upon which mankind depends, or (b) the national level of development with necessary focus on issues of public health, sanitation, ecologically sound agricultural and industrial development, etc., at one end, and similar focus on pollution, transportation, etc., at

83

the other extreme, or (c) global and recurrent concerns such as population growth or urban and housing planning.

Alternatively, one could say that the scientific realities or criteria of environmental quality provide the first principles from which the others are deductively derived with reference to actual conditions to provide order and priority. Thus both deductive and inductive analytical methods take their point of departure from the scientific reality and concept of environmental quality.

(2) Formulation of responsibilities of governments needs to be examined in relation to both the responsibilities already assumed by States (e.g. planning, requirements of environmental impact statements, transportation and housing authorities, etc.) and the needs not yet embodied in government conduct.

Not all States presently have the will or the resources to initiate environmental programs; nonetheless an international standard for States to aim for could be framed. In so doing a lasting quality is needed and principles of government functions should be couched in broad terms of responsibilities, leaving the means and specific duties to definition within each country compatible with national cultures, patterns of government, etc.

(3) It should be clear that the Declaration is not an attempt to limit national sovereignty or to graft wholly new powers onto the international community. Rather, environmental concern involves a new understanding of existing jurisdictional bases of power. It emphasizes that there is within these jurisdictions an environmental dimension which permeates all aspects of activity. Just as economic or statistical analysis is automatically considered and monetary costs are factored into decision-making, so now environmental costs must be reviewed and assessed.

(4) Although the Declaration text appreciates the importance of technology and its proper use, it shows no recognition of the role of technology assessment. It should be a responsibility of every land to engage in technology assessment as discussed above.

(5) The Declaration should not be a reaction to the alarms about environmental dangers. It cannot be infected either by unexamined fears of developing countries or by greedy preoccupation with cleaning up the excesses of pollution in the overly developed lands. Rather the Declaration must be anticipatory; it must reach out and say where the international community ought to go and with what standards of conduct. Without such a progressive orientation the Declaration will not achieve the lasting impact which some wish it might.

(6) The Declaration should be clearly framed in terms of maintaining environmental quality, thus placing the developed versus developing country issue aside as best as possible. Preamble ten and such of the principles as deal with development can be consolidated on this basis.

84

(7) Those elements of the Declaration which merely restate the obvious or existing governmental authority, such as principles seven, eight, nine, ten, and twelve, all ought to be deleted. The Declaration should embody new understandings of rights and responsibilities and not be specific about governmental duties. The financing debate in sixteen is really operational and belongs in that forum rather than in the forum of general principles.

It would appear preferable to recast all the principles in terms of mankind's rights and responsibilities. Diversity of expression would be assured.

(8) The Declaration as a statement of general principles ought not be confused with agreed international law. Issues of liability specifically should be referred to the International Law Commission in the U.N. and not imperfectly analyzed in the Declaration. A general expression of responsibility would be appropriate in the Declaration, but not an announcement of legal principles. Eventually, of course, the general principles may win acceptance and as such become general principles subscribed to and binding on all civilized lands; state conduct does not permit this to be the case at the present.

(9) Principle four is inadequate to its task in light of the long-standing U.N. interest in urban matters and the specific recommendations of the U.N. Symposium on the Impact of Urbanization on Man's Environment held in June 1970.

(10) The issues discussed in Section IV C & D of this essay, especially as to population control, must be synthesized in the Declaration. Just as the UNESCO charter observes that the defenses of peace must be cast in the minds of men, so the reframing of institutions to cope with environmental needs will require new commitments, new values and new thinking patterns.

Essential to recasting the Declaration is the right to life in a healthy environment and the fundamental principle that to maintain this right man finds himself in the position of the trustee: we are the surrogates for those who in the past put their hopes in us and passed on the mantle of cultural heritage; we are the stewards of the present quality of life; we are the guardians for the generations not yet conceived. None of our acts having impact on the environment can be viewed solely in short-range terms. No such breach of our fiduciary responsibilities will be accepted by tomorrow's generation.

V. CONCLUSIONS

The many specific observations and criticisms set forth herein need not be repeated in closing. Some general conclusions, however, suggest themselves.

No easy consensus as to the "proper" criteria for determining international environmental concerns can be found. The elements of such criteria, those empirical as well as those derived from value judgments, can be discerned, but it is too early to codify them into a fixed set of criteria. What shape they will take in Stockholm at the 1972 Conference or thereafter can only be surmised.

It can be concluded, nonetheless, that environmental quality is taking and will take an equal status with international concerns for development, arms and security, and world trade. It is a chief topic of transnational impact and concern. The problems of the environment, however, will not soon be dealt with despite their importance, since both funds and trained personnel are lacking and will be so for at least a generation to come. Environmental concerns are also likely to be given a lower priority simply because the global community lacks the capacity to quickly reorder its priorities which until now has scant concern for environmental issues as such.

Maintenance of environmental quality as a guiding principle of conduct resolves the dichotomy between the developing country's environmental ills and the developed country's pollution troubles. It does not, however, reorder *ipso facto* the priorities of States. Unless military spending is curbed, funds for development and pollution abatement will remain limited. Poverty and the attendant environmental ills will likely continue for some time to come, since funds will be scarce and the rich lands will be slow to find a greater empathy for the poverty environmental ills of the poor lands.

The reluctance of the international community to come to grips with the population growth problem in the context of environmental troubles is yet another indication that the environmental symptoms of poverty will persist. The established but still nascent global concern for housing and urban problems and the poorly co-ordinated international attention given to energy generation are both symptoms of the underlying population growth and the needs it produces. It is naive to factor the politically charged population element out of the central position it ought to hold in any serious evaluation of environmental problems.

Education and new environmental attitudes and values will take several generations to fully produce a new ethic favoring maintenance of environmental quality. In light of this reality, the Declaration on the Human Environment ought to be framed prospectively as a standard for achievement and aspiration. Failing this it will hold transitory and limited political impact.

Short of generational change, man must start immediate restructuring of societal institutions at all levels to better provide for environmental planning, for technology assessment, for study of environmental impact and for similar functions.

The mutual concerns for environmental quality will find their way into programs of the various States or international organizations. Issues will crop up in the global arena depending upon what part of the international community chooses to give the issue priority. Broad classifications can help structure responses to these unanticipated problems as they arise.

The structuring of responses to the issues as they are raised necessitates in the first instance an accurate and objective understanding of environmental facts, of the problems and of possible solutions. In the next instance, ideally, such restructuring would depend on the political postures of the various elements of the international community; this would be the political decision-making phase.

Since it is most doubtful that the trusteeship concept can quickly take hold to provide guidance and consensus for state conduct, there will be a need for creating independent consensus on each separate environmental concern raised. This reality strongly suggests the need for a continuing international program into which global environmental data is fed and which would have the capacity to convene *ad hoc* interstate or transnational conferences mandated to study a specific issue and to pose means for solutions. As environmental problems are varied yet always present, the need for these meetings would be constant but the participants not always the same. Some flexible yet on-going system might be created — a refined environmental "GATT" perhaps.

The consensus for action on any given environmental issue can be expected to coalesce around informed self-interest. Repeated experience may produce a consensus for the trusteeship concept, and accordingly the trusteeship principle must be calculated as a part of the system and *ad hoc* meetings. The system must have ways of assessing consequences of trends and actions and selecting a priority order for the issues treated.

Within each nation, as well as globally, concern must be paid to the reordering of priorities. Population control and curbing the arms race must be given primary attention with nearly simultaneous efforts at socio-economic development (both ecologically sound development and the elimination of poverty-induced environmental ills) and at the elimination of threats to the quality of the environment by technological or industrial activity. These priority reorderings represent political decisions of the first magnitude; decisions in favor of environmental needs will result in trade-offs and although certain trade-offs would be more desirable than others, there is no assurance of what these will be.

In short, even though the proper international environmental concerns cannot always be identified, the international community has agreed there is a need for principles to guide conduct in relation to these concerns. It follows that there is a need for an orderly and systematic institutional response to concerns. Only experience will indicate what criteria can be employed in setting priorities among global environmental concerns and structuring programs to cope with them.

NOTES

[1] *U.N. Monthly Chronicle*, Oct. 1970, at iii.

[2] P.C. Jessup, *Transnational Law* (Storrs lectures on Jurisprudence, 1956) — quotation condensed from dedication page of *Colum. J. Transnational Law.*

[3] Finney, "Senate Unit Says Costlier Weapons May Cut Defense," *N.Y. Times*, Sept. 9, 1971, at 1, col. 6.

[4] "Development and Environment," Report submitted by a panel of experts convened by the Secretary-General of the U.N. Conference on the Human Environment, 4-12 June, 1971, Founex, Switzerland, U.N. Doc. GE 71-13738 at 22-30 (1971).

[5] *Id.* at 27.

[6] For quotations in this paragraph see *id.* at 27-30.

[7] *See also* Kasdan, "Third World War — Environment versus Development," 26 *The Record of the Association of the Bar of the City of New York*, June 1971, at 454.

[8] *See generally* as to this discussion Study of Critical Environmental Problems (SCEP); *Man's Impact on the Global Environment: Assessment and Recommendations for Action*, Report of the Secretary-General, U.N. Doc. E/4667 (1969); Russell & Lansberg, "International Environmental Problems — A Taxonomy," 172 *Science*, June 1971, at 1307-14.

[9] *See* discussions of quality control techniques in W. Friedmann and J. Beguin, *Joint International Business Ventures in Developing Countries: Case Studies and Analysis* (1971).

[10] *See* "Problems and Priorities in Human Settlements," Report of the Secretary-General, U.N. Doc. A/8037 (1971).

[11] Ochs, "Can India Cope with Its Environmental Problems?" 1 *International Wildlife*, Sept.-Oct. 1971, at 18, 19.

[12] *See generally* addendum to vol. II, "World Plan of Action for the Application of Science and Technology to Development," Report of the Advisory Committee on the Application of Science and Technology to Development, U.N. Doc. E/4962/Add 1. (Part X) (1971).

[13] "Technology: Processes of Assessment and Choice," Report of the National Academy of Science for the Committee on Science and Astronautics of the U.S. House of Representatives (July 1969).

[14] F.F. Darling, *Wilderness and Plenty* (1971).

[15] P.L. No. 91-190, 83 Stat. 852, codified at 42 U.S.C. 4321, 4331, *et seq.*

[16] For agenda *see* "Report of the Preparatory Committee for the U.N. Conference on the Human Environment," U.N. Doc. A/Conf. 48/PC. 9, paras. 7-89 (1971).

[17] 3 U.N.R.I.A.A. 1905 (1938).

[18] *See* U.N. Documents with titles as set forth in text, A/AC. 105/C.1/VIII/CRP. 1, and A/AC.105/C.1/VIII/CRP.2.

[19] *See generally* for discussion of problems and recommendations for use of satellites by the U.N. "Space Communications: Increasing U.N. Responsiveness to the Problems of Mankind," A Report of a National Policy Panel Established by the U.N. Association of the U.S.A. (1971).

[20]*Supra* note 13, at 13.

[21]*See generally,* "World Population — A Challenge to the U.N. and Its System of Agencies," A Report of the National Policy Panel Established by the U.N. Association of the U.S.A. (1969).

[22]*Supra* note 16, at 13-14.

[23]R. Arvill, *Man and Environment* at 253 (1970 Pelican ed.).

[24]*See, e.g.,* "Report of the Preparatory Committee for the U.N. Conference on the Human Environment," U.N. Doc. A/Conf. 48/PC/6, para. 29 (1970).

[25]*See* U.N. Doc. A/Conf. 48/PC.9, para. 9 (1971).

[26]*Id.* at para. 32.

[27]*See* U.N. Doc. A/Conf. 48/PC/W.G. 1/CRP.4/Add 2, (1971).

[28]*See* U.N. Doc. A/Conf. 48/PC/W.G. 1/L.1/Rev. 1. (1971).

[29]*See* U.N. Doc. A/Conf. 48/PC 12, annex 1 (1971).

[30]*See* U.N. Doc. A/Conf. 48/PC 12, annex 2 (1971). "Report of the Rapporteur on Reservations and Observations on the draft preamble and fundamental principles expressed by members of the Intergovernmental Working Group."

[31]*Supra.* note 29.

[32]*Ibid.*

[33]*Ibid.*

[34]*Ibid.*

[35]*Supra* note 4, at iii.

[36]U.N. Press Release, HE/65 (Sept. 13, 1971).

[37]U.N. Press Release, HE/66 (Sept. 14, 1971).

[38]U.N. Press Release, HE/68 (Sept. 14, 1971).

[39]U.N. Press Release, HE/88, ECLA/189 (Sept. 21, 1971).

[40]U.N. Press Release, HE/74 (Sept. 16, 1971).

[41]U.N. Press Release, HE/86 (Sept. 21, 1971).

[42]*Ibid.*

PART THREE

TOWARD AN INTERNATIONAL LAW OF
ENVIRONMENTAL PROTECTION

PART III.
TOWARD AN INTERNATIONAL LAW OF ENVIRONMENTAL PROTECTION

EDITORIAL ANALYSIS

A. *A glance at the present legal landscape.*

Is there presently an international law of environmental protection? If so, what is its scope and content? For the moment, we may take "international law" as encompassing legal rules establishing reciprocal rights and obligations of national states or international organizations. And we may take the law of "environmental protection" to embrace not only legal arrangements designed or intended primarily for regulating pollution or some other activity injurious to some environment, but to include more generally all legal rules which might be invoked in the course of an effort either to justify, or to prevent, abate, or obtain other remedy for, an environmental injury. From the vantage point of such a definitional platform as this, a glance at some very general features of the contemporary international legal order will be instructive in pointing toward answers to the questions posed above.

The two most pervasive features of that landscape, insofar as a law of environmental protection is concerned, are the two great *laissez-faire* principles of national sovereignty and freedom of the high seas. Taken together, they may be said as a general rule to put nations in a legal position, within their own respective territories and within most of the great common area of the planet, to conduct such activities injurious to the environment as they please, up to the limits permitted by the state of development of the relevant technologies and by their own unilateral assessment of their political, economic, military, or other requirements.

It is true, of course, that these general features of the international legal order are a part of the framework of the international law relating to many areas of inter-state relations. What distinguishes the law of environmental protection from many other such areas of international law is the overriding extent to which it remains dominated by these two *laissez-faire* principles. By contrast, well-developed fields of international legal regulation of state conduct — such as the law of international trade, of the use of force between states, of contractual relations between states, or of exchange of official governmental representatives — are dominated by large bodies of regulatory legislation which have the effect of carving out extensive exceptions to the principle of national sovereignty and, in some cases, the principle of freedom of the high seas.

Professor L. F. E. Goldie's paper appearing at page 104 of this book sets out a description and an appraisal of present international environmental law. The picture that emerges from such an analysis as Professor Goldie's, as to both customary and conventional law, is that of a rather motley collection of limited and often still-emerging limitations on the freedom of action conferred on states by the two fundamental principles referred to above. These limitations are particularly scant with regard to "dry land" activities impairing environmental quality, insofar as general international law, as distinguished from rights and obligations established by special bilateral or regional treaty arrangements, is concerned. Here, principles which might impose responsibility and liability for acts injurious to another state are still embryonic and vaguely defined, and little effort at general regulation through treaty has been undertaken (Article 12 of the Chicago Convention on International Civil Aviation is an exception).

Within the law of the sea, the collection of legal rules and principles directly relevant to protection of the environment is somewhat ampler, since there has been considerable effort at general regulation of certain highly specific polluting activities, and since treaties in the field confer certain competences on coastal states in geographic areas beyond their territorial jurisdiction which place them in a position to regulate activities injurious to the environment in those areas. Moreover, arguments have been put forward for a right on the part of a state threatened with environmental injury from sources beyond its territorial jurisdiction, at least where those sources are located on the high seas, to take reasonable action to prevent or abate that injury. Such a right has been recently written into treaty law with respect to a specific form of polluting activity, in the 1969 IMCO Convention Relating to Intervention on the High Seas in cases of Oil Pollution Casualties, discussed by Professor Goldie at pages 117-120. But its present existence and scope, as a matter of general international law, would be matters of controversy.

As to both activities within territorial jurisdiction and activities in the ocean beyond territorial jurisdiction, it is clear that any principle obligating states to refrain from injury to the environment itself, as distinguished from injury to the environment of a particular state, is as yet in only the most rudimentary stages of development. This state of affairs contrasts with situations prevailing in some national legal orders, in which environmentally injurious activities may be subject to regulation not only through the law of torts, providing injured individuals a mode of redress invokable only on their own initiative, but through the criminal law as well.

B. *Some observations on principles, present or prospective.*

1. *Responsibility, liability, and the measure of injury.*
It comes quite naturally to lawyers, in considering alternative arrangements for protecting the environment, to think of establishing principles which impose legal responsibility for injuries on those who caused them or were in a position to prevent them. Concomitantly, lawyers think of imposing liability to rectify such an injury through compensation in an amount commensurate with the harm inflicted. Professor Goldie's paper discusses the various and scattered bases in customary and conventional international law upon which one might seek to ground an assertion that such principles were already an emerging part of international law (see particularly pages 105-106, 129-139).

It is safe to assume that the question of the extent to which the responsibility-liability approach should be relied upon to do specific jobs of environmental protection will arise repeatedly in the course of the next few years, as it has in the recent past (for example, in connection with the 1969 IMCO Convention on Civil Liability for Oil Pollution Damage).

Among the general considerations which will bear on this question are those set out in the following paragraphs.
(a) *The relation between problems of proof and the selection of legal strategy.*
The oil-spill catastrophe is perhaps the paradigm case in which the planners of environmental protection policy are likely to think of the responsibility-liability strategy. In such a case, problems of proof — at least of the existence and cause of injury, if not its extent — are likely to be comparatively easy. By contrast, the same problems of proof in the case, say, of an injury inflicted in Scandinavia by airborne effluents discharged elsewhere in Europe, are likely to be formidable. The same would be true in the case of injury to a fishery stock at considerable distances offshore from petroleum discharges from land-based sources, or from ocean-based sources discharging in relatively small quantities on a relatively large number of occasions. For problems like the latter two, considerations of economy and efficiency argue against a system of legal control based primarily on determination of responsibility and imposition of liability, and in favor of a system which seeks to prevent the injurious activity primarily through regulatory regimes establishing precise standards of permissible conduct.
(b) *Specific regulatory regimes as a remedy in particular cases.*
It may be that even in the case of injurious activities which readily lend themselves to an economical determination of responsibility, the most effective remedy will not be the imposition of liability, but instead — or additionally — the establishment of a specific regulatory regime. The second decision, in 1941, of the arbitral tribune in the

Trail Smelter case (one of the few international litigations which may have precedental bearing on the question of responsibility and liability for environmental injury) established such a regime, having the effect of laying down permissible levels of emission on the part of the smelter whose operations had been the cause of the dispute.

(c) *Determining tolerable levels of the externalization of costs.*

It is commonplace to think environmental injuries as "external costs" imposed by persons engaged in economic activity on persons who are not so engaged, and who benefit only indirectly from the activity, if at all. One important problem in the legal control of environment injury will be that of determining the point below which such externalization of costs should be deemed warranted by the value to the community of the activity that entails it. There is reason to doubt that the technique of ascription of responsibility and imposition of liability is a very effective one for making such determinations. There are several reasons why this is so. Determinations of liability are episodic. Moreover, any particular such determination will provide a standard only as to a level of externalization that is *not* permitted, but will not of itself provide information as to what may be permitted. And to the extent that the legal order imputes precedental value to such determinations, the body of jurisprudence developing from them will grow at an erratic rate. Perhaps more fundamentally, the legal concept of liability for injury does not readily lend itself to a process which aims at allocating external costs of economic activities by determining permissible levels of injury. The theory upon which liability generally proceeds is that injuries, once determined, are to be compensated in full; it is the added costs, either of compensation or of reducing the level of future injury, that perform the allocative function by being passed on by the operator to the end user.

At the same time, it is worth noting again that the *Trail Smelter* case resulted not merely in a determination of responsibility but also in the establishment of a particular regulatory regime. Leaving aside the question of the legal competence of particular international tribunals to devise such a remedy, this case suggests that in some situations, litigation of particular disputes might serve the dual function of both imposing responsibility for past acts and allocating the costs of future ones.

In any event, it is clear that an exploration of the limits of usefulness of the legal concepts of responsibility and liability quickly brings one to the problem of permissible levels of injury, a problem which will pervade efforts at environmental control whether pursued through litigative proceedings in international tribunals, through setting standards of conduct by treaty, or through the exercise of regulatory functions by international agencies. And it should be clear also that determining permissible levels of injury is not a scientific judgement, any more than deciding whether a superhighway should be built through a residential neighborhood is scientific.

Both are judgments of public policy, although such judgments in the environmental field will depend especially heavily on scientific information in many cases.

2. *The concept of injury to the environment.*

The developing law of responsibility and liability discussed above is grounded, for the most part, on the principle that international law forbids injury of one state by another. It regards preservation of a state's own environment as a legally protectable interest of that state, and injury to that environment, accordingly, as giving rise to legal liability. It is not predicated on the theory that international law obligates states to refrain from injury to, or to protect, the planet's environment, and that default on these obligations may give rise to liabilities within the legal order even in the absence of a showing that some state has suffered what has heretofore counted as a legal injury. We have already observed that both of these theories of legal injury are often exhibited in the law of environmental protection found within national legal systems: not only are individuals sometimes permitted to sue to prevent or abate environmental injuries which impair their own individual proprietary rights; there are also obligations to refrain from injuring the environment itself which are regarded as protecting a public interest in environmental quality and which are enforceable most characteristically through the processes of the criminal law. Discharging polluting wastes into a stream, for example, may give rise not only to civil liability to the owners of downstream tracts, but also to criminal liability under laws or regulations prohibiting or restricting the discharge.

It is fairly easy to see what kinds of jobs of environmental protection on a global basis an effectively working system of state responsibility and liability for injury to other states might be expected to do fairly well, and what kinds it could not be expected to do (leaving aside, for the moment, problems of proof such as those discussed in the preceding section). Such a system could be expected to cope with injuries to the territory of one state arising from activities in the territory of another, or from activities by that other state or its nationals in an area beyond national jurisdiction. It could not be expected to cope very well with injuries to the environment lying in areas beyond national jurisdiction, where no legally recognized injury to the territory, property, or nationals of another state could be shown. (A clear example would be the destruction of a guyot or of marine life systems by a nuclear explosion in the ocean.) Even more clearly, such a system could not be expected to deal adequately with injuries by a state to portions of the planet's environment lying within its own national jurisdiction, even if of such a scope and magnitude as to be regarded as offending against an interest of the international community as a whole or of mankind itself.

The notion that mankind itself has a proper interest in the integrity of the whole planet, without regard to the vagaries of political jurisdictions or allocations of power at any historical moment, may be finding a place in the moral awareness of modern man. If so, however, this does not mean that it has yet found its place in existing international law, or even that the international community is well on its way toward carving out such a place for it. In fact, one can discern only fragmentary evidences of such a development. The 1970 Declaration of the United Nations General Assembly on Peaceful Uses of the Sea-Bed (Res. 2749 (XXV) asserted that the sea-bed beyond the limits of national jurisdiction is the "common heritage of mankind". The 1972 United Nations Conference on the Human Environment is expected to have a treaty before it creating a "world heritage trust", which would have the effect of establishing a list of designated sites within various national territories to be preserved because of unique natural, cultural or historical value to mankind as a whole.[1] Another treaty would have unique wet-lands areas lying within national territories designated in a similar way.[2] Article 25 of the 1958 Convention on the High Seas obligates "all states" to "co-operate with the competent international organizations for the prevention of pollution of the seas or air space above, resulting from any activities with radio-active materials or other harmful agents".

Certain of the language considered by the Intergovernmental. Working Group established within the United Nations to draft a declaration on the human environment (discussed at length in Mr. Robinson's paper appearing at pages 74-85 above) suggested a general interest in protection of the environment as such. The Working Group's draft discussed by Mr. Robinson asserted, for example, that "everyone has a responsibility to protect the environment", that "states shall carefully husband their natural resources and shall hold in trust for present and future generations the air, water, land, plants, and animals on which all life depends;" and that "each state has the responsibility to compensate for damage to the environment caused by activities carried on within its territory."

The present lack of any solid international legal basis for asserting a public interest on the part of the international community in protection of the planet's environment is only a natural reflection of the state of political organization of the planet generally. It remains to be seen to what extent states will be willing to articulate explicit principles asserting such a community interest, or to agree to regulatory regimes or institutional devices by which it could be effectively vindicated.

3. *A right of states to take unilateral protective action.*

It can be argued that the cardinal principle of a strategy of environmental protection must be the principle of unilateral national action. This argument would be grounded on the fact of the primitive state of development of international law as regards both responsibility and liability for environmental injury, on the one hand, and the concept of an international community interest in the environment as such, on the other. This fundamental principle being recognized, the primary problem in the progressive development of international law would be, for the time being, the delimitation and regulation of the right of self-help or other unilateral action.

One may discern a certain analogy here between the law relating to environmental injury and the law regulating the use of force in international relations. Ideally, the use of force would be regulated through the universal multilateral institution established for that purpose, the United Nations. In fact, however, since the inception of the United Nations our experience has been that responses to allegedly illicit uses of force usually take the form of individual or collective national action, the multilateral agency being incapable in fact of responding effectively. In the case of protection against environmental injury, it is argued, the case for unilateral national action is even more compelling, in view of the lack of international institutions with even the legal power to prevent or abate particular environmental threats.

(a) *National action to protect one's own environment: Self-help.*

Unilateral action predicated on a theory of a right to protect oneself is the paradigm case of national action to prevent or abate environmental injury. Professor Goldie's paper outlines, at pages 117-120 below, the possible bases on which an argument might be grounded for the existence of such a right in general international law, and indicates something of the limits of any such right which those grounds suggest. An effort to develop the law simply by means of the *ad hoc* exercise of such a right with respect to particular threats as they arise, would confront a complex of difficulties — difficulties which are present even in the case of action in the ocean beyond national jurisdiction.

For one thing, to an even greater extent than in the case of an act of force in self-defense, an act of self-help to abate environmental threat, not governed by a treaty regime, will be self-judging in character. And we can by no means be assured that the proprieties will be perceived alike by all reasonable men of goodwill.

Moreover, it must be presumed that on some occasions the effective exercise of such a right of self-help would entail the exercise of force against another state, its property, or its nationals. At that point, self-help for environmental protection becomes not merely analogous to the unilateral exercise of force but an instance of it, and must be judged by the same standards as those applied by the U.N. Charter to the use of force generally. Those standards, of course, envisage permissible national force only in exercise of the right of self-defense, recognized by Article 51. There is nothing in the language of that article to suggest that the exception to the prohibition on the threat or use of force which it contains is broad enough to include action designed simply to prevent environmental injury. And a decision as a matter of legal policy to seek so to broaden it is hardly a step to be taken lightly. The international community has enough difficulty as it is with various national efforts to stretch beyond any utility the concept of "armed attack", which most U.N. members that have addressed the question profess to take as limiting the right of self-defense.

From the point of view of a government which asserts a right of self-help in areas beyond national jurisdiction, the solution — in point of legal theory, at any rate — is clearly for that government state to make a claim of continuing national jurisdiction to exercise certain kinds of regulatory prerogatives within a stated geographic zone. If (as has not always been the case) that state is willing to assert that such an exercise of jurisdiction is grounded in a right presently existing in international law, it will at least avoid the embarrassment of being unable to assert any other than a domestic legal basis for actions which may in fact give rise to considerable international friction. It is understandable that states making such claims would seek to induce the community at large to validate them by general delegations of authority to coastal states to regulate in matters of environmental protection in designated coastal zones.

(b) *National action to protect an international interest in the environment: Custodial Protection.*

As a matter of existing law, there is even less basis for asserting the legal right of a state to take environmental protective action on behalf of the international community than for an asserted right to take self-protective action. In the latter case, there is at least the traditional principle of self-defense, incorporated in whole or in part by the Charter, which provides a certain argument-by-analogy in support of unilateral action. As to activities which are injurious to the planet's life systems, but cannot be said to amount to a legal injury against any particular state, the broad thrust of international law — as already emphasized — has been strongly adverse to the development of any right on the part of one state to intervene in such injurious activities by another state or its nationals. On the contrary, the general effect of the twin principles of national sovereignty and freedom of the high seas has been to leave each national state free to impair its own environment in the course of pursuing its own objectives, and free to compete with other states in impairing the environment of the planet's common areas.

100

Nonetheless, if the concept of a legally protected international community interest in the environment develops at all, it will doubtless come to fruition much faster outside the areas generally acknowledged to lie within national jurisdiction. The natural concomitant of such a development would be a right on the part of states, and in some cases a duty, to take action to protect that interest. The legal problems entailed by such a development would be closely analogous to those discussed earlier with reference to help. The delegation by the international community of authority to the coastal state to act as environmental "custodian" over a portion of the ocean adjacent to its own coasts, currently suggested by some, could be predicated on the theory of an international community interest, although in practical fact its proponents are understandably more likely to be motivated by an interest in self-protection than in protecting the community at large.

4. *A declaration of principles as a legal strategy.*

From an early stage, a broadly supported declaration of states on the human environment has been among the strategies discussed in planning toward the 1972 United Nations Conference on the Human Environment. It has not been clear, and at the present writing remains uncertain, precisely what would be the intended role of such a declaration, whether adopted by the Conference or by some other body such as the U.N. General Assembly. A wide variety of possible roles are conceivable, even if one limits consideration to the precedents of previous U.N. General Assembly declaratory exercises. Examples include the Universal Declaration of Human Rights (Res. 217 (III) A), the 1960 "Anti-Colonialism" Declaration (Res. 1514 (XV)), the Declaration of Legal Principles on Outer Space (Res. 1962 (XVIII)), the Declaration of Principles of International Law concerning Friendly Relations (Res. 2625 (XXV)), and the Declaration of Principles concerning the Sea-Bed and Ocean Floor Beyond the Limits of National Jurisdiction (Res. 2749 (XXV)).

For one thing, a declaration by a United Nations conference or other body might well have no role as a *legal* strategy at all — except in the indirect way of identifying problems which might in due course be made the subject of legal action. Each of the United Nations resolutions mentioned above, however, whatever its legal effect, was concerned with an area regarded at the time as in need of further legal development. This is sure to be the case with any declaration or set of declarations on international environmental problems, whatever the nature of the legal role such utterances might be intended to play. There are at least three principal ways in which a declaration of environmental *principles* (not to speak of other kinds of declarations), adopted by a universal intergovernmental body, might serve directly as a kind of legal strategy.

First, it could identify particular jobs of international legislation which are needed and record agreement in principle to proceed with them, describing each with as much particularity as feasible.

Secondly, it could formulate legal-looking substantive principles — couched in the law-like language of rights and obligations of states — but explicitly intended not as statements of law but as agreed guides to the development of law through treaty-making or otherwise. In this case the principles might be explicitly described as reflecting an agreement on what ought to govern the conduct of states (but does not presently do so as a matter of law).

Thirdly, it could articulate principles, either explicitly asserting them to be reflections of existing international law or leaving open the question of their legal status.

In making declarations of the first two types, states would be acting outside the law-making process itself, and addressing themselves collectively to the question of what should be done within that process. A declaration of the third type raises problems of greater subtlety and complexity than the first two, as it amounts to an act by states within the law making process. It proceeds on the theory — for which there is a considerable body of support in the practices of U.N. organs and statements of U.N. members — that a virtually unanimously supported formal assertion of what the law is, by such a body as the U.N. General Assembly, is in itself strong evidence of international law, even if it may go beyond what could properly be described as existing international law in the absence of such an assertion.

This power to make "instant international law" on the part of the General Assembly or a plenary United Nations conference is neither as instantaneous nor as radical as this nomenclature might suggest. The process of reaching near-unanimous agreement on a declaration of international law on matters of any consequence is a long and arduous one. And the power of any individual state or group of states to abort the effort if it takes an unsatisfactory turn, or to influence its outcome, is considerably greater than its power over a treaty-making negotiation. Moreover, the end result will usually be no more (although no less) effective in influencing the conduct of states than other highly general principles of customary international law, disembodied as they are from any specific procedural or institutional arrangements designed to insure that states actually take them seriously.

Nevertheless, this potential means of progressive development of international law can be a useful and powerful one if carefully husbanded. This fact itself should be a governing consideration in deciding what role would be played by any declaration about problems of the human environment. For example, it would be a mistake, as regards both the potential usefulness of the U.N.'s law-making powers and the development of the law of environmental protection, to try to do a more ambi-

102

tious law-making job through a declaration of principles than the political traffic will bear, resulting in a declaration which turns out to be strongly controverted as to its substance and law-making effect.

In Part II of this book, at pages 38-39, a number of other grounds for caution in drafting and promulgating broad declarations of principle were set out. The moral suggested by all these considerations is that general declarations may have an important legal role to play, at this early stage in the formulation of international public policy on the environment, but that role must be played with extreme judiciousness if more harm than good is not to be done.

NOTES

[1] *See:* Introductory Note by the Secretary-General of the Conference on the World Heritage Foundation, U.N. Doc. A/Conf. 48/IWGC. 1/2, July 26, 1971.

[2] Draft Convention on Conservation of Wetlands of International Importance, U.N. Doc. A/Conf. 48/IWGC.1/4, July 30, 1971.

DEVELOPMENT OF AN INTERNATIONAL ENVIRON-
MENTAL LAW — AN APPRAISAL

by *L. F. E. Goldie**

Introduction

From its inception writers have presented international law as a limited system governing only the relations of states in their public interactions, namely "the system of right and justice which ought to prevail between nations or sovereign states".[1] The present era of accelerated change is reflected in the rapid expansion of the scope of international law. Its scope is continuously broadening and has come to include, not only the interactions of states within the arenas which international and regional agencies provide in addition to the arenas of traditional diplomacy, but also relations of states with international agencies and those of international agencies *inter se*, the transnational interpenetrations of communities and activities, and the increasing capacity, at least in certain regions, to vindicate individual claims of recognition, protection and participation in the social system. But when these dramatic developments are compared with the present international law governing pollution, the latter (apart from some conventions which remain unimplemented, in part) appears to have hardly moved out of the traditional rut at all.

In contrast with the law of nations's traditional limitations and contemporary shortcomings, an international environmental law should be a flexible instrument capable of protecting the environment at a number of levels of action. It should regulate government interactions, impose minimum standards for national legislation and administration, require all international agencies, be they regional or universal, to include the protection of the environment as an inherent and uncontrovertible measure of policy in the process of decision, build into regimes governing the exploration and exploitation of the seabed resources special standards and duties of environment protection, and establish international agencies which should flexibly impose minimum universal and regional standards for preventing further environmental degradation. It would be no part, however, of such an international environmental law's function to prevent absolutely the transformation of the environment into energy and useful or enjoyable commodities.

---

*The author is Professor of Law, Director, International Legal Studies Program, Syracuse University College of Law.

I. The Present Scope Of An International Environmental Law

A. *State Responsibility*

The view has long prevailed among jurists and publicists that doctrines of national sovereignty and autonomy are inconsistent with a thesis that in international law states may be held to act at their peril. Hence the great majority of respected writers who have contributed their considered opinions in this area have rejected arguments claiming that either strict or absolute liability may be imposed on states. This is not only true of general arguments, it is equally true of proposals which have only contemplated certain special situations and certain narrow sectors of legal relations as being apt for absolute and strict accountability in the event of catastrophic harms. Thus we find the following statement in Oppenheim:

An act of a State injurious to another State is nevertheless not an international delinquency if committed neither wilfully and maliciously nor with culpable negligence. Therefore, an act of a State committed by right, or prompted by self-preservation in necessary self-defense, does not constitute an international delinquency, no matter how injurious it may actually be to another State.[2]

According to this view, massive oil pollution disasters no more than, for example, nuclear catastrophes, and disasters caused on the earth's surface by space activities, would not, *de lege lata*, attract strict, let alone absolute, liability. Furthermore, customary international law would not appear to provide other institutions and doctrines for the regulation or restraint of activities having very high risks of catastrophic and polluting accidents or the restraints of pursuits which have a continuous and cumulative, if barely measurable under traditional legal doctrines, degrading effect on the environment. Indeed, in wide areas general international law would still appear to either permit or be uncertain about pre-emptive policies whereby the first comer is entitled to "shut-out" the other participants in the activity, or at least permanently reduce the utility of a resource to those others. Examples include the interference with an international stream by upper riparian states so as to deny full use of it to the lower riparians, the raising of radioactive fallout health hazards by bomb testing in the atmosphere so as to inhibit other states from so doing (unfortunately the Nuclear Test Ban Treaty would not appear to have become recognized as embodying a universal rule binding signatories and non-signatories alike), the taking of the population of a fishery so as to destroy its effective reproduction so completely that the taker may be said to be "mining" the resource rather than fishing, and the pollution of lakes and even sea areas so as to deny their utility to others.

Some international arbitral decisions and recent conventions would appear to provide some doctrinal mitigation of this gloomy picture. One may, however, ask to what extent these developments indicate widely-binding rules and doctrines. With this caveat in mind they should be examined as possibly standing as fingerposts pointing to legal change.

Apart from Article 12 of the Chicago Convention on International Aviation, some aviation regulations, the emerging principle of good neighborliness, and the limited, although possibly developing, doctrines of liability in international law, there has been little to encourage environmentalists in the law governing the dry land transnational control of pollution. The law of the sea may, however, lend itself to international regulation more readily. Accordingly, the types of present-day maritime jurisdiction which lend themselves to state control of pollution offshore will be examined, followed by discussions of the use of the high seas as an "infinite sink" and the need to restrain this proclivity, the misleading "creeping jurisdiction" issue, the formulation and limits of states' rights to abate polluting activities threatening their land territories and territorial sea, the "principle of good neighborliness," and liability for harms under international law.

B. *Maritime Zones of State Competence to Restrain Pollution Activities*

The existing legal framework available for governing maritime pollution activities includes both international and domestic law competences. The transnational nature of environmental law problems calls for the co-ordination and mutual interpenetration of both bodies of law. Accordingly, a review of offshore competences of states to regulate maritime pollution activities should provide an appraisal of how the developing system of environmental law could call upon nations to exercise unilaterally, or mutually, their individual competences. Furthermore, in order to present a complete picture, that appraisal should also indicate the contexts for common and concerted action to be taken on the basis of the desirability of controlling polluting activities beyond the area of states' unilaterally exercisable competences.

Traditionally, international law has divided the seas into two great legal categories: those under the sovereignty of coastal states (and in which states are free to pursue their own domestic policies of environmental protection), for example, internal waters and territorial waters, and those beyond the sovereignty of any state, historically designated as the "free high seas". This latter zone may be seen as a "common" and so has been treated as "infinite sink" for the world's waste materials. At the present time an increasing number of state claims to exercise exclusive coastal state authority over additional sea areas are being brought within the same class of exclusive jurisdictional claims as the traditional territorial sea and internal waters (including historical

106

waters). Claims of these additional jurisdictional zones have, at times, been predicated on demands to protect the claimant state's environment. These claims, whether based on environmental or other considerations, were unknown to traditional international law. Those of them which are receiving international legal recognition embrace contiguous zones; special fisheries zones; zones of special jurisdiction, for example customs' zones beyond the territorial sea and zones of a temporary nature within which exclusive control is claimed for various kinds of weapons testing with possible disastrous effects on the environment. (This last type of claimed authority still includes, in the cases of Communist China and France, nuclear and hydrogen weapon-testing in maritime areas). In addition to the sea areas subject to the recognized claims of states, there are lawful seabed claims extending beyond territorial limits — namely those over adjacent continental shelves. Again, increasingly, states are establishing fishery conservation zones by agreement. Other types of coastal state claims which currently lack, even in this generally permissive world, the necessary recognition and acceptance which is essential to erect them into customary law concepts are the "CEP" claims,[3] and the "archipelago" claims of Indonesia and the Republic of the Philippines to draw baselines around their island systems from their outermost headlands and islands.[4]

(1) *Internal Waters.*

In law, the status of internal waters tends to be assimilated to that of the land of the coastal state.[5] That is, coastal states' authority with respect to seas which are classified as internal waters is, juridically speaking, assimilated to their sovereign authority over their land territory — except in so far as the nature of the actual quality of the watery medium may impose factual as distinct from juridical differences. These waters include historic bays and bays with straight base or closing lines of 24 miles breadth,[6] waters lying landward of straight baselines where the coastline is deeply indented and cut into, or where there is a fringe of islands along the coast and in its immediate vicinity, or, finally, where account may be taken of economic interests peculiar to the region concerned whose importance is clearly evidenced by long practice.[7] Examples of historic bays abound: Chesapeake Bay is a very long-standing and internationally accepted one. As states' exclusive competencies in internal waters are limited, under international law, only in the same way as those over dryland territory are, it follows that states have authority to protect the environment in their internal bays and estuaries as they have above the high water mark. Accordingly, their power to take protective action on behalf of such activities conducted in those locations as battery fish farming enterprises and sedentary fisheries are just as plenary as their authority to protect their inland orchards and farms from contamination.[8]

(2) *Ports, Harbors and Roadsteads*

Ports, harbors and roadsteads present a complicated picture. While ports and harbors are nearly always internal waters, roadsteads may be territorial waters or contiguous zones, or even, possibly, high seas. Hence coastal states have full control (since harbors and ports fall within the category of internal waters) over all vessels and activities within their ports and harbors. On the other hand, history and comity have brought them to subscribe, for reasons of convenience and reciprocity, to policies which recognize that control over the domestic discipline of ships in their harbors should be left to their masters and so be governed by the laws of the flag state — unless the "peace of the port" becomes involve.[9] But this is a discretionary withdrawal of jurisdiction by the coastal state for purposes of convenience, reciprocity and amity. It is not a privilege or immunity which international law accords to foreign flag ships within the ports of coastal states. Hence, the port state is entitled to treat all matters which affect the "peace of the port" as beyond its discretionary withdrawal of authority and subject to its domestic laws. Furthermore, it does not permit polluting activities in harbors contrary to the law and policies of the port state. Roadsteads are different from ports and harbors and fall within the regimes of either internal waters or the territorial sea, depending on location.[10] They may even be high seas, although this would be a most unusual case since the historic regulation of traffic in the roadstead and its use for quarantine and customs inspection purposes will generally place roadsteads within the category of contiguous zones. Be these classifications as they may, it is arguable that a port state has competence to hold a ship within its ports accountable for pollutions committed:

   (i) within the port contrary to its laws;

  (ii) in its territorial sea also contrary to its laws;

  (iii) on the high seas, so as to injure the port state's coasts and territorial sea;

  (iv) also on the high seas and contrary to the port state's international obligations.

In connection with item (iv), the proposal is that the United Kingdom, for example, should be permitted to hold accountable a Liberian-flag ship which has entered its ports for discharging oil on the high seas and in the North Sea when that discharge is contrary to her rights under the Bonn Agreement.[10a]

The resistance one finds to the incorporation of principle (iv) above seems to this writer to be unduly based on an anachronistic respect for the traditional prerogatives of ship masters. The *Lotus Case*[11] has provided for a long time an indication that international law is prepared to mitigate the monopoly of the flag state by recognizing the jurisdictional claims of the port state. The dramatic arrest, just as she was quitting Singapore's territorial sea of the *Lake Palourde*, in order to give the

108

British plaintiffs a leverage for obtaining *in rem* jurisdiction of their claims against the Union Oil Company with respect to the *Torrey Conyon*[11a] casualty provides a further illustration. In such cases traditional rules of admiralty law appear to find no difficulty with acceding to port state claims which countervail those of the flag state, despite admiralty's traditional sympathy with the laws and customs of mariners. The additional element in this proposal is that the port state's traditional rights (which include the accepted right of closing its ports to an offending ship) should be made available to allow that state to require ships's compliance with its legal obligations and its common interests with other states as embodied in treaties, regarding the protection of the high seas.

(3) *The Territorial Sea.*

The territorial sea is distinguishable from ports and harbors as well as from internal waters in that, while the territorial sea is subject to the sovereign power of the coastal state, it is also subject to the rights of shipping which may navigate freely through it — provided that navigation is "innocent". As the traditional language phrases this situation, ships may exercise the right of innocent passage, but not that of "free navigation", through the territorial sea of coastal states.[12] Innocent passage may also be exercised, according to the United States doctrine and according to the Geneva Convention on the Territorial Sea and Contiguous Zone, by warships.[12a] This view of the right of innocent passage was shared by the International Court of Justice in the *Corfu Channel Case*.[13] On the other hand, the Soviet Union does not recognize that warships are entitled to enjoy the right of innocent passage. But the Soviet's position on this is not altogether clear, as on so many other points of international law. Although ships may exercise the right of innocent passage, aircraft may not. Finally, ships may lose their right of innocent passage if during transit they disturb the peace of the coastal state in any way or engage in activities which are non-innocent. Clearly, this would include any activities which the coastal state may regard as polluting its territorial or maritime environment. I would suggest, furthermore, that an inhibition of polluting activities would not be limited to those which have an effect on the coastal state's territory. Within the territorial sea the coastal state may regard any polluting activity contrary to its own regulation of its territorial sea as a breach of the passing ship's duty to maintain the innocence of its passage.

(4) *Contiguous Zones.*

The contiguous zone of seas under international law is distinguishable from the territorial sea on a basis which has been widely and surprisingly misunderstood. This misunderstanding has profound implications for problems arising out of the development of a global environmental law. It leaves unsettled the criteria of the kinds of pollution activities in the contiguous zone which the coastal state may prohibit, or regulate, and those which fall outside the coastal state's competence. If the coastal state were to exercise power in the latter context, its conduct would constitute an unjustifiable interference with a foreign ship's freedom to navigate on the high seas. Conduct on the high seas must be controlled by different legal agencies and principles from those which stem from coastal states' exclusive competences in offshore maritime zones subject to their authority.

Many international lawyers tend to assimilate it to the territorial sea and refuse to make meaningful and necessary distinctions between these two regimes of offshore waters. In this, they are completely and clearly wrong.[14] Contiguous zones, properly defined, consist of areas of waters offshore over which states may exercise specialized jurisdictions for specific purposes having direct or immediate effect within the territorial sea, internal waters, or adjacent dry land.[14a] For example, should a ship passing through the zone engage in a polluting activity, an internationally justifiable exercise of jurisdiction by a coastal state could only arise if that act could be shown to have a potentiality for deleterious effects on shore or in the state's territorial or internal waters. For it can be claimed only if the protection of the coastal state's territory (including its territorial sea) is involved. Thus the claim, by the United States in the Water Quality Control Act of 1970 of the United States Congress, providing that the United States can enforce the Act in the contiguous zone of the United States, seeks to give more than international law allows. That is not to say that the United States courts would not uphold that authority. But should they do so, they would be consciously choosing the legislation of Congress in preference to the rules of customary international law and of Article 24 of the Convention on the Territorial Sea and Contiguous Zone.

The confusion is compounded today because the Geneva Convention on the Territorial Sea and Contiguous Zone limits the extent seaward of contiguous zones to 12 sea miles. The assumption underlying this limitation was that territorial sea would be no more than 3, or at the most, 6 sea miles in breadth. Since then, however, an inexorable trend has developed whereby a number of states have been expanding the outer limits of the territorial sea they claim to 12 sea miles and even beyond. Accordingly, the 12 sea miles limit of the contiguous zone is losing its significance as a means for expanding out from the low water mark, coastal states' specific claims to exercise specialized authority over events having direct results ashore.

In addition, there are contiguous zones which must be recognized and respected which extend far beyond 12 sea miles from the shore.[14b] For example, the United States has for a long period of time exercised authority over special customs zones and other special areas for distances of over 60 miles from our shores. Then there is also, of course, the ADIZ

110

(Aircraft Defense Identification Zone), which is, to my way of thinking, an application of the contiguous zone concept under unique conditions. This zone extends some 500 sea miles offshore. By means of this last, jurisdiction is exercised over aircraft only when they are approaching and intend to land within the United States. In the context of pollution and environmental protection, coastal states may, under general international law, only exercise authority to prevent polluting activities which have an impact on their land territory, shore, internal waters and territorial seas. They are not entitled to vindicate, in their contiguous zones, the universal moral claim for unpolluted high seas (or even contiguous zones!).[14c]

(5) *The Continental Shelf.*

The maritime zones I have discussed so far — apart from some types of contiguous zones — would appear to be relatively traditional in nature. Although, in its general terms, the Continental Shelf Doctrine has come to be recognized as a form of customary international law, it is of relatively recent provenance.

Insofar as the Continental Shelf Doctrine (and the Convention which embodies it) reflect an acceptance of the inevitable by international lawyers,[15] one may regretfully assume, once technology made exploitation of submarine areas beyond the territorial waters possible, that the only remaining question was whether the oceans (beyond 3 sea miles from the low water mark) were to be exploited under the rubric of the freedom of the high seas or under that of the Continental Shelf Doctrine. In either case, the environment would be, as the oil blow-outs in the Santa Barbara Channel in January-April 1969[16] and subsequent blow-outs and fires in the Gulf of Mexico well illustrate, the most likely victims.

On the other hand, as political events arising out of the Union Oil Company's "miscalculation" in the geology of the Santa Barbara Channel tend to illustrate, a coastal state may more easily be held accountable for its actions in the adjacent continental shelf region by a national constituency dedicated to protecting the environment. Such a constituency is more likely to be effective in insisting on its own polity's responsibility towards its continental shelf areas when those areas concerned may not then be exploited by the nationals of other states invoking the doctrines of the freedom of their common high seas and their bed.

What is the Continental Shelf? First, it is necessary to distinguish between the physical geographical shelf, which is purely descriptive, and the legal idea of the shelf. The latter is the child of policy and is purely prescriptive. First, the concept in physical geography: every dry-land mass stands upon a pedestal which plunges down into the ocean abyss. The geological formation of this pedestal begins, generally speaking and with certain dramatic exceptions (for example, the west coast of South America, and parts of the California coast, the coast of British Columbia and the southern coast of Alaska) from the dry land perspective, as a fairly gentle gradient, or shoulder, extending out under the sea to a point marine geographers have named the "break in slope". This break in slope may occur at any point between 35 and 400 fathoms — or even 500 fathoms. But most frequently it seems to occur at around 100 fathoms or 200 meters of depth. Lawyers have argued, in order to impose uniformity of measurement on a geographical concept which can only be accurately measured with difficulty and evidences no uniformity, that no matter where the break in slope may in fact occur, the continental shelf boundary should be drawn as the average, or general, specific line of 200 meters. Beyond the break in slope the shoulder disappears and the land mass tends to plunge into the abyss at a far steeper gradient. At the foot it meets the bed of the ocean floor at depths of between 3,500 and 4,500 meters. Here a major geological change takes place. The chemical and geological formation of the seabed is different qualitatively from that of both dry land and the pedestal.

Secondly, although the legal definition of the continental shelf is enshrined in Article 1 of the Continental Shelf Convention, this definition has a far wider reach of legal authority than merely among the states who have ratified the treaty. In 1969 the International Court of Justice laid down in the *North Sea Continental Shelf Cases*.[17] that the first three articles of the Convention codified pre-existing customary international law. Accordingly, these provisions reflect norms binding on all states, not merely the adherents to the treaty alone.

Article 1 of the Continental Shelf Convention defines the outer limits of the legal continental shelf as being either at the 200 meter bathymetric contour line, or, alternatively, where, beyond 200 meters of depth, the resources of the seabed are exploitable. This is an extremely open-ended definition; so much so that organizations like the National Petroleum Council are now arguing that the "true" location of the continental shelf's outer limits under international law is not at the break in slope, or shoulder of the shelf, let alone at the 200 meter bathymetric line indicated by Article 1 of the Convention, but at the place of geological change, namely the foot of the pedestal and just beyond — this area being known as the Continental Rise. This change of definition from the 200 meter bathymetric contour line to one which lies between 3,500 and 4,500 meters has resulted from a seemingly plausible but over-elaborate juggling with the "adjacency" and "exploitability" tests as providing the continental shelf's true outer limits. This prestidigitation has been due to the unreflectiveness of those who have sought to give "exploitability" its meaning and operational significance. It has merely been seen as indicating the depths at which submarine holes can be drilled, regardless of the consequences. This is a singularly crass appraisal in this day and age when "exploitation" and its grammatical variants have become perjorative terms.

The Santa Barbara Channel disaster of January-April 1969[18] underlines for us all that it is easier to drill a submarine oil well than to cap it after a blow-out. If newspaper reports of the fire and blow-out at the Chevron Oil Company's well near Venice, Louisiana,[19] are any indication, the lessons of Santa Barbara have not yet been learned. In his comments on Senator Pell's Senate Resolution 33 of 1969[20] this writer has proposed that:

Senate Resolution 33 [should] contain a pledge that no exploration of exploitation activities will be espoused or licensed by states, or by any international organizations, at depths greater than the feasibility of closing of blow-outs. Nor should pipelines be permitted below . . . depths [at which they may be rapidly repaired].[21]

The pledge referred to in this quotation is, of course, a promise by states party to the "Declaration of Legal Principles" which Senator Pell included in his Resolution, that they would promulgate the necessary domestic legislation to prohibit drilling wells and pipelines below the depths of rapid and complete repair. Indeed, while "exploitability" remains a test for determining the outer limits of the continental shelf, the technological capacity to control the consequences of drilling holes in the seabed, rather than the mere capability of promiscuously inflicting them on the environment, should set both the outer limit of exploitations and of the meaning of "exploitability" as a criterion of the extent of coastal states' continental shelves under Article 1 of the Continental Shelf Convention.

(6) *The Canadian Claims Respecting Arctic Waters: A Special Case.*
Canada's recent declaration of a protection zone of 100 sea miles in width,[22] which is additional to her new territorial sea claims of a 12 mile belt, would appear to have been devised so as to comply with the general international law right of abatement of high seas pollution activities threatening a state's territory.[23] That declaration (and its implementing legislation) has been misunderstood in the United States public press to the extent that it has been represented as an attempt to extend Canadian sovereign jurisdiction seaward in a manner resembling the maritime assertions of Chile, Ecuador and Peru (as well as other South and Central American countries).[24] Canada is not claiming to exercise sovereignty over an offshore zone of 100 sea miles in width wherein she may exercise a comprehensive authority for all purposes, or even for a wide spectrum of purpose. Rather, she is merely designating an appropriate area in which she intends to exercise a limited authority to vindicate a specific national purpose, namely the protection of the delicate ecological balance of her Arctic tundra.[25]

C. *The Free High Seas*

Over against the proliferating legal categories which have just been adumbrated and which are all alike in their function of clothing (or pretending to clothe) exclusive state claims with legal justifications for enclosing increasing areas of the high seas, there remain the free high seas. The doctrine which asserts this freedom clearly vindicates the long-term, common interests of all states.[26] Be that as it may, it is less than four centuries old and has only won universal recognition as a result of bitter struggles at sea, no less than by bitter polemics in the study and at the negotiating table. In the Middle Ages and on through the Renaissance and, indeed into the seventeenth century, many states claimed to exercise sovereignty over the special sea areas; for example, Venice claimed sovereignty over the Adriatic, as did Genoa over the Ligurian Sea, England over the English Channel, the North Sea, and the Atlantic between the North Cape (Stadland) and Cape Finisterre, Denmark and Sweden over the Baltic, the Dano-Norwegian Kingdom over the North Atlantic and especially the waters between Iceland and Greenland. But, most extravagant of all, Spain and Portugal claimed to divide all the oceans between them under the Bull of Pope Alexander VI (the famous Borgia Pope) *Inter Caetera* (1493) and the Treaty of Tortesillas.

Today the free high seas are still (but decreasingly so from their heyday in the nineteenth century) a common resource of all mankind. As with a common, so with the oceans, all the states see their greatest mutual advantage as stemming from the general exercise of restraint by all, so that the high seas' resources and cleansing properties are not overstrained, and its areas lying near coastal states are not enclosed. On the other hand, each state sees its own individual profit as pre-empting to itself as much of the common resources as possible, of enhancing its own use and abuse of the commons' resources, and of maximizing its own enclosures. Thus each state is impelled, in seeking its own short-term profit, to work remorselessly against both the general welfare and its own long-term advantage.

The contemporary trend of eroding the freedom of the high seas has stemmed from its largely negative character and its dependence on customary international law in an age which seeks to emphasize the concretization of justice and places a greater trust in public intervention than in private enterprise than in the past. Being negative, the doctrine is largely one of prohibitions. So far it has not been built into institutions wherein the equal rights of all states provide the bases of affirmative policies of concrete distributive justice. This negative character, indeed, provides the ammunition for arguments that, like any common, the richer and more powerful states can obtain disproportionally greater benefits from the ocean at the expense of the smaller states. Its second weakness, that of its validity being largely based on customary international law, makes it dependent upon the continued practice and affirmance of states. Neither practice nor affirmation give it, today, the support it previously enjoyed. Its diminution today is also, in part, concurrent with the contemporary dwindling in significance of customary international law.[27] Furthermore, both of these characteristics have (in the absence of special conservation treaties) permitted states to engage in unlimited high seas fisheries, so that the survival of some species (for example blue and sperm whales) is threatened. Again, the negative character of the doctrine has increased the use of the ocean as if it were an infinite sink for all kinds of damaging materials — from dumping fissionable waste and testing nuclear bombs, to the constant flow of raw sewage, mercury and DDT into its waters. While the problems of open access to fisheries are of great and increasing importance, this presentation will necessarily concentrate on the problems which arise from the permissive climate of the law that permits conduct to be based on the assumption that the seas have an infinite capacity to absorb the world's garbage for the indefinite future. Before this is taken up, however, the tasks of international law in the environmental field might be discerned more clearly as the result of a brief survey of some emerging activities which might well become as sensitive to the need for legal change as a result of technological developments as have problems of oil pollution damage.

D. *Excursus — "Creeping Jurisdiction"*

"Creeping jurisdiction" (or "Craven's" Law[28]) is being increasingly used as a pejorative phrase for indicating the danger of recognizing coastal states' limited unilateral claims to exercise jurisdiction beyond zones sanctified by tradition or by international law. The propounders of this theory (or "law") tell us that whenever a state enjoys exclusive offshore rights for some purposes, it tends to acquire further exclusive rights for other and perhaps all purposes, jeopardizing regional, international and community interests in the freedom of the seas. Professor Bilder's recent article on the Canadian Arctic Water Pollution Prevention Act provides an example:

... the precedents established by the Act are clearly capable of widespread abuse by other, perhaps less responsible states, with potentially harmful consequences for traditional principles of freedom of the seas. If a nation of the international stature of Canada may establish a 100-mile contiguous zone to control pollution, other coastal states may also seek to do so; and the range of regulation justified under the rubric of pollution control may in practice differ little from that asserted under claims of sovereignty over such zones. Moreover, if 100-mile contiguous zones can be established for pollution control purposes, why not for other purposes as well.[29]

One response to the "creeping jurisdiction" argument is that the Canadian claims of pollution control are predicated on the unique problems

115

of Arctic ecology and on the extreme precariousness of the web of life in that region. Thus the title prescribes the Act's purpose as being merely:

... to prevent pollution of areas in arctic waters adjacent to the mainland and islands of the Canadian arctic.

Again, the Canadian Note handed to the United States Government of April 16, 1970, has been summarized as asserting, *inter alia:*

It is the further view of the Canadian Government that a danger to the environment of a state constitutes a threat to its security. Thus the proposed Canadian Arctic waters pollution legislation constitutes a lawful extension of a limited form of jurisdiction to meet particular dangers, and is of a different order from unilateral interferences with the freedom of the high seas such as, for example, the atomic tests carried out by the USA and other states which, however necessary they may be, have appropriated to their own use vast areas of the high seas and constituted grave perils to those who would wish to utilize such areas during the period of the test blast.[30]

If this is held to be the core quality of the claim, then there can be very few states who can treat it as a precedent. The Canadian claim can only become a precedent, and that precedent then can only become a means of allowing coastal states to add to their maritime authority by means of "creeping jurisdiction", if the necessary restrictions of purpose placed on the definition of Canada's pollution control contiguous zone are lost sight of. But if those limitations of purpose are lost sight of, the fault does not lie with Canada's claim, but with those who fail to identify the points of necessary distinction and find in "creeping jurisdiction" an excuse for either their own ineptitude or pusillanimity. States' exclusive jurisdiction can only creep forward if the contraposed community interests withdraw them. A failure of will should not be disguised behind a pseudo-law. There is, furthermore, a need to distinguish between Pecksniffian claims in the name of pollution-prevention (but whose real function is greed, bellicosity, or cartographical chauvinism) and the real article. "Creeping jurisdiction" theories are useful for absolving the timid from this invidious task. Perhaps the strongest criticism that can be levelled against the current belief in "creeping jurisdiction", as a real and existing phenomenon, is that such a belief provides the groundwork for inducing states to deny acceptance to what may be an intrinsically constructive and acceptable proposal of specific exercises of competences which could be conducive to the general welfare, merely out of a fear that such proposals might become the first steps in a creeping towards accretions of coastal states' sovereignty.

E. *Coastal States' Rights of Abatement Beyond Their Jurisdictional Limits*

(1) *General International Law*

Despite the apparently clear-cut situation outlined in the introduction to this Section, writings about the international law doctrines of self-help, self-preservation and self-defense testify to basic disagreements. The boundaries they set between these concepts are blurred. Indeed, it may well be that writers can only spuriously incorporate "self-preservation" into the body of international law, for it is an instinct rather than a legal right.[31] Be that as it may, self-help permits a state confronted by a major calamity to exert sufficient, but no more than sufficient, force to avert the danger or abate its effects. Furthermore, the exercise of this right requires the observance of the rule of proportionality. The measure of this rule's application and scope was well prescribed (in a context of armed self-defense rather than in the type of abatement envisaged here, but still, nevertheless, instructive) by Secretary of State Daniel Webster in the case of *The Caroline.* He stated that a government taking defensive or abatement action must "show a necessity of self-defense, instant, overwhelming, leaving no choice of means, and no moment for deliberation. It will be for it to show also that it ... did nothing unreasonable or excessive, since the act, justified by the necessity of self-defense, must be limited by that necessity and kept clearly within it."[32] The *Torrey Canyon* casualty in March, 1967, provided the present writer with an application of Daniel Webster's standard:

A case, surely, could have been made for a swift abating action on the part of the British Government, provided it did not involve risking the lives of the stricken vessel's officers and crew. Could there have been a valid characterization of such steps by the British Government to save its coasts, and the livelihood of its inhabitants, as the excessive, over-hasty use of force which the *Corfu Channel* case condemns as contrary to international law? A clear distinction can be drawn between the case where a country goes into the territorial sea of a distant nation and sweeps mines so that it can pass through that territorial sea, and the case where a coastal state, instead of passively awaiting catastrophe, destroys a potentially harmful entity off its shores but on the high seas. Would there have been doubts or delays if a disabled B-52 armed with hydrogen bombs had plunged into the waters adjacent to Pollard's Rock? The means of averting harm would have been different, naturally, but no one would have questioned haste.[33]

(2) *A Recent Treaty Formulation: The 1969 IMCO (Public Law) Convention.*[34]

Although it points to a clearer and more definitive formulation of the rights of states to prevent and abate oil pollution damage arriving within their territories from the high seas, the IMCO Public Law Convention has not yet come into force. Accordingly it merely stands as a public document expressing the desires of the states which have signed it. Furthermore, even if it were to come into force, it would still only bind the states parties to it in any particular where it did not either formulate existing customary international law or constitute an instrument of change in customary law. The International Court of Justice's decision, in 1969, in the *North Sea Continental Shelf Cases*[35] underlines the difficulty of resorting to a treaty to establish both of these points and, most especially, the latter. While the discussion which follows reviews the IMCO Public Law Convention as *lex lata*, the treaty faces both the present of settled law and the future of legal change. It should be read, therefore, in the light of both its present status of being in the limbo of all treaties which have not yet been brought into force and its Janus-like quality of facing both the past and the future.

Before examining the IMCO Public Law Convention, perspectives should be formed by reviewing two earlier IMCO treaties on pollution of the ocean, namely the International Convention for the Prevention of the Pollution of the Sea by Oil and Amendments to the International Convention for the Prevention of Pollution of the Sea by Oil, 1954.[37] As their titles indicate, these treaties were drawn up as instruments for diminishing the rapid increase of the oil pollution of the sea. They prohibited the discharge of oil in stated zones[38] by almost all the most significant classes of ships.[39] These zones were, in the main, contiguous to coastal areas dependent on clean seas. The conventions' effectiveness was limited, however, since their enforcement lay within the jurisdiction of the states of registry.[40] They contained no recognition of a coastal state's right of abatement, even in the defined "prohibited zones." Nor did they deal with the vexed issues of liability for harm.

To remedy these defects, the Inter-Governmental Maritime Consultative Organization (IMCO) called an International Legal Conference on Marine Pollution Damage which met in Brussels from 10 to 29 November, 1969. It prepared and opened for signature and accession two conventions: the International Convention Relating to Intervention on the High Seas in Cases of Oil Pollution Casualties[41] and the International Convention on Civil Liability for Oil Pollution Damage.[42] These conventions were accompanied by three resolutions: Resolution on International Co-operation Concerning Pollutants other than Oil;[43] Resolution on Establishment of an International Compensation Fund for Oil Pollution Damage;[44] and Resolution on Report of the Working Group on the Fund.[45] The Conference also set out, in an annex to Article 8 of the Public Law Convention, rules governing the settlement of disputes by conciliation and arbitration procedures.

Of these instruments the Public Law Convention is the agreement calling for treatment in the present context. It authorizes the parties to take necessary measures on the high seas "to prevent, mitigate or eliminate grave and imminent danger to their coastline or related interests from pollution" or the threat of it by oil "following upon a maritime casualty or acts related to such a casualty."[46] Warships and other public ships en-

118

gaged on "governmental non-commercial service",[47] however, are not subject to such measures. After setting out consultation and notification requirements with which a coastal state must comply, except in cases of extreme urgency, before taking preventive or curative measures,[48] the Convention stipulates that those measures "shall be proportionate to the damage actual or threatened".[49]

Were it to come into force, would this Convention change the customary international law rights, duties and exposures of the parties? An answer to this question would center around four points: (1) the limitation of the Convention to "pollution by oil", (2) the Article 3 provision of procedures for notification and consultation, (3) the Article 5 requirement that measures should be "proportionate" to the damage, and (4) the Article 6 obligation to pay compensation if the damage caused by the measures taken exceed what may be "reasonably necessary" to cure the harm.[50]

Clearly the Convention can only be invoked in the case of oil pollution, but this does not of itself repeal the general right of self-help in such matters. In addition, IMCO's Resolution on International Co-operation Concerning Pollutants Other than Oil recognizes that "the limitation of the Convention to oil is not intended to abridge any right of a coastal state to protect itself against pollution by any other agent."[51] It recommends that the contracting states exercise their general law rights in the light of the Convention's applicable provisions when confronted by pollution dangers from other agents. The procedures in Article 3 for consultation and notification do not unduly limit or restrict the general law right of abatement. They provide the means of exercising, in an appropriate fashion, the rights recognized by general customary international law, and add the amenities of co-operation and good neighborliness while precluding the possibility of an Alphonse-Gaston routine preventing any positive action.[52]

The Public Law Convention's paragraph 1 of Article 5 makes the general demand that the coastal state's response to a casualty and the ensuing harm of threat thereof shall be "proportionate". This, in itself, may be no more than the incorporation of the general customary law principle. Paragraphs 2 and 3 of the same Article are as follows:

2. Such measures shall not go beyond what is reasonably necessary to achieve the end mentioned in Article 1 and shall cease as soon as that end has been achieved; they shall not unnecessarily interfere with the rights and interests of the flag State, third States and of any persons, physical or corporate, concerned.

3. In considering whether the measures are proportionate to the damage, account shall be taken of:
(a) the extent and probability of imminent damage if those measures are not taken; and
(b) the likelihood of those measures being effective; and
(c) the extent of the damage which may be caused by such measures.[53]

Clearly these provisions do no more than spell out the general law requirements for the lawful exercise of the contemporary circumscribed right of self-help as applicable in the special case of averting or abating the consequences of a catastrophic casualty at sea.[54]

Finally, the obligation under Article 6 to pay compensation for harms caused by excessive measures is an embodiment of a very conservative view of customary international law. It may be that under special circumstances a case could be made for compensation when losses are inevitably incurred in the "proportional" exercise of force. Be that as it may, the conclusion from the consideration of these four points is that, insofar as the Public Law Convention is related to pollution by oil, it codifies the pre-existing rights of coastal states to abate actual or threatened harms. It leaves the rights of these states untouched when the polluting agent is some substance other than oil.

F. New Technology and Pre-emptive Activities

(1) *Introduction—Emerging Technologies and Their Risks of Harm.*
While the sanction underlying the threat of liability, especially strict liability, may provide a scruple against reckless or pre-emptive conduct, it may not offer the only, or even the most effective deterrent. Regulations and control of uses of the sea and of the land, including the outright prohibition of some activities and substances, surveillance, experimentation and the search for antidotes or alternative beneficial uses, and their imposition when proved, are also necessary. In this wider context liability tends to operate as an *ad hoc* peripheral and incomplete means of enforcement, just as it tends to remain a less than one hundred percent satisfactory remedy for the injured. This part of the paper is intended to bear upon the good neighborliness and liability issues while attentive to the latter's standing as a relatively inferior, insensitive and unsatisfactory weapon in the armory of remedies and controls.

Secondly, analysis of the control of pollution activities will be further served by identifying some examples of emerging deep-sea mining activities which will increase the hazards of pollution from deep-sea mining and connected harms and by investigating other emerging or possible maritime uses which may be more than usually vulnerable to those harms. It will then be possible to indicate liability issues in terms of conduct which operates pre-emptively (or expropriatively) by throwing the burden of risks onto others as contrasted with conduct which is vulnerable to expropriation through the creation of risk by others.[55] Activities in the latter class, on the other hand, tend to be inclusive, and other uses of the sea may be conducted alongside these activities without increased risk of harm. This classification is intended to indicate the main contours of risk-creation and risk-exposure. It does not seek dogmatically to impose any final classificatory dichotomy.

(2) *Activities Which Increase Risks to Others.*

Many large-scale enterprises operating on the frontiers of science and technology engage in operations having a high degree of cost and risk. They all illustrate how some of the emerging scientific uses of what the ocean has to offer, which are generally thought of as justified by man's Scriptural mandate to exercise mastery over nature for the general benefit, may greatly threaten the environment and bring waste, poverty and misery in their train. They may, indeed, constitute not merely a risk of economic loss, but at times a possibility of bodily harm and even sudden death. Resultant economies may at first seem attributable to technological break-throughs and to size. However, on more careful review they may come to be seen, at least in part, as savings made at the expense of third parties or of the environment. Such economies will precipitate increased hazards of pollution. Furthermore, these two items, cost and risk, may be seen as reciprocal. The more an enterprise is called upon to shield third parties and the environment from the risks of disasters which may result from its operations, the higher its operating costs tend to become. Conversely, the more such an enterprise is permitted to expose third parties to harm, or the environment to devastation, the more it will be in a position to reduce its operating costs. The costs of protection, however, still remain. They become "social costs"[56] and are merely transferred from the enterprise to the environment, or to society — or some sectors of it. Enterprises which enjoy the privilege of passing on their costs clearly increase the risk of harm to other users. In doing so they deliberately create risks which expropriate from members of the public expectations of continued enjoyment of the environmental amenities of living — the emerging "amenities rights"[57]

Examples of this group of expropriative activities include the following:

(a) *Winning Mineral Resources from the Ocean*

(i) Fossil Fuels under the Seabed.

For a considerable time oil has been taken from shallow seabed areas. But recent improvements in technology have allowed economically feasible oil drilling to take place beyond the 200 meter bathymetric contour line[58] (the outer limit of the legal continental shelf as defined in terms of depth).[59] This technological trend[60] will become intensified as demand increases.[61] Thus, *Our Nation and the Sea* tells us:

Twenty-two countries now produce or are about to produce oil and gas from offshore sources. Investments of the domestic offshore oil industry, now running more than $1 billion annually, are expected to grow an average of nearly 18 per cent per year over the coming decade. Current free world offshore oil production is about 5 million barrels per day, or about 16 per cent of the free world's total output.[62]

As claims to develop more offshore oil and gas resources go into deeper and deeper regions, they will inevitably give rise to more acute problems of polluting the seas and the coasts.

The *New York Times* reports between January 31 and April 3, 1969 of the events which constituted the sorry history of the oil drilling catastrophe in the Santa Barbara Channel, should indicate to thoughtful people the pressing need to take immediate measures for the protection of our environment against the time when powerful enterprises engage in widespread deep-ocean submarine oil drilling exploitations. As exploration and exploitation activities extend further into the deep oceans, so must the risk of blow-outs increase with the consequent difficulty of getting them under control if rigorous conditions and regulations are not imposed.

In addition, the requirement of absolute liability[63] has a necessary place here, just as it has with regard to the obligation of the operators of giant tankers and the sub-ocean trains and pipelines. With the possibility of blow-out wells in the deep oceans and damaged or deteriorated pipelines discharging their polluting contents into the ocean environment, absolute liability should be imposed for harms done. These possibilities also point to the risk of great harms to the environment and to those who look to the sea for their survival, livelihood, health, therapy and recreation. Furthermore, as new uses of the sea develop (*e.g.*, undersea hospitals, laboratories, recreation centers and store houses), so will the exposure to harm increase.

More injurious to the environment than dramatic blow-outs such as that of Santa Barbara, and more recently that in the Gulf of Mexico, or even massive oil spills from giant tanker casualties (*e.g.*, *Torrey Canyon*), are the day-to-day minor spills and leaks of oil from a multitude of activities. The Commission on Marine Science, Engineering and Resources has said:

... [T]he most pervasive pollution comes not from headlined oil spills but form the many activities that take place every day underwater. There are about 16,000 oil wells off the continental United States, and the number is increasing by more than one thousand a year. There is rightful concern that oil well blow-outs, leaks in pipelines, and storm damage can cause pollution that could ruin large parts of commercial fisheries, sportsfishing and recreational areas.[64]

(ii) Surficial Deposits

Writing some five years ago, Dr. John Mero could claim:

... [S]ubstantial engineering data and calculations show that it would be profitable to mine [from the sea] materials such as phosphates, nickel, copper, cobalt and even manganese at today's (1964) costs and prices. And I firmly believe that within the next generation, the sea will be a major source of, not only those metals, but of molybdenum, vanadium, lead, zinc, titanium, aluminum, zirconium and several other metals as well.

122

... But most important, the sea-floor nodules should prove to be less expensive sources of manganese, nickel, cobalt, copper and possibly other metals than are our present land resources.[65]

While these minerals may be won increasingly from the sea, they undergo a cycle of constant renewal[66] which, for the foreseeable future, will continue to add a greater quantity of nodules to the store already on the seabed than could be taken for human use.

This possible future source of wealth and well-being, however, like the winning of oil and gas from the subsoil of the deep oceans, carries risks of polluting the environment. The Commission on Marine Science, Engineering and Resources explains:

Mining operations conducted completely independent of land (as in the deep sea or remote shallow banks) will result in entirely different processing and transportation problems. Ore will be loaded directly in barges, tankers, or ore transports. Immediate initial beneficiation or processing may be necessary at sea to reduce weight or bulk although this may require large processing equipment on the dredging ship. If all operations are conducted from a single vessel, this will further reduce the amount of ore collected in each trip. If multiple vessel operations are anticipated, one collecting and processing vessel could operate continuously while transport vessels shuttle to port.[67]

What this does not tell us is that the waste products, including acids and other processing chemicals, will be dumped into the sea by the mobile processing ship.[68] A number of such ships could turn sea areas (perhaps of no great extent initially) into maritime equivalents of slag heaps, causing considerable ecological change and deleteriously affecting the food web.

(iii) Minerals in Suspension

Apart from the metal-rich waters of such special, and currently little understood, phenomena as submarine hot brines (*e.g.*, those of the deeps of the Red Sea and the Atlantic II deep),[69] the sea carries many chemicals and metals in suspension. Substantial industries already extract sodium chloride (in the form of common salt), potassium chloride, magnesium chloride, sodium sulphate, magnesium metal and bromine from the ocean.[70] Processing the extraction of these resources,[71] like the beneficiation of nodules from the sea floor, could give rise to waste and pollution problems. It also should be remebered that seawater could become an increasingly important source of fresh water serving urban areas and irrigating arid lands.[72] It is possible to imagine political and legal problems arising in such areas not unlike those now presented by the need to distribute the waters of international river basins.

(b) *Generating Power from the Sea*

In Volume 2 of its *Panel Reports*, the Commission on Marine Science, Engineering and Resources distinguished between two categories of "[m]ajor power generating concepts to exploit the ocean's potentials,"[73]

123

namely (1) the use of the sea as an environment, and (2) harnessing the energy in the sea.

(i) Use of the Sea as an Environment.

The seabed may well provide an environment for establishing nuclear power stations. At 150-200 foot depths they would be below the level of all except major disturbances caused by storms. Because this ideal depth is not found on the Atlantic and Gulf coasts of the United States sufficiently close to shore (approximately within twenty miles of the coast), certain added costs, such as those of building relay stations or embedding the structure in the seabed, might be necessary in such places. Indeed, an embedded reactor design, appropriate even for less than optimal areas, has been studied.[74] On the other hand, the main savings of submarine nuclear power plants would be: eliminating land cost; low costs in constructing the radiation shield; averting (or at least delaying) the obvious and expensive aspects of thermal pollution problems; avoiding possible expensive claims for the causation of such illnesses as leukemia by gradually "leaking" radioactivity; and eliminating the possibility of the multitude of claims occurring in the event of a nuclear disaster on the scale which might arise on dry land.

Should power stations located on or under the seabed be used increasingly as a means of easing the problems of population growth and crowding on land, important legal problems of protecting the marine ecology will arise. It should be remembered that such stations could create risks, not only of radioactive pollution, but also of thermal pollution leading to local eutrophication and other deleterious losses to the quality of the area's animal and plant life. Thus, building and running these power stations might adversely affect the use of the sea as a widespread source of knowledge, beauty, health and pleasure. Issues of the sort of liability to be imposed on operators for the harms their underwater stations might create should not be deferred. And finally, issues of the degree of pollution of the sea which is to be accepted as "tolerable" would have to be faced. Here again, the traditional "free for all" would be most inappropriate.

(ii) Harnessing Tidal Energy[75]

Possibly because of the friendly and relaxed atmosphere of the dispute (reflected in the French Judge Basevant's delivering of a very learned opinion unfavorable to his own country's claims), the recondite investigations of Anglo-Norman feudal land tenures and the learned disquisitions on the history of the Norman Duchy in which the International Court of Justice indulged itself, the *Minquiers and Ecrehos Case*[76] litigation has seemed to lack both drama and modernity to commentators. Yet, in reality, more so than in most of the cases adjudged by the ICJ, the underlying conflict which led to this display of antiquarian erudi-

124

tion pointed to the future. France did not dispute English Normandy's rule over the islets and reefs of the Bay of Granville out of a pious duty to vindicate dead heroes' titles. She needed to exclude Jerseymen who engaged in the mundane pursuits of collecting crabs, oysters and lobsters for the London market from the locations where the Commission du Plan had called for the building of power stations[77] to generate from the English Channel's tides, approximately a quarter of France's electricity.[78]

The French desire to harness tides for the generation of electrical power is not unique, although it would appear to be in advance of other countries. Nearly one hundred sites for commercially feasible tidal power plants exist in the world:[79] Great Britain, the United States, Canada, India, Australia, New Zealand, the Soviet Union, Argentina, Brazil, Spain, Germany and Mexico are all engaged in studying the possibilities of this source of power.[80] In fact, Great Britain has had the possibilities of harnessing the Bristol Channel's tides under review since 1918.[81] However, only France, Canada, the United States and the Soviet Union have begun to implement their plans.[82]

This new use of the sea, although seemingly so beneficial and apparently without harmful side effects, could also impose difficult legal problems of answerability and of deprivation. The *Minquiers and Ecrehos Case* highlights the potential conflict of such a use with that of fisheries. In addition, barrages, channels and holding basins could clearly change the whole complex dynamic of an estuary — perhaps greatly and irreversibly accelerating its decay into a swamp. Where an estuary is international,[83] perhaps a supranational agency or a multinational public enterprise with built-in safeguards to protect other uses might well provide the only effective institutional blueprint.

On the other hand, a supranational agency directed to the shared use of an estuary for the purpose of generating electric power might so strongly reinforce the interests supporting that specific use that, reciprocally, it could further weaken the effectiveness of those claiming recognition for its fishery, recreational, residential and aesthetic uses. Such a supranational agency would, accordingly, have to be widely enough conceived to include at least some representation of the interests its power-generating activities might threaten. Alternatively, its mandate should include a deference to those threatened interests. A system of compensation for the substantial diminution or exclusion of existing uses should also be formulated.

(c) *Transportation*

As the great corporations which are exploiting the planet's petroleum resources move their activities out into the deep ocean, they will need to transport their crude oil and their gas to centers of population. The logistical problem this need presents will be solved in the main, at least

125

for this century, by means of giant tankers.[84] Although pipelines may well come to provide means of transporting the great bulk of gaseous, liquid and fine-grain materials between continents, or from seabed operations in the deep ocean, many decades will elapse before the greater proportion of bulk cargoes will cease to be carried in ships of increasingly gigantic dimensions.[85] This observation does not imply a negation of the probability that, in the near future, pipelines will be used increasingly to bring gaseous, liquid and pulverized products of deep-ocean mining ashore; it is intended merely to emphasize that this mode of transportation faces not only great technological problems, but also problems of the political stability of the coastal state onto whose lands the pipelines debouch.

The economies of scale of giant tankers, submarine trains and pipelines increase the hazards of pollution for the livelihoods of coastal and insular populations and for the environment. These increased hazards will be, moreover, commensurate with the tankers' and submarine trains' increased size, and the pipeline's increased diameter and length.

The *Torrey Canyon* casualty and the ensuing widespread pollution of the English and French coasts in March 1967 illustrate the risks to which the operation of great tankers expose coastal populations. This point is underscored when it is remembered that with its gross tonnage of approximately 120,890 deadweight tons[86] the *Torrey Canyon*, when she was impaled on Seven Stone Rocks, was the third largest tanker afloat, while she is dwarfed by a new generation of giant tankers. One heard surprisingly little about Shell's 207,000 ton *Marpessa* breaking in half on Monday, December 15, 1969;[87] at the time she was not carrying the cargo for which she had been built — namely oil.

Not only are tankers and bulk ore carriers increasing greatly in number, size and cargo capacity, but there is also a possibility in the near future of nuclear-powered cargo fleets. For example, *The Economist* recently reported, in a critical review of the British shipbuilding industry, that:

Prospects for nuclear cargo ships have radically altered since 1964 when the Padmore committee reported, correctly, that neither the speed nor size of ship required by the shipping lines justified nuclear propulsion. The project still needs to be treated with great caution, but there are few signs that anyone in this country is watching to see when ship size will reach the point where it justifies reopening the question on nuclear propulsion.[88]

The same article points to the potential of hydrofoils, pusher barges, lighters-aboard-ships as well as nuclear propelled cargo ships "and other developments" which all could become "more important" than hovercraft.[89]

As hydrofoils and nuclear powered cargo ships, in particular, increase in size and speed, they probably will create very important problems of safety to their users and to the environment.

126

(3) *Some Risk-Exposed Activities*

(a) *Development of Biological Resources*

Edible fish constitute perhaps the oldest, and certainly the most valuable of the biological resources of the sea. But, from the most far-off times to the present, mankind has had only the more primitive approach to the winning of this resource — that of the hunter and collector. This is as true of the Australian aborigine wading in a mangrove creek at low tide as it is of a modern radar-equipped trawler fleet. Today we stand on the brink of great changes. In order to survive, mankind may eventually need to change his means of gathering food from the sea. The hunter of fish might become the herdsman and shepherd of some species, and the farmer and cultivator of others, thereby changing fundamentally his ecological, social, economic and legal relations to the sea.[90] It may well become necessary for him to cultivate and process algae and plankton, even if only to feed the fish and animals which he himself will eat. These activities could qualify for a very high level of protection from exposures to harm since they are especially vulnerable to destruction by pollution and to risk-creating, pre-emptive activities generally.

(b) *Health, Therapy and Recreation*

In addition to winning drugs from the sea,[91] mankind may use it for health, therapy and recreation. Dr. Cousteau has described how cuts and sores, which proved obstinate and hard to cure on account of the heat and other adverse conditions ashore, healed in 48 hours or less under the Red Sea, in Conshelf II.[92] Perhaps hospitals for personal injury and accident victims and major surgery cases might be established underwater. In addition, psychotherapy may develop concepts calling for restful sanatoria, especially for hypertension and anxiety cases, to be developed in the oceans or on the seabed.[93]

With the spread of leisure, education and the popularity of scuba diving, underwater activities may become increasingly popular. The appeal of underwater hobbies and interests may even come to exceed those of the surface, since they offer an intellectual dimension lacking in surface water sports, while possessing an equally physical dimension in the form of exercise and excitement. Amateur scuba diver naturalists could become interested in being observers of and reporters on submarine phenomena, thereby making important contributions to the many nascent underwater sciences. Would it be beyond the realm of practicality to foretell the mass production of inexpensive underwater recreation and/or research vehicles and vessels? What would be the liability of extra-hazardous submarine enterprises, such as nuclear power stations, to persons engaging in uncerwater naturalist and observation activities? What precautions should be demanded?

(c) *Scientific Research*

At the outset a definition of scientific research should be stipulated. Unless otherwise expressly stated or demanded by the context, the term "scientific research" and its grammatical variations and synonyms will be used to indicate disinterested academic, scholarly or naturalistic investigations by qualified presons and institutions. It should not be confused with either "exploration" for commercial purposes, or experimental defense activities which, incidentally, might include scientific research. On the other hand, publication of the results of such scientific research should not be mandatory, it should be at the professional discretion of the research worker or institution involved.[94]

In addition to the factors mentioned in the immediately preceding subsection, academic marine sciences are developing very rapidly. This burgeoning may well provide one of the major confrontations of exclusive and inclusive claims of uses of the oceans' depths and florr. At a time when more and more countries have scientific research ships flying their flags — whether owned by university, private or government laboratories[95] — many coastal states are seeking more than ever before to restrict scientific research activities off their shores.[96]

Ocean and outer space research activities may become intimately connected in an increasing number of ways. The oceans seem to provide the preferred location for the recovery of space vehicles on their return to earth. In addition, various large floating platforms may well provide valuable links in combined ocean-outer space research and communications activities. Reciprocally, space vehicles have an enormous capacity for monitoring the state of the oceans.

Finally, the freer marine scientific research is allowed to become, the more likely pollution, radiation, eutrophication, ecological imbalance and other man-made abuses of the sea may be discovered and rectified by appeals to public opinion. Claims made in this connection may well vie with many of the most time-honored uses of the sea, including its treatment as the ultimate depository of all kinds of garbage (for example, the dumping of poison gas containers, chemical and bacteriological weapons and waste nuclear materials) and as the arena of contemporary pre-emptive military competition. In evaluating a viable system of priorities it will be necessary for international law to determine the protections it will accord to research, an inclusive use of the sea, and those which will consecrate the pre-emptive, exclusive uses which may curtail the free advancement of science.

(d) *Weather Forecasting*

Weather prediction increasingly has come to depend upon reports from ships at sea. More recently, weather satellites and buoys (Ocean Data Acquisition Systems — ODAS) have provided additional dimensions of prediction. A system of long-range forecasting may come into operation which could be conducted by means of a complex and computerized combination of weather and communications satellites, buoys and the more traditional modes of collecting weather data which already exist. Thereby, a comprehensive inter-governmental knowledge of the "ocean-earth-atmoshpere" physical system would be continuously and accurately kept up to date[97] by means of a highly sophisticated "World Weather Watch".[98] Ultimately, perhaps, technological advances and developed procedures of inter-governmental co-operation may lead from weather prediction to weather control on a comprehensive basis. Unlike weather prediction, however, weather control leaves us with an uneazy suspicion that this may become an exclusive pre-emptive activity, exposing other uses of the sea (and possibly even the land) to risks of undue harms. In addition, the Intergovernmental Oceanographic Commission (IOC) has, at least on paper, gone one stept beyond the World Weather Watch towards a pollution surveillance system. It has formulated a long-term proposal to the effect that losses to or impairments of the oceans through pollutants should be monitored on a global basis.[99] This, possibly, may be performed by the proposed Integrated Global Ocean Station System which it is developing in conjunction with the World Meteorological Organization (WMO). Such a system of world-wide ocean surveillance of pollution could, furthermore, become an integral part of a wider organization of international control. This of international control. This organization could be given added support by a system of registration for such contaminating activities as the ocean dumping of wastes of all kinds (from military materials and radio-active waste to city garbage and including waste and tailings from deep ocean mining and beneficiation and the oily ballast from tankers).

G. *The Principle of Good Neighborliness*

"Good neighborliness"[100] is an emerging principle of international law with many transnational law qualities. It calls for a broad standard of respect and recognition. It obligates states, enterprises and individuals to respect the rights of others to participate in the social process. These values of respect, recognition and participation are, in their turns, founded on a higher value, namely the Human Rights to Life as assured in Article 3 of the United Nations Universal Declaration of Human Rights. It is not proposed that either the human right to life or even the principle of good neighborliness has become formulated into specific rules capable of providing the major premises of decisions in international and domestic courts. Rather they provide the perspectives for directing the future development of the law and the guidelines for the formulation of future rules governing decisions. Indicating fundamental policy concepts, they should be viewed as having a higher significance than merely being justifications for some previously decided cases.

The *Trail Smelter Arbitration*[101] provides some interesting and instructive analogies and guidelines. This case, in brief, arose out of a dispute between Great Britain (on behalf of Canada) and the United States concerning the pollution of air currents by sulphur dioxide fumes from a Canadian smelter built in a valley which was in both the Province of British Columbia and the State of Washington. The injury complained of took the form of the chemical contamination of the valley's soil, streams and air, resulting in the poisoning of trees and crops on the U.S. side of the border. Complaining of the damage this pollution occasioned to its side of the boundary, the United States successfully contended that Canada was liable for past losses and was obliged, further, to ensure that the injury should be abated in the future. It is suggested that, in fact, the pollution complained of provides an example of the pre-emptive conduct discussed earlier in this paper. For the complaint related to an exclusive pre-emption of the use of the air in that the smelting operation complained of was carried on regardless of the claims of other legitimate interests. This pre-emption, indeed, was so detrimental to the affected lumber, fruit-growing and agricultural interests as to prevent their effective pursuit in the area affected by the effluent smoke. In polluting the atmosphere, rivers and soil of the valley, the company was failing to recognize and respect the claims of its "neighbors"[102] by pre-empting the use of the air-flow to carry off its gases.

In the law of international rivers, customary international law would appear to be in the process of consolidating a broad standard of recognition and respect of the alternative uses of the waters which has come to be called "good neighborliness".[103] The Permanent Court of International Justice gave this expression a concrete foundation in the case of the *International Commission of the River Oder*[104] where it enunciated the principle that:

... when consideration is given to the manner in which States have regarded the concrete situations arising out of the fact that a single waterway traverses or separates the territory of more than one State, ... it is at once seen that a solution ... has been sought not in the idea of a right of passage ... but in that of a community of interest of riparian States. This community of interest in a navigable river becomes the basis of a common legal right, the essential features of which are the perfect equality of all riparian States in the use of the whole course of the river and the exclusion of any preferential privileges of any riparian State in relation to others.[105]

Indeed this duty of recognition and respect of alternative uses which the Permanent Court enunciated in the *Oder* case was also continued in the *Trail Smelter Arbitration* itself. The formulation of doctrine giving rise to this latter decision was in the following terms:

The Tribunal, therefore, finds the above decisions, taken as a whole, to constitute an adequate basis for its conclusions, namely, that, under principles of international law, as well

130

as the law of the United States, no State has the right to use or permit the use of its territory in such a manner as to cause injury by fumes in or to the territory of another or the properties of persons therein, when the case is of serious consequence and the injury established.[106]

In its decision of April 16, 1938, the Commission refrained from setting up a permanent regime regulating the smelter works' emissions of sulphur dioxide. But it took this decision only because the necessary scientific information for establishing such a regime was still wanting.[107] After the necessary information had been gained, the Commission, in its Award of March 11, 1941, did prescribe a permanent regime regulating, as it were, the permissible degree of pollution, and, therefore, the amount and extent, or proportion of the shareable atmosphere at the disposition of the Smelter Company.[108] The function of the regime was thus to bring about the use of the atmosphere as a shareable rather than as a unilaterally appropriated and pre-empted resource.[109]

Although the principle of good neighborliness provides a very general standard, the *Trail Smelter Arbitration* and the *Oder River* cases provide examples of its specific utility in the process of international decision. On the other hand, there are many situations in which such a concept could be in danger of becoming no more than an empty and a formal category. Hence law and science should seek to provide it with specific modalities and meaning for application by means of subsidiary rules. These should be designed so as to give it a content reflecting the varying standards, needs and capabilities of the time and place. While remaining a general directive, its operation becomes dependent upon those modalities which are developed in the vernacular of each international ecological system, while other contexts call for its universal application on a global basis. Above all a spectacular "progressive development" of international law could be gained in this sector from a cross-fertilization of the international law standard of good neighborliness and the concept of the pre-emption of a common resource, with the French decisions which have so greatly developed the abuse of rights doctrine.[110]

H. *Liability for Harms under General International Law*

Despite the restrictive theory of liability in international law which was adumbrated in an earlier section of this paper,[111] some arbitral and judicial decisions indicate the incipient reception of strict liability as a category of public international law. Some treaties, too, reflect this trend. Thus the *Trail Smelter*,[112] *Corfu Channel*,[113] and *Lac Lanoux*[114] cases testify to this reception — the first and third of these were abritral decisions and the second a decision of the International Court of Justice. In none of these cases was the issue of fault primary. Although *Trail Smelter* appeared to turn, at least in some of the Tribunal's formulations, on the Anglo-American doctrine of nuisance, this was due to the inclusion, in the *compromis*, of a reference to the decisions of the United States Supreme Court in the exercise of its original jurisdiction in settling controversies between the states of the United States. In exercising this jurisdiction, it should be noted, the Supreme Court sits as a quasi-international tribunal.[115] Hence the precedent the two countries stipulated as acceptable were not drawn from domestic law strictly so called. But it can be argued that the *compromis*'s stipulation reflects a special acceptance of non-general international law derived from the fact that the two countries were governed by the common law, and therefore accepted it as specially governing. My suggestion is that the value of *Trail Smelter* derives, not so much from the *compromis* or the Tribunal's opinion, as from the regime it established for monitoring and governing the emission of sulphur dioxide. This aspect of the case reflects a clear vision of the parties' international rights and obligations, since the Tribunal focused on levels of emission, not on the intentions or negligent failures of the smelter works.

If *Trail Smelter* is to be viewed, as it should be, as an application of public international law, rather than of common law, the irreducible minimum of the relevant general principles of law contained therein is the strict liability which Canada owed to the United States. This interpretation is strengthened, further, by pointing out that no issue of fault was tried in that case. Again, in the *Corfu Channel* case Albania's liability stemmed from the presence of the mine in her territorial waters, not from any malevolence or neglect which would have had to have been proved by the applicant state. In the *Lac Lanoux* arbitration the Tribunal clearly considered strict liability to govern in the event of a finding for Spain. The Tribunal stated:

It could have been argued that the works would bring about a definitive pollution of the waters of the Carol or that the returned water would have a chemical composition or a temperature or some other characteristic which could injure Spanish interests. Spain could then have claimed her rights had been impaired ... [116]

In addition to these three cases, the United States Government's *ex gratia* payments to the Japanese Government for injuries sustained by Japanese fishermen as a result of the 1954 hydrogen bomb tests in the Pacific have an auxiliary, but only an auxiliary, law-indicating function. During March and April of 1954 the United States carried out a series of nuclear tests at the Pacific Proving Grounds in the Marshall Islands. As a result of miscalculations, some Japanese fishermen and some of the inhabitants of the Marshall Islands (*e.g.*, those on Rongelap Island)[117] were injured by hydrogen bomb tests carried out on March 1. (It should, perhaps, be noted that although Professor McDougal and Mr. Schlei wrote of a "series of miscalculations" as occasioning the injuries,[118] negligence on the part of the United States has not been established. Furthermore, it is doubtful whether a case could be made against the United States in terms of *res ipsa loquitur*.[119])

After the incident, diplomatic action culminated in an Exchange of Notes between Japan and the United States. The resulting agreement entered into force on January 1, 1959.[120] The United States paid two million dollars to the Japanese Government on the understanding that the sum would be distributed in an equitable manner at the discretion of that Government.[121] This payment reflects the United States' concern and sense of moral obligation, despite the lack of proven fault on its part. Its concern reflects a basic sentiment of justice and stands as an important signpost in the legal evaluations of the liability to be ascribed to developing scientific activities, particularly when placed in perspective with the *Trail Smelter, Corfu Channel* and *Lac Lanoux* cases.[122]

In the light of these developments and of the emerging international values which underlie them, this writer has suggested the following policy argument in support of incorporating the more stringent obligations of good neighborliness in international law which strict and absolute liability call for:

A municipal system has sufficient authority to prohibit ultrahazardous activities which are not socially beneficial. International law, on the other hand, is still largely a system of permissive and facultative norms. The practicality, therefore, of seeking to outlaw many activities which are not conducive to the general utility may be questioned. It would be more in keeping with the present stage of international law's development to argue for the regulation of these activities, and for the imposition of stringent responsibilities and high maximum monetary levels of liability upon them. Hence, if they may not be prohibited, their potentiality for harm can be reduced by the imposition of either strict liability or absolute liability.[123]

This emerging principle and its development into the principle of "channelling"[124] already has become incorporated into the international law treaty governing the liability for nuclear harms.[125] Before examining the treaties which embody this principle, its development as a concept of absolute liability should be reviewed.

I. *Absolute Liability*

(1) *A Proposed Definition*

While some writers may use the terms "strict" and "absolute" liability interchangeably, this writer would distinguish between them and accept Sir Percy Winfield's view that in the *Rylands* v. *Fletcher*[126] type of case such terms as "strict liability", and "liability without fault" are preferable to "absolute liability."[127] Professor Winfield has convincingly argued that the exculpating rules which the courts have developed to mitigate the rigor of the defendant's liability under *Rylands* v. *Fletcher* render the adjective "absolute" someting of a misnomer; hence the phrase "strict liability" has come to be preferred. In the present article, however, the term "absolute liability" has been revived, not in order to enter any debate with Professor Winfield, but to indicate a more rigorous form of liability than that usually labelled "strict".

It is more correct to say that absolute, rather than strict liability was imposed in the international agreements on liability to third parties in the field of nuclear energy which have just been indicated. The principle of channelling found in these treaties[129] traces liability back to the nuclear operator, no matter how long the chain of causation, nor how novel the intervening factors (other than a limited number of exculpatory facts). These agreements also admit of fewer exculpations than does the rule in *Rylands* v. *Fletcher*.[129] For example, Article 9 of the Paris Convention on Third Party Liability in the Field of Nuclear Energy (1960) provides for the exculpation of the operator only when the acts complained of are:

... directly due to ... disturbances of an international character such as armed conflict and invasion, of a political nature such as civil war and insurrection, or grave natural disasters of an exceptional character which are catastrophic and completely unforeseeable on the grounds that all such matters are the responsibility of the nation as a whole.[130]

Even these may be eliminated by national legislation.[131] Furthermore, as the Explanatory Memorandum to the Paris Convention indicates, the operator's liability is "not subject to the classic exonerations for tortious acts, *force majeure*, acts of God or intervening acts of third persons."[132] Where the incident was caused, either in whole or in part, by the plaintiff's act, the defendant operator is not completely exculpated. But a competent court may weigh the effect of his negligent conduct upon the plaintiff's claim.[133]

The concept of absolute liability developed in the nuclear liability treaties, more effectively than any other concept presented so far, prevents the creator of a risk from passing that risk onto the public and thus expropriating wealth and security from other people. The formulation by the Legal Sub-Committee of the General Assembly's Committee on the Peaceful Uses of Outer Space, however, is an exception to the above rule. The Sub-Committee has developed a stricter form of liability than that reflected in the treaties imposing liability for the civilian uses of nuclear energy; the limited exculpatory circumstances permitted in these treaties have not been repeated in the Sub-Committee's 1963 Draft Declaration of Legal Principles.[134]

In contrast to the level of responsibility called for in the nuclear energy treaties, the 1963 Draft Declaration and the Outer Space Treaty impose concepts totally dissimilar from fault liability. They would not appear to permit an operator who deliberately creates a risk to pass at least some of the cost of that risk onto others, thereby to expropriate from them. This writer has suggested the following connection between absolute liability and risk-creation as an expropriation:

134

Perhaps a principle may be seen as emerging whereby an enterprise, which in the course of its business engenders the possibility of injuries to the members of the public who consume its wares or come into contact with its operations, is liable for damage arising from the risks it creates. To exonerate such an enterprise would have the effect of enabling it to conduct its operations at the expense of others and throw a valid operating cost onto the shoulder of its neighbors, or onto those of the ultimate consumers of its products or services. Professor Cowan has aptly called the emerging judicial policy which gives recovery under these conditions "the policy of viewing a deliberately created risk as [as] expropriation."[135]

When risks are created, amenities are threatened by expropriation.

(2) Recent Treaty Developments

(a) A Perspective

Like the discussion of the IMCO Public Law Convention in an earlier section of this paper,[136] the following review of certain liability conventions is oriented towards the testimony they offer of trends in the development of public international law, rather than towards the change in legal relations those of them which have come into force establish among a limited number of states. They testify to the felt need, among states, for stricter levels than traditional public international law permits[137] of obligation and of compensation when harms have been the result of the impact of technological developments on social and legal relations. But clearly, they are only peripherally affecting, if they are affecting at all, the present-day legal relations of states.

(b) The Brussels Convention on the Liability of Operators of Nuclear Ships (1962)[138]

This treaty is one of four[139] which have been negotiated to formulate the basis of liability for nuclear harms. All four have two characteristics which are of immediate relevance to the present discussion (1) they are drawn with a view to treating the relevant nulcear operations as a common problem, be the operators private corporations or government agencies, and (2) they impose the standards of liability which the term channelling indicates and impose the elimination of the usual exculpatory circumstances which strict liability permits.[140] The former of these characteristics indicates that the signatory states are mutually prepared to regulate transnational[141] nuclear situations and problems with transnationally effective rules. The second indicates that, despite the traditional theories of international law, these states have accepted a form of absolute liability to govern nuclear disasters within the treaties' terms. The first of these four agreements has now been signed by seventeen member states [142] of the Organization for European Economic Co-operation. This agreement (known as the Paris Convention) attaches liability for injury or loss of life to any person, or for damage or loss of property, to the operator of a nuclear installation involved in a nuclear incident.[143]

Article III of the 1962 Brussels Convention makes the operator (*i.e.*, not only the owner but a demise or bare-boat charterer as well) of a nuclear ship liable for damage caused by the escape of ionising materials from his ship, even if fault can be proved against other parties[144] (except for the narrow limits of Article II (5)). Similarly, when a conventional ship collides with a nuclear ship and causes the release of ionising radiation, the owner or operator of the conventional ship is not liable for injuries resulting from that radiation, but only for the damage which would be attributable to his vessel independently of the nuclear-caused or nuclear-induced injuries. In this way the operator of the nuclear ship is made the insurer of others suffering specifically nuclear injuries occasioned by the operation of his ship. This liability is imposed without any reference to the manner of the nuclear ship's navigation or handling. Engaging in this hazardous activity is the causal factor for designating the party liable to those who might be harmed by a nuclear accident.

As with nuclear activities, so also the laying of submarine pipelines and the undertaking of many other technological wonders, including the further development, to the point of hypertrophy, of giant tankers, the outer limits of scientific and engineering knowledge are quickly reached, so that catastrophic accidents result in which people unconnected in any way with the activity may suffer injuries caused by unforeseen hazards. The progressive development of an international liability law for these activities calls for the application of the principle of the channelling of responsibility to the tanker operator, or to the operator of a submarine cargo train, pipeline or other technological innovation carrying a considerable risk of pollution. For it was those operators' decisions to engage in their ultrahazardous activities which exposed others to the consequential risks of injury especially attributable to those activities. In this regard, namely the attribution of particular types of harms to specific types of activities, the analogy between what should be the liability of the operators of these technological innovations and what has been formulated as the appropriate liability of the operators of nuclear ships is convincingly close.

(c) *The Brussels IMCO (Private Law) Convention on Pollution (1969)*
The conservatism which generally appears to prevail in international maritime law affairs is reflected in some of the background of this Convention's drafting. Even after the British Government's initiative, prompted by the *Torrey Canyon* catastrophe,[145] calling for reconsideration of existing rules of liability,[146] there was still a substantial, although a diminishing support for fault liability. For example, after a considerable division of opinion among its national associations and among the delegations at the plenary session in Tokyo from March 30 to April 4, 1969, on the opposing claims of fault and strict liability,[147] the Comite Maritime International (CMI) formulated the liability article of its draft con-

vention in terms of fault with a reversal of the burden of proof.[148] This middle position was accepted only after a note had been appended to the draft convention stipulating:

This Convention is based upon the concept of fault by the shipowner with liability limited at an insurable figure.

If higher authorities should not adopt these concepts, the question whether liability should be on the shipowner or on the cargo owner or on both should be reconsidered.[149]

This CMI draft was part of a close working relationship with IMCO, but the latter's conference at Brussels in November adopted a more far-reaching standard. It defined the liability to be imposed as follows:

1. Except as provided in paragraphs 2 and 3 of this Article, the owner of a ship at the time of an incident, or where the incident consists of a series of occurrences at the time of the first such occurrence, shall be liable for any pollution damage caused by oil which has escaped or been discharged from the ship as a result of the incident.

2. No liability for pollution damage shall attach to the owner if he proves that the damage:
    (a) resulted from an act of war, hostilities, civil war, insurrection or a natural phenomenon of an exceptional, inevitable and irrestible character, or
    (b) was wholly caused by an act or omission done with intent to cause damage by a third party, or
    (c) was wholly caused by the negligence or other wrongful act of any Government or other authority responsible for the maintenance of lights or other navigational aids in the exercise of that function.

3. If the owner proves that the pollution damage resulted wholly or partially either from an act or omission done with intent to cause damage by the person who suffered the damage or from the negligence of that person, the owner may be exonerated wholly or partially from his liability to such person.[150]

Article 7 requires that owners of tankers carrying more than 2,000 tons of oil cargo in bulk maintain insurance or other financial security, including a certificate from a projected international compensation fund, to the limit of liability. The state of registry is required to certify that this requirement is complied with.[151] Furthermore, the Convention gives a right of direct action against the insurer, guarantor or other obligor of the owner's liability.[152]

The Convention limits liability to 2,000 francs per ton of the ship's net adjusted tonnage,[153] not to exceed 210 million francs.[154] The franc in question (the "Poincare franc") is a unit of account of sixty-five and a half milligrams, fineness nine hundred.[155] The amount per ton is approximately $134.40 with a maximum of about $14,112,000 in round figures. The owner may not, however, limit his liability if the incident was a result of his actual fault or privity.

Note should also be made of the strict liability which Article 3 imposes on owners. Despite the exculpatory provisions of paragraph 2,[156] this is clearly stricter than the usual formulations of strict liability, be they under the rule in *Rylands* v. *Fletcher*[157] or under the American Law Institute's doctrine of liability for ultrahazardous activities.[158] It may, therefore, be designated appropriately as absolute liability.

(3) *Variables for Liability Issues Arising from Maritime Catastrophic Accidents*

Even though this writer welcomes the advent of strict and absolute liability in international law, he does not look forward to the elimination of the less stringent doctrines from the areas of their appropriate application. The strictness of the liability to be imposed should depend upon the type of activity causing the harm, the type of activity harmed or through which an individual is harmed, and the juxtaposition of the operator and the injured.[159]

A scale of liability, reflecting the degree of pre-emptiveness of the activity to which liability is attached and exemplified in five social situations and their consequential regimes[160] is proposed. It should be emphasized that these have not been developed in order to render the question of liability dependent on the location of the accident (*i.e.*, in the exclusive zone of coastal state jurisdiction or on the high seas); rather liability is to be seen as a function of the activities giving rise to the ensuing injury — that is, dependent on the social relations created by the incident. The following are five examples of social situations and their suggested levels of liability:

(i) When harm to a coastal population or its livelihood is occasioned by a use of the sea which gains economies from exposing others to increased risks, absolute liability, channelling accountability to the operator (possibly subject to a maximum limitation of liability sum) should be imposed on the risk-creating operator for causing the harm;

(ii) When fish-farming, including intensive or "battery" fish farming activities, health (including submarine therapy), submarine recreation and scientific research activities are harmed by the types of activity indicated in (i) above, absolute liability, subject to a maximum limitation of liability figure, should be imposed;

(iii) When harms caused by activities in (i) above are suffered by other activities in the same category, the injury calls for no higher level of compensability than that given by fault liability;

(iv) When traditional maritime activities such as fishing with trawls, lines and nets (including purse-sein nets) cause injury to activities which reap economies by exposing others to risk — for example, submarine pipelines or tankers, or mining activities — the liability applicable should be in terms of fault, but negligence should be presumed. The actor, for example, the fisherman should be permitted to exculpate himself on such grounds as want of notice and knowledge on his part, due care, or inevitability. When traditional fishing activities are

138

the immediate cause of harm in traditional fishing grounds, or under other circumstances which the operator of the tanker, submarine pipeline or train, or other risk-creating activity knowingly increases the risk to others, the fisherman may show that those facts represent an assumption of risk by the operator. Indeed, the application of channelling proposed in (i) above may well leave the operator of the risk-creating enterprise as the party liable rather than the fisherman whose net or trawl may have been the immediate cause of the harm;

(v) When traditional maritime activities such as those indicated in (iv) above are the agents of harm to the vulnerable[181] types of emerging activities, for example those indicated in (ii) above, then liability should be strict in the traditional sense, but not absolute.

Each of the five sets of social relations inherent in these different classifications of liability varies from the others in terms of the balance of risk and power to inflict harm. They also vary in terms of the degree of effective expropriation which the creation of risk in each relationship entails. The regime appropriate to each set of social relations should be viewed as restoring the balance of risk and power by adopting the appropriate concepts of liability, so that one group of interests is not permitted to take risks or carry on its operations at the expense of the others. On the other hand, those "others," while entitled to protection, should not be protected against the consequences of risks resulting from their own prior conduct. Furthermore, their own protection should be in terms of the risks to which they expose their own operations, their social desirability, their relative immunity from harm, and the risks they create for yet other activities. In this way each set of social relations which is brought into being by the creation of risk is seen as being subject to the degree of liability appropriate to the exposures it creates for others, to its own social value, and to its own vulnerability to harm.

II. FLAGS OF CONVENIENCE[162] AS RESPONSIBILITY-AVOIDANCE DEVICES[163]

As long as individuals find certain laws objectionable they will seek to develop legal devices in order to evade legally the operations of those objectionable laws. When a law-avoidance practice becomes widespread, it generally comes to be supported by a morality alternative to the traditional one embodied in the existing rule of law (e.g., the relation between flags of convenience shipping and the fleets of "traditional maritime states"). Although the flags of convenience issue has traditionally been couched in terms of its labor-management aspects, this is myopic, since such flags can be equally useful in avoiding higher international law standards of accountability than those traditionally prescribed, just as they have been resorted to in the past to avoid fisheries restrictions[164] or paying the wages for which American seamen had bargained successfully.

139

Indeed, world-wide acquiescence in flags of convenience could greatly stultify, if not render completely ineffective, an international regime for controlling pollution from tankers, pipelines, deep-sea mining and high seas mineral extraction from seawater. All that is needed for the avoidance of the regime is that some state (no matter how small) should remain outside the regime, freely register ships and mining corporations under its domestic laws and irrespective of the nationality of their management and the sources of their capital, and rely on its rights (and hence those of the ships and enterprises it registers) under customary international law to treat the high seas as a common (and thereby "capture" hydrocarbons, hard minerals and chemicals in suspension in sea water through *occupatio res nullius* as fish are captured today, dump tailings and refuse, lay pipelines, and generally treat the high seas as an infinite sink).

Since its advocates hold that flags of convenience practices are unassailable, a brief review of some of their inherent logical contradictions and an appraisal of their juridical background becomes relevant to the issue of evolving a body of international environmental law. The United States has entered into agreements with her citizens who are owners of flag of convenience shipping providing for "effective United States control" of such vessels in times of emergency. In defense of this policy "Project Walrus" explains:

U.S. owners can register foreign-built shipping under any friendly flag of their own choice, or transfer from one flag to another at will. In the case of foreign-built PANLIBHON-flag ships, the Maritime Administration normally negotiates agreements with the U.S. parent companies that the ships will be made available to the United States in the event of a national emergency.[165]

Thus a contradictory situation presents a number of anomalous situations coming into existence. On the one hand the traditional international law doctrine of the freedom of the high seas can be invoked to justify the exercise of discretion (except insofar as this may be limited by some states' domestic law restrictions on registration under their flags) by ships' owners in their selection of an appropriate nation of registry. Yet on the other, "effective United States control", while seeking to invoke this privilege, denies its corollary which has traditionally provided that a ship may not lawfully have dual or multiple nationality.[166] Yet, under the Project Walrus thesis, the flag nationality is clearly intended to be subordinated to the "effective control nationality". If that is the case, then a number of bizarre possibilities present themselves, of which the following are examples:

(1) Contrary to international law, the ship is recognized as having dual or multiple nationalities; or

(2) Despite the flag the ship wears, her single nationality is her purportedly dominant one, namely that of her "effective control". If this

is to be the outcome, then the whole device of avoiding United States treaty obligations regarding the pollution of the high seas would be rendered negatory; or

(3) The "effective United States control" agreements entered into between the United States Government and citizens are regarded as illegal and therefore void, leaving the flag-of-convenience state in sole legal and validly effective control of the ship; or

(4) The flag-of-convenience state refuses to recognize, or be bound by, the "effective United States control" agreements, or rejects them as a derogation from her sovereign authority; or

(5) States with which flag-of-convenience states are in contention may choose to disregard the "effective United States control" agreements, arguing that these do not bind third parties.

All five of these variables are relevant to show how flawed the international and transnational accountability of states and enterprises for catastrophes caused by the management of flag of convenience ships would remain, in spite of attempts by the majority of ship-owning states to improve contemporary international law by making it more responsive to urgent environmental claims. It seems unconscionable that these flaws, which may provide a handsome return to the states of flags of convenience registry and to the owners of such ships, constitute a danger to the world community and the global environment. Thus building giant tankers which take refuge in a flag of convenience fleet may create pollution problems of far greater seriousness than the labor-management issues in the maritime field which usually seem to monopolize the attention of writers on flags of convenience. One responsible comment may suffice: *The Economist* has pointed out that it is doubtful whether Liberia, for example, has the means, even if it had the will, to prosecute breaches of the IMCO Conventions regulating (and eventually prohibiting) the pumping out of oily ballast onto the common high seas of mankind.[167] This juxtaposition of the flags of convenience and the freedom of the high seas once again points up the inveteracy of the tragedy of the commons.[168] Usually the participants in a common right welcome the development of an equitable regulatory system for the utilization of their common which effectively restrains each from inexorably working against both the good of all the others and his own long-term advantage. But where even the most insignificant party stays outside the regulatory system and insists on exercising his commonage rights, his capacity to destroy that regulatory system remains a threat. He will supply the incentive for his competitors in the common to remain outside the regulatory system, or to use his commonage rights for taking advantage of the regulatory system's restrictions on all the other participants who are also his competitors in the common. It is for these considerations of competitive advantage that flags of convenience threaten any regime which imposes common restraints in order to advance the interest of environmental protection. They assume the existence of a regulatory system which ties the hands of those who honor it in order to avert the tragedy of the commons and still provide the means of dishonoring that regulatory system for the few who insist on their rights to ravage the common. In this way flags of convenience exacerbate the tragedy of the commons; furthermore, they nullify attempts to avert it.

III. APPRAISAL OF CONTEMPORARY PUBLIC INTERNATIONAL LAW

A. *Traditional Law*

The continued denotation of the doctrine of the freedom of the high seas as licensing states to use the oceans as an infinite sink reflects a gross insensitivity towards the consequences of the continuous outpouring of their wastes of all kinds into the sea. This facet of the "tragedy of the commons" is inherent in the present system; any alternative regime must nullify that particular evil, at least. At the present time, all states may deplore the dumping of oil, yet the major maritime oil-spills, the sinking of nuclear waste and nerve gas into the sea, still hasten to maximize each state's own tragic role as participating in polluting the seas. There is, thus, a competitive race to degrade the high seas by those who deplore this action while acting without restraint. This paradoxical situation of states can only be ended when either the seas cease to be capable of receiving more garbage, or when all states mutually agree to restrain themselves (through mutually accepted standards), or are restrained by some external authority, or a mixture of these two. International law is only standing on the threshold of restraining the use of the seas as the ultimate dumping ground.

B. *Current Developments Pointing to Necessary Restraints*

Although the conventions on liability for nuclear damage and the IMCO Private Law Convention were treated as part of contemporary international law, they cannot be viewed as codifying pre-existing customary norms. And, although those of the conventions which have come into force bind the parties to them, their adhering states are so few, in comparison with all the states whose agreement would be necessary to a basic legal change, that the burden of proof lies heavily upon anyone seeking to adduce them as evidence of a widespread *opinio juris sive necessitatis*.

The treaties which have been cited to support arguments that they indicate a wind of change in international law, it must be confessed, were usually drafted with a fire brigade mentality on the part of the diplomats who negotiated and drafted them; a specific problem of exposure to the risk of harm from possible nuclear catastrophes or giant oil tanker casualties was foreseen and guarded against. (Or, as in the case of the *Torrey Canyon* oil spill and the consequential formulation of the 1969 IMCO Conventions and legal provisions they were drafted *post hoc* against repetitions.) There has not been an attempt to embody all the single instances into a general principle of international law which has been universally accepted and is capable of transnational application.

One may doubt, however, whether a too-pessimistic view of the restricted scope of the recent oil and nuclear liability conventions is any more realistic than a too-optimistic one which sees them as embodying and reflecting into the current international arena an emerging, but currently binding, principle of general international law. When coupled with the developments reflected in the *Trail Smelter, Corfu Channel,* and *Lac Lanoux* cases,[169] perhaps some amelioration can be found of the difficulty of establishing a timely legal change which is consonant with technological developments. For legal change, no matter how desirable, is not an inevitable consequence of social and technological change. It is a matter of conscious reform and development through the available law-making or law-indicating criteria and institutions. While law does not necessarily change so as to remain in harmony with material developments, if it does not do so, justice becomes increasingly maldistributed as distance between the law's prescribed assumptions and social reality increases. Legal fictions (namely the pretense or contrivance of untrue statements of fact or characterizations of existing facts so that possibly desirable, but otherwise legally irrelevant, legal prescriptions can be brought in to govern situations) may be resorted to by a desperate community. These devices can become particularly grotesque in international law and relations where, unlike domestic legal systems, there are no courts which remain in strict control of the fictions they permit the parties to formulate or invoke. Accordingly, in the international environment, legal fictions become untrammelled proliferations of the Theatre of the Absurd where no final script has been written and where each party can, free of direction, *ad lib* his responses as he receives his cue from his opponent by surprise. Should he fail to do so, he will then cue the other to develop further uncontrolled strategems in the manipulation of the fiction.[170]

In the meantime, and for want of a more developed legal order, states tend to stretch analogies into legal fictions and are prone to use conservation pretexts in Pecksniffian maneuvers to extend their maritime claims. Peru's utilization of Aristotle Onassis' whaling venture off the western coasts of South America in 1954[171] in order to justify and consolidate the then incipient CEP policy of claiming to exercise jurisdictional authority for at least 200 sea miles from her coasts, which had begun in 1952,[172] provides an example of how a pretended claim to act on behalf of the world community can be utilized to forward particularist goals. Clearly, decision-makers in the international arena need to be aware of the misuses of contemporary sensitivity towards pollution to guard against them. In addition, the transnational nature of environmental problems, no less than the *realpolitik* of national selfishness, calls for transnational solutions, perhaps primarily on a regional basis, since regional problems can be presented to the effective public constituencies within states as having greater and more persuasive immediacy than universal ones.

IV. LIABILITY AND MULTINATIONAL PUBLIC ENTERPRISES

A. *Accountability*

Underlying the discussion so far has been the assumption that a risk of pollution-creating activity has the national character of a single state. This assumption has been equally true of privately as of publicly owned enterprises. In either case, the state of the enterprise's nationality creates the necessary conditions of assuring full responsibility to those who may be harmed. The position becomes complicated, however, when a group of states forms a consortium to engage in an economic or ocean-exploration activity which enhances the risk of pollution injuries to others. Should each of the states severally and cumulatively be held liable? Should all be held jointly liable? Should the agency their consortium creates be the sole party liable? Should that agency be held primarily liable and its member states only secondarily liable? Should there be some system for registering international agencies whereby only registered agencies are liable and their member states exonerated from further duties to compensate for pollution damage?

It is submitted that the constituent treaties of such agencies should expressly confer international legal personalities on them. Such a conferral may not, however, entirely dispose of their problem. In addition, the establishment of a central registry for such agencies could well dissipate current doubts regarding their international legal personality.

While the *Injuries Case*[173] tells us that the United Nations and, by implication, universal agencies like it, may possess a restricted international legal personality appropriate for enabling them to carry out their functions, the position may be different in the case of agencies which have a limited membership. Opponents of recognizing the international legal personality of these latter entities could well argue that the contracting states may not impose their creation on unwilling third states, but should await its recognition by the family of nations. On the other hand, if the agency's international personality, as established in its

144

constituent treaty, is necessary for the tasks the consortium is structured to perform, then, surely, an objective juridical personality may well be created over and above that established merely amoung parties to the agreement[174] But third states may well be slow to recognize the existence of a legal personality necessary for the performance of tasks common to a group of states when the issue is whether a claim should be pursued against an agency having limited purposes and being merely the instrument of a limited number of states, or pursued agains the member states themselves.

The policy considerations which should be paramount are the pragmatic inducements for vindicating, the consortium's international legal personality; they also include the protection of the public and the fulfillment of the establishing states' blueprints and purposes. Contemporary international law does not possess the institutions and rules which could best accord such personality. Accordingly, a convention governing pollution matters should include the provisions of a system for registering consortia as international legal entities. The United Nations would, at the present time, appear to be the most suitable authority for carrying this task of registration. Therefore, it is suggested that the pollution convention include provisions whereby international public enterprises engaged in exploration and exploitation activities can be registered with the appropriate United Nations authority. The convention should, as a corollary, then call upon all the parties to it to recognize the international legal personality of all interstate agencies registered under its terms. In such a case, at least among the parties to the convention, the agency would be primarily liable and its constituent states only secondarily liable. In order to protect states who are bound to recognize agencies registered under the convention, the registration system should require states which establish such agencies to post a guarantee or insurance fund sufficient to cover all possible claims within the maximum amounts laid down in the pollution treaties. Alternatively, whether either no system for registering consortia of this type is provided or, if provided, is not availed of, then the agency and the constituent states should be held jointly and severally liable for the full amount of loss caused by any pollution damage an enterprise governed by the agency may have caused or permitted.

B. *Actio Popularis?*

If the accountability of international entities *per se* came to be accepted, then similarly those, or analogous entities could be evolved which would be charged with the task of bringing claims against polluting activities if negotiations were to fail. That is, possibly starting with regional arrangements, international entities, both governmental and non-governmental, could come to exercise similar representative rights and reflect similar concerns on an international footing to those envisaged for citizens and citizens' groups in the *Michigan Envirnmental Protection Act of 1970*.[175] In effect, such entities would come to be the pursuers of an *actio popularis* in the international arena where individuals are only too likely to be inhibited by delays, costs and the inherent resistance of the system to individuals having the privilege of pursuing their own courses of action and where states are only too prone to be diverted by diplomatic considerations and the temptations of trade-offs in different and indeed, irrelevant (from the environmental policy angle) contexts of interaction.

An international *actio popularis* would be especially relevant for vindicating shared environmental claims with respect to the protection of the oceans and the atmosphere. In addition, a world-wide system of environmental monitoring[176] conducted, for example, by IOC and WMO (and possibly other entities such as IMCO) might usefully assist in providing the evidence necessary for pursuing such an action. (Accordingly, these, or closely related agencies specifically evolved for the purpose, could be empowered to bring these actions.) Recently, the International Law Commission began to take an interest in the possibilities which an international *actio popularis* could provide.[177]

V. ENHANCEMENT OF THE ENVIRONMENT

A. *The Contemporary Dilemma*

Capitalist and socialist societies alike assume that human welfare advances by transforming the raw materials of the universe into the means of production and consumer goods. Generally speaking, neither type of society has come to accept the harsh fact of life that this process of converting "nature" into "goods" has its own spillover costs, indeed its own dangers to human welfare. That this could be the case, indeed, is the perception of only a small minority in the most advanced societies. Amongst the vast majority of humanity such a position is still greeted with skepticism, even as the enunciation of a cruel joke — being held to be sophistry for preventing the full economic development of the underdeveloped areas of the world or, in the industrial states, as a confidence trick to undermine our traditional trust in technological virtuosity and managerial competence. Despite the lag in public opinion, however, the development of safeguards against harmful side effects resulting from the transformation of "nature" into "property" and the formulation from the modalities of liability for the harms those transformations bring in train are becoming urgent tasks for lawyers. It is thus becoming increasingly urgent to define alternative base values which can be built into the contemporary exploitative consumer values of free enterprise and social-

146

ist societies alike. One such value is that of amenities.

B. *Amenities Rights*

Amenities rights should not be confused with the traditional common law's concepts of nuisance or its civil law and international law equivalents.[178] Rather, the concept of these rights is to articulate a basis of claim against the "spillovers" (harmful side effects) of industry[179] which individuals, communities and nations should be able to vindicate. Furthermore, the concept of amenities is not merely preventive, negative or conservationist. It provides administrators with guidelines for the betterment of a region.

Both internationally and domestically, amenities rights should include the recognition of a right to health by enjoining the pollution of the air by chemicals and noise, the right to the environment's beauties (by requiring the replacement of "unspoilt nature" by artifacts of equal beauty and dignity), and of a right of integrity (by enjoining the erosion of the countryside and the blight of cities). The right to amenities should be seen, in domestic law, as both a personal and a property right. In international law, analogies with both of these categories should be received and developed in terms both of the territorial integrity of states and their sovereign rights to enjoy their natural resources, but in such a manner as not to waste those of their neighbors' or to erode their neighbors' amenities. Again, international law should be developed whereby the transnational recognition of private amenities rights should be recognized. In this way an international law of amenities rights would become effective at two levels. On the first level states would be entitled to protect their territorial integrity against an invasion of polluting materials or the erosion of their natural resources, for example air and water, through environmental degradation and depreciation or the polluting exploitation of such common property natural resources as flowing water and air from outside their territories. On the second level they should be entitled to vindicate their citizens' transnational rights against disamenities. Amenities rights should be seen as additional to the rights already outlined as arising under or emerging from existing international customary and treaty law. The functions of international agencies and non-governmental entities formed for the vindication of amenities, the enhancement of a sector of the environment undergoing transformation from "nature" into "property" and the protection of the environment would be those of official, quasi-official and unofficial Attorneys General bringing *actiones publica*. Finally, the claim that each state should be able to make with respect to the environment of the region of its location should include the capability of insisting upon the observance of minimum standards for planning developments. *Quis custodiet ipsos custodes?*

C. Perspectives

While much of what has been said in these pages seems oriented from the point of view of accountability and liability, these are not the only envisioned premises of conduct for protecting the environment. They should, rather, be viewed as the means of distributing the loss when breakdowns in the orderly and regulated conduct of exploitation occur. Liability and accountability fit into the total protective context as supplementary to complex regional and international systems of interlocking regulations through preventive laws and treaties. These last may well be conceived of in terms of regionally preserving and enhancing amenities and including the regulation and control of uses of the air, sea and land. Regulation under these circumstances requires the outright prohibition of some activities and substances and the surveillance, experimentation and the search for antidotes or alternative beneficial uses with respect to others. In this wider context, liability merely becomes a peripheral and incomplete means of enforcement. Being piecemeal, fortuitous and oriented to the specific and unique circumstances of an immediate claim, it is too microscopically focused to provide the most effective means of social control, just as it must always remain a less than one hundred percent satisfactory remedy for the injured.

Thus the demand for amenities should be implemented administratively by ensuring that planners establish requirements reflecting the recognition and respect for the amenities of the life of a region when establishing industries, communities, centers of merchandising or transportation, and generally transforming the raw stuff of our environment into the commodities of better living. For the enjoyment of those goods by their destined consumers will eventually be stultified if their production engenders the abuse of the environment and its transformation into a slag-heap.

NOTES

[1]Vattel, *The Law of Nations* vi (4th American Edition, Joseph Chitty ed. 1835)

[2]1 Oppenheim, *International Law* 343 (8th ed, Lauterpacht, 1955) [hereinafter cited as "1 *Oppenheim*"]. (Footnotes omitted.) At footnote 1 on the same page there is the following statement:

> "There is an increasing tendency among modern writers to reject the theory of absolute liability and to base the responsibility of States on fault ..." (citations omitted)

At footnote 2 on the same page we find, however, the statement that injurious acts done in pursuit of a right or in self-preservation:

> "... can, therefore be repelled, and indemnities may be demanded for damage done..." (citations omitted)

See also Sohn and Baxter, "Convention on the International Responsibility of States for Injuries to Aliens" (Draft No. 12 with Explanatory Notes) at 43-44, 50-52, 171-76, 188-90, April 15, 1961 (mimeographed materials) [hereinafter cited as "Sohn and Baxter"]; *see also, infra*, Section IV *passim*. Compare, Hardy, "International Protection Against Nuclear Risks", 10 *Int'l & Comp. L.Q.* 739, at 752-53 (1961).

[3]The "CEP" claims are claims to exercise "sovereignty" (this term is given varying meanings as time and circumstances require) over sea areas within a belt of "at least" 200 sea miles from the shores and the island possessions of the claimant states. "CEP" itself represents the initials of the three founder states (Chile, Ecuador and Peru) who were parties to the Declaration on the Maritime Zone, Santiago, Chile, Aug. 18, 1952. For an English translation of this and the parties' accompanying declarations and agreements (together constituting the "Santiago Declaration"), as well as subsequent and supplementary declarations and agreements, see B. MacChesney, *Situation, Documents and Commentary on Recent Developments in the International Law of the Sea* 265-89 (Naval War College Blue Book Series No. 1, 1956). *See also* B. Auguste, *The Continental Shelf — The Practice and Policy of the Latin American States with Special Reference to Chile, Ecuador, and Peru* 187-92 (1960); S. Bayitch *Interamerican Law of Fisheries, an Introduction with Documents* 42-47 (1957); U.S. Department of State, *Santiago Negotiations on Fishery Conservation Problems* (1955). For a polemical defense of the CEP claims and policies, *see, e.g.,* Cisneros, "The 200 Mile Limit in the South Pacific: A New Position in International Law with a Human and Juridical Content," ABA Section of *Int'l & Comp. Law,* 1964 *Proceedings* 56 (1965). Note particularly the criticism of the CEP claims in Kunz, "Continental Shelf and International Law: Confusion and Abuse" 50 *A.J.I.L.* 828, 835-50 (1956) [hereinafter cited as "Kunz"].

Until 1970 Chile, Ecuador and Peru had been able to add only Nicaragua and El Salvador to their band — President Trejos having vetoed, on Nov. 21, 1966, the ratification of the Declaration of Santiago by Costa Rica's Legislative Assembly. On the other hand, Argentina, by Law No. 17094, dated Jan. 4, 1967, has asserted a double claim: out to 200 miles from the mainland coast as well as from the coasts of islands, and out to the 200 metre isobath. While it is true that a number of South and Central American states have added to their continental shelf claims, claims to the "epicontinental sea" (*i.e.,* the volume of the waters superincumbent upon their continental shelves) off their coasts, and to the superambient air above that "sea", this type of claim is still asserted (albeit spuriously, cf. Continental Shelf Convention, art. 3) in terms of the international law regime of the continental shelf. Thus, this type of claim is distinguishable from the CEP type. So far the six "CEP countries" (including Argentina) have not been successful in persuading other Latin American states to assert specifically CEP claims to adjacent seas, nor has the Organization of American States adopted this position as that of the collectivity of Western Hemisphere nations. Indeed it has not, as a body recognized as valid state claims to epicontinental seas. Thus, for example, at the Inter-American Specialized Conference on "Conservation of Natural Resources: The Continental Shelf and Marine Waters," Cuidad Trujillo, Dominican Republic, March 15-28, 1956 (see the *Final Act* of the Conference *Organization of American States Conference & Organizations Series*, No. 50, Doc. No. 34.1-E-5514 (1956)) the CEP states were unable to gain the Conference's agreement to the "bioma" and "eco-system" theories, or to declare that either the waters above a continental shelf region, or waters extending from the shores of coastal state for some distance such as 200 sea miles, appertain to the coastal state either on the basis of the continental shelf doctrine or on some other theory. The Conference observed (in Resolution I of the Conference, the "Resolution of Ciudad Trujillo," *Final Act supra* at 13-14) that:

"2. Agreement does not exist among the states here represented with respect to the juridical regime of the waters which cover the said submarine areas.

...

"6. Agreement does not exist among the states represented at this Conference either with respect to the nature and scope of the special interest of the coastal state, or as to how the economic and social factors which such state or other interested states may invoke should be taken into account in evaluating the purpose of conservation programs.

...

"Therefore, this Conference does not express an opinion concerning the positions of the various participating states on the matters on which agreement has not been reached..."

For the views of inter-American legal experts, see *Inter-American Council of Jurists,* "Resolution XIII, Principles of Mexico City on the Juridical Regime of the Sea, Section C: Conservation of the Living Resources of the High Seas," *Final Act of the Third Meeting* 37 (English CIJ-29) (1956). Note should be taken of Dr. Garcia Amador's comments (as representative of Cuba) on the "Principles of Mexico City" at the Geneva Conference on the Law of the Sea, 1958:

"As to the Principles of Mexico City, the validity of that document should be considered in the light of the resolution unanimously adopted by the Inter-American Specialized Conference held in Ciudad Trujillo in 1956." 3 U.N. Conf. of the Law of the Sea, Geneva 1958, Official Records 37, U.N. Doc. A/Conf. 13/30 (1958).

For the 1956 Resolution of Ciudad Trujillo to which Dr. Garcia Amador is referring, see *supra* this note. For comments of governments, *see id.,* 50-59; *Inter-American Juridical Committee, Opinion on the Breadth of the Territorial Sea* at 24-42, OEA/Ser. I/VI.2 (English CIJ-80) (1966).

For the United States point of view, see U.S. Department of State, *Santiago Negotiations on Fishery Conservation Problems* at 1-15, 19-20, 26-30, 36-41, 50-58, 59-66 (1955). For the CEP countries' position and their criticism of the U.S.' point of view, see *id.,* 30-35, 41-44, 45-50.

Be that as it may, on May 8, 1970, Argentina, Brazil, Costa Rica, Ecuador, El Salvador, Nicaragua, Panama, Peru and Uruguay participated in the Declaration of Montevideo on the Law of the Sea whereby the above-named states announced:

"That in declarations, resolutions and treaties especially inter-American, as well as in multi-lateral declarations and agreements reached among Latin American states, juridical principles have been consecrated which justify the right of states to extend their sovereignty and jurisdiction to the extent necessary in order to conserve, develop and exploit the natural resources of the maritime zone adjacent to their coasts, its seabed and subsoil;

"That, in accordance to said juridical principles, the signatory states have extended, because of their special circumstances, their sovereignty or their exclusive jurisdictional rights over the maritime-zone adjacent to their coasts, its seabed and subsoil, to a distance of 200 maritime miles, measured from the baseline of the territorial sea."

[4]Indonesia, the Andaman Islands, Fiji, and the Philippines Republic claim, on the basis of the "archipelago theory", all waters within baselines joining the outer promontories of the outer islands of their groups as internal waters and they measure their territorial seas outward from those baselines. This writer does not agree with those who sould see resemblances between the claims which Indonesia, the Philippines Republic and the others put forward, and the Canadian claim of protective jurisdiction. In finding similarities, there are necessarily errors of labelling a contiguous zone which has been defined for a single purpose (protection of the Arctic ecology of the Canadian Tundra) as a claim of sovereign competence for all purposes (namely the category of claims which the term internal

waters indicate). If, on the other hand, some other "archipelagic" claim is implied, which is distinguishable from those made by Indonesia and the Philippines Republic, then this distinction should be clearly given. In this connection, however, *see now* Fishing Zones of Canada (Zones 1, 2 and 3) Order, given Dec. 15, 1970, 104 *Canada Gazette*, Part I, Dec. 26, 1970, at 3035-37. For further discussion of this issue *see, infra* Sections II B(6) *and* III E.

[5]Note, however, that art. 5, para. 2, Convention on the Territorial Sea and the Contiguous Zone, done at Geneva, Apr. 29, 1958, (1964) 2 U.S.T. 1606, T.I.A.S. no. 5639,516 U.N.T.S. 205 (effective Sept. 10, 1964) [hereinafter cited as "Convention on the Territorial Sea"], derogates, in some cases, from the proposition in the text. It provides:
"Where the establishment of a straight baseline in accordance with article 4 has the effect of enclosing as internal water areas, which previously had been considered as part of the territorial sea or of the high seas, a right of innocent passage, as provided in articles 14 to 23, shall exist in those waters."

[6]Art. 7, para. 4, Convention on the Territorial Sea.

[7]New section 11 (c) (1), (m), inserted by section 102 Water Quality Improvement Act of 1970, 84 Stat. 91.

[8]*See, e.g., Trail Smelter Arbitration*, 3 UNRIAA 1905, 1938 (1938 and 1941).

[9]*See*, for example, *Cunard S.S. Co. v. Mellon*, 262 U.S. 100 (1923), and note especially *id.*, at 125; *Wildenhus' Case*, 120 U.S. 1 (1886), and note especially *id.*, at 11, 12; *see also, The Creole* (1853), 2 Moore, *Digest of International Law* 351, 358 (1906) [hereinafter cited as "Moore"]. This is often known as the "English Rule". It originated in the dictum of Best J., in *Forbes v. Cochrane*, 2 B & C 448, 467, 107 E.R. 450, 457 (K.B., 1824); *Caldwell v. Vanvlissengen*, 9 Hare 415, 68 E.R. 571 (V. Ch., 1851); and *Savarkar's Case*, Scott, *The Hague Court Reports* 516 (1911). For some additional cases see *Reg. v. Keyn*, per Phillimore, J., L.R. 2 Ex. D. 63 at 82 (C.C.R., 1876). The American cases would appear to favor the "English Rule"; see, for example, *Cunard S.S. Co. v. Mellon and Wildenhus' Case, supra*. See also *Patterson v. Bark Eudora*, 190 U.S. 169 (1903). Frequently the "French" or "Continental Rule" is contrasted with it; see, for example, *The Sally* and *The Newton*, 5 *Bulletin des Lois de l'Empire Francais* 602 (4th ser., 1807); *The Tempest*, Dalloz *Jurisprudence Generale* 92 (1859); 1 *Oppenheim* 502-4; Brierly, *The Law of Nations* 223-5 (6th ed., Waldock, 1963) [hereinafter cited as "Brierly"].]
On the other hand, *see*, as a little known example of the "English Rule", *In re Sutherland*, 39 N.S.W. Weekly Notes 108 (1922) and *see*, for a presentation and discussion of this case, Charteris, "Habeas Corpus in Respect of the Detention of a Foreign Merchantman," 8 *Journal of Comparative Legislation* 246 (3rd ser., 1926). Briefly the facts were these: two French convicts who had been sentenced to transportation to New Caledonia, and who were named Tulop and Szibar, escaped from the French ship *El Kantara* whilst she was in the port of Newcastle, New South Wales, en route for the French penal colony. She sailed without them. The New South Wales authorities later arrested the convicts and handed them over to another French ship, *La Pacifique*, in which they were destined to continue their voyage to Noumea. Before the vessel sailed, an application for a writ of habeas corpus rule on behalf of the convicts was made by Sutherland. The Full Court of the Supreme Court of New South Wales refused the rule on the ground that to grant it would be to ignore the immunity of matters of internal management aboard the French ship from Australian law. Sir William Cullen, the Chief Justice, said (*id.*, at 108-9):
"If there were anything to show that the master of the French ship was acting without authority under French law, then the question might arise whether there was authority under Australian law for his keeping the men on board in Australian waters."
This Australian version of the "English Rule" was delivered whilst the Court was sitting *en banc*. The concurrence was unanimous. When such cases as *In re Sutherland* are said to exemplify the "English Rule" it is submitted that perhaps the traditional distinction between the "English Rule" and the "Continental" or "French Rule" may well have become more a matter of formulation than of application and practice. *See*, for a discussion

151

of this, and for a similar conclusion, "Brierly" at 225-6. Moreover, examples abound which illustrate the point that terms such as the "public order" or the "tranquility" of the port are indeterminate, leaving their application to considerations of policy. To juxtapose the two Philippine cases of *People v. Wong Cheng*, 46 P.I. 729 (1922) and *United States v. Look Chaw*, 18, P.I. 573 (1910), will suffice to illustrate this point.

For examples of diplomatic action to protect the immunity of the internal management of foreign ships in port, *see* protests by Belgium, Denmark, Great Britain, Mexico, Netherlands, Norway, Portugal, Spain, Sweden, in 1923 against the assumption of jurisdiction by the United States over liquor carried (but not sold) aboard their ships in United States waters and harbors 1 *U.S. Foreign Relations* 113 (1923).

[10]*But see People v. Wong Chen*, 46 P.I. 729 (1922), *distinguish United States v. Look Chaw*, 18 P.I. 573 (1910).

[10]a. Agreement for Co-operation in Dealing with Pollution of the North Sea by Oil, *done* June 9, 1969 [1969] Gr. Brit. T.S. No. 78 (*CMND* 4205).

[11][1927] *P.C.I.J.* Ser. A, No. 10; *But see* United Nations Convention on the High Seas, *done* April 29, 1958, art. 11, [1962] 2 U.S.T. 2312, T.I.A.S. No. 5200, 450 U.N.T.S. 82 (effective Sept. 30, 1962).

[11]a. For an outline of these events *see* E. Cowan, *Oil and Water: The Torrey Canyon Disaster* at 193-96 (1968).

[12]For a definiton of innocent passage, *see* arts. 14-23 Convention on the Territorial Sea.

[13]*Id.*, art. 4, para. 1. *See also, id.*, art. 23.

[14]For a discussion of the solecism *see* Goldie, "International and Domestic Managerial Regimes for Coastal, Continental Shelf and Deep-Ocean Mining Activities," *The Law of the Sea: National Policy Recommendations* 226, 227-30 (Proceedings of the 4th Annual Conference of the Law of the Sea, June 23-26, 1969, University of Rhode Island, 1969).

[14]a. *See*, for a vigorous explanation of this point, McDougal & Burke, *The Public Order of the Oceans* 45, 518-19 (1962) [hereinafter cited as "McDougal & Burke"].

[14]b. For a convincing argument that the International Law Commission's limitation of the contiguous zone to 12 miles and the incorporation of that limitation into art. 24(2) of the United Nations Convention on the Territorial Sea and Contiguous Zone, *done* April 19, 1958 [1964] 2 U.S.T. 1606, T.I.A.S. No. 5639, 516 U.N.T.S. 205 (effective September 10, 1964) was "anachronistic", *see, id.* 605.

[14]c. *Id.* 77-78, 516-18.

[15]Professor Georges Scelle was representative of the small band who refused to join the ranks of the international lawyers who saw virtue in the reception of the Continental Shelf Doctrine in international law or who were resigned, or complaisant, about its inevitability. *See* Scelle, "Plateau Continental et Droit International", 59 *Revue Generale de Droit International Public* 5 (1955) [hereinafter cited as "Scelle, Plateau Continental"]. *See also* the report of his comments in 1956 1 *Y.B. Int'l L. Comm'n.* 133 which states:
"Mr. Scelle observed that, as he did not attribute any scientific value, far less any legal validity, to the concept of the continental shelf, he welcomed any discussion which might further obscure the concept and thereby lead to its rejection."

[16]*See, e.g., N.Y. Times*, Jan. 31-April 3, 1969.

[17][1969] I.C.J. 3.

[18]*See supra*, note 16.

[19]*See N.Y. Times*, March 2, 1970, at 17, cols. 1-6.

[20]S. Res. 33, 91st Cong., 1st Sess., 115 *Cong. Rec.* 1330 (1969), which recommends that the President should place a resolution endorsing basic principles for governing the activities of nations in ocean space before the United Nations Committee on the Peaceful Uses of the Seabed and Ocean Floor beyond the Limits of National Jurisdiction. Also printed in *Hearings on S. Res. 33 Before the Subcommittee on Ocean Space of the Senate Committee on Foreign Relations.* 91st Cong., 1st Sess. at 9 (1969).

[21]"Memorandum by L.F.E. Goldie on Senate Resolution 33," *Hearings on S. Res. 33, id.* at 290, 300.

[22]Arctic Waters Pollution Prevention Act, 18-19 Eliz. 2, c. 47 (Can. 1970). Royal Assent given June 26, 1970. This Act has not yet been proclaimed as having come into force, *see id.,* Section 28. *See also New York Times,* April 9, 1970 at 13, cols. 6-8; *id.* April 10, 1970, at 13, cols. 3-4; *id.* April 16, 1970, at 6, cols. 1-2; *id.* April 20, 1970, at 38 (editorial) col. 2; *id.* April 26, 1970, Section 4 (Week in Review) at 3, cols. 5-8.

[23]For a further discussion of this issue, *see infra,* Section II E.

[24]These countries, and their associates in the "200-mile Club", claim "sovereignty" over their offshore sea areas for a distance of at least 200 sea miles. For a discussion of these claims *see* Goldie, "The Oceans' Resources and International Law — Possible Developments in Regional Fisheries Management," 8 *Colum J. Transnat'l L.* 1, at 31-38 (1969). *See also* Montevideo Declaration on the Law of the Sea, *adopted* May 8, 1970 and communication of 28 May, 1970 from the Delegation of Uruguay to the Secretary General of the United Nations, 64 *A.J.I.L.* 1021 (1970), 9 *I.L.M.* 1081 (1970). In addition, Indonesia and the Philippine Republic assert claims of similar dimensions, if, presumably, of different antecedents and provenance, *see supra,* note 4.

[25]For a clear enunciation of the validity of the distinction relied upon here, *see* McDougal & Burke at 518-19.

[26]Professor Joseph Kunz cogently argues that "the long-established principle of the freedom of the high seas" is a norm *juris cogentis* of general customary international law; *see* Kunz at 828, 844-45, 853.

[27]*See* De Visscher, *Theory and Reality in International Law* 162 (Corbett transl. 1968).

[28]For this appellation of creeping jurisdiction *see* Henkin, "The Continental Shelf," *The Law of the Sea: National Policy Recommendations* 171, 175-76 (Proceedings of the 4th Annual Conference of the Law of the Sea Institute, June 23-26, 1969, University of Rhode Island, 1969).

[29]Bilder, "The Canadian Arctic Waters Pollution Prevention Act: New Stresses on the Law of the Sea," 69 *Mich. L. Rev.* 1, at 30 (1970).

[30]House of Commons Debates 6027 (April 17, 1970). *But see R. v. Tootalik* E4-321, 7 W.W.R. (n.s.) 435 (Northwest Territorial Court 1970) rev'd on other grounds, 74 W.W.R. 740. Noted in Green, "Canada and Arctic Sovereignty," 48 *Can. B. Rev.* 740, 755-56, 773 (1970). *See also* Auburn, "International Law — Sea Ice — Jurisdiction," *id.* at 776-82.

[31]This writer, for one, is most resistant to the uncivilized notion that self-preservation may justify making lawful that which would otherwise be unlawful. Brierly was correct when he said, citing the cannibalism case of *R. v. Dudley and Stephens,* 14 *Q.B.D.* 273 (1884):
"The truth is that self-preservation in the case of a state as of an individual is not a legal right but an instinct; and even if it may often happen that the instinct prevails over the legal duty not to do violence to others, international law ought not to admit

153

that it is lawful that it should do so."
Brierly 405. For clarity, and because of the important moral issues outlined by Brierly in the passage just quoted, it is necessary to distinguish between self-preservation on the one hand and self-help on the other. *See* McDougal & Feliciano, *Law and Minimum World Public Order* 213 no. 204 (1961) for a critique of the "subsumption of disparate things under a common rubric."

[32]Moore, 409-14 (1906). *See also* Jennings, "The Caroline and McLeod Cases," 32 *A.J.I.L.* 82 (1938). Hall characterizes the quoted formula as "perhaps expressed in somewhat too emphatic language ... [but] perfectly proper in essence." *See* Hall, *A Treatise on International Law* 324 (8th ed. A. Higgins 1924). For reasons stated in the preceeding footnote, Oppenheim-Lauterpacht's characterization of the case of *The Caroline* as "self-preservation" is respectfully disagreed with. *See* 1 *Oppenheim* 301. For a reasoned justification of the use of the term "self-defense" to describe the coercive protective measures open to the British Government in the *Torrey Canyon* casualty, see Utton, "Protective Measures and the 'Torrey Canyon'", 9 *B.C. Ind. & Com. L. Rev.* 613, at 623 (1968). This writer, however, prefers the term "self-help" to indicate justifiable action in oil disasters of the type under discussion.

[33]Goldie, Book Review, 1 *J. Maritime L. & Com.* 155, 158 (1969).

[34]*See infra* note 41.

[35][1969] I.C.J. 3. *See,* for a general discussion of this complex issue and of the different positions taken by the members of the Court on it, Goldie, "The North Sea Continental Shelf Cases — A Ray of Hope for the International Court?" 16 *N.Y.L. Forum* 325, at 336-59 (1970) [hereinafter cited as "Goldie, North Sea Cases"].

[36]*Done,* May 12, 1954, 1961 3 U.S.T. 2989, T.I.A.S. No. 4900, 327 U.N.T.S. 3 [hereinafter cited as the "International Pollution Convention"] (entered into force July 26, 1958).

[37]Adopted April 11, 1962, [1966] 2 U.S.T. 1523, T.I.A.S. No. 6109 (entered into force as to amendments to arts. 1-10, 16 and 18, May 18, 1967 and as to art. 14, on June 28, 1967) [hereinafter cited as "Pollution Amendments"]. Further amendments were made in 1969, Amendments to the International Convention for the Prevention of Pollution of the Sea by Oil, 1954 (as amended), annexed to IMCO Ass. Res. A. 175 (VI) *adopted* Oct. 21, 1969. *See Two Conventions and Amendments Relating to Pollution of the Sea by Oil* (Message from the President, May 20, 1970), 91st Cong., 2nd Sess., at 29-32. *See also* 62 *Dept. State Bull.* 756-57, 758-59 (June 15, 1970).

[38]*See* Annex A to the International Pollution Convention replaced by Section 14 of the Pollution Amendments.

[39]*See* the four exceptions listed in art. 2, para. 1 of the Pollution Amendments, *supra* note 37.

[40]*See* art. 2 of the International Pollution Convention, *supra* note 36, as replaced by Section 2 of the Pollution Amendments, *supra* note 37.

[41]*Done* Nov. 29, 1969, 9 *I.L.M.* 25 (1969) [hereinafter cited as the "Public Law Convention"].

[42]*Done* Nov. 29, 1969, 9 *I.L.M.* 45 (1969) [hereinafter cited as the "Private Law Convention"].

[43]9 *I.L.M.* 65.

[44]9 *I.L.M.* 66.

[45]9 *I.L.M.* 67.

[46]Public Law Convention art. 1, para. 1, *supra* note 41.

[47]*Id.* para. 2.

[48]*Id.* art. 3. Art. 4 provides for the list of experts contemplated in art. 3.

[49]*Id.* art. 5, para. 1. Paragraphs 2 and 3 set out the limits of state action.

[50]Art. 7 saves all existing rights "except as specifically provided" in the Convention. *Id.* The question is, therefore, whether the express limitation of the Public Law Convention and the express provisions in arts. 3, 5 and 6 limit or enlarge the rights of coastal states.

[51]*Supra* note 43.

[52]The treaty among Belgium, Denmark, France, the Federal Republic of Germany, the Netherlands, Norway, Sweden and the United Kingdom, the Agreement for Co-operation in Dealing with Pollution of the North Sea by Oil, *done* June 9, 1969, [1969] U.K.T.S. No. 78 (*CMND* 4205) (entered into force Aug. 9, 1969), formulates some of the amenities of good neighborliness in this context.

[53]Public Law Convention, *supra* note 41, at 29.

[54]This position has recently been affirmed by the United Nations General Assembly in paragraph 13 of the Declaration of Principles Governing the Sea-Bed and the Ocean Floor, and the Subsoil Thereof, Beyond the Limits of National Jurisdiction, G.A. Res. 2749 (1970) which reads:
Nothing herein shall affect
...
"(b) The rights of coastal States with respect to measures to prevent, mitigate or eliminate grave and imminent danger to the coastline or related interests from pollution or threat thereof resulting from, or from other hazardous occurences caused by, any activities in the area, subject to the international regime to be established."

[55]This thought was basic to this writer's "Liability for Damage and the Progressive Development of International Law," 14 *Int'l & Comp. L.Q.* 1189 (1965) [hereinafter cited as "Goldie, 'Liability for Damage'"] and his "International Principles of Responsibility for Pollution," 9 *Colum. J. Transnat'l L.* 283 (1970) [hereinafter cited as "Goldie, Responsibility for Pollution"]. *See* Goldie, "Liability for Damage" 1222-24, 1254-48 and Goldie, "Responsibility for Pollution" 284-85, 312, 317-19. Many of the thoughts in these studies will be central to the pages which follow.

[56]*See* Goldie, "Liability for Damage" 1189 *passim*, and especially 1212-13 for a discussion of this issue of the thesis that transferring the costs of extra-hazardous activities to those who are exposed to the risk of harm should provide a basis for compensation. *See also* Goldie, "Responsibility for Damage Caused by Objects Launched into Outer Space," British Institute of International and Comparative Law, *Int'l L. Ser.*, No. 6, spec. pub. No. 9, *Current Problems in Space Law* 49, 54, 56-57 (1966).

[57]*See*, for a brief indication of the "amenities rights" question, Goldie, "Amenities Rights — Parallels to Pollution Taxes," 11 *Natural Resources Journal* 274 (1971) [hereinafter cited as "Goldie, 'Amenities Rights'"], *and see* Section VI *infra*.

[58]*See* Goldie, "The Exploitability Test — Interpretation and Potentialities," 8 *Natural Resources Journal* 434-36 (1968), especially notes 1 and 2 and the accompanying text and Appendix I for an outline of this trend off the coasts of the United States.

[59]*See* Convention on the Continental Shelf, *done* April 29, 1958, [1964] 1 U.S.T. 471, T.I.A.S. No. 5578, 499 U.N.T.S. 311 (effective June 10, 1964). The other conventions which the 1958 United Nations Conference on the Law of the Sea at Geneva produced were: Convention on the Territorial Sea and the Contiguous Zone, *done* April 29, 1958, [1964]

155

2 U.S.T. 1606, T.I.A.S. No. 5639, 516 U.N.T.S. 205 (effective Sept. 10, 1964); Convention on the High Seas, *done* April 29, 1958, [1962] 2 U.S.T. 2312, T.I.A.S. No. 5200, 450 U.N. T.S. 82 (effective Sept. 30, 1962); Convention on Fishing and Conservation of the Living Resources of the High Seas, *done* April 29, 1958 [1966] 1 U.S.T. 138, T.I.A.S. No. 5969, 559 U.N.T.S. 285 (effective March 20, 1966).

[60]Experimental drillings have already been conducted through over 11,000 feet of water into the sediment beneath. *See, e.g.*, the report of the *Glomar Challenger's* drilling through 11,720 feet of water and a further 472 feet of sediment in the Gulf of Mexico to discover oil in submarine salt domes, *N.Y. Times*, Sept. 24, 1968, at 44, cols. 2-5. This report indicates that the depth of 17,567 feet was also drilled. *See also id.*, Sept. 1, 1968, at 45, cols. 3-7, and Nov. 26, 1968, at 28, cols. 2-7. For a report of discoveries by the U.S. Navy research ship *Kane* of clues to "oil rich salt domes" in the deep ocean off the west coast of Africa *see N.Y. Times*, May 13, 1969, at 29, cols. 1-5. For reports on oil exploration plays on the continental shelf and slopes of the United States and Canadian Atlantic coasts, *see N.Y. Times*, Aug. 30 1968, at 25, cols. 6-7. This article reported that: (1) permits have been issued for the exploration of 260 million acres or nearly 410,000 square miles of seabed; (2) the Shell Oil Company will use a semi-submersible rig, the Sedco H, which will drill as deep as 25,000 feet while sitting on the seabed under 1000 feet of water, or afloat through 800 feet of water; (3) most of the areas now being explored are within 200 miles of the largest cities of the United States (other areas are close to major Canadian cities); and that (4) most of this area is extremely turbulent, like the North Sea, and in contrast with the Gulf and Southern California coasts.

[61]*See*, Commission on Marine Science, Engineering and Resources, *Our Nation and the Sea* 122-30 (1969) for projection of increases in both demand for and production of offshore oil "twenty years from now". In addition to *Our Nation and the Sea*, the Commission has published three volumes of *Panel Reports*, *i.e.*, vol. 1, *Science and Environment* (1969); vol. 2, *Industry and Technology: Keys to Ocean Development* (1969); vol. 3, *Marine Resources and Legal-Political Arrangements for their Development* (1969) [hereinafter cited as *Panel Reports* and prefixed by the appropriate volume number].

[62]*Our Nation and the Sea*, *supra* note 61, at 122.

[63]*See* Goldie, "Liability for Damage," *supra* note 55, at 1215-20, 1241-44, 1246-49 and Goldie, "Responsibility for Pollution" at 309-12, for a revival of the term "absolute liability" with a new content and operation. *See also* sections II I-J *infra*.

[64]1 *Panel Reports*, *supra* note 61 (111) 52-53.

[65]Mero, *The Mineral Resources of the Sea* 275, 280 (Amsterdam 1965) [hereinafter cited as "Mero"]. *See also* Mero, "Review of Mineral Values on and Under the Ocean Floor," in *Exploiting the Ocean* 61 (Transactions of the Second Annual Marine Technology Society Conference and Exhibit, Washington, June 27-29, 1966) [hereinafter cited as "Mero, 'Mineral Values'"]; 1 *Panel Reports*, *supra* note 61, at (I) 32; 3 *Panel Reports*, *supra* note 61, at (VII) 106-71) and Troebst, *Conquest of the Sea* 180-93 (B. Price and E. Price transl. 1962) [hereinafter cited as "Troebst"].

[66]*See, e.g.*, Mero, "Mineral Values" at 76.

[67]2 *Panel Reports*, *supra* note 61, at (VI) 186; *see also id.* at (V) 184-85, and *Our Nation and the Sea*, *supra* note 61, at 134-35.

[68]*But see* 2 *Panel Reports*, *supra* note 61, at (VI) 183 where the following recommendation was made:
"Research on the problem of waste disposal ... Unwise dumpings of the tailings, if not carefully planned, could quickly foul a mining operation. Furthermore, the compatability of a marine mining operation with exploitation of the other resources of the sea, particularly the food resources, will depend principally on the effectiveness of the tailings-disposal system."

156

[69]*See* 3 *Panel Reports, supra* note 61, at (VII) 107 and the authorities cited therein at notes 23-27.

[70]*See, e.g.,* Mero, *supra* note 65, at 25-52. Note especially Table II for a list of the degree of concentration and of total quantities of 60 of the elements in sea water.

[71]*See* 3 *Panel Reports, supra* note 61, at (VII) 101, however, for an indication of the cost which would, at the present state of the art and of demand, make this development prohibitive in most parts of the sea where special concentrations do not occur.

[72]*See* G. Young, "Dry Lands and Desalted Water," 167 *Science,* Jan. 23, 1970, at 339 for an outline of this process. *See also* 3 *Panel Reports, supra* note 61, at (VII) 223-32 especially for the concomitant problems of disposal of waste and pollution.

[73]2 *Panel Reports, supra* note 61, at (VI) 213. *See also id.* at (VII) 223-34.

[74]*Id.,* (VI) 215.

[75]There are other potential sources of power in the ocean — wave motion, currents, thermal gradients and geothermal sites. An attempt to harness wave energy to operate a generator has been made on the Algerian coast. *See* 2 *Panel Reports, supra* note 61, at (VI) 217. But these are all in the far more distant future than the plans to generate electricity from the tides.

[76][1953] I.C.J. 47.

[77]*See* Judge Carniero's closing comments, *id.,* at 66.

[78]*I.e.,* the La Rance Tidal Project near St. Malo, *see* 2 *Panel Reports, supra* note 61, at (VI) 216.

[79]R. Charlier, "Harnessing the Energies of the Oceans," 3 *Marine Tech. Soc. J.* 59 (1969).

[80]*Ibid.*

[81]*Id.* at 63. Had either the 1933 or the 1945 River Severn project been brought to fruition, "they would have paid off within ten years."

[82]*Id.* at 59. *See also id.* at 65-67, and 2 *Panel Reports, supra* note 61, at (VI) 217-19.

[83]An international power project has been proposed for Passamaquoddy Bay, on the Bay of Fundy between the State of Maine and the Canadian Province of New Brunswick. *See* 2 *Panel Reports, supra* note 61, at (VI) 217-19.

[84]*See* Table 4, 1 *Panel Reports, supra* note 61, at (III) 67 for a projection of the growth of tankers and bulk carriers over the period 1970-2000. *See also* the textual matter accompanying this Table.

[85]*See* Troebst, *supra* note 65, at 97-98, where the author projects the following possible developments in ocean transportation:
"Eventually man will use regular convoys of submarine barges, towing behind them a chain of enormous, sausage-like containers. The United States Rubber Company and several European firms have already designed rubber containers for surface transportation of various liquid cargoes. Bigger versions, 20 feet in diameter and 360 feet long, would be ideal for high-seas traffic. Every "rubber sausage" of this size could hold 182,000 gallons of freight and several of them could be towed by a single submarine tanker. Admiral Momsen is convinced that by 1980 such submarine barge trains will be almost a mile long, transporting some seventy-five different liquieds ranging from oil, petrol, alcohol and acids to fine-grained materials like cement or grain. One great advantage would be that no reloading would be necessary if the

purchaser was located inland. Tugs could continue to convey the goods by river to the point nearest the final destination."

[86]This was the tonnage given in *Republic of Liberia Board of Investigation, Report in the Matter of the Standing of the S.S. Torrey Canyon on March 18*, 1967, at 1 (1967).

[87]*See* 233 *The Economist*, Dec. 20, 1969, at 62-63 for a brief mention of this casualty, and of a number of others occurring to giant tankers in recent months around the world. At the time of that issue's publication there were 75 *Marpessa*-sized tankers at sea and 300 under construction.

[88]*See* "Shipping Faces the Rapids," 235 *The Economist*, Apr. 11, 1970, at 50, 51.

[89]*Id.*, at 51.

[90]Experiments are already being conducted into fish farming by analogues of battery methods. *See* "On Flatfish Farm," 234 *The Economist*, Jan. 24, 1970, at 51.

[91]*See* 2 *Panel Reports, supra* note 61 at (VI) 190-97.

[92]Cousteau, "Working for Weeks on the Sea Floor," 129 *National Geographic*, April, 1966, at 498.

[93]*See* Wilford, "Learning from a Sojourn under the Sea," *N.Y. Times*, July 12, 1970, section 4 (The Week in Review), at 10, cols. 1-2, for an interesting confirmation of this theoretical possibility.

[94]This requirement in art. 5, para. 8 of the Convention on the Continental Shelf, *done* April 29, 1958 [1964] 1 U.S.T. 471, T.I.A.S. No. 5578, 499 U.N.T.S. 311 is not necessarily beneficial to research. Indeed, it should be properly viewed as creating, in favor of coastal states, restrictions on the freedom of the sea which had not existed previously. Because applications to conduct even purely scientific projects off their shores may arouse some states' suspicions, those applications will probably be met by time-consuming delay in receiving the consent which cannot "normally" be withheld — delays, moreover, which may well be as effective as withholding consent by rendering the research plan useless. In this way apprehensive states could prevent the scientific publication of discoveries concerning their coastal regions.

[95]*See, e.g.*, list of scientific research ships registered by the maritime nations of the world in 1 *Panel Reports, supra* note 61, at (I) 14. For a survey of the growth of marine science research activities *see id.* at (I) 2-3, (I) 13-19.

[96]Sullivan, "Freedom of Scientific Inquiry," *Law of the Sea: National Policy Recommendations* (Proceedings of the 4th Annual Conference of the Law of the Sea Institute, University of Rhode Island, June 23-26, 1969) 364 (1970); Cheever, "International Organizations for Marine Science: An Eclectic Model," *id.* at 377.

[97]*See, e.g.*, 1 *Panel Reports, supra* note 61, at (II) 11-14, (II) 58-62.

[98]*See*, on this concept, and possible military adaptations, Goldie, "Submarine Zones of Special Consideration under the High Seas," *The Law of the Sea: the Future of the Sea's Resources* 100, at 103-13 (L. Alexander ed. 1967).

[99]*See*, U.N. Doc. A/7750 (mimeo Nov. 10, 1969).

[100]For a discussion of this concept, *see* Goldie, "Special Regimes and Pre-emptive Activities in International Law," 11 *Int'l & Comp. L.Q.* 670, 687-91 (1962) [hereinafter cited as "Goldie, 'Special Regimes'"].

[101]3 U.N.R.I.A.A. 1905, 1938 (1938 and 1941).

158

[102]For a discussion of "good neighborliness" *see* Berber, *Rivers in International Law* 211-23 (1959).

[103]*See, supra* note 102.

[104][1929] P.C.I.J., Ser. A, No. 23.

[105][1929] P.C.I.J., Ser. A, No. 23 at 27. *See also* "The Helsinki Rules, International Law Association, Report of the Fifty-Second Conference (Helsinki) 477 (1966).

[106]3 U.N.R.I.A.A. 1934-37, 1966 (1938 and 1941).

[107]*See*, 3 *Reps. Int'l Arb. Awards* 1907, 1934-37, 1966 (1938).

[108]3 U.N.R.I.A.A. 1966-82 (1938 and 1941).

[109]*Id* at 1965, where the Commission stated: " ... the regime hereinafter prescribed, will, in the opinion of the Tribunal, be 'just to all parties concerned,' as long, at least, as the present conditions in the Columbia River Valley continue to prevail."

[110]For an early discussion of the doctrine of the abuse of rights in international law *see* Lauterpacht, *The Function of Law in the International Community* (1933) Chapter XIV. Generally on this topic the late Sir Hersch Lauterpacht wrote *id.* at 298:
"The doctrine of the abuse of rights plays a relatively small part in municipal law, not because the law ignores it, but because it has crystallised its typical manifestations in concrete rules and prohibitions. In international law, where the process of express or judicial law-making is still in a rudimentary stage, the law of torts is confined to very general principles, and the part which the doctrine of abuse of rights is called upon to play is therefore particularly important. It is one of the basic elements of the international law of torts."

[111]*See, supra*, section II A.

[112]3 U.N.R.I.A.A. 1905, 1938 (1938 and 1941).

[113][1949] I.C.J. 4.

[114]12 U.N.R.I.A.A. 281 (1957), 53 *A.J.I.L.* 156 (1959).

[115]*See, e.g.*, Chief Justice Fuller's appraisal of the Court's function in such cases, in *Kansas v. Colorado*, 185 U.S. 125 at 146-47 (1902) where he said:
"Sitting, as it were, as an international, as well as a domestic, tribunal, we apply Federal law, as the exigencies of the case demand."
Compare with this statement, however, that of Mr. Justice Butler in *Connecticut v. Massachusetts*, 282 U.S. 660, 670-71 (1931) *and note* his emphasis on the Supreme Court's decision in terms of an "interstate common law." *See also Hindenlider v. La Plata River & Cherry Creek Ditch Co.*, 304 U.S. 92, 110 (1938); Scott, "The Role of the Supreme Court of the United States in the Settlement of Interstate Disputes," 3 *Selected Essays on Constitutional Law* 1540 (1938).
In conclusion it is suggested that although the Court applies a special "federal common law" it leans heavily on international law sources for its materials of decision.

[116]12 U.N.R.I.A.A. 281, 303 (1957), 53 *A.J.I.L.* 156, 160-61 (1959).

[117]*See* Settlement of Japanese Claims for Personal and Property Damages Resulting from Nuclear Tests in Marshall Islands in 1954, *done* Jan. 4, 1955 [1955] 1 U.S.T. 1, T.I.A.S. No. 3160. *See also* 30 *Dept. State Bull.* 598-99 (1954); 31 *Dept. State Bull.* 492, 766 (1954); 32 *Dept. State Bull.* 90-91 (1955).
A similar *ex gratia* payment on compassionate grounds has been appropriated for certain residents of Rongelap Island in the Pacific Island Trust Territory in respect of fall-

out injuries following the explosion of an atomic bomb at Bikini Atoll on March 1, 1954. *See* Committee on Interior and Insular Affairs, "Providing for the Settlement of Claims of Certain Residents of the Trust Territory of the Pacific Islands," *H.R. Rep No.* 1193, 88th Cong., 2d Sess. (1964); and Pub. Law No. 88-485 (Aug. 22, 1964); 78 Stat. 598 (1964).

[118]*See* McDougal & Schlei, "The Hydrogen Bomb Tests in Perspective: Lawful Measures for Security," in McDougal & Associates, *Studies in World Public Order* 763, 764 (1960).

[119]The difficulty of characterizing this case in terms of *res ipsa loquitur* is illustrated by *Williams v. United States*, 218 F. 2d 473 (5th Cir. 1955) in which a jet aircraft (an Air Force B-47) exploded in mid-air causing deaths, personal injuries and property damage. The Court of Appeals for the Fifth Circuit held that at the time of the trial the engineering and scientific knowledge necessary for the manufacture, maintenance and flying of jet aircraft was so novel and specialized that a court could not confidently extrapolate from circumstantial evidence to find the defendent negligent. *See, however, Ybarra v. Spangard*, 25 Cal. 2d 486, 154 P. 2d 687 (1944). *But see,* for criticism of this latter case, Seavey, "Res Ipsa Loquitur: Tabula in Naufragio," 63 *Harv. L. Rev.* 643 (1950). For an explanation of special circumstances in *Ybarra v. Spangard, see* Prosser, *Selected Topics of the Law of Torts* 302, 362-63 (1953). *See also* Goldie, "Liability for Damage," *supra* note 55, at 1197-99, 1232-33.

[120]*See, supra* note 117.

[121]32 *Dept. State Bull.* 90-91 (1955).

[122]*See, supra* notes 112-114.

[123]Goldie, "Liability for Damage," *supra* note 55, at 1221 (footnotes omitted), and Goldie, "Responsibility for Pollution," *supra* note 55, at 308-09.

[124]This was the term used in the English version of the Explanatory Memorandum of the Convention on Third Party Liability in the Field of Nuclear Energy, *done* July 29, 1960 [hereinafter cited as "Explanatory Memorandum to the Paris Convention"]. The Convention itself is at 8 *Europ. Y.B.* 202 (1960) [hereinafter cited as the "Paris Convention"].
   Currently three other nuclear liability treaties are in existence:
   (1) International Convention on Civil Liability for Nuclear Damage, opened for signature May 21, 1963, IAEA Doc. CN. 12/46, 2 *I.L.M.* 727 (1963) [hereinafter cited as the "Vienna Convention"];
   (2) The Brussels Convention on the Liability of Operators of Nuclear Ships, 57 *A.J.I.L.* 268 (1963);
   (3) Convention Supplementary to the (OEEC) Paris Convention, 1960, Jan. 31, 1963, 2 *I.L.M.* 685 (1963). There is a fifth embryonic agreement in a draft sponsored by the Inter-American Nuclear Energy Commission.

[125]It should be noted, however, that the treaty governing the liability of the operators of nuclear ships is not, technically, a part of "international treaty law" since it has not yet come into force. *See* note 132 *infra.*

[126]L.R. 3 H.L. 330 (1868).

[127]*See* Winfield, "The Myth of Absolute Liability," 42 *L.Q.R.* 37 (1926).

[128]"Channelling" in this context denotes the tracing of liability for nuclear injuries back to the operator of a nuclear ship or reactor, notwithstanding the length of the causal chain or the intervening acts, except for wilful acts of the plaintiff. *See, e.g.,* art. 2 section 1, Vienna Convention, *supra* note 124 (1), at 730-31. *See also* Goldie, "Liability for Damage," *supra* note 55, at 1215-18, 1241-44, and Goldie, "Responsibility for Pollution," *supra* note 55, at 309-17.

[129]Its many exceptions place limitations on the rule of *Rylands v. Fletcher*. For example,

Winfield lists eight. Winfield, *Tort* 449-63 (7th ed. Jolowicz and Lewis 1963).

[130]Explanatory memorandum to the Paris Convention, *supra* note 124, section 48, at 249. *See also* Secretariat of the International Atomic Energy Agency, *Article by Article Comments on the Draft International Convention on Minimum International Standards Regarding Civil Liability for Nuclear Damage* (IAEA Doc. No. CN12/2). International Atomic Energy Agency, "Civil Liability for Nuclear Damage," *Official Records*, International Conference, Vienna, April 29-May 19, 1963 IAEA Legal Series No. 2 (1964) at 77, asserts "56. The absolute liability of the operators is not subject to the classic exonerations of tortious acts, *force majeure*, acts of God or intervening acts of third persons ..." In section 57, allowable exonerations are listed. These are the same as the exculpations in the Paril Convention. *See* Cigoj, "International Regulation of Civil Liability for Nuclear Risk," 14 *Int'l & Comp. L.Q. 809 (1965)*.

[131]Art. 9; *see* The Explanatory Memorandum to the Paris Convention, *supra* note 124, at 249. The signatory states to the Paris Convention may eliminate even these exceptions to the operator's liability for purposes of their own domestic law. *See* art. 9. Parties to the Vienna Convention may eliminate the exceptions "grave natural disaster of an exceptional character" from their national laws. *See* art. 4 (3) (b).

[132]Explanatory Memorandum to the Paris Convention, *supra* note 124, at 249.

[133]*Ibid.*

[134]Declaration of Legal Principles Governing the Activities of States in the Exploration and Use of Outer Space, G.A. Res. 1962, 18 U.N. GAOR Supp. 15, at 15, U.N. Doc. A/5515 (1963). *See also* Treaty on Principles Governing the Activities in the Exploration and Use of Outer Space, Including the Moon and Other Celestial Bodies, opened for signature Jan. 27, [1967], 3 U.S.T. 2410, T.I.A.S. No. 6347 [hereinafter cited as "Outer Space Treaty"].

[135]Goldie, "Liability for Damage," *supra* note 55, at 2121-13. *See also* Goldie, "Responsibility for Pollution," *supra* note 55, at 312.

[136]*See, supra* section II E:2.

[137]*See, supra* note 2 and the accompanying text for a brief indication of the prevailing standards under the accepted and traditional rules of public international law.

[138]*See, supra* note 124. Art. 24, para. 1, provides: "This Convention shall come into force three months after the deposit of an instrument of ratification by at least one licensing State and one other State." It has not yet come into force since it has not been ratified by either the United States or the Soviet Union. *See also* Hardy, "The Liability of Operators of Nuclear Ships," 12 *Int'l & Comp. L.Q.* 778 (1963), and Konz, "The 1962 Brussels Convention on the Liability of Operators of Nuclear Ships," 57 *A.J.I.L.* 100 (1963).

[139]The three other treaties are listed *supra* note 124.

[140]*See, e.g.*, Paris Convention, art. 9, *supra* note 124, at 214, 215 and Explanatory Memorandum to the Paris Convention, *supra* note 124, at 248, 249 for the denial of exonerating circumstances other than those which "are the responsibility of the nation as a whole" (*supra* note 123 and the accompanying text). *See also supra* note 120 and the accompanying text.

[141]*See* Goldie, "Liability for Damage," *supra* note 55, at 1189-90 for a discussion of the connotation of "transnational" in the context of catastrophic accidents. *See also* Goldie, "Responsibility for Pollution," *supra* note 55, at 313.

[142]The signatory states are Austria, Belgium, Denmark, France, the Federal Republic of germany, Greece, Italy, Luxembourg, the Netherlands, Norway, Portugal, Iceland,

161

Spain, Sweden, Switzerland, Turkey and the United Kingdom.

[143]See Paris Convention, arts. 3, 4 and 6, supra note 124, at 206-11.

[144]Art. III (1) reads as follows:
"1. The liability of the operator as regards one nuclear ship shall be limited to 1500 million francs in respect of any one nuclear incident, notwithstanding that the nuclear incident may have resulted from any fault or privity of that operator; such limit shall include neither any interest nor costs awarded by a court in actions for compensation under this Convention."
See, in addition, art. II, which provides:
"1. The operator of a nuclear ship shall be absolutely liable for any nuclear damage upon proof that such damage has been caused by a nuclear incident involving the nuclear fuel of, or radioactive products of waste produced in, such ship.
2. Except as otherwise provided in this Convention no person other than the operator shall be liable for such nuclear damage."

[145]See Brown, "The Lessons of the Torrey Canyon," 21 Current Legal Prob. 113, 114 (1968) for an indication of this initiative.

[146]The other items related to legal problems concerning preventive measure against oil pollution and means of limiting the extent of harm caused thereby.

[147]See Healy, "The CMI and IMCO Draft Convention on Civil Liability for Oil Pollution," 1 J. Maritime L. & Com. 93-98 (1969) for an outline of this debate.

[148]CMI Draft of an International Convention on Civil Liability for Oil Pollution Damage, art. 2, [1969] CMI Documents 42.

[149]See Maritime Law Association of the United States, Document No. 537, April 30, 1969, at 5779 (mimeographed material).

[15] Private Law Convention, supra note 42, art. 3, paras. 1-3.

[151]Id. art. 5, para. 1.

[152]Id. art. 7, para. 8.

[153]Art. 5, para. 10 of the Convention, id., defines the ship's net tonnage for purposes of para. 2 as follows:
"For the purposes of this Article the ship's tonnage shall be the net tonnage of the ship with the addition of the amount deducted from the gross tonnage on account of engine room space for the purpose of ascertaining the net tonnage."
The paragraph then adds that if this mode of measurement cannot be used then the "ship's tonnage shall be deemed to be 40 per cent of the weight in tons (2240 lbs) of oil which the ship is capable of carrying."

[154]Id. para. 1.

[155]Id. para. 9.

[156]See text accompanying note 130 supra.

[157]L.R. 3 H.L. 330 (1868).

[158]3 Restatement of Torts, sections 519-24 (1938). Note especially the comment to section 520:
"a. Ultrahazardous activities distinguished from negligence and nuisance. The rule stated in this Section is applicable to an activity which is of such utility that the risk unavoidably involved in carrying it on cannot be regarded as so unreasonable as to

make it negligent to carry it on, as the word "negligence" is defined in §282. If the utility of the activity does not justify the risk inseparable from it, merely to carry it on is negligence, and the rule stated in this Section is not necessary to subject the actor to liability for harm resulting from it."

[159]This concept of the relativity of liability in international law to risk creation, exposure and social desirability was first outlined by this writer in Goldie, "Liability for Damage," *supra* note 55, at 1220-24, 1254-58. *See also* Goldie, "Responsibility for Pollution," *supra* note 55, at 282-85, 307-09, 317-19.

[160]The concept of "regimes" used there and elsewhere in this essay is taken from Goldie, "Special Regimes" 11 *Int'l & Comp. L.Q.* 670 (1962). *See also* McDougal, "The Prospect for a Regime in Outer Space," in *Law and Politics in Space* [Proceedings of the First McGill Conference on the Law of Outer Space, 12 and 13 April, 1963] at 105, 106-109 (M. Cohen ed. 1964).

[161]*See* sections II F (1) and II F (3) *supra*.

[162]The phrase "flags of convenience" has been defined in the following terms:
The term "Flags of Convenience" is commonly used — and is used in this Report — to describe the flags of such countries as Panama, Liberia, Honduras and Costa Rica whose laws allow — and indeed make it easy for — ships, owned by foreign nationals or companies to fly these flags. This is in contrast to the practice in the maritime countries (and in many others) where the right to fly the national flag is subject to stringent conditions and involves far reaching obligations.
Maritime Transport Committee, Organization for European Economic Cooperation, "Study on the Expansion of the Flags of Convenience Fleets and on Various Aspects Thereof," Jan. 31, 1958, at 2 (mimeographed material).
This phrase has been used in pejorative, commendatory, and neutral contexts. An example of the first may be found in the statement of Hoyt S. Haddock, Executive Secretary of the AFL-CIO Maritime Committee, "Hearings on Study of Vessel Transfer, Trade-in, and Reserve Fleet Policies Before the Sub-Committee on the Merchant Marine of the House Committee on Merchant Marine and Fisheries," 85th Cong., 1st Sess., ser. 12, pt. 2, at 694 (1957). *See also* Omar Becu, "Fighting the Pirate Flags," 124 *Free Labor World* 59 (1959). Examples of the commendatory use may be found in "Liberia's Merchant Fleet," 9 *Liberia Today* 12 (1959), and in Boczek, *Flags of Convenience: An International Legal Study, passim* (1962) [hereinafter cited as "Boczek"]. Neutral uses of the term can be found in *West India Fruit and Steamship Co.*, 130 N.L.R.B. 343, 364 (1961); National Academy of Sciences, National Research Council, *The Role of the U.S. Merchant Marine in National Security* (1959) (Project Walrus Report by the Panel on Wartime Use of the U.S. Merchant Marine of the Maritime Research Advisory Committee, National Academy of Sciences Publication 748) [hereinafter cited as "Project Walrus"], and "Chasing the Runaways," 202 *The Economist*, Feb. 24, 1962, at 709.
It may be noted that although the definition quoted at the outset of this footnote names Panama, Liberia, Honduras and Costa Rica as 'flag of convenience' states, it does not, by its use of the words "such countries as," close the list. Thus, the Venezuelan flag flies from the sterns of a small American-owned fleet. On the other hand, Costa Rica has repealed her flag of convenience legislation (*N.Y. Times*, Oct. 31, 1958, at 57, col 4). Costa Rica's decision may be contrasted with the fact that two nations, at about the same time as Costa Rica's repeal, decided to join the group of states which offer easy terms for the registration of ships. These are Lebanon (*N.Y. Times*, May 27, 1958, at 62, col. 6) and Tunisia (*N.Y. Times*, Oct. 30, 1958, at 61, col. 4). It is perhaps likely that more states will be added to the list for prestige or revenue purposes from time to time, especially if the original members should increase their taxes or improve their standards of seaworthiness. In this regard coincidences in the history of Panamian tax law and the statistics of Panamian registration are illuminating, *see* Mender, "Nationality of Ships: Politics and Law," 5 *Arkiv for Sjorett* 126, 279-80 (1961), especially notes 19 and 20 and the text which they accompany.
For connotations of the phrase "PanLibHon" with reference to shipping (formerly "PanLibHonCo" when Costa Rica's laws offered that nation's flag as a convenience to

163

foreign-owned ships), *see* the definition given by the National Labor Relations Board in *West India Fruit and Steamship Co.*, 130 *N.L.R.B.* 343, 364 and note 82 (1961): "PanLib-Hon is the term usually employed in referring to 'flag of convenience' ships of Panamanian, Liberian and Honduran registry."

A further point of definition may be made regarding the reference to the term "flag." It is taken as the indicator of a ship's nationality and as a short form of the more technically accurate phrase "colours and pass"; *see The Vrouw Elizabeth,* 5 C. Rob. 2, 5, 165 *Eng. Rep.* 676, 677 (Adm. 1803) (opinion of Lord Stowell's phrase would be "flag and documents of registration). As Reinow, *The Test of Nationality of a Merchant Ship* 140-41 (1937) [hereinafter cited as "Reinow"] points out: "The significance of the flag is internationally recognized. It symbolizes nationality in actual practice as well as in the terminology of international engagements." (footnotes omitted). The term "flag" is taken in many modern writings as a shorthand term for referring to, and as the outward symbol of, a ship's nationality. *See also* Comment, "The Effect of the United States Labor Legislation on the Flag-of-Convenience Fleet," 69 *Yale L.J.* 498 (1960); Comment, "The 'Effect of the Genuine Link' Principle of the 1968 Geneva Convention on the National Character of a Ship", 35 *N.Y.U.L. Rev.* 1049 (1960); Comment, "PanLibHon Policy and the Problems of the Courts," 60 *Colum. J. Rev.* 711 (1960). On the importance of the flag in this sense, *see e.g., Case of the S.S. "Lotus,"* [1927] P.C.I.J., ser. A, No. 10, at 25; *The Creole* (United States v. Great Britain), 2 *Moore,* 358, 361; *R. v. Keyn,* 2 Ex. D. 63 (1876); *Marshall v. Murgatroyd,* L.R. 6 Q.B. 31 (1870); *R. v. Anderson,* 11 Cox Crim. Cas. 269 (1860). *See also United States v. Flores,* 289 U.S. 137 (1933). Contrast the predicament of a ship without a lawful flag: *see Movan v. Attorney-General for Palestine* [1948] A.C.351 (*J.C.P.C.*). However, for a critical comment on the general acceptance of "the flag" as synonymous with a ship's nationality, *see* Reinow, *supra* at 140-53, especially 146-51, 152-3 and note 54, and compare with the broad general use of the phrase, his statement (at 152): "It is the authorization behind the flag which is significant."

[163]This section is based on section V of this writer's article "Responsibility for Pollution," *supra* note 55, and on section IV of his article "Recognition and Dual Nationality — A Problem of Flags of Convenience," 39 *Brit. Y.B. Int'l L.* 220, 254-61 (1963) [hereinafter cited as "Goldie, 'Flags'"].

[164]*See, e.g., Mortensen v. Peters,* 8 Sess. Cas. (5th Ser.) 93 (1906), *and* comments thereon in Goldie, "Flags" 224-25, note 4.

[165]Project Walrus, *supra* note 162. *See also* Report by Leo A. Hoegh, Director of the Office of Defense Mobilization, Dec. 29, 1960, at 16 (mimeographed material); *and* Brief for the United States as Amicus Curiae at 20-21, *West Indian Fruit and Steamship Co.,* 130 *N.L.R.B.* 343 (1961).

[166]*See* McDougal, Burke & Vlasic, "The Maintenance of Public Order at Sea and the Nationality of Ships," 54 *A.J.I.L.* 25, 57 (1960) which states:

"The one necessary limit upon the discretion of states, and a limit which appears universally accepted, is that, once a state has conferred its national character upon a vessel, other states may not confer their national character as long as the original national character remains unchanged."

See also, McDougal & Burke, *supra* note 14a, at 1058, *and see* the categorical statement in 1 *Oppenheim, supra* note 2, at 595 which reads: "But no state may allow a vessel to sail under its flag which already sails under the flag of another State." *See also* the Geneva Convention on the High Seas, art. 6, sec. 1 of which provides: "Ships shall sail under the flag of one State only and, save in exceptional cases expressly provided for in international treaties or in these articles, shall be subject to its exclusive jurisdiction on the high seas."

[167]"The Channel: Playing Canute with Pollution," 239 *The Economist* 77 (April 10, 1971), *but see* "Plugging Some Leakages," 239 *The Economist* 80 (May 8, 1971).

[168]*See, supra,* section II C.

[169]*See, supra,* notes 112-114 and their accompanying text.

[170]For an example of a proposal for a legal fiction in international law which equally lacked the needed oredering and controls and possessed the qualities of the Theatre of the Absurd (as well as Grand Guignol), *see* Goldie, "Legal Aspects of the Refusal of Asylum by U.S. Coast Guard on 23 November, 1970," 23 *Naval War College Rev.* 32, 39 at note 11 (May 1971).

[171]*See, e.g.,* "Sovereignty Over Coastal Waters — U.K. Attitude on Seizure of Onassis Fleet," *Financial Times* (London), Nov. 20, 1954, at 5, cols. 1-2; "A Man at War," *Financial Times* (London), Nov. 22, 1954, at 6, cols. 4-5; "Sea Dogs," *id.,* at col. 5; *and* "Gilbertian Fantasy," *id.,* at cols. 5-6.

[172]For a discussion of the history of consolidation of the CEP claims and of the utilization of Peru's arrest of Onassis' whaling fleet, *see* Kunz 834-36.

[173]Advisory Opinion on Reparations for Injuries Suffered in the Service of the United Nations [1949] I.C.J. 174. *See also* Advisory Opinion on Certain Expenses of the United Nations [1962] I.C.J. 151.

[174]For a discussion of problems regarding the utility of international organizations, *see* Fitzgerald, "The Participation of International Organizations in the Proposed International Agreement on Liability for Damage Caused by Objects Launched into Outer Space," 3 *Can. Y.B. Int'l L.* 265 (1965).

[175]*Mich. Comp. Laws Ann.* section 691. 1201 (Supp. 1970). *See* Goldie, *Amenities Rights* 274, 276-77. A representational type of precedure permitting citizens to be "private attorneys general" to protect aesthetic, recreational and conservational interests would appear to be evolving in the United States federal courts, *see, e.g., Associated Data Processing Service Organizations Inc. v. Camp,* 397 U.S. 150 (1970); *Scenic Hudson Preservation Conference v. Federal Power Commission,* 354 F. 2d 608 (2d Cir. 1965). *C. f. Sierra Club v. Hickel,* 433 F. 2d 24 (1970), cert. granted 401 U.S. 907 (1970). *But see now Committee for Nuclear Responsibility v. Seaborg,* 3 ERC 1126 (D.C. Cir. 1971); *and Calvert Cliffs v. Atomic Energy Commission,* 2 ERC 1779 (D.C. Cir. 1971).

[176]*See, supra* section II F (3) (d).

[177]U.N. Doc. A/CN.4/237.

[178]On this latter *see Trail Smelter Arbitration, supra* note 112.

[179]*See, e.g.,* Mishan, "The Spillover Enemy," 35 *Encounter* 3 (Dec. 1969); Ramsey, "We Need a Pollution Tax!" 26 *Bulletin of Atomic Scientists* 3 (April 1970). For a legal formulation, *see* Goldie, "Responsibility for Pollution," *supra* note 55, at 325-27.

PART FOUR

DEVELOPING INSTITUTIONAL PROCESSES AND STRUCTURES

PART IV.
DEVELOPING INSTITUTIONAL PROCESSES AND STRUCTURES

EDITORIAL ANALYSIS

A. *The nature of the system.*

If we are to organize the international community to cope with environmental problems, we must keep clearly in view the institutional character of the system within which this organizing is to be done.Even the most innovative environmental management plans capable of commanding a serious hearing in the foreseeable future will not, of themselves, entail fundamental changes in the institutional make-up of international society. That society will remain a rather loosely organized community of independent entities in which the principle of national sovereignty predominates. The United Nations will remain. Less fundamentally, the United Nations Specialized Agencies will continue, and their own constitutional independence within the family of international organizations is unlikely to be affected. Various regional international organizations with more remote connection with the United Nations will persist, and whatever is their present competence in law or in fact to concern themselves with environmental problems will likely continue. All these things it is reasonable to predict regardless of whether new institutions for the protection of the environment are created in the immediate future, and regardless of the extent to which conceivable environmental functions to be performed by international organizations may be centralized in a single institution. In sum, then, the system within which planners for the environment — like planners in any other area of international co-operation — must operate is one in which the vast preponderance of power to act reposes in sovereign states, and in which the multi-lateral structures which bind those states loosely together for special purposes are themselves diverse and only loosely interconnected one with another.

The chief executors of policy on environmental matters, at the point where that policy entails compliance with standards of conduct aimed directly at abating or preventing injuries to the environment, will be national governments. Consequently, it is only prudent to expect that the chief makers of environmental policy must be national governments, even though in this role they will often act in concert through multi-lateral structures, and sometimes may act only indirectly through the exercise by multilateral instrumentalities of authority previously delegated to them by governments. It is an over-simplification to say that

169

governments will not accept standards of conduct or plans of action "imposed" upon them by international agencies. But it must be borne in mind, without any slackening of enthusiasm for bold and imaginative international institutional arrangements, that in a world community organized as ours presently is, the limits on what the traffic will bear by way of such imposition — even at the hands instrumentalities previously agreed to and authorized — can be reached very quickly.

B. *How much law-making?*

If it is important to keep an eye firmly fastened on the nature of the system within which one operates, it is equally important to try to make at least a rough assessment, in advance, of the kinds of functions which can be expected to be needed. The current aphorism is "form follows function".

One way to ask this question — and at the same time, perhaps, to reflect the lawyer's bias — is: How much international law-making is required, in relation to other kinds of institutional functions? By "law-making" here we mean the establishment of standards of conduct for states or other actors affecting the environment, and having the force of law whether derived from treaties or regulatory action by an international agency.

The short answer to the question "how much law-making?" is an acknowledgement that it is really too early to tell with precision. What the question calls for is the application of what were called, in Part II of this book, "criteria of efficacy" regarding various alternatives within a range of possible modes of attack upon particular problems. And for many apparent environmental problems, as we have already observed, the state of human knowledge is inadequate to permit reliable judgments as to the most efficacious means of coping with them ultimately. This fact in itself, however, is important, because it tells us that as to such a problem, whatever it may require in the long run, what it requires in the *short* run is not law-making but something else. In other words, the clear connection between the data-base and the mode of action — on which comment was made in Part II — is an important consideration in estimating what proportion of international environmental-management energies should be expended on law-making activities.

When we take into account, also, the necessity for developing an adequate political consensus for a particular law-making enterprise, even where an adequate data-base has been accumulated, then it is apparent that the problems on which major law-making can be expected in the near future are only a handful at most. In the field of marine pollution, for example, it may be that problems of dumping and other pollution from vessels will ripen fairly shortly for further legislative

170

action. But the same can hardly be said for the much more extensive and complex problem of marine pollution from land sources. In general, it is safe to say that for every environmental problem which appears ready for law-making action in the foreseeable future, there are likely to be many others which for the time being will need to be dealt with by a wide range of what might be called "management processes". Some of these processes will be aimed at eventual law-making, and others of them at influencing the conduct of states or private persons by other devices.

C. Centralization: How much and of what kind?

"The environment problem", so denominated, is for the most part still fairly new on the agenda of concerns of the international community. Despite this newness, however, it is probably fair to say that the thinking of those national and international bureaucracies most concerned with the matter and that of their constituencies in the private sector, have undergone very considerable change under the stimulus of discussions within the United Nations and elsewhere. The concept of a single, new international agency with an all-encompassing jurisdiction over environmental problems and with a mandate to set about from the outset producing international legislation on a wide range of problems, is likely to attract much less adherence now than would have been the case in the first flush of enthusiasm for the newly-discovered environment issue a few years ago.

Nevertheless, there remains a compelling logic in the conviction that there is something about "the environment problem" which sets it apart from some other areas of international co-operation, insofar as the need for centralizing some of the functions of international agencies is concerned.

It is clear at a glance that "the environmental problem" embraces such a wide and disparate collection of individual problems, falling within the present mandate of a wide variety of public agencies both international and national, that there is a need for someone at the center to do what is usually called "coordination". More fundamentally, however, it is argued that the structure of the existing complex of international organizations, like that of national governments, mirrors an important part of the reason for the *existence* of the planet's environmental problems. To understand why there *is* "an environmental problem" of global scale, one must understand the wide range of important human activities around the globe that for many generations have characteristically gone their separate ways, pursuing their own respective objectives, accommodating among themselves where those objectives clashed, but none of them counting their impairment of the livability of the planet among their costs. Existing organizations were created to function as part of this same system. Consequently, it is argued, if what is needed is an infusion of a single environmental perspective into international public policy-making across the board, it cannot be reliably achieved through existing international institutional structures, established for other purposes to meet the needs of the system within which the problem arose. How, for example — it is asked — can organizations established in response to the interests of nations in shipping, in economic development, in agricultural enterprise, or in nuclear energy, be expected to serve as spokesmen for the environment?

This perception is only partly true of the roles that have been played, for example, by the U.N. Specialized Agencies.

While none of these agencies was established solely or even primarily for what would now be regarded as an "environmental" purpose, this fact has not prevented a number of them from undertaking, sometimes quite concretely, environmental protection efforts in particular fields within their range of competence — of which the work like that of IMCO in the field of marine pollution by oil and that of FAO in soil conservation may be only the most obvious. But from the point of view described above, the question of centralization becomes not whether there should be any centralization of functions, but how much there should be, and of what kind. The following paragraphs sketch some of the issues that are likely to be confronted in answering these questions.

1. The "coordination" function.

The long years of experience of the United Nations system in the pursuit of "coordination" will be of very direct relevance in the environmental field both in making institutional choices and in carrying out programs of action. That experience has not been unmitigatedly successful, and "coordination" as a concept does not enjoy a good reputation within the system. In any event, if "coordination" is to be one of the functions of a central agency in the environmental field, its scope and content will require thorough thinking-through in the light not only of this prior experience but also of any peculiar demands of environmental problems such as those suggested in the preceding paragraphs. We may tentatively predict conclusions along the following lines:

First: the "coordination" function will have to be broader than simply the elimination of duplication among various international organizations pursuing environmental activities — a brand of "coordination" which some have come to regard as a codeword for uncritical budget-cutting. It is not clear, indeed, that duplication in the operation of environmental management agencies would in all cases be undesirable; a certain amount of planned overlap — for example, in scientific research — might sometimes be a wise investment.

Secondly: "coordination" should reasonably go on to embrace such

172

additional functions as identifying and seeking to eliminate conflicting activities; identifying gaps in activities underway; seeking to establish priorities; and making judgments about the most efficacious way to get particular activities performed. Presumably it would be generally accepted that such fairly conventional-looking functions need to be performed somewhere. In theory they might be performed, at least for the United Nations family, by the system's existing inter-agency coordination machinery.

Thirdly: in the field of environmental management however, performing such functions as these will itself require in turn that the co-ordinating agency be able to command a wide range of supporting capacities that do not look like conventional "coordination" at all, and which in any event lie well outside the capabilities of conventional United Nations coordinating devices whether inter-governmental or inter-secretariat. Gaps in activities underway cannot reliably be identified in the absence of a comprehensive frame of reference within which to make judgments as to what activities *ought* to be underway, and such a framework cannot be developed by professional coordinators. Priorities among competing activities cannot be intelligently set without the means to ascertain the scope and urgency of the problems with which each is intended to cope, and an understanding of the nature and limitations of available resources for action. International environmental priorities will not be authoritatively set until firmly fixed in the environment policies of individual governments, and this requires a vigorous catalyst to unify the policies of the disparate departments or ministries within an individual government whose functions impinge on environmental matters.

A central agency taking on such jobs as these would clearly require formidable resources of substantive competence: it would require, in brief, the competence to discharge a number of what were called "criteriological tasks" in Part II of this book, with a view to making assessments regarding the existence and significance of environmental problems, the way in which available resources should be allocated to them, and the wisdom and effectiveness of those allocations viewed in retrospect. Moreover, it would have to work in close relationship with government policy-makers in the environmental field.

2. "Coordination" vs. mobilizing the power of knowledge.
The argument for limiting a central agency to a "coordinating" role more narrowly conceived than the mushrooming role just described, would proceed from the assumption that the existing system already contains various pieces of institutional equipment capable — if only they were given the necessary political and financial support — of performing the various functions which an ideal environmental management system might perform. There is an important kernel of truth in this hypothesis.

173

Many of the activities embraced in any reasonable taxonomy of such functions fall within the legal competence and experience of a specialized agency or some other part of the existing system, and might be adequately performed as to some environmental problems by that agency. Such functions cover the whole spectrum, from research and data collection to promotion, notification and alerting, monitoring, planning, dispute settlement, and formal regulation or other standard-setting (any Specialized Agency can call a plenipotentiary conference to draft a treaty).

It is of great importance, however, to note that this fact does not of itself imply that no central function other than a classic "coordination" function should be performed at the center. If the international warehouse already contains an adequate collection of machinery, what is lacking is the motive power to get that machinery moving, and moving on the right job. It is not as if the equipment were all already in operation at top capacity, and required only some central direction to prevent various pieces from bumping into one another or from taking on the same tasks. It has already been emphasized that this state of affairs is hardly the fault of the agencies themselves — that is to say, of their international bureaucracies — and that any "performance gap" in international organizations is first to be laid at the feet of governments as the principal executors of policy in the international community. The dominant problem in organizing the international community to cope with environmental problems is marshalling the requisite motive force that is to be found only in the political and financial commitment of governments. And this problem is not one of "coordination" alone, but is better described as one of bringing the power of knowledge to bear on the effective makers of government policy. Several brief points of explanation are in order.

First, one must emphasize the term "effective". For, as some of the comments in the preceding section indicate, it would be a mistake to assume that for practical purposes it is the same government that is represented in each of the Specialized Agencies behind the name-plate of a single member state. It is probably the case that most foreign offices, to say nothing of most governments as a whole, regard the bulk of policy issues dealt with in international organizations as fairly close to the periphery of their interests. Consequently even two people from the same foreign office, representing a government in different international agencies, may adopt conflicting positions whose inconsistency is never purged by a vigorous in-house policy review. There are other symptoms of the same malady. Governments often fail to take seriously the commitments to policy objectives which they have permitted their representatives to accept in an international organization. A government's participation in international organization policy-making is sometimes paralyzed, when it is found to impinge on conflicting national policy objectives and the conflict is regarded as important enough to immobilize policy but not important enough to resolve. To be sure, devising new international structures or re-arranging the old will not of itself insure that the whole range of policy-making within a single government is imbued with an environmental perspective at an effectively high level. But it is safe to say that creating a forum in which international environmental policy is addressed comprehensively, even if the execution of that policy may be done elsewhere, should greatly assist those responsible for environmental matters within a government in unifying and thus putting muscle into that government's environmental policy.

Secondly, it is in this light that we should consider any controversy with respect to the proper relationships of formal authority between a central agency and the component agencies of the existing system. Apprehension is sometimes expressed on the part of the Specialized Agencies, for example, that a central body would be given the power to "tell the agencies what to do". Disparagers of the Specialized Agencies are inclined to insist that something like this *must* be done, in order to insure proper "coordination" and protect against bureaucratic aggrandizement by the component parts of the United Nations family or by regional organizations. Such a controversy misses the point: assuming that a central agency should be empowered to formulate views on the question of what jobs need to be done and where they might best be done (which is likely to be admitted by many people on both sides), the important thing is not whether those views are expressed in a form which is in some sense legally binding on the component agencies.

Indeed it would probably be a waste of energy at the present juncture to undertake the fairly elaborate revisions of existing institutional structures which would be necessary to make this possible. The important thing is, rather, who participates in these assessments and is committed to them, and the effective force of those commitments within governments.

Thirdly, bringing the power of knowledge to bear on governments cannot rest on any naive assumption that individual governments, if only they are confronted with the facts, will preceive the common good and pursue it even at the expense of more immediate and narrowly national policy objectives. It is true that a central agency should provide the scientific facts: it should serve as a single dissemination point in an information system designed to gather, interpret, and disseminate knowledge of the relevant scientific data. But the power of that knowledge to move governments stems from a grasp by policy-makers of the full panoply of consequences that may flow from a failure to adjust national policy so as to take it into account: not simply consequences injurious to the environment, but political consequences both international and domestic, economic consequences, repercussions for a government's moral stature or prestige, and perhaps others.

Here, as in any system in which the role of knowledge is to move to action, the source of information and the mode of its presentation within the system may be as important as its content. The policy impact of scientific information regarding the polluting effects of the activity of a government or its nationals may well differ radically, depending on whether that information is communicated to it by means of a confidential investigation by the government's own experts, an international executive acting in the alerting role of an ombudsman, the report of an international body of scientists that may contain some of that government's own nationals, or disclosures produced in the course of complaints brought before an international body by a private citizens' group. All of the prospective information-gathering and disseminating functions of a central environmental agency should be considered in light of the need not simply to produce a routine flow of facts, but to produce those facts under circumstances that will maximize the probability of political action.

Finally, the *routine* character of the flow of facts is itself of considerable importance in moving governments to action, as the traditional skittishness of many governments toward permanent international fact-finding machinery attests. Clearly governments will find it more difficult to avoid accepting and acting upon information produced by the normal operation of processes they themselves have previously established. Governments should be fully committed at the outset to the establishment of the various components of an information system, whether concerned with scientific research or otherwise; and the occasions on which fresh political authorization for the operation of the system is required should be minimized. Arrangements have been suggested by which governments themselves would transmit information regarding the environmental consequences of major governmental or private undertakings (similar to the "impact statements" required by United States legislation), and information about national environmental legislation or regulation. For similar reasons such arrangements should place these submissions on a routine basis, well insulated from day-to-day policy-making within the government.

D. *Sub-global systems.*

The question of centralization of functions has been discussed in the foregoing sections in reference to the *global* system comprising the U.N. family of organizations. This system is "global" in two senses: (a) formal membership in the constituent bodies is global, and (b) the scope of the system's concern might theoretically reach any international environmental problem whether the problem itself is global or merely regional. It is clear, however, that a substantial proportion of international activity on environmental matters will involve systems organized on a sub-global basis, which fall outside the United Nations family. (This fact accounts for the inclusion in this volume of the papers prepared by Professor

Slouka, Mr. Stein and Professor Bilder, respectively.) The existence and scope of legal authority of these sub-global organizations, as already indicated, are unlikely to be substantially affected by any institutional decisions on environmental management taken in the near future. Moreover, as a class, these organizations differ from the constituent organizations of the United Nations family in that a number of them — such as bilateral or regional river commissions — were established in whole or in part for explicitly environmental purposes.

One general point about these sub-global systems should be borne in mind in making institutional decisions for the environment: In a world system in which the two overlapping problems of "coordination" and "mobilization of the power of knowledge" are to be dealt with at the center, there is no reason why sub-global systems could not be as much part of a world system as the U.N. Specialized Agencies or various other constituent agencies of the U.N. family. The institutional features which will be necessary to make this world system work, will tend in equal measure to make it work for sub-global organizations not formally a part of the United Nations family as for the constituent organizations of that family. As already indicated, the most important single factor in any such system is not likely to be devising the proper formal relationships of hierarchical authority within the system, but rather engaging those who make effective policy for national governments in the process of international policy-making.

INTERNATIONAL CO-OPERATION FOR POLLUTION CONTROL

by *Daniel Serwer**

Introduction

Underlying this discussion is a notion of what pollution and pollution control are as well as some ideas concerning the purposes of international co-operation in this area. Pollution is viewed as that part of the flow of materials and energy from man's activities to the environment that may cause undesirable effects. The definition, or more accurately the choice, of what is undesirable may vary with the physical, legal, economic, social and cultural context. Pollution control is viewed as the management of this flow in order to achieve objectives such as the protection of human health, the protection of organisms or populations other than man or the protection of other resources, including the stability of the environment itself. Thus, not only are the means of controlling pollution considered a matter of choice, but so are the targets, though the choice among these is not discussed here.

Thus, the discharge of pollutants as such is not viewed here as either illegal or immoral, and the control of pollution is viewed as a matter of choice rather than necessity. This is not to say that legal norms and moral values have nothing to do with pollution or its control. Legal norms are among the most important means of pollution control, and moral values are both a fundamental consideration in determining goals and an important constraint on the use of means. These are, however, only part of the means, considerations and constraints; there are others that are more economic, social and cultural than legal or moral. Complete prohibition is but one of a number of means, and even the strictest definition of objectives would require its use only occasionally if compliance with other means were assured. It would be much simpler if there were a moral imperative, "Thou shalt not pollute," but this is not the case now and is not likely to be the case so long as the environment has a capacity for receiving many materials without undesirable effects occurring and so long

*The author is a Research Associate at the United Nations Institute for Training and Research.

This paper was originally prepared at UNITAR in consultation with Mr. Oscar Schachter, Director of Studies of UNITAR, as a "basic paper" for the United Nations Conference on the Human Environment. It has benefitted greatly from comments received from officials of several international secretariats as well as from participants in the Conference on Legal and Institutional Responses to Problems of the Global Environment. These comments are gratefully acknowledged, but the views, opinions and interpretations are those of the author. UNITAR takes no position on the questions studied under its auspices; the Institute does, however, accept responsibility for determining whether a study merits publication and dissemination.

as economic and social development is a fundamental goal.

As for the purposes of international co-operation in this area, it should be apparent that not all pollution problems are intrinsically of international significance. Many of the most acute problems are local and can be solved without any international co-operation. Even in this case, however, international co-operation may be useful, for not all states possess sufficient technical and legal expertise to formulate appropriate measures, and even states that do may find the recommendations of international organizations useful. Moreover, international co-operation on developing means to control commonly occurring, local pollution problems may contribute significantly to the achievement of shared goals regionally and even globally.

There are, however, several kinds of pollution problems that to some extent require international co-operation for their solution rather than merely benefiting from it. First, there are pollution problems that literally do not respect national jurisdictions; pollutants can cause undesirable effects outside the state in which they are discharged to the environment. Harm may be caused to other states or to the interests of other states in shared resources, or to those large areas of the biosphere which do not belong to any one state. In some cases, pollution from a single source may even be distributed globally. Moreover, the situation may become extremely complex when the pollutants are discharged in more than one state, when more than one pollutant is involved, and when the victims are themselves contributing to at least some of the problems. International co-operation in such cases may be needed not only to establish common objectives but also in apportioning the burden of meeting these objectives among the states in which the sources of pollution are located.

Second, international co-operation may be needed even if the physical impact of the pollutants in question lies strictly within national jurisdictions insofar as there is international trade in a) goods that may contain potential pollutants or whose use or transport may cause pollution, or b) in goods whose production may cause pollution. In the case of goods that may contain a potential pollutant or whose use or transport may cause pollution, the need for international co-operation arises primarily from the desire of producers to avoid the creation of non-tariff barriers through the imposition of a variety of anti-pollution standards by importing states, or from the desire of users to avoid having needed supplies of useful materials cut off. This raises the important question of who should be involved in international co-operation in this case. Producers alone are likely to push for uniformity in policies, since for them uniformity is likely to be easiest and cheapest to comply with. Such uniformity may not, however, be appropriate to all consumers; uniform standards may be either too lax for some importing states or unnecessary and costly as well to others.

In the case of international trade in goods whose production may cause pollution, the need for international co-operation arises not from the interests of producers or consumers as such, but from the interests of those states that either have relatively low levels of the pollutants in question in the environment or would like to reduce these levels. For the former, the added cost of controlling pollution problems of this type in states that have higher levels of pollutants may bring a comparative advantage in international trade. For the latter, these added costs may pose obstacles to taking needed measures. The basic problem to be faced here is what kind of equitable international solutions can be reached, given the great physical, economic and social variations that may exist among competitor states, both to remove some of the obstacles and to assure the realization of the comparative advantage of a relatively clean environment.

Thirdly, the need for international co-operation may arise in the case of pollution problems that can be solved through action by a single state but where such unilateral action has an international impact. One instance is intervention on the high seas in cases of oil pollution casualties, for which the 1969 IMCO Convention will provide a basis for international co-operation if it comes into force. This is, however, a rather unusual case. Such unilateral actions as the imposition of product standards, the limitation or prohibition of the manufacture of certain materials, exclusion from national jurisdictions of ships or aircraft that do not conform to reasonable standards of construction or operation, and the extension of anti-pollution jurisdictions are likely to be more common. Precisely what can be done about international co-operation in cases of this type varies with the situation. Generally, it would appear reasonable to suggest that states announce their intent to take unilateral action for pollution control and consult in advance with other states that may be affected even though there may be no legal obligation to do so. It should be apparent, however, that one of the better ways of avoiding the difficulties that may arise from unilateral action is to provide sufficient international controls on the problems that arouse states to take such action.

The focus of this paper is on the measures that can be taken in this regard. These are divided into two categories: means of controlling pollution, including protection standards, discharge standards, technological standards, complete prohibitions and effluent charges and price adjustments; and means of promoting compliance with these, including liability, registration and licensing, technical assistance, subsidies and compensations, and planning and forecasting. Each of these is discussed separately, although in practice they are often used in combination. The list of means may well be incomplete, although it is hoped that the most important are included even though they may not be given the names by which others know them (see *A Note on Terminology*, p. 206-207). The over-all aim to display the range of means available rather than to analyze each in detail. Accordingly, the discussion of each is brief and attempts to indicate basic issues in the choice of means, to suggest how

180

these might be used in solving problems of current international interest, and to consider the organizational implications of taking action along these lines. This can hardly be considered the final word; much more experience and detailed scholarly analysis will be needed before we learn how each of these tools works and how each may be used effectively.

I. CONTROLLING POLLUTION

A. *Protection Standards*

Protection standards are maximum acceptable levels of a pollutant (or its indicator) in specified media or targets, or maximum acceptable intakes of a pollutant into the target. These standards are usually expressed as concentrations in air, water, food or soil as well as in human, animal and plant life. The protection standards set for different media and targets are often related. For example, in order to protect human health from harm due to lead, a protection standard for lead in human body tissues may be set, but compliance with this primary standard may depend on complaince with other protection standards, known as "derived working limits," for lead in the food man eats and in the air he breathes.

Protection standards can play a number of useful roles in controlling pollution because they provide a rational basis for further action. Thus, rather than deciding to monitor a pollutant, to issue an alarm, to impose standards or liability on the sources of pollution, or to take other actions involving significant efforts or costs merely on the basis of a qualitative notion of what is acceptable or unacceptable behavior on the part of those who discharge pollutants, or because a pollutant has been detected in an unlikely place, action can be based instead on explicit quantitative norms for pollutants in media or in targets. Indeed, without protection standards a great deal of effort may be lost or misdirected in controlling individual sources of pollution beyond that which is necessary or desired. This is obviously the case for those pollutants for which there exists a threshold below which there are no undesirable effects, but even when no such threshold exists there may exist a level below which the effects are considered acceptable. Little may be gained, and much may be lost in terms of time, money and effort, in seeking the reduction of pollution below such a level. Thus, although achieving compliance with protection standards in general requires the use of a variety of other measures, basing the use of these on an evaluation of the physical situation relative to protection standards may offer significant savings.

The level at which protection standards are set depends on a weighing of costs and benefits, and these depend on the nature of the effects themselves, the goals it is desired to achieve and the uses to which the given medium is put. Effects may vary with the physical environment, as is clearly the case with oil in the Arctic and in tropical zones since temperature is a major factor in the persistence of oil. Different objectives may be set, including the protection of human health, the protection of organisms or populations other than man and the protection of other resources. Media may be used for different purposes: water that is not potable may still be useful for industrial cooling. There may, however, be some objectives that are commonly held, some pollutants whose effects do not vary greatly with the physical environment and some common uses. In such cases protection standards may be widely applicable. A number of protection standards for human health have in fact been set internationally, including standards for various contaminants in drinking water, for pesticide residues and other contaminants in food, for air pollutants in working places and for radiation doses to man.

The potential wide applicability of some protection standards is in sharp contrast to the much narrower applicability of many other means of controlling pollution that focus on the sources. The extent to which releases of pollutants from individual sources need to be controlled in order to achieve a given level of protection varies not only with the local meteorological and hydrological conditions and the characteristics of local plant and animal life, but with the number of sources in the area as well. The possibility of setting protection standards on the international level does not, however, lead necessarily to the conclusion that they should be set on the international level, and in many cases states may prefer to set their own protection standards since the desire for environmental protection and the willingness and ability to meet its costs vary. Even where purely local problems are involved, however, there may be a considerable economy of effort and a significant contribution to the pursuit of common goals in putting at the disposal of states recommendations for protection standards made by competent international organizations, particularly since the development of such standards often requires a complex and costly effort. Moreover, as noted above, there are some situations where international action to control pollution is to some extent required. In two of these cases, namely where the physical impact of pollutants is not confined to a single state and where there is international trade in goods whose production causes pollution, protection standards may be particularly useful.

Where the physical impact of pollutants is not confined to a single state, internationally agreed protection standards could provide the basis for international co-operation not only in protecting states from pollution discharged in other states but also in protecting areas of the biosphere beyond national jurisdictions. Protection standards would not themselves solve such problems, for compliance with them would usually depend on the control of the sources of pollution, but they would provide clear, quantitative goals on which to base the apportionment of allowed discharges. Thus, rather than basing the control of the sources of pollution on the fact that pollutants have crossed a national jurisdiction and caused some kind of harm, protection standards would allow states to decide what types of risks are unacceptable and to base further action on the occurrence of levels of pollution known to cause such unacceptable effects.

Where the need for international action arises from international trade in goods whose production causes pollution, internationally agreed protection standards might provide the basis on which states could avoid obstacles to pollution control caused by reluctance to impose added costs on producers as well as assure the full realization of the comparative advantage of having relatively low levels of pollution in the environment. How compliance with protection standards set for this purpose would be achieved could be left up to individual states. Differences in the number of polluters involved and in local environmental conditions, as well as in economic and political systems, would mean that states would be likely to choose different measures for bringing about compliance. It is just this flexibility that is needed in this case. If one state were able to avoid imposing discharge standards because its producers were located on a river with a large capacity for the pollutants in question, then it might have a comparative advantage in international trade, but this would be derived from a natural resource with which it happened to be richly endowed rather than from any lack of diligence about pollution control. Many developing countries might find international co-operation for pollution control based on protection standards to their advantage since they may often have fewer industrial polluters and lower levels of industrial pollutants in the environment. Again this would be a result of the objective conditions rather than any special exception.

Irrespective of the purpose of international co-operation in setting protection standards, some basic considerations concerning the organizational implications of setting these on the international level are appropriate. It may appear reasonable to suggest that the responsibility for developing at least some protection standards lies with existing international organizations competent with respect to particular media or targets. This proposition, however, ignores the need to take account of the costs of avoiding undesirable effects as well as the benefits of doing so. The protection of human health may lie clearly within the competence of the World Health Organization (WHO), but the degree to which human health should be protected from, for instance, the risks of heavy metals accumulating in human body tissues should be evaluated in the light of the costs of controlling their discharge from a variety of sources. Setting protection standards, in particular the primary protection standards on which the design of other means is based, may, therefore, require combinations of existing competence as well as special arrangements for taking into consideration costs and benefits that do not fall within the competence of existing organizations.

In addition to the organizational implications of actually setting protection standards on the international level, there are implications arising from the need for information on which these are based and for achieving consistency and completeness of protection standards. As idyllically rational as it is to set protection standards in the light of the costs and benefits of avoiding risks, the present state of knowledge with respect to most pollutants allows no more than a start in this direction. This situation is not only due to the difficulties of evaluating costs and benefits and of expressing them in comparable terms, but in the first place to ignorance of the risks themselves. A great deal of information is, of course, available on the effects of pollutants, but in order to set protection standards this information needs to be translated into quantitative assessments of the risks, that is of the expected frequency of undesirable effects at various levels of a pollutant in the targets and in the media. Only for ionizing radiations is a sufficiently expert and prestigious assessment of risks available; the results have received wide acceptance internationally. Ionizing radiation is, of course, a pollutant with a long history as well as with a number of characteristics that may make it relatively easy to assess risks. It is not, therefore, possible to suggest that all the procedures and methods applied in this case should be followed for other pollutants. It is, however, possible to suggest that what has been done for inoizing radiations is needed for other pollutants and that the use of an expert, intergovernmental committee could be an organizational model.

As for achieving consistency and completeness of protection standards, the organizational implications would be significant as well. The problems of consistency and completeness arise because a given pollutant may have undesirable effects on a number of targets, because en route to each of these it may pass through a number of media and because it may be released from a number of different types of sources. Consistency would, first, be served by authoritative assessments of the sources and pathways of pollutants as well as of their risks; it would appear reasonable to have these assessment functions performed by the same body. The problems of consistency and completeness are, however, complicated by the fact that the competence to set various standards for a given pollutant often lies with different international organizations. Thus, in addition to the need for assessments of pathways and sources, there would be a need for over-all review to assure that measures with respect to a given pollutant in various media are taken and that they are consistent with each other. The need for this over-all review function is in a sense the ultimate lesson for international organizations of the many recent discussions of ecological systems: if international organizations are to handle environmental problems, they shall have to behave much more like a self-conscious system than like the family that they still are in fact. Judging from past experience, the formal legal links among international organizations and the many co-ordination committees of their representatives are not likely to provide the solution.

B. *Discharge Standards*

A discharge standard is a maximum acceptable release of a pollutant from a given source to a specified medium under specified conditions. These standards differ fundamentally from protection standards, for they establish norms for the behavior of individual polluters while protection standards establish norms for targets or media in the environment.

Discharge standards have been set on the international level only infrequently, and their potential role in future international action does not appear to be as great as that of protection standards. As noted above, the need for limiting the discharge of pollutants in order to achieve a given level of environmental quality varies with factors such as climate, topography, hydrology and the number of sources of the pollutant in question. Thus, it may not be necessary to impose the same discharge standards on automobiles, for instance, in Calcutta as in New York in order to keep the pollutants discharged from automobiles below the level at which they adversely affect human health. Indeed, international discharge standards applied uniformly would in many cases place a burden on developing countries that cannot be justified even in strictly environmental terms because developing countries usually have fewer sources of industrial pollution. As a result, the setting of discharge standards, even where common objectives are concerned is often best left to national and even local authorities.

There are, however, some cases in which international agreements on discharge standards may be needed. For many pollution problems there exist "problem-sheds" — areas within which the levels of pollution are relatively or even completely independent of the discharge of pollutants elsewhere. The boundaries of these problem-sheds do not necessarily correspond to national jurisdictions and do not necessarily lie within a single state. Thus, international co-operation may be required in setting discharge standards in the basins of international rivers, semi-enclosed ocean basins and international "air-sheds." The situation is particularly complex since parts of any single state may lie in several problem-sheds since the sheds for different pollution problems do not in general coincide and since the problem-sheds do not necessarily correspond to the regions which have been defined for other purposes. The likely result is that special regional intergovernmental arrangements will be formed to deal with specific pollution problems. These pollution control arrangements will not necessarily be congruent with other regional arrangements such as the Economic Commissions of the United Nations, the FAO Fisheries Commissions, regional security arrangements or regional economic communities.

In each of these special intergovernmental arrangements, one of the major problems is likely to be the apportionment of the allowed discharges of pollutants. This type of problem is always a knotty one, as the negotiation of commodity agreements shows. It may be particularly difficult in the case of pollution control because states are likely to find themselves co-operating with other states with whom they do not normally co-operate in other regional matters and with states whose social and economic systems and development vary widely. Some formulas for apportioning the allowed discharge of pollutants may be worked out, such as uniform percentage reduction in discharges, equal per capita discharges or even uniform discharge standards. Each of these ways of determining discharge standards would, however, shift the burden of pollution control so that bargaining may arise. If it were possible for the international community to provide some guidelines indicating either how the allowed discharges should be apportioned or how the bargaining process should be conducted, such guidelines might contribute significantly to reaching agreements.

The need for international discharge standards may also arise in the case of those few pollution problems for which the "problem-shed" is global or near-global rather than regional. The number of such global problems is, fortunately, very limited. At present, the most likely candidates for inclusion in this category appear to be DDT and other persistent chlorinated hydrocarbons, mercury and other heavy metals, carbon dioxide in the atmosphere and oil in the oceans. Apportioning the allowed discharge of pollutants among the many states contributing to each of these problems, even if agreement could be reached on the goals desired, may be quite difficult. In some cases, these problems may pose greater risks locally than internationally, and standards based on national interests may contribute significantly to lessening the international impact. For oil in the oceans, the apportionment problem has already been solved in part: the discharge standards imposed by the 1954 Convention for Prevention of Pollution of the Sea by Oil (as amended 1962 and 1969) are the same for all ships irrespective of the flags they fly. No special provisions were made for variations in the costs to different shipowners of complying or for variations in the economic and social development of the flag states. The results are not entirely unsatisfactory: eighty per cent of the world's oil tankers are equipped to comply with the Convention. The fact that non-compliance appears to be more common among developing countries is not, however, entirely satisfactory either.

More important, perhaps, than compliance or non-compliance with the 1954 Convention is the possibility that the deliberate discharge of oil by ships may not be the major source of oil in the oceans. It now appears as if more oil may be reaching the oceans from land-based sources — either via the atmosphere or via rivers and direct discharge into the oceans — than from ships. If this is the case, the discharge standards imposed on ships may be placing an unduly heavy burden on a single source; perhaps discharge standards or other restraints should be imposed on land-based sources of oil as well. The problem at present with such a suggestion is that there is no international body within whose competence the setting of such discharge standards clearly lies. If, as seems to be the case, "oil in the oceans" is the proper definition of this problem rather than "oil from ships," then there is a need for some revision or extension of the legal machinery dealing with this problem.

Similar considerations apply to the other global or near-global problems cited above, as well as to the many other problems of regional international significance and, for that matter, to more localized problems. If discharge standards are to be set, the burden of control may be unfairly distributed and control itself less effective than it might be unless all the sources of the problem are taken into account, though it may be well that different approaches will be taken to limiting the release of a pollutant from different sources. The importance of this comprehensiveness of approach, even where only a single pollutant or set of problems is in question, has been explicitly recognized in the preparations for dealing with with marine pollution at the United Nations Conference on the Human Environment. The Intergovernmental Working Group on Marine Pollution is charged with considering all sources of marine pollution: ship-based, land-based and bottom-based. Any future organizational arrangements concerned with discharge standards — even if only in an advisory capacity — should probably also be given this breadth of scope in dealing with sources of pollution.

C. *Technological Standards*

Technological standards are norms concerned with the performance and design of those technologies or operations leading to the release of pollutants. Thus, technological standards, like discharge standards, are concerned with the behavior of sources of pollution; indeed, discharge standards might have been considered as a special case of technological standards applied to a single aspect of the operations of a polluter, namely the discharge of pollutants. This has not been done because the problems that arise in using technological standards as a means of controlling pollution are not the same as those that arise in the case of discharge standards. In particular, since technological standards are usually applied uniformly to all sources of pollution of the same type, for example to all oil tankers or to all manufacturers of benzene, the problem of apportioning the allowed discharges may not arise.

In addition, technological standards differ from discharge standards in that they tell a polluter precisely how to comply rather than setting a limit with which he can comply in any way he sees fit. This means that those setting technological standards need to know not only what is required in the way of limiting the discharge of pollutants in order to achieve the desired levels of environmental quality but also what means are available to a given polluter in order to limit the discharge of pollutants. Aside from the added burden upon those setting the standards, there is the possibility that various polluters, even though engaged in the same type of activity, would limit their discharge of pollutants in different ways if given the choice. If, for instance, one steel manufacturer prefers to limit his discharge of sulfur dioxide by installing a particular cleaning device while another prefers to limit the discharge by changing the process by which he manufactures steel, a technological standard that requires all steel manufacturers to install the cleaning device would not be well received by the latter. Such a standard may in fact impose unnecessary costs and increase resistance to pollution control.

Despite these difficulties, technological standards may often prove useful, particularly when there is no wide choice as to the means of control or where one means of control is clearly superior to others. Moreover, where pollution arises from the use of products in which there is international trade, uniformity in product standards, some of which may be considered a special case of technological standards, may be desirable in order to avoid the creation of non-tariff barriers by the imposition of various standards by different national governments. At present, product standards for the control of emissions from automobiles are probably the most important kind of technological standard, it might be called a "use" standard, for products like DDT and other pesticides in which there is international trade. These would specify not the design of the product in question but appropriate uses for it, so that if it were decided to reduce the use of a substance like DDT through international co-operation, this could be done for those uses for which substitutes are available while maintaining supplies for what might be considered essential uses. Otherwise, individual states might prohibit the manufacture of DDT altogether, thus cutting off supplies needed urgently in developing countries for malaria control.

A number of technological standards have been set on the international level, though in many cases these are concerned primarily with safety and may contribute to pollution control only incidentally. The problems that arise from the uniform imposition of technological standards without regard to the preferences of individual operators are not so crucial in the case of many of these international technological standards because they are recommendations with little binding force; in formulating national legislation states may adapt the standards to their own needs. This is not, however, entirely the case since the International Atomic Enerby Agency (IAEA) Standards, among others, may possess considerable binding force. These usually apply, however, to activities in which there has been a long-standing concern with strict safety precautions from which arises a consensus on "good practices."

It has been possible to set these technological standards, irrespective of their binding force, because some international organizations possess the necessary technical competence to deal with the details of the operations conducted within their areas of legal competence. This technical competence often derives from agency activities which aim primarily at promotion rather than at control. In some cases the international organizations are themselves involved in activities for which they recommend technological standards; in others they are in close contact with those who are involved in these activities. This is unavoidable in many instances, for the expertise needed for technological standard-setting can often be obtained only at first hand. Thus, as desirable as the separation of promotional and control activities may be in principle, in the case of technological standards there is a need for close ties between the promoters and the controllers.

If only safety — in the sense of protecting those directly involved in dangerous activities — were in question, this need for close ties between promoters and controllers in setting technological standards might not raise serious difficulties except in those few cases where operators are truly irresponsible.

No shipowner or captain wants to wreck an oil tanker, and no public utility wants to have a nuclear reactor run wild. Pollution control may, however, be a somewhat different matter. The operator of a factory in which mercury is used may be willing to take every precaution to avoid danger of poisoning the factory workers, but the effects of the mercury discharged from that factory on those who eat the fish in which the mercury has accumulated are far removed from his immediate concerns. Technological standards that aim at controlling pollution may even conflict with those that aim at safety since one possible safety measure in dealing with dangerous materials is to discharge them into the environment. In some cases, the interpretation given to safety has been broad enough to avoid such conflicts in technological standards, as in the case of many activities in which radioactivity is used. The needed concern for pollution control — whether there is a conflict between this goal and safety or not — does not, however, necessarily arise from the immediate concerns of those engaged in activities that lead to the discharge of pollutants or from the most immediate concersn of those setting technological standards for the safety of these activities.

As a result, there may be a need for a continuing review of the situation with respect to technological standards from the point of view of controlling pollution. A body whose primary concern is environment may not be able, for lack of the technical expertise that derives from engaging in the activities that lead to the discharge of pollutants or from promoting these activities, to set technological standards for pollution control. It may, however, be able to point out where new technological standards or the revision of existing technological standards are needed and where there appears to be a conflict between the concerns for safety and for pollution control. The actual setting of technological standards, as well as the revision of existing standards and the reconciliation of conflicts between safety and environmental concerns, might remain with those specialized bodies that already possess the legal and technical competence required or, where lacking, be delegated to specialized *ad hoc* bodies. Such a division of responsibilities would not only help to avoid duplication and to limit the size of any new body concerned with environment, but would also allow for the fullest use of existing resources.

D. *Complete Prohibitions*

Any standard may imply a prohibition in the sense that non-conformance with the standard is prohibited. This is not, however, the type of prohibition in question here. Rather, it is the complete prohibition of either the discharge of pollutants or activities which lead to the discharge pollutants. In a sense, the former type of prohibition is an extreme case of a discharge standard and the latter type of prohibition is an extreme case of a technological standard. What is common to prohibitions of this type is that they tell a polluter precisely what he must avoid doing in order to comply.

Prohibitions are, as a result, a common means of legal control where the objective is the elimination of undesirable activities, as is the case in much criminal law. Just for this reason, however, prohibitions have only a limited usefulness in pollution control, for the object of pollution control is rarely to eliminate a pollutant from the environment altogether. More often, it is the control of discharges so that the level of a pollutant in the environment is below what is considered acceptable, and only rarely does the achievement of such levels involve the elimination, as opposed to the limitation, of pollutant discharges. This is the case both because the environment often has some capacity to receive pollutants without harm and because some damage may be considered acceptable in the light of the cost of prohibiting the discharge of pollutants or the activities producing them. If, as some proponents of pollution control have urged, we were simply to "turn off the tap" wherever pollutants were being discharged, the effects might, in many instances, be a great deal more catastrophic than those of present environmental problems. The capacity of the environment to "re-cycle" pollutants is an important natural resource. This resource, like others, may need to be managed and conserved, but economic and social development would not be possible without using it as well.

Prohibitions do, however, have a role as a means of controlling pollution. The discharge of some pollutants under certain circumstances may entail risks so great that they cannot be justified even in terms of significant benefits. This argument has been used in favor of the prohibition of super-sonic transport and of DDT, though in both of these instances the

190

proposition that the risks so overwhelm the benefits that a prohibition is appropriate has not, at least up to now, been proven. In other cases, the risks or costs may not be so great, but a prohibition may still be considered justifiable because there are less dangerous courses of action available. The validity of this argument depends on the availability to the parties involved of the expertise and resources needed to make use of the alternatives. In a case like the ocean dumping of chemical weapons, there are viable alternatives available to those few states involved in this practice, since these are in general among the most technologically advanced and economically developed states. In the case of the use of DDT or in the case of the ocean dumping of radioactive wastes, however, the alternatives may be available only in theory to many of the states involved.

In still other cases, the distribution of the risks and benefits as well as their absolute or relative magnitudes may make a prohibition appropriate. It matters little to a non-nuclear state receiving fall-out from atmospheric testing of nuclear weapons that the tests are justified to the state conducting them on the basis of the benefits to its own national security. This may be part of the reason why there is now a Nuclear Test Ban Treaty, though the availability of underground testing as an alternative to atmospheric testing and the magnitude of the risks involved in the latter played a part as well. The distribution of costs and benefits may also be part of the reason why there is a Convention on Prevention of Pollution of the Sea by Oil that prohibits the intentional discharge of oil in specified zones; there is also growing pressure for the complete prohibition of intentional discharges. Though the costs of this practice in terms of damage to beach amenities may be considerable, it is not clear that avoiding these costs is justified on a purely economic basis when the costs of installing the necessary equipment on ships and in harbors is taken into account. The fact that all coastal states may suffer damage to beach amenities, irrespective of the benefits they may derive from the tanker trade, along with the existence of alternatives to the deliberate discharge of oil that are not prohibitively expensive may contribute to the appropriateness of a prohibition in this case.

Similar considerations may apply as well to other pollutants of current concern, including the deliberate discharge of mercury from factories into rivers and oceans: the alternative of preventing such discharges altogether appears to be technologically feasible and economically reasonable, and the costs of mercury pollution in terms of both damage to human health and to fishing industries through the seizure of contaminated fish have been considerable. Moreover, these costs are incurred irrespective of any benefits a state may derive from factories that are discharging mercury. The prohibition of such discharges of mercury may be a subject that is becoming ripe for intergovernmental agreement.

In the present international system, prohibitions are normally imposed by the conclusion of a formal treaty, and effective prohibition does ap-

191

pear to depend on intergovernmental agreement. The conclusion of a formal treaty is, however, both costly and time-consuming. It may be that where the risks of pollution are readily apparent and the costs of prohibiting the discharge of a pollutant or an activity that leads to the discharge of pollutants are not so great, that the need for action can be satisfied more readily through resolutions and declarations rather than treaties. Moreover, where international transportation activities are involved — like the super-sonic transport or the deliberate discharge of oil — it may be argued that individual states can protect themselves by prohibiting the vehicles in question— in these cases either the super-sonic transport itself or ships that are not equipped to avoid discharging oil deliberately - from their national jurisdictions. Such unilateral action does, however, have its disadvantages and is likely to be used only rarely.

Multilateral complete prohibitions are likely to be imposed rarely as well for the reasons cited above, but when they are needed, existing international organizations may well provide appropriate forums in which intergovernmental agreements can be reached. The sources of pollution often fall within the legal and technical competence of these organizations, as in the case of deliberate oil pollution from ships. In such cases, existing organizations may appropriately handle any need for a prohibition, though where there is a conflict between the promotional and control functions, a body concerned with environmental problems generally might be useful in prompting the consideration of a prohibition. In other cases, the sources of a pollutant may not fall within the competence of a single organization or any existing organization. Again, a body concerned with environmental problems generally on the international level might prove useful in reconciling conflicts and promoting co-ordinated action as well as in taking up the substance of those problems which do not fall to any existing organization.

E. *Effluent Charges and Price Adjustments*

Effluent charges and price adjustments can be used either in combination with various standards imposed on the sources of pollution or by themselves as a means of controlling pollution under certain conditions. Where the discharge of pollutants can be measured accurately and routinely, charges levied on this discharge are a disincentive to pollute. Unless the cost of these effluent charges, as they are usually called, can be passed on by the polluter, he must take them into account. Some polluters may institue controls while others may prefer to continue discharging pollutants and pay the charges, but by adjusting the charges the desired levels of pollutants in the environment may be reached. Even when the discharge of pollutants cannot be measured accurately and routinely but the discharge of pollutants is inherent in the use of a given material, adjustments in the price of this material can be used in much the same way as charges levied on its discharge. Such effluent charges and price adjustments differ from standards, whether technological or discharge, and prohibitions in that they do not set norms for what is to be done to control pollution but rather leave up to those discharging pollutants the choice both as to the means of control and the extent of control.

This flexibility allowed by effluent charges and price adjustments is unique among the means of controlling pollution discussed here, and it may often be a significant advantage. Discharge standards and technological standards could be tailored to suit the varying needs and preferences of those discharging pollution, but this is difficult to do without raising the possibility of bargaining in each individual case. Moreover, the use of standards, particularly technological standards, requires that a great deal be known about how the sources of pollution can be controlled, whereas effluent charges and price adjustments leave this burden with the polluter. Moreover, effluent charges and price adjustments provide a continuing incentive, so long as pollutants are being discharged, for the discovery of new control techniques, recycling wastes, and the use of less polluting processes and materials. Standards may also provide some incentive in this direction, but once compliance has been achieved the incentive is solely for cheaper rather than better means of control.

For these reasons, effluent charges and price adjustments appear to be gaining popularity in many countries as a means of controlling pollution, although in some countries there still appear to be constitutional inhibiabout using these means. It remains to be seen how they will work in practice in different types of economies. The most extensive experience with effluent charges appears to have been in the Ruhr River basin, where they have been used with considerable, though not unqualified, success. The United States Government has proposed a price adjustment on leaded gasoline in the form of a tax on lead. It is, however, of interest to note that this has been proposed as an interim measure, intended explicitly as an incentive to oil companies to find ways of making satisfactory non-leaded gasolines, which is to be followed by a complete prohibition of leaded gasoline.

Internationally there would in many cases be serious practical difficulties in reaching agreements among states to impose effluent charges and price adjustments, although it is not clear that the difficulties would be any greater than those encountered in reaching binding agreements for the imposition of many standards. If agreement could be reached, however, there would appear to be no fundamental reason why effluent charges and price adjustments could not be used as a means of controlling pollution in many international "problem-sheds," such as the basins of international rivers, semi-enclosed ocean basins and international airsheds. States might be unwilling to permit international administration of the funds collected, but so far as the effect on the release of pollutants is concerned who administers these funds is largely irrelevant.

This is not to say, however, that the use of effluent charges and price adjustments internationally would not be faced with some serious practical problems. It is difficult to picture these charges and adjustments being used unless they were mandatory, whereas discharge standards and technological standards, and even prohibitions, may be effective even if they are only recommendations. States could, in the absence of binding agreements, institute a kind of effluent charge or price adjustment through the imposition of tariffs on materials whose production or use causes pollution, but in addition to being effective only insofar as there is international trade in the materials in question, such unilateral action could lead to a tariff "war" with many adverse effects. Moreover, effluent charge and price adjustments may be highly inequitable in terms of the economic position of those who would bear the costs. It has been proposed, for instance, that pollution due to DDT could be reduced by raising its price, but both within individual countries and internationally this would impose heavy burdens on those least able to pay, namely farmers and developing countries. This inequity might be solved by providing special subsidies, but this would greatly increase both the complexity and difficulty of implementation.

Using either effluent charges or price adjustments on the international level would be a major innovation, although in the case of price adjustments there may be precedents in areas other than pollution control. Effluent charges, in particular, would require close international co-operation among states in a given "problem-shed" area not only in imposing and revising the charges as necessary but also in monitoring the discharge of pollutants. Effluent charges may, however, have an advantage over discharge standards insofar as they can be applied uniformly, thus avoiding the problem of apportioning the allowed dishcarges. On the other hand, price adjustments do not require measurements of the discharge of pollutants and might be imposed through existing tariff agreements and national tax or price policies, though the possible problems arising from the inequitable distribution of the added costs would remain.

II. PROMOTING COMPLIANCE

A. *Liability*

Liability for damage can promote compliance in two ways: through the deterrent effect on a polluter of knowing that he may be required to pay compensation for the damage he causes and through the technological standards imposed on a polluter as conditions for insurance. These two mechanisms are to a large extent mutually exclusive, for a polluter seeks insurance in order to avoid paying the full costs of compensation. The polluter, therefore, reduces the deterrent effect of liability for damage at the same time that he becomes subject to standards imposed as conditions for insurance.

Whether operating through the mechanism of deterrence or through the mechanism of standards imposed as conditions for insurance, the usefulness of liability as a means of promoting compliance requires that it be possible to show that particular damages were caused by pollutants from a particular source, where the notion of damages is dependent on the existence of a legal right to undamaged possession or enjoyment. This is a serious limitation in a world where knowledge is far from complete, where many polluters may contribute to a single pollution problem, where synergistic effects may occur and where there exist common-property resources. Pollution problems frequently resemble traffic jams more than automobile accidents: there are many participants rather than just one or two; the cause of the problem lies in the individual decisions of these many to do what, except for the existence of so many others, might be acceptable rather than in a single error or unlawful act; and there often exist thresholds below which no problem would exist. Traffic lights, rules of the road, tolls and many other means of control that do not require the assignment of responsibilities may not work well, but they are surely more useful in controlling traffic than the imposition of liability on each driver for lost time and frayed nerves caused to others. Similarly, though liability is an appealing means of promoting compliance insofar as it assigns to the polluter the costs of damage caused by pollution, its usefulness is very limited.

There are, however, some instances in which liability may be useful. In the case of the Trail Smelter, it was possible to trace specific damages to property in one state causally to a specific source of pollution in another state, though the fact that this could be done was due in part to the relatively unpolluted air in the vicinity and the absence of other possible sources of the pollutant in question. In terms of complexity and difficulty of proof, the "black snow" in Sweden which is allegedly caused by air pollutants from Great Britain is probably more typical, so it is unlikely that the Trail Smelter case has been an effective deterrent. Liability is likely to prove more useful in cases where large-scale pollution incidents are involved, particularly if caused by an accident against the occurrence of which insurance may be obtained. The 1969 Inter-governmental Maritime Consultative Organization (IMCO) Convention on Civil Liability for Oil Pollution Damage is the outstanding example on the international level. The deterrent effect of the liability imposed can be of little importance: liability for damage due to oil pollution arising from the wreck of a tanker can hardly increase the deterrent to a tanker owner of losing a ship at sea. Along with the liability imposed, however, is a requirement for

195

owners to maintain insurance or other financial security; the technological standards imposed as conditions for obtaining this protection are most likely to contribute to pollution control.

Technological standards imposed as conditions for insurance are particularly important on the international level because the capacity and authority to impose binding standards and to bring about compliance with these is limited. Moreover, the setting of technological standards by international organizations is often a slow process involving negotiations among experts, as well as among the representatives of states in those cases where the standards are more than recommendations. A truly independent and responsible insurer may be able to act more quickly and, in many cases, as effectively, though the standards imposed by insurers may not be the same as those that would be imposed by governments and by international organizations. The same degree of effectiveness cannot be expected from insurers who are not truly independent and, in particular, from self-insurance arrangements. These may provide adequately for compensation, but they cannot be expected to impose technological standards.

Besides oil pollution, the most likely candidates at present for liability imposed internationally would appear to be pollution arising from the transport of "dangerous cargoes" other than oil and from the disposal of noxious agents in the oceans. In both of these cases, it appears likely that when damage occurs it should often be possible to trace it to a specific source. In the case of dangerous cargoes, technological standards imposed as conditions for insurance could well serve to prevent damage, but it is not clear whether it would be possible to obtain insurance in the case of the disposal of noxious agents in the oceans considering the routine, as opposed to accidental, nature of this practice and the long time lag which may pass before damage occurs. Moreover, in both these cases liability is relevant only where there exists a right to undamaged enjoyment and may, therefore, be relatively ineffective so long as damage is done only to the high seas or the fish therein.

In terms of organizational implications, the imposition of liability can probably be handled readily by existing international organizations in the cases of the transport of dangerous cargoes and the disposal of noxious agents in the oceans, if states are willing to take action along these lines. Other cases may arise in which the competence to bring states together in order to prepare the necessary legal instrument will not be so clear, but since the imposition of liability is a one-time event and need not require continuing evaluation or revision, it can probably be handled on an *ad hoc* basis.

B. *Registration and Licensing*

Registration, despite its apparently mild character compared to licesning,

196

can be an important means of promoting compliance. The information obtained can be used in the formulation of measures for controlling pollution so as to minimize the costs and difficulties of compliance. Indeed, in the absence of information such as how much radioactive material is dumped in the oceans and where, or what polychlorinated biphenyl compounds are being manufactured and for what purposes, it is almost impossible to begin to formulate appropriate control measures other than complete prohibitions. Where an international problem-shed is involved, knowledge of the sources of pollutants and the amounts released to the environment is of particular importance. Registration must be carefully designed in order to reveal this information since, for instance, a user of coal may not even know that when he burns coal he releases mercury to the environment, but with careful design a major contribution can be made to accounting for the presence of various pollutants in the environment and to clarifying the various approaches which may be taken to limiting them to acceptable levels. Thus, even if the burning of coal is a major source of mercury in the environment it may still turn out that limiting the levels of mercury can be accomplished more readily and less expensively through controlling its release from factories which use it as a catalyst. Such a determination may, however, require that the amounts of mercury being discharged from both types of sources be known, whether though registration or some other means.

Licensing is different from registration because it involves not only a transfer of information but also a determination as to whether given activities that may lead to pollution or the release of pollutants are permissible prior to the event itself. Licensing may, therefore, be viewed as a combination of registration with some type of standard, with determination as to whether compliance with the standard is achieved being made prior to the occurrence of a violation. Clearly, such a permit system has significant advantages over a system in which compliance is checked only after the event, but it has significant administrative costs as well. There is as well the issue of "licenses to pollute," but so long as licensing is not used to make special exceptions that make compliance with set protection standards impossible or difficult, this would appear to be an emotional rather than a substantive charge. Licenses are, in fact, used effectively to control many activities. It can hardly be said that a driver's license is a license to kill pedestrians or that a pilot's license is a license to crash airplanes; the purpose of such licenses is in fact to prevent damage from what in many ways are important and beneficial activities. The same applies to licenses issued for many activities which, in the absence of controls, would cause damage due to pollution.

In addition to the usual practice of issuing licenses or permits to individuals or to enterprises on condition of fulfilling certain standards, there exists a proposal for a variant of licensing which would combine registration with effluent charges. Under what is usually called a scheme of "discharge warrants," licenses for the discharge of pollutants would be sold, with the total warranted amount of discharge being less than that which is known would cause protection standards in a given problem-shed to be exceeded. This would create a market in what is sometimes referred to as "assimilative capacity" of the environment for a given pollutant, although assimilation may be a misleading term since protection standards may be set at a level higher than that at which no damage at all is known to occur. If more polluters want to enter a given problem-shed or if those already there want to expand, they would either have to purchase discharge warrants or, if they considered the price too high, limit their release of pollutants. Such a scheme shares the advantages and disadvantages of effluent charges. It has the added advantage of eliminating the need for administrative manipulation of the prices charged since these would be governed by a market mechanism.

On the international level, intergovernmental agreements and recommendations of international organizations may provide for registration with or licensing by national governments or international organizations themselves. Pesticides, for example, have been registered by national governments in accordance with the recommendations of the World Health Organization (WHO) and the Food and Agricultural Organization (FAO). Licensing by national governments in accordance with intergovernmental agreement has been proposed by the United States Draft Convention for ocean dumping, although international organizations may possibly play a role in the setting of standards as conditions for the issuance of permits by national governments if something like the U.S. Draft Convention comes into force. Examples of registration by international organizations are the IAEA register of radioactive materials dumped in the oceans and the United Nations register of space satellites. There are, as well, a number of arrangements for reporting to international organizations which, although not called registration, are closely analogous to it; such arrangements may also prove useful in the formulation of measures for controlling pollution.

A number of proposals have been made for registration or licensing by international organizations beyond what is now being done. In the preparations for the Stockholm Conference, proposals have been put forward for a Registry of Chemical Compounds and for inventories of pollution discharges to the marine environment. The many difficulties with such proposals include the sensitivities of governments concerning the information involved, determining criteria for what should be reported or registered, administrative and technical complexities for both international organizations and governments in collecting and processing the information, and assuring the compatibility of information from many sources. Even before these difficulties are faced, however, it must be asked what purposes registration would serve, for these may vary from purely technical and scientific purposes to the more political and administrative purpose of formulating control measures. The requirements of the different users involved are not necessarily the same, and the design of a registration scheme will have to take this into account.

C. *Technical Assistance*

Technical assistance can be used as a means of promoting compliance in two ways: directly, by providing those who have pollution problems with aid in obtaining the technical means to comply; and indirectly, by making the provision of technical assistance, whose primary purpose may not be pollution control but rather the promotion of economic or social development, conditional on compliance with standards concerned with pollution control. These uses of technical assistance as a means of controlling pollution are independent, and the issues involved in each are distinct.

As for the provision of technical assistance on environmental problems themselves, the need is already considerable and can be expected to grow. Just as technology has played a role in the creation of pollution problems, it can also play a role in their solution. Many of the methods available for solving pollution problems — including treatment plants for water pollution, precipitators for air pollutants, recycling materials which would otherwise become waste, as well as many of the methods for detecting pollution and for avoiding it through the use of alternative means — are technology-intensive. Moreover, the need for technology-intensive methods of pollution control is not limited to those countries or to those polluters who are technologically advanced. Industry is but one of many sources of pollution. Agriculture, particularly when it is aided by modern fertilizers and pesticides, can produce eutrophication in lakes, hazards to wild life and, where poultry or livestock is raised on a large scale, major problems in waste management. Population density, regardless of the state of economic development, can contribute significantly to pollution problems. Modern agricultural methods and urbanization are not limited to the technologically advanced countries.

International organizations have already provided technical assistance on the analysis and solution of pollution problems, although this is often done in the context of technical assistance on natural resource management rather than being limited to pollution control alone, and such technical assistance is not usually provided in order to promote compliance with specific standards. This is especially true in the case of water pollution and water resources management, a topic of concern to a number of United Nations bodies, where the goals of economic development and pollution control are often mutually reinforcing or at least compatible. The provision of technical assistance by international organizations is not, however, limited to the sending of experts to developing countries. The setting of various standards relevant to pollution control by interna-

199

tional organizations is also a kind of technical assistance insofar as it enables states to utilize expertise that is not available locally or that is needed for other tasks.

The need for technical assistance, whether on pollution problems themselves or as part of natural resources management, is likely to grow with both economic development and the increasing awareness of environmental problems. Moreover, measures taken on the international level to control pollution may increase even further the need for technical assistance. Thus, for example, compliance with the limits on the deliberate discharge of oil imposed by the 1954 (as amended 1962 and 1969) Convention on Prevention of Pollution of the Sea by Oil requires the installation of special equipment on tankers and in ports; some of the non-compliance with the Convention may be attributable to the lack of the technical, as well as financial, resources needed to do this. Whether the increasing demand is to be met from existing resources or whether new finances and expertise are to be made available to those organizations, national and international, that provide technical assistance internationally remains a question to be resolved, insofar as the United Nations system is concerned, at the Stockholm Conference.

However this question is answered, fulfilling the increasing need for technical assistance on pollution problems and their solutions would not appear to necessitate any major organizational rearrangements or innovations. Existing international organizations given adequate financial resources would appear to be capable of handling most requests for technical assistance on pollution problems. Where this may not be the case, there must be some question as to whether a body concerned with environmental problems generally would be able to respond either, for such a body could not be expected to possess technical expertise adequate to every contingency. Indeed, there is some question as to whether any new body concerned with environmental problems should even attempt, at least at first, to provide technical or other assistance on specific projects, because many of the needs can be fulfilled by existing agencies and because this might draw resources away from other priorities.

Making the provision of technical assistance whose primary purpose is not controlling pollution conditional on compliance with pollution control standards is done to only a very limited extent at present by international organizations. The most striking example is the IAEA Standards, compliance with which may be made mandatory in activities for which the IAEA provides assistance as well as in the activities of the IAEA itself. The IAEA case is, however, unusual in that the IAEA is an organization whose purposes and competence are linked directly to a single type of material that may become a pollutant. No other United Nations body is in quite the same position. There may be a number of national bodies which provide technical assistance internationally in this position, but there are both practical and legal difficulties in one state dictating to another stan-

200

dards or other measures for controlling pollution as conditions for receiving bilateral technical assistance.

In the United Nations system, there may be some room for expansion to other organizations of the IAEA approach, although where this is appropriate could only be decided after an extensive study of the impact in each case, in order to avoid interference with other priorities. Moreover, constitutional revisions may be required to institute the mandatory application of standards to projects aided by international organizations. It is more likely, at least in the immediate future, that international organizations will follow the lead of the International Bank for Reconstruction and Development which, rather than making the provision of assistance contingent upon compliance with set standards, evaluates proposed projects from an environmental point of view and includes this evaluation in its over-all decision-making process. This practice could be readily extended to other organizations.

It might also be possible to delegate responsibility for evaluation of United Nations-aided projects from an environmental point of view, or for receiving and evaluating "impact" statements from sponsoring agencies, to an independent body. This could raise problems with respect to interagency relations, and the competence to conduct evaluations might in some cases be difficult to obtain. Independent evaluation by bodies not providing assistance would, however, have its advantages, particularly if the body conducting them did not itself provide assistance. There appears to be a tendency in national governments toward establishing independent high-level bodies responsible for such evaluations; the United Nations might benefit by moving in this direction as well.

D. Subsidies and Compensations

Controlling pollution, except in unusual cases, costs money. Moreover, depending on what measures are taken, the costs may not be equitably distributed. These costs and inequities can be significant hindrances to controlling pollution; subsidies and compensations are, respectively, aids to overcoming these hindrances. Both subsidies and compensations may take many forms — direct payments or grants, tariff concessions, trade concessions — but in general they provide some sort of financial incentive to compliance. Neither subsidies nor compensations have in the past been used extensively on the international level to promote pollution control, but subsidies are frequently used for other purposes: the promotion of exonomic development and the maintenance of political, military and economic alliances or co-operation. No fundamental reason is apparent why subsidies and compensations should not be used more extensively for environmental purposes, although there are clearly limitations on the resources available, even among the richest countries, for this purpose.

The situation with subsidies is in part similar to the situation with respect to technical assistance, as discussed above. Environmental problems are not limited to wealthy countries any more than they are limited to technologically advanced countries. Though developing countries are relatively better off with respect to environmental quality and therefore have the opportunity to avoid some of the mistakes made by the developed countries, there are sometimes financial difficulties in doing so, and subsidies may help to overcome these difficulties. Moreover, as in the case of technical assistance, measures taken on the international level, such as internationally agreed standards, may increase further the need for subsidies. And again, the question of whether these needs are to be met, if at all, from existing resources remains unresolved; it appears highly unlikely, however, that in the case of financial assistance either developed or developing countries would favor taking resources away from economic development for the promotion of pollution control.

The usefulness of subsidies may not, however, be limited to those cases in which a state is in great financial need. Subsidies may also be useful where pollution discharged in one state causes damage to another state, irrespective of the economic development of the two, for the state in which the damage occurs could offer to subsidize the necessary measures for the control of pollution. Such a subsidy, sometimes referred to as a bribe, would be unlikely except that under certain conditions the state paying the subsidy might still be better off than it would if the pollution were allowed to continue. As unappealing as this may appear from the point of view of equity since it places the burden of the solution on the victim, it remain to be seen whether it might not in some cases work.

If the source of pollution were in a developing country and the victim were a developed country, there might be a greater incentive for the provision of subsidies discussed above. Due to the geographical distribution of developed and developing countries, this might appear unlikely, but where a pollutant has a global or near-global impact the control of pollution in both developing and developed countries may be required. Thus, if the prevention of damage due to DDT in developed countries requires restrictions on its use in developing countries because of its worldwide distribution in the atmosphere, it may be that developed countries can come out better off by providing developing countries with subsidies for the use of alternatives to DDT. Both would share in the benefits of the consequent reductions in the use of DDT.

In this case, however, as well as in others, what appears to be a subsidy might better be called compensation. The DDT being released to the environment through its use in developing countries would not be causing as serious damage if it were not for the DDT that has already accumulated in the environment, most of which appears to come from the earlier use of DDT in developed countries. Accordingly, it might be fair for those who have benefitted from the uncontrolled use of the environment to compensate those who have only recently had the opportunity to discharge pollutants, if this opportunity is to be denied in order to control pollution. Otherwise, international control of the discharge of pollutants places an inequitable burden on those who come latest to pollute; this inequity may force developing countries to oppose control and to avoid participating in needed agreements.

Compensations of this type have been used internationally in the past, including the direct payments in return for agreements not to exploit common-property resources. Unfortunately, the payment of compensation may create an incentive for states to increase undesirable activities in order to receive compensation when they agree to stop. In the case of abatement of pollution, however, this difficulty, if it arises, can probably be avoided by paying compensation partly on the basis of percentage reductions in the discharge of pollutants and partly on the basis of the absolute size of those reductions. Formulas of this type might not lead to the payment of compensation in the amount that is strictly speaking the value of the opportunity given up, but this would in any case be extremely difficult to determine; a more pragmatic approach with the desired result may be appropriate.

Many subsidies could be handled through existing bilateral and multilateral assistance programs, but this raises the problem of having pollution control compete for resources with the promotion of economic development. It might be preferable if, whenever internationally agreed measures are taken for pollution control, provisions were made for subsidizing at least part of the costs of compliance on the part of those who would otherwise be unable to comply for lack of sufficient financial resources. Similarly, whenever internationally agreed measures are taken, appropriate consideration might be given to whether some states should be compensated for the lost opportunity to pollute without causing harm that others have taken advantage of in the past. If this is to be done, however, it is necessary for countries that have contributed little, or even not at all, to environmental problems, in particular developing countries, to participate in such agreements.

E. *Planning and Forecasting*

On the national level, planning may play a major role as a means of promoting pollution control in general and compliance in particular, just as it has come to play a major role in many countries as a means of promoting economic and social development. Indeed, one important measure that can be taken on the national level is to incorporate pollution control goals into economic planning. Land-use planning may also be of particular importance. Pollution control is but one of a number of possible factors in determining appropriate land-uses but by including it among the relevant factors states can, to some extent, control the development of concentrations of various types of human activity that may produce pollution and locate such concentrations in those areas where pollutants will cause the least damage. Considerable savings in both pollution control and economic development can be derived by utilizing this means of control.

On the international level, the usefulness of this type of planning is very limited, although where common property resources such as international rivers, semi-enclosed ocean basins and even the oceans themselves are concerned a need may arise for international co-operation in planning for various uses. One case of particular importance is planning for the exploration and exploitation of the resources of the sea-bed and ocean floor beyond the limits of national jurisdiction. In this case, pollution control, as well as successful exploitation, may depend to a large degree on planning the areas to be subject to exploitation in such a way as to both open up rich deposits of minerals and to avoid interference with other legitimate uses of the marine environment, in particular shipping and fishing. Thus the object of pollution control in this case may not be so much the control of the discharge of pollutants as such, but rather the separation of mineral exploitation activities from other activities in order to reduce the likelihood that, for instance, the turbidity caused by gathering manganese nodules will cause damage to known stocks of living resources. The machinery for instituting such control does not yet exist, but the recent Declaration of Principles adopted by the United Nations General Assembly would appear to leave the way open for "sea-bed" or "ocean floor" - use planning by whatever regime is set up.

Types of planning other than land-use planning may also have a role as a means of achieving environmental quality on the international level, though these in general are subordinate to other means discussed above. There is, in the first place, the planning by international organizations of their own activities, which is usually undertaken at least one or two years in advance. This planning is not intended as a means of controlling pollution, but it may in fact contribute insofar as it puts states on notice that certain types of activities are to occur and thereby encourages both national and international action. Thus, the planning for events like th ECE Conference on Problems of the Environment (Prague 1971) and the United Nations Conference on the Human Environment (Stockholm 1972) is important not only for what occurs in Prague and Stockholm, but also because the preparations catalyze national awareness and actions. The preparation of national reports for these conferences appears to have been particularly important in this regard.

Secondly, international organizations can and do develop for subjects within their competence plans of action, the fulfillment of which depends on activities and events largely, though usually not entirely, beyond their immediate control. FAO's Indicative World Plan for Agricultural Development, the United Nations Strategy for the Second Development Decade and the Intergovernmental Oceanographic Commission's Long-

Term and Expanded Programme of Oceanographic Research are some of the more recent examples of this type of planning on the international level. So far as environment is concerned, it is not clear whether something like a "Comprehensive World Plan for the Human Environment" would be either feasible or useful at present, though a plan of action for the control of marine pollution and a plan of action for soil conservation may be two of the results of the Stockholm Conference. There are disadvantages to fragmenting environmental problems in this way, but there are also disadvantages in attempting to handle all subjects at once. Marine pollution and soil conservation are at present the subject of planning on the international level because they are topics of immediate, widespread international concern. It is only realistic to expect that planning on the international level will advance more rapidly on the more pressing common problems.

Such planning to deal with problems of current interest is not, however, sufficient for controlling pollution since environmental problems do not often stand still. Indeed, even in the case of marine pollution and soil conservation, action is being planned not only because these are current problems, but also because they are expected to become more acute in the future. There are, moreover, other developments that can be considered problems largely, or even solely, in the sense that they can be expected to cause damage in the future. Carbon dioxide and particulates in the atmosphere may be taken as examples of this type of problem, though the very nature of such problems is that even the determination of what is a problem is subject to considerable uncertainty. The need for planning on problems such as these does not arise solely because problems can be handled better if they are anticipated, but in some cases also because remedial action, to be effective, must be taken in advance of the time when the problem would otherwise have its greatest impact. For carbon dioxide and particulates to accumulate to the levels at which they may cause serious problems may take years; likewise, some time may be necessary before controls on their discharge are reflected in lower levels in the atmosphere.

The existence of problems with long lead-times creates a need for forecasting future problems as well as planning to deal with the growth in current problems. International organizations do forecast some developments relevant to environmental problems, such as population growth, industrialization, urbanization, and economic growth. Other environmental problems have been the subject of occasional forecasts by international organizations, such as the prediction by an expert panel convened by the World Health Organization that water supply problems will become more severe more quickly in developing than in developed countries.

There may, however, be a need for a more comprehensive, continuing approach to forecasting the future impact of specific pollution problems of international significance. Such forecasting might be only the first step in controlling pollution, but it could be an essential step insofar as it alerted governments and the competent organizations of the need to initiate action.

The need for such a continuing forecasting capability is made particularly acute by the environmental fashion of recent years. So many forecasts, reliable and unreliable, have been made that a point is being reached at which those responsible for taking action may not be able to respond to alarms because the alarm bell is ringing continuously. It would hardly do to remedy this situation by granting a monopoly on alarms to a single body, but it may be that there is a need for a "watchdog" body to evaluate the forecasts of others as well as to make its own. Such a body could then alert governments and international organizations in order that plans could be made in time for the various means of achieving environmental quality to be used. If, for instance, a forecast of the present problem of mercury in the oceans had been available even five years ago, protection standards for mercury could have been set, discharge standards imposed on factories and technological standards set for the use of mercurial fungicides. It can hardly be imagined, however, that this would have been done on the basis of forecasts as uncertain as those available today on many potential future problems.

If such an "early-warning" capacity were set up, it could not operate in isolation. Close ties to governments and international organizations would be required in order to carry out its "alerting" function. The "forecasting" function would require close ties to sources of scientific expertise in order to receive and evaluate the forecasts of others and to make its own forecasts. In addition, any monitoring of actual levels of pollutants in the environment and their effects would be useful both for "forecasting" and "alerting".

A Note on Terminology

An attempt has been made, throughout the text of the present paper, to use the terms defined by the Preparatory Committee for the United Nations Conference on the Human Environment at its third session (13-24 September 1971) for the discussions of pollution at Stockholm, or to use terms that are consistent with these. The relevant definitions of the Preparatory Committee are as follows:

Exposure: the amount of a particular physical or chemical agent that reaches the target.

Target (or *receptor*): the organism, population or resource to be protected from specified risks.

Risk: the expected frequency of undesirable effects arising from a given exposure to a pollutant.

Primary protection standard: an accepted maximum level of a pollutant (or its indicator) in the target, or some part thereof, or an accepted maximum intake of a pollutant into the target under specified circumstances.

Derived working levels (or *limits*): maximum acceptable levels of pollutants in specified media other than the targets designed to ensure that under specified circumstances a primary protection standard is not exceeded.

Discharge (or *effluent* or *emission*) *standard* or *release limit:* the maximum acceptable release of a pollutant from a given source to a specified medium under specified circumstances.

Technological standards (or *codes of practice*): concerned with the performance and design of those technologies or operations leading to the release of pollutants.

In addition, for the purposes of the present paper the term "protection standards" has been coined to cover both primary protection standards and derived working limits.

It should be noted that throughout the paper the term "standard" is used in the sense of a measure of what is acceptable or unacceptable, irrespective of binding force.

INTERNATIONAL ENVIRONMENTAL CONTROLS IN THE SCIENTIFIC AGE

by *Zdenek J. Slouka**

Introduction

This paper examines the role of science and technology in the politics of international environmental management. The scientific and technological component is one of the pervasive influences in all issues of environmental control. Yet critical inquiries into the relation between science and policy on the international level are scarce. How does the need for scientific and technical knowledge, the foundation of all environmental management, affect the political processes through which new international norms and mechanisms are being established?

In the pages below I argue two fundamental and related points.

The first is this: that efforts to create new global norms and institutions for environmental control by the slow traditional means such as multilateral conferences are very seriously misguided if they are relied upon as the primary mechanisms for the management of environmental alteration, that is, if they are not accompanied by decisive international responses to environmental issues on regional and bilateral levels, or if they weaken or sidetrack such more limited responses.

The second point is that even if the world community were capable of efficiently creating world-wide intergovernmental institutions and policies in some areas of environmental management, the question remains whether they should be created in every case. My argument is that we should critically assess every such instance on several discrete levels. Will the new global institution have enough flexibility to respond to the swift and largely unpredictable tides of scientific and technological change? How brittle may the initial political consensus prove to be under the stresses of change? Will the new intergovernmental institution

*The author is a Research Associate at the Institute for the Study of Science in Human Affairs, Columbia University; Fellow, Woodrow Wilson International Center for Scholars, Washington, D.C.

The work on this study was made possible by the Institute for the Study of Science in Human Affairs, Columbia University. I wish to express my thanks for extensive critical comments on earlier versions of this paper to Louis Henkin, Oliver Lissitzyn and Christopher Wright of Columbia University and to Warren S. Wooster of the Scripps Institution of Oceanography, University of California. I am also very grateful for numerous helpful comments offered by members of the Panel on International Law and the Global Environment of the American Society of International Law, by several participants of the Conference on Legal and Institutional Responses to Problems of the Global Environment, Arden House, N.Y., September 1971, and by Fellows of the Woodrow Wilson International Center for Scholars, Washington, D.C.

displace, weaken, or fortify other already existing or emerging non-governmental efforts in the same direction? Proposals have been advanced for the establishment of an international scientific research institute to be appended to a U.N. environmental unit for policy planning and review.[1] If it is at all possible, is it also wise? How would such an institute affect the complex web of co-operative relationships spun by non-governmental scientific organizations and by individual scientists across the world? Will it enhance, or will it undercut, the total contribution of international science to environmental management?

In essence, I question the general validity of several assumptions: that global institutions should be always preferred to more fragmented systems; that central direction is always better than a more diffuse decision-making structure; that intergovernmental commitment to international problem-solving is always more important, more functional and more desirable than the involvement of non-governmental groups; that we are somehow automatically helping along the United Nations and the world peace if we house under the U.N. roof every environmental problem that the international community encounters.

These points are derived primarily from an examination of four specific phenomena generated by the interplay of science and technology with international politics. Identified and discussed in the main body of this paper, the phenomena are described as interrelated traits representing a science-technology syndrome in international policy-making.

One prominent trait is the transfer of concepts and perspectives from the world of science to the world of politics. When scientific and technical data show an environmental problem to be global in scope, the demand follows almost automatically that the problem be solved by global norms and institutions; the question whether such a solution is politically feasible is often not even raised.

Another characteristic is the political role played by the collection and dissemination of scientific and technical data in international policy-making. In general, these processes are shown to expand and diversify the field of participants in the policy-making process and to make that process more complex and time-consuming.

The third trait has similar impacts. This is the futuristic orientation of international policy problems in which science and technology are significant ingredients; practically all questions of environmental management fit that category. The scientific and technological content of these issues is capable of mobilizing into political action even groups which are not as yet in any way affected by the issues, but seek to insure that their possible future interests, however they may define them, will not be adversely affected by the actions of others.

Finally, the high-level concern with economic values which characterizes all problems of technological management, especially on the international scale, is the fourth trait of the science-technology syndrome;

it makes the policy-making process even more complex, the field of participating interests even more diverse.

Examined in greater detail below, the four traits of the science-technology syndrome appear to lead not to a unification of international order for the global environment but to a diffusion of decision-making loci in the international community. When a policy-making process becomes too complex and protracted and its product too soft and uncertain to serve the felt need for the regulation of technological change on the global level, specific policies begin forming on lower levels — regional, local, bilateral or unilateral. The questions of how to manage such diversity — how to live with it in political peace and environmental order — is one of the central concerns of this paper.

The inquiry touches two sensitive points. It raises the possibility that, in the international system, increased flows of scientific and technical data and increasing participation by scientists in policy-making processes are mixed blessings. But nowhere is there even a faint implication that information flows should be cut and scientists pushed aside. On the contrary, more of both will be needed in the very center of policy-making processes for effective international management of environmental alteration. The problem is that we do not as yet understand the impact of scientific knowledge on international policy-making well enough and that our attempts to mesh the scientific worlds with the political ones — without one seriously disrupting the other — are, at best, very awkward. Commenting on an earlier version of this paper, a colleague whose judgment I respect highly wrote to me: "It is repugnant to me to think that information can hurt." Yet sometimes it is necessary to think repugnant thoughts in order to find out what makes them so.

The second sore spot is touched by my conclusion that in many areas of international environmental management — even in those where global ecological phenomena are involved — we would not only do better but, indeed, have no choice but to act on levels very much below the United Nations, or outside the traditional intergovernmental frameworks, or through soft and unstable political accommodations rather than firm legal norms and institutions. Here again, I have no apologies beyond stating my bias: I find the role of the United Nations in an effective management of environmental alteration absolutely crucial; how that role will be fulfilled depends on how wisely and selectively the organization is used and how carefully it is loaded with new tasks.

A considerable amount of evidence and illustrative material in the pages below has been drawn from the field of international marine affairs. This is not, however, a simple recourse to some distant analogy in the absence of other, more direct data. International ocean policy is, indeed, a direct and sizeable segment of what is emerging as an international environmental policy because the ocean is a very sizeable segment of the total human environment. The experience derived from

210

international management of the ocean, and particularly from its mismanagement, may prove to be one of the greatest assets we now have.

I. DATA, POLITICS AND POLICY FOR THE GLOBAL ENVIRONMENT: AN IMBALANCE.

On any level of analysis, problems of environmental management display the normal characteristics of all issues of public policy. The problem must be first identified and understood in terms of its social significance. Next it must be recognized as potentially susceptible to a rational solution through public policy. Then comes the crucial step of actually covering the distance between the two, between cognition and solution. The distance is political; it must be measured by the pulse of the political process which alone determines whether or not the recognized need will be adequately served by an organized authoritative response.

The distance between cognition and solution of environmental management questions is often greater than other issues of public policy which do not so much depend for their definition on scientific and technical data and on the extrapolation of the data into a set of alternative futures. In dealing with environmental problems, whether nationally or internationally, the relevant data must first be politicized by mobilizing social interests of sufficient intensity to generate the process of public policy-making, in itself a potentially difficult task.

When environmental tasks are handled on the international level, the difficulty of crossing from cognition to action and solution is further multiplied by the very fact that the world political process is so much more diffuse than the national one, and that effective public policies may be had in so many more shapes and sizes, from flickering bilateral understandings to formal institutions of global dimensions.

Perhaps just because the international political processes — the roads spanning the distance from the recognition of an environmental task to the decision on the social response to it — are often so long, so multifarious and so intertwined, we often avoid exploring and charting them.

Much is done at the cognitive stage where environmental issues are being identified. Highly sophisticated methods are used to define how the expanding and proliferating technologies affect the global environment, what opportunities for environmental use and control they present, and which tasks are critical today and which will be tomorrow. There is as yet no program underway for a comprehensive investigation of global environmental problems, nor is environmental quality being systematically evaluated and measured, or its over-all changes being reliably recorded. The report of an international conference on the use and conservation of the biosphere, convened in 1968 in Paris by UNESCO, clearly reflected the gaps in available knowledge.[2] The M.I.T. sponsored and globally oriented "Study of Critical Environmental Problems" was held in 1970; its seventy participants, representing more than a dozen disciplines, set out to determine what could be said authoritatively about global environmental problems, and they too found the data base very inadequate.[3]

Scientific and technical expertise, however, is growing quite rapidly, and the body of knowledge is expanding through multiple efforts at private, institutional, national, transnational, and international levels. Much of what is being done in the United States in scientific and technological assessment of environmental issues directly reflects international dimensions of the problems[4] On the international level, various environmental monitoring programs are in action or under preparation; the effort to accumulate more comprehensive data reflecting the global interface of technology and environment is being accelerated.[5] It is possible, of course, that we are losing ground, that our technology disturbs the natural balance much faster than we gather ecological data to guide our actions; nevertheless, in scientific and technical terms we are learning more and are doing so more systematically.

We also seem to be doing rather well at the other end of the policy-making process where rational solutions for environmental tasks are being drafted. Straining our imaginations to the limit and sometimes beyond, we blueprint optimal rules and mechanisms to deal rationally with environmental problems and opportunities. Recognizing that both technologies are generated and controlled on the national and lower levels and that the international community has no direct or easy recourse to technological fixes capable of alleviating some of the ecological strains, we design for the management of the global environment various types of social, political and legal solutions of international proportions. By far the greatest number of attempts at large-scale social engineering originate at the private level, particularly in the United States. Illustrative of this type of sincere and sometimes sophisticated blueprinting of global systems of environmental order are George Kennan's proposed International Environmental Agency capable of setting international standards for the uses of the global environment and eventually of making and enforcing its rules governing environmental activities;[6] or Richard Baxter's International Environmental Authority designed to deal "with the sea, with rivers, with ground water, with lakes, with natural resources generally, with conservation, with land use, and perhaps even with this vexing problem of limiting the number of human beings on the earth."[7] Private institutions are sometimes effective stimuli as well as instruments for developing such schemes of international order; among them the Center for the Study of Democratic Institutions,[8] the Commission to Study the Organization of Peace,[9] and

212

the International Institute for Environmental Affairs[10] are particularly active and visible in a populous and lively field. On the nation-state level, policy designs for environmental controls are often developed as responses to what appear to be opportunities for international quasi-legislation or treay-making by multilateral conference.[11] In some instances such national initiatives do lead to international initiatives: the rapidly progressing preparations for the 1972 U.N. Conference on the Human Environment and for the U.N. Conference on the Law of the Sea now scheduled for 1973 are the most prominent cases in point. Other important efforts at developing schemes for international environmental controls emanate from regional contexts: the Conference on Environment convened by the U.N. Economic Commission for Europe held in Prague in May 1971 is an outstanding example.

On the international level we know much more about what the environmental problems are, and what we would like to do about them, than about how to do it. On its way to an agreed social solution, a recognized social problem must pass through a political process which, like a complex set of filters, determines whether any particular solution is or is not feasible. However, the political feasibility of proposed political and legal responses to recognized environmental needs of the international community have not been systematically studied, and the criteria for such feasibility studies are yet to be formulated.

II. THE SCIENCE-TECHNOLOGY SYNDROME AND GLOBAL POLICY

The prominent scientific and technological component in international policy-making for environmental management brings about certain characteristic phenomena in need of closer examination. These phenomena or traits represent a science-technology syndrome; they mutually support one another so that one-way causal sequences between them are difficult to identify.

A. *Scientific Ethos and Policy-Making.*

The impact of scientific and technological perspectives on international policy-making is pervasive: the global, comprehensive dimensions of modern science and technology stimulate demands for systems of order on a comparable scale.

The comprehension of the fundamental unity of all nature, including man himself, represents an essential ingredient of the modern scientific ethos. The new science of ecology and the ecological perspectives developing in many fields of scientific inquiry rapidly define innumerable links connecting individual phenomena and their systems and build them

213

into gradually higher structures. Many research projects are and must be undertaken on an international scale and through multidisciplinary approaches. Many modern technologies have truly global reach; their impact on the natural environment is potentially or actually universal in scope.

A typical case of the necessity to match the scope of scientific inquiry with the scope of the phenomenon under study was stated by Warren S. Wooster, a Scripps oceanographer and president of SCOR:

The processes operating in the waters are of large scale and are driven by forces of planetary dimensions. Life in the ocean is affected by these processes, so that the type, number and distribution of organisms may be controlled by events occurring in distant places. Because of this immense unity, investigation of the world ocean is inherently an international affair, requiring cooperation ranging from the simplest exchange of information to the most complex integration of research programs.[12]

While difficult to fulfill, this requirement is not only proper and eminently sensible: it is, in fact, inevitable if the knowledge of oceanic phenomena is to be advanced in meaningful patterns. However, problems multiply exponentially as the range of demanded social controls moves from the accumulation of scientific knowledge to the satisfaction of other social values, be they technology development and control or the allocation of economic goods. The fact of the world ocean being a unity provides a rationale for a similarly unified scientific effort to understand the ocean; but does the same fact support equally well a demand that, because of its immense unity, the world ocean and all its uses should be subjected to a comprehensive global regime?

Given the expanding perspective of science and the underdeveloped state of international society, there must obviously be a point beyond which the latter can no longer keep up with the former, where the scientific perspective does not easily translate itself into a corresponding social action. It is one thing to argue that the biosphere, having evolved as a whole and functioning as a whole, should be studied through a broad, comprehensive international scientific effort; but it is very different to say that, because of that unity and wholeness, the use of the resources of the biosphere should be rationalized on a world-wide scale.[13] Undoubtedly it should, but the social instruments for such a monumental task are not as yet at hand.

The scientific imperative takes the form of a quantum jump from the realm of knowledge to the arena of politics in many areas along the science-policy interface, from broad designs for global environmental management systems to the regulation of a particular fish stock. In favor of regulatory systems "tailoring fishing effort to the size of the resource," John L. Kask, former Director of Investigations of the Inter-American Tropical Tuna Commission, stated the case for a world-wide convention regulating the use and conservation of tuna:

Tunas are found in most tropical and temperate waters of the world. Many make trans-ocean and inter-ocean migrations. Most of the five species ... in whatever ocean they occur are already fully or nearly fully exploited... To deal effectively with this developing situation nothing less than a world tuna convention seems indicated.[14]

Writing later on the same topic, Kask's successor in IATTC, James Joseph also argued that "on the basis of the biology of the tunas there is good reason to suggest that geographical areas of responsibility need to be based more on biological parameters and less on political ones." And also like Kask, Joseph argued that tunas are highly migratory fish, crossing oceans and even traveling among oceans; with the fishing fleets also increasingly mobile and the tuna market widespread, the establishment of "a world tuna commission, or some such similar body," is then proposed as a "straightforward," "efficient" approach.[15]

Proceedings of scientific meetings and writings by scientists on public issues are replete with examples of the yardsticks of science being used for the measurement of the required social response. But if the scientific ethos, especially in its ecological variety, leads to what appear to be excessive demands on the law-making and institution-building capability of the international society, the scientists who generate that ethos are certainly not its only and, perhaps, not always its primary carriers into politics. The scientific ethos with its strong underpinnings of rationality is a pervasive force because it corresponds to the aspirations of the scientific age. The sense of ecological unity, of global interrelations among natural phenomena, evokes parallel concepts in those concerned with the social and political divisions in the world. It is eagerly seized upon by people devoted to the building of universal and rational systems of order and tirelessly searching for sources of inspiration and strength. International organizations are the natural habitat of this breed of men of vision, be they international civil servants or social scientists dealing with international organizations. And international organizations are also the forum where international policy processes of global scope are most often initiated. When U Thant urgently recommended the creation of a global authority to deal with the problems of the environment,[16] the scientific sense of ecological unity was visibly fused with his strong preference for political unity.

In all this there is a remarkable contrast. In their efforts to understand and effectively build international institutions, students and practitioners of international organization rather readily adopt scientific concepts. But, even when they are seeking to expand their own scientific effort through a better system of international co-operation, there is little evidence that natural scientists are similarly motivated to seek guidance from the repertoire of experience and data accumulated by the social sciences or from the expertise of social scientists. Is it, perhaps, because the social sciences have too little to offer? Could it also be a problem of attitudes?

The question of who is learning more from whom is not a crucial one in the present context. The central point is that scientific perspectives embodied in the ecological imperatives are assimilated not only into the pronouncement of the practitioners of international organizations but also into the thinking of social scientists. Daniel S. Cheever, concerned with the establishment of effective international administration for particular environmental functions, made a simple argument: "After all, the world ocean is a system, a bio-system. Its continued equilibrium, therefore, requires a matching adminsitrative system to regulate its use."[17] Richard N. Gardner, arguing that the United Nations should "lead the environmental parade" as an appropriate instrument for effective action and would in turn be made a better and stronger organization through such an endeavor, employs the argument of ecological unity as a self-evident imperative:

We are beginning to comprehend the unity of the world's ecological system, which means that all nations may be affected by how any one of them treats its air, water and land ... The international community will be increasingly involved in environmental issues. ... Indeed, the most powerful impetus to world order may no longer be the threat of nuclear war, but rather the urgent necessity of new transnational measures to protect the global environment.[18]

To Richard A. Falk, the ecological imperative points toward a complete transformation of the international system:

From an ecological perspective, the political fragmentation of mankind into separately administered states makes no sense whatsoever. The basic ecological premise posits the wholeness and interconnectedness of things. Up until very recently, the scale of human life on the planet did not present any dangers to the system as a whole, but, more recently, technological developments, together with rapid population expansion, have removed this margin of safety and have started building up levels of pressure that threaten to disrupt the delicate balance of links in the cycle of life on earth. To moderate this pressure responses by man will be required to embrace the whole earth; there is need for central guidance of human activities in relation to natural surroundings.[19]

As a cultural trait of the scientific age, the scientific ethos or, more specifically, the ecological imperative pervades and shapes the orientations and preferences of scientists and non-scientists alike. This trait is a powerful force behind demands — and is often their very source — that environmental problems be assessed and attacked from the global level and in a comprehensive fashion wherever their nature is not glaringly local and isolated. The ecological imperative causes the nature and scope of proposed social solutions for environmental problems to be determined by scientific and technological criteria; questions whether or not such solutions are also politically feasible are obscured. That the world ocean is a unity, or that the biosphere is a unity, are ascertained facts as uncompromising as other sets of scientific data. But policies, environmental as well as any other, are essentially sets of compromises.

216

Under the impact of the scientific ethos, the programatic spirit of the policy-making process becomes dominant and its pragmatism weakens; the trend moves toward manifestoes, less in the direction of operational norms.

B. *Data for Decision-Making.*

Technical information plays a conspicuous role in environmental policy-making. The injection of massive doses of scientific and technical data into such policy-making processes is partly a product of the scientific ethos. Science, and modern science in particular, solves its tasks by expanding and deepening the knowledge of the problem area until all its elementa are known and thoroughly understood; for science the problem then no longer exists, the task has been completed. And this scientific and technological problem-solving style seeps into the policy-making process in the form of a powerful illusion that masses of scientific and technological data will help generate the right policy for environmental management, that more data, and more precise data, will stimulate greater and firmer social and political consensus on what is to be done collectively. Of course, every policy and, in particular, every policy in areas with considerable scientific and technological components must be made in conditions of relative ignorance if there is to be any policy at all. The question then is how much one must know in order to decide. And the scientific ethos enveloping the environmental issues manifests itself in the tendency of the participants in the decision-making process to call for more research time and more data rather than less. The policy-making process becomes more complex and protracted.

But it is also very obvious that reliable and balanced scientific and technical data are an absolute necessity for environmental policy-making, not just a fancy of the scientific age. For our analytical purposes, then, the high input of scientific and technical information into policy-making is a separate factor, a distinct trait of the scientific-technological syndrome with distinct consequences for the efficiency and outcome of the policy-making process and its structure.

The dissemination of scientific and technical data is in itself a part of the political process. Data activates or even creates political interests. A few well-chosen facts neatly plucked from a wider body of knowledge and properly interpreted and sharpened for action can provide a ready rallying point for political forces and their policy goals. The issue of the deep ocean floor was ushered into the political realm of the General Assembly by the rather inconspicuous initial stratagem, employed in 1966 in ECOSOC and in the Second (Economic and Financial) Committee of the General Assembly, of requesting surveys of marine resources and of the state of marine science and technology.[20] Technical information condensed from scientific and technical knowledge and properly disseminated has the unquestionable potential of generating many environmental issues into issues of international policy-making.

Beyond this, the need for scientific and technical data is also the access road for various types of expertise into the mainstream of the political process. Almost invariably, this access directly reinforces the cultural tendency to view better and more plentiful technical data as reliable clues to better policies. When in 1967 the First Committee of the General Assembly was debating whether or not the seabed issue should be kept on the agenda, a spokesman for UNESCO and its Intergovernmental Oceonographic Commission (IOC), arguing that it was far too early to start the formulation of a policy, said:

one cannot ... envisage any solution without realizing that to do so mankind should have at its disposal all the knowledge of the ocean accumulated over the years, and much new knowledge which may be gathered only through persistent scientific research ... .[21]

In 1969 a group of eminent scientists acting as the Executive Committee of the Scientific Committee on Oceanic Research (SCOR) offered to ease the international controversy over the deep ocean floor by providing the policy-makers with more adequate information disseminated in the form of annual volumes comprising scientific reports based on marine research done by laboratories around the world.[22]

The improved access of expertise to the international policy-making process, in itself a symptom as well as a stimulus of increased receptivity of technical data by policy-makers, has still other effects. Above all, it diversifies the fields of interests participating in the political process. As democratization of international policy-making, this is a positive element. But this type of democratization also lowers the decision-making efficiency. The trend, though has set in: when issues as complex as environmental control come up, the United Nations almost automatically seeks all the expertise available in the specialized agencies and other governmental as well as non-governmental organizations. And with the expertise inevitably comes the organizations' interests in the promotion of their purposes and in their own self-perpetuation and growth. The potential influx of such interests into the policy process is massive. The General Assembly resolution to convene in 1973 a comprehensive conference on the law of the sea specifically invites six major specialized agencies to co-operate with the Seabed Committee in preparing scientific and technical documentation and explicitly calls on still other organizations to join the effort.[23] In its resolution on the preparation of the 1972 Conference on the Human Environment, the General Assembly invites all the specialized agencies and all other inter-governmental and non-governmental organizations concerned to close collaboration with the Secretary General and the Preparatory Committee.[24] It is true that such invitations are routine wherever policy matters with significant scientific and technological components are to be acted upon by the inter-

218

national community. But the significance of this phenomenon may lie precisely in the routine character of the invitations coupled as it is with a lack of systematic study assessing the impact of such co-operative relationships.

To act effectively on environmental issues the international community evidently needs many types of scientific and technical information. But it is not obvious that it is getting what it needs or that it knows how to use it. Oxcar Schachter and Daniel Serwer stressed that "the problem of how technical matters of widespread concern are to be presented reliably for national and international consideration and action remains unsolved, particularly on the international level."[25] This probably will always be so, considering the difficulty and, in the author's opinion, impossibility of obtaining reliable, "reliable" meaning "entirely objective", reporting of technical matters; the very selection of some data and the exclusion of other involves subjective judgments.

Yet, there is still another side to this. Even when technical information is effectively communicated to international decision-makers, it may or may not ease the policy-making task. The same solid data guiding some nations to policy action may lead others to inaction. It was the high reliability of scientific data supplied to the policy-makers of the Inter-American Tropical Tuna Commission that helped to undercut, at least temporarily, the effectiveness of IATTC and of its conservation policy.[26] Reliable scientific data was supplied to the International Whaling Commission to promote better conservation policies and practices; some IWC countries used the information on the distribution of the diminishing stocks to whale more efficiently.[27]

So we have a thesis: scientific and technical information is needed to make international policy-making for environmental controls not only more rational but, in fact, possible. Next comes the antithesis: the need of scientific and technical data brings into the policy process new concepts and new interests diluting and fragmenting the general policy consensus. The data, used by different participants for different ends, becomes disfunctional. And the synthesis? Possibly and hopefully, the beginnings of a synthesis may lie in a better understanding of this inner conflict as the first step toward its control and eventual management.

C. *Technological Futures and the Political Present.*

The futuristic orientation of international policy-making in areas as rich in scientific and technological implications as environmental affairs is a particularly significant and far-reaching feature of the science-technology syndrome. It further expands the field of participants in the policy process and multiplies the diversity of their interacting goals.

Almost every international policy-making effort is future-oriented in the sense that it seeks to regulate the subsequent behavior of states.

However, most policy issues before the United Nations traditionally arise in response to actual or imminent crises in the real, material world — crises highly visible and keenly felt. The Middle East, Kashmir, Congo, the arms race, West Irian, decolonization — all these and many others reflect the fact that conflict in the real world is still the main stimulus of international efforts to establish order. In general, the international community is inexperienced in long-range policy planning[28] necessitated by technological flux; it lacks the basic political competence and mechanisms for acting today on problems of tomorrow.

In policy-making processes such as those involving the seabed and the various environmental issues, the futuristic orientation is pronounced because of the heavy ingredient of science and technology. Technologically and geopolitically, the deep ocean floor is still far from becoming a field of active contention among nations; the problem of man's impact on the global environment is still defined more by extrapolating present trends than by simply measuring them. The policy-mobilizing force is largely only the force of social interpretation of scientific and technical data; the conflict is still much more in the minds of men than in the sea or atmosphere. Bargaining over issues of this type, governments act out roles conditioned by their assumptions of future technologies and the consequent opportunities and challenges.

The primary ramification of this futuristic trait is its effect on the field of active participants in the policy-making process. Where an issue before the United Nations reflects a real and defined contemporary problem in need of corrective action, the definition of the problem itself determines the main field of interested parties. In future-oriented issues, where the primary policy goal is the prevention of future loss and the allocation of future values, everyone is a potential participant; the field of participants is uncertain because it is determined by the perception each state has of its own stake in a given socio-technological future. But the future is infinite, and the economic and social pressures governments feel are immediate, heavy and diverse; the seabed, water pollution, pesticide control, or conservation of resources are all issues with entirely different meanings for different societies.

In the case of the deep ocean floor, the extrapolation of available data regarding mineral resources and marine engineering skills brought about such a rush of expectations and mobilized many governments to political action, however uninvolved in marine affairs they may have been until then.[29] In the case of a global environmental policy process, the main problem may be how to arouse active interest among members of the international community and how to maintain the momentum. The end structure of the two policy-making processes may not be so dissimilar. While the field of participants in the seabed issue is virtually global[30] and interest runs generally high, for many states the question of a future allocation of seabed resources is no longer the primary

220

or even secondary issue. National governments are political entities motivated by political pressures, and political pressures are generated, or at least affected by the needs of political constituencies. Since the unborn constituencies apply little pressure, the seabed policy-making process has become an instrument for the satisfaction of present needs rather than future visions. To some countries it offers an opportunity to negotiate a more advantageous sphere of exclusive maritime jurisdiction; others use the seabed politics to protect their fishery interests; still others are concerned with preventing minerals obtained from the seabed from flooding the markets and depressing world prices. Some are skeptical about the practicability of a seabed resource-sharing system but find their participation in the policy issue useful for other ends, whether to boost their national prestige in a general sense or to increase their bargaining power in other issues.[31]

In the environmental field national interests are gradually recruited for international action even where the individual states are not too concerned about the environment. This in itself sets the stage for a "routinization" of the policy process similar to that experienced with reference to the seabed current interests are again grafted onto future concerns, often layer by layer. Such extreme, multidimensional pluralism could be fatal to any attempt to articulate policy, particularly in the international system with its fragmented and discontinuous authority structures.

D. *Economic Concerns in Technology Management.*

Relatively intense economic concerns are an essential trait of the science-technology syndrome in global policy-making because science and technoloby always imply economic costs, and expendable economic values are neither endlessly abundant nor evenly distributed in the international community. Every aspect of environmental management involves costs, mostly formidable. Global environmental monitoring is costly. Technological restraint demanded by imperatives of environmental protection may be as costly as the development of technologies preventing or correcting undesirable environmental change.

In the present context one important aspect of the massive economic implications of technology-based policy issues is the problem of international burden-sharing. The economic trait brings into the policy issues of environmental management the concept of public goods[32] which pervades many areas of international co-operation.[33] The economic theory of public goods applied to international policy processes aimed at environmental protection emphasizes that so far as technological damage to environment is of international or global dimensions, whoever corrects the damage or prevents its aggravation creates a public good in which many others share without necessarily paying.

This in turn raises the question whether the nations participating in a global policy process aimed at the correction or prevention of undesirable environmental alteration will be motivated toward some equitable burden-sharing which would provide the basis for an effective system of order.

This is a problem of considerable intricacy. First, the economic theory of public goods may be used to support the argument that national propensity to international co-operation will be low if the public goods obtainable through co-operation can be had without it;[34] this argument assumes a large degree of rationality on the part of the individual actors. Second, the public goods concept cannot very well account for situations in which a state might be willing to share the costs of producing one public good it would get anyway (as when a downstream community benefits from anti-pollution efforts by upstream riparians) only because it thereby obtains some other value which is often not visible to or recognized by outsiders (*e.g.*, in cases of bloc-politics and other systems of vote- or policy-trading).

On balance, the prevalent indications are that economic considerations tend to push the international policy-making process aimed at the global environment in the same direction as the other traits of the science-technology syndrome: it has the potential of bringing into the policy process a considerable number of participants seeking a diversity of goals which may or may not reflect a concern with the quality of the global environment. To many participants, then, it may be relatively unimportant whether or not the process will result in the formulation of a new system of order in international environmental management. Such increments in their relative positions as they may derive from their participation in the policy-making process, not from its culmination, may become the primary or the only value they seek.

III. GLOBAL SCHEMES AND PARTICULAR SOLUTIONS FOR ENVIRONMENTAL TASKS

A. *Global Policy for the Global Environment: A Misfit?*

The science-technology syndrome raises serious doubts about the productivity of global policy-making efforts aimed at comprehensive reforms in the field of environmental management. As yet, we have little historical experience with global policy-making by which a highly pluralistic world would seek to respond in unison to the challenge of technological change. The seabed issue now before the United Nations is unique in many respects, and the policy concern with global environment is steadily assuming comparable characteristics. The uniqueness of the seabed issue is that it marks the first time a world-wide allocation of significant material values is to be accomplished through political bargaining in a global field of participants. This is a process quite different from that through which changes in the law of the sea and the new regime of the continental shelf were being negotiated in the 1950's. The U.N. International Law Commission and the Sixth (Legal) Committee were then the main arenas of interaction. That process, and its culmination in the 1958 Geneva Conference, was rather isolated from other political issues before the United Nations, and inter-issue bargaining was limited. The continental shelf regime was to a considerable extent shaped and codified in the relative coolness of legal analysis and in the politically almost antiseptic climate of jurisprudential reasoning; the seabed issue is being debated in the hothouse of the First (Political) Committee and of the General Assembly itself.

By its nature, the U.N. policy-making for the global environment is more akin to the unfinished business of creating an international regime for the deep ocean floor than to the continental shelf policy-making of the 1950's. Pressed by the scarcity of empirical data, however, some indicators may be drawn from the 1950's experience of international law-making for the ocean. One striking feature of that process is the time-span involved. For the four major conventions produced by the 1958 Geneva Conference on the law of the sea, the policy-making time-spans were on the order of two decades, plus or minus five years depending on where one designates the beginning of the policy-making process.[35] However, even when the conventions entered into force, they were far from global in their extent. The Convention on Fishing and the Conservation of the Living Resources of the Sea — an area of international activity also greatly affected by technological change — required seventeen years to mature into a legal document; at the end of this period it was binding on twenty-two countries whose combined catches at that time made up less than 14 percent of the total world catch of sea fish.[36]When the Convention on the Continental Shelf entered into force in 1964 after nineteen years of policy-making, its twenty-two participants controlled only about 34 percent of the total global length of all national sea-coasts (Antarctica excluded).[37]

That the global policy-making process was contributing throughout its course to the formulation of international norms independent of the formal treaties being negotiated is a point to be taken up below. As a technology-stimulated, conscious striving for new departures institutionalized on a global level, the effort was a failure. The scope of the outcome was very limited. The process was protracted to the point of resulting in technological obsolescence: the technology-based definition of the outer limits of the continental shelf was visibly disfunctional even before the Convention entered into force.[38]

Nothing among the potential effects of the science-technology syndrome in global policy-making suggests that the tempo of the bargaining process will now increase so as to approximate the tempo of scientific and technological change. Neither does anything suggest that such processes, whether they aim at a seabed regime or at environmental management systems, will become more purposive, more clearly targeted on salient issues. The indications are to the contrary. The ethos of the scientific age with its ideal of matching the scale of social organization to the scale of known ecological relationships tends to cast the policy-making process into the exalted form of a comprehensive remodeling of whole systems. The need, real or imagined, to have a steady supply of scientific and technical data and studies as decision-making tools further prolongs a process which is already unwieldy due to the great number of actors who have been mobilized into participation by learning about the significance of the issues or by the promise of reaping other pay-offs from such participation.

Other students of the processes of problem-solving and decision-making, following different routes, arrived at conclusions similar to those to which the science-technology syndrome points: that policy-making by a very large field of participants seeking to institute a major systemic change is likely to be unproductive as the primary rational instrument for such change. A recent study on the role of African states in the United Nations, noting the exaggerated tendency of those states to maneuver major policy issues before the United Nations — such as the nuclear non-proliferation treaty — to gain marginal bargaining power on colonial issues, concludes that:

to the extent that such behavior becomes the norm a significant incentive has been created for avoiding, where possible, United Nations consideration of major issues. Inter-issue bargaining is, of course, not unknown in traditional diplomacy. However, the extent to which the procedures of the United Nations facilitate such inter-issue connections is sufficiently greater than that available in traditional diplomatic negotiations to qualify as a qualitative difference. The ease with which bargaining advantages on other issues can be extracted when coupled with the independent and unpredictable negotiating positions of the African missions will tend to mitigate against the new and complex issues of the 1970's being submitted to the Organization for its consideration.[39]

In a different context, a study by James Buchanan and Gordon Tulloch of the costs of decision-making points to a similar conclusion stressing the unproductivity of the large-scale, multilateral policy process.[40] The findings of the study, extended for the international system by Bruce Russett, "can be read as a conservative statement on the continued uses of the nation-state in the international system and the undesirability of transferring functions to a supranational organization."[41]

More formidable than high bargaining costs are other obstacles to effective large-scale decision-making as identified by Robert Dahl and Charles Lindblom. Concerned primarily with comprehensive planning for economic developmnet, Dahl and Lindblom singled out (a) extreme analytical difficulty, and perhaps impossibility, of identifying for policy

224

purposes the complex and dynamic linkages between multiple phenomena and of envisaging the possible consequences of the decisions being made, (b) the problem of forecasting rapid technological change, and (c) the rigidity with which complex institutions meet innovative tasks of major dimensions.[42]

Many of these arguments are persuasive. They may have their intrinsic weaknesses, but they stand because no empirical evidence is available to disprove them. Only one major phenomenon raises some doubts: the unflinching stubbornness of human aspirations to organize and reform international life into rational and comprehensive patterns. If our earlier interpretations of the effect of the scientific ethos of this age on policy-making structures are basically sound, comprehensive decision-making efforts on the global level are likely to proliferate, not diminish — a possibility still to be critically assessed.

B. *Particular Solutions as Diffusion of Global Authority.*

The accelerating efforts in the United Nations to generate a global framework for environmental management may simply reflect a case of organizational self-energization: numerous and diverse interests cluster around a newly defined task, then keep the new problem-solving mechanism alive to obtain various advantages from the process. However, the substantive issue is there: the impact of human activities on environmental quality is recognized as adverse; it is of international scope; it is dynamic. The need for international regualtion is real. One may then hypothesize that where global policy-making processes are perceptibly slower than scientific and technological change which stimulated them, a trend toward a proliferation of international policy subsystems sets in; seemingly the more exalted the level of decision-making, the greater the proliferation of subsystems.

The states will simply try to satisfy their needs of environmental management by different means as the needs arise. This problem of international diffusion of authority must be examined before the mutual compatibility of the policy-making processes taking place on different levels can be evaluated.

The little evidence so far accumulated by decision-making experience does support the hypotheses and the prognosis of a continued diffusion of decision-making loci in international environmental management. The political and legal system of the oceans — to use again the issue-area broadly comparable to that of environmental controls — contains a number of instances reflecting the relationship between the global pull and the local push.

In the case of the continental shelf, there is today one weak convention obtained through a long and arduous global effort, and a growing number of particular agreements, mostly bilateral, serving in various ways the particular needs of states. These subsystemic agreements pertain to the North Sea, the Baltic, the Persian Gulf, the Adriatic, and the Asian Mediterranean Sea.[43] The fact that in none of the Mediterranean areas of the world, concentrating the greatest expanses of technologically and economically accessible shelf, have all the coastal states subscribed to the 1958 convention increases the possibility that further particular systems will be created. The Latin American response to the early stages of the continental shelf policy process — the 1952 Declaration of Santiago by Chile, Peru and Ecuador proclaiming coastal sovereignty over the seabed and the waters above to a distance of 200 miles offshore — may have been somewhat atypical of the diffusive trend. Considering how Latin American particularism has grown since then,[44] one could legitimately ask to what extent this particularism may have been in fact exacerbated by the lack of international responsiveness to Latin American problems, and to what extent this non-attention could have resulted from the notion that the "capricious" Latin American policies could be overcome by the weight of a general new regime of global scope and at great centripetal force. There is but little force in the occasional argument that the 1958 Convention on the Continental Shelf, while not regulating all aspects of the global regime, did establish the global principle of exclusive national control; that rule had arisen long before the Convention became valid and is independent of it. The growth of international custom was in this case swifter than the institutionalized global law-making.

The difficulty of negotiating the 1958 Convention on Fishing and Conservation of the Living Resources of the High Seas was greater than in the case of the continental shelf; it commanded weaker adherence and took longer to become valid for a smaller number of parties.[45] In the seventeen years needed to produce the treaty, the knowledge of conservation problems and techniques expanded and new efficient fishery technologies were developed. This only accentuated the existing differences between states and led to rapid proliferation of particular agreements and political understandings. D.W. Bowett's thorough examination of the law of international fisheries led him to the following conclusions:

Thus, in this matter too, given the ratifications of the Convention, the Society of States has no general rules or regime, and we are forced again to consider partial solutions, reached between small groups of States, in special areas or in relation to special stocks of fish. ...

Recent years have seen partial solutions, in particular areas, and it is now quite evident that these very difficult problems of adjustment of the economic interests involved can only be made in relation to specific areas, between limited groups of States, and cannot flow from any universally-accepted principles.[46]

Symptoms of the diffusive tendencies, intensified by the growing discrepancy between the rapidity of technological change and the labored

226

progress of global policy-making, are appearing in several areas. The new Canadian policies for the protection of the Arctic have been proclaimed in an unfortunate manner from the point of view of both international law and of the effectiveness of the pollution-control program. However, the substance of the Canadian concern is real and legitimate. Again the question arises to what extent the unilateral move — the ultimate international diffusion of authority — reflects the lack of confidence that multilateral and global efforts at environmental protection, as those mounted in the United Nations, are effective.

The issue of environmental protection involves complex and varied technologies and rapid changes in the social perceptions of environmental tasks. The push toward unilateral, bilateral, regional and otherwise limited responses is likely to be greater in this area of policy-making than in many other fields of international concern. In one of the valuable recent discussions of the international problem of marine pollution, Oscar Schachter and Daniel Serwer argue that "marine pollution control measures must be tailored carefully to fit particular problems,"[47] then conclude that along with more comprehensive efforts:

there has come to be a greater recognition of the need for regional pollution control organs since it is apparent that, although pollution is a global problem, it is not uniformly global. Regional arrangements in the Baltic, the North Sea, Mediterranian, Caribbean and perhaps in the Arctic are now under way, and it is likely that these organs will have a decisive part to play in achieving day-to-day practical controls.[48]

On a more theoretical level, John Ruggie finds that while technological innovations are likely to lead in the future to increased international activities, "the impact of most will be limited to the technical operation of tasks"; additionally, "a diffusion of decision-making loci, specific to sets of tasks and actors", is to be expected.[49]

C. A Two-Tier Policy-Making Process.

The probability is high that under conditions of technological flux the global policy-making process involving major allocations of material resources will be even less productive than in the past and that increasingly smaller subsystems will proliferate. This is not an argument that for the purposes of international environmental management the comprehensive approach should be abandoned and the diffusive one more heartily embraced.

The global, comprehensive approach cannot be easily abandoned. The ecological aspirations reflecting the scientific ethos of this age are likely to generate global policy-making processes and keep them alive, however futile they may appear to be with their endless cacophony of multiple interests and apathies. The important point here is that the appearance of futility may be misleading. To observe that global policy-making processes are largely unproductive is to make one assumption:

that their primary, if not their sole purpose, was to produce a specific new multilateral treaty or to create a new global agency. Then let's ask what went wrong. Was the policy-making process a failure because it did not produce what we thought it should have produced or was the expectation itself unsound?

When an issue reaches a high policy-making stage in the United Nations, as the seabed problem has and the environment may, a massive flow of confrontations, compromises, fact-finding, vote-trading and other forms of international interactions take place. Much of what is injected into the process may be irrelevant, some of it may be misleading and even disfunctional: the amorphism of the process deepens when some policy inputs are in fact intended to bring pay-offs in other, often substantively remote areas. But here and there the cacophony breaks into more harmonious, consensual notes, and one may detect notions difficult perhaps to translate into firm policies but clear enough to suggest an emerging spectrum of available policy choices by indicating the limits of political feasibility. During the subdued but global ocean policy process in the fifties, the main coutours of the continental shelf regime emerged relatively rapidly. Through the same process, general concepts of conservation responsibilities and rights in high sea fisheries were perceived with reasonable clarity, and some limits of political feasibility also were charted: it became rather obvious that more than persuasion might be needed if the coastal states' special interests were to be given less than full priority over other user's. The deep ocean floor policy process of the sixties and early seventies, more intensely political, has produced over the past six years a set of new policy perspectives; the spectrum of politically feasible seabed regimes has been clarified although no particular and formal solution may be in sight. In this sense, that policy process has covered a remarkable distance since 1966.

The comprehensive, global, policy-making process in fields heavily affected by modern science-based technologies is probably the nearest available approximation of a policy-oriented international technology assessment. The incessant interplay of data and goals on the global level provides a running overview — however rumbling and often inarticulate — of the international technological stresses and perceived opportunities, their social implications, and the available political responses. If, in this sense, the global policy-making process is an end in itself, it should be as global, comprehensive and intensive as possible. The greater the number of countries, organizations and individuals actively participating in the process, and the larger the amount of assembled relevant data, the more balanced the eventual assessment may eventually become. If assessment, rather than regulation and centralization of authority, is the primary function of the policy debate, Richard Gardner's suggestion that all nations, including the individual segments of divided states, should participate in the Stockholm Conference[50] is truly a functional suggestion. Assessment is a cognitive process, regulation a political one; their structures are very different. Richard Falk's approach also reflects a recognition of this dichotomy and the relation of the two different processes in his comment that:

possibly an awareness of the dimension of the problems and the direction of solutions will generate political processes in various parts of the world which will work out trade-offs as the basis for adjustment.[51]

The need for the policy-making process to be intensive in order to spin-off a broad and continuous international technology assessment poses a problem. What makes governments participate in international policy-making and what makes experts and their organizations pour in data and evaluations is the notion that the stakes are real, that definite policies are being shaped and perfected, that values are being allocated, and that policy stands bring tangible rewards. Once this notion is lost, the process may be lost. A bargaining process through which a General Assembly resolution is being formulated will be sufficiently intensive only if the participants believe that the resolution will have direct and timely political effects. There is no easy way out of this eat-it-and-have-it-too dilemma unless it be found in a somewhat greater sophistication with which we adjust our expectations of what the global policy-making process could and should bring — when and how.

The global and comprehensive policy-making process performing the role of problem-oriented international technology assessment is especially important for environmental tasks. The early functionalist and regionalist notions that larger systems of order can be brought about by spill-over or incrementalism or both appear quite illusory in international environmental management. In 1967 several European states working through the Organization for Economic Cooperation and Development and through the European Nuclear Energy Agency in a joint operation dumped 35,800 barrels containing 10,900 tons of radioactive wastes into the northeast Atlantic.[51] This co-operative venture may or may not be another grain of cement in the foundations of an integrated Europe. What it may represent in terms of the global environment is another question, and what ten or a hundred such successful disposals of waste would mean — all regionally organized and perfectly harmonious — is still another.[53] A continuous, intensive policy-making process aimed at global control of marine pollution may never be achieved but in its course may provide the pressures and tensions needed to sensitize the global responsiveness of states and their organizations.

This argument goes further than Schachter's and Serwer's when they stress that what is needed for international control of marine pollution is "a many-sided institutional approach to achieve the right balance."[54] In the present analysis, the global and the particular policy processes are not seen running side by side, one scoring here and one there. They are hierarchical rather than complementary. They are fused together to form a single two-tier process in which the understandings, apprehensions and goals, continuously articulated, assessed and re-evaluated on the global level, are allowed to seep down to the second tier of the sub-systems and gently civilize the harsh but unavoidable particular solutions to which individual states, pressed by technological flux, will increasingly resort.

The practical implications of this two-tier concept of international policy-making in technologically rich areas can be illustrated by the case of the current United States policy for the deep ocean floor. As announced by the President in May 1970 and as subsequently submitted to the U.N. Seabed Committee in the diluted form of a draft convention styled as "a working paper for discussion purposes,"[55] the U.S. policy was an input into the global decision-making process. The policy has been widely acclaimed for its internationalist orientation; devoted advocates of rapid expansion of global governmental authority have seen in it an important victory for their cause.

Whatever it may prove to be in the future, it represents an initiative not only taken on the global policy-making level, but also left there. It presumably waits until "a sufficient number of other States also indicate their willingness"[56] and join the policy. An explicit agreement by an unspecified number of states is obviously needed to activate the policy internationally. Yet, if the two-tier concept of the policy-making process is followed, the United States policy proposal appears in a different light. As an input into the global process of assessment, it is politically perfectly feasible and functional. It will retain its political feasibility if it is taken as a guide and stimulus activating compatible policy processes on subsystemic levels in various bilateral and regional contexts. The United States, to test and enhance the strength of the policy, could seek treaties implementing various parts of the envisaged international seabed regime. Or other states, such as the group now negotiating the division of deep ocean floor resources in the Red Sea, could let themselves be guided by those parts of the U.S. proposal which best reflect the general views of the international community.

The two-tier approach is not really a call for innovative policy actions. The system of international order has always been built through policy initiatives taken on the global level and on the levels below — overwhelmingly on the latter. The only novelty contained in the two-tier concept is the stress it places on the critical need — especailly for international environmental tasks — to see the two levels of decision-making as a hierarchical structure in which the global level guides and modifies the lower. In order to obtain policy action at a speed commensurate with that of technological change, and at the same time not to end up with an amorphous mass of inequalities and self-centered practices with low levels of international responsiveness, the action has to start from below — guided by the light coming from the global assessment process above, however dim and flickering that light may be.

NOTES

[1]Several such proposals emerged during 1971. Outstanding among them is that outlined in Chayes, "International Institutions for the Environment," elsewhere in this volume.

[2]UNESCO, "Final Report of the Intergovernmental Conference of Experts on the Scientific Basis for Rational Use and Conservation of the Resources of the Biosphere," (Paris: 4-13 September 1968), U.N. Doc. SC/MD/9 (1969).

[3]Study of Critical Environment Problems (SCEP), *Man's Impact on the Global Environment: Assessment and Recommendations for Action* (Cambridge, Mass.: MIT Press, 1970). At 6, the SCEP Report states: "... it is important to note the deficiencies in the data and projections related to problems of global concern. In the process of making judgments we found that critically needed data were fragmentary, contradictory, and in some cases completely unavailable. This was true for all types of data — scientific, technical, economic, industrial, and social. These conditions existed despite a year of planning, extensive preparation of background materials, the presence among Study participants of some of the world's leading scientists, and the generous access to data provided by virtually every relevant federal agency."

[4]Some of the work is reflected in a number of congressional documents and executive reports issued over the past several years. For an illustrative listing of 1963-69 materials of this type *see* L. Caldwell, *Environment: A Challenge to Modern Society* 267 Fn. 23 (1970). For a good survey of the state of science and technology regarding the oceans as an element of the total geophysical system, *see* the Report of the Panel on Environmental Monitoring in U.S. Commission on Marine Science, Engineering and Resources, 1 *Science and Environment*, Panel Reports (D.C.: U.S.G.P.O., 1969).

[5]Several international organizations in different functional fields have their own data-collecting divisions or participate in broadly organized programs. Within the United Nations general system, the major organizations concerned with various types of environmental monitoring include the World Meteorological Organization, International Civil Aviation Organization, International Atomic Energy Agency, U.N. Scientific Committee on Effects of Radiation, Economic Commission for Europe, International Labor Organization, UNESCO, Intergovernmental Maritime Consultative Organization, Food and Agriculture Organization, World Health Organization, and U.N. Development Program. Outside the U.N. system, organizations such as the Organization for Economic Cooperation and Development, European Economic Community, or NATO Committee on Challenges of Modern Society play more prominent roles in the accumulation of scientific and technical knowledge of environmental phenomena. Among non-governmental international organizations the International Union for the Conservation of Nature and the groups associated in, or the various committees of, the International Council of Scientific Unions generate considerable input into environmental monitoring. Furthermore, these various organizations often jointly man and coordinate specific international monitoring programs such as the World Weather Watch, International Biological Program, International Hydrological Decade, Endangered Ecosystem Monitoring Program, and International Decade of Ocean Exploration, among many other projects already operational or in various preparatory and planning stages.

[6]Kennan, "To Prevent a World Wasteland: A Proposal," 48 *Foreign Affairs*, April 1970, at 401-413.

[7]Baxter, "International Co-operation to Curb Fluvial and Maritime Pollution," in *International and Interstate Regulation of Water Pollution: Conference Proceedings* 77 (New York: Columbia Univ. 1970).

[8]Prior to its *Pacem in Maribus* international convocation (Malta 1970) which resulted in a number of proposals, the Center stimulated the formulation of a statute for the world ocean. *See* E. Borghese "The Ocean Regime," 1 *Center Occasional Papers* no. 5 (Santa

Barbara: Fund for the Republic, 1968).

[9]Commission to Study the Organization of Peace, *The United Nations and the Bed of the Sea*, Nineteenth Report (New York: 1969). The report recommended the establishment by the General Assembly of an international authority governing the seabed and outlined its functions and structure.

[10]IIEA, "Toward a Working Alliance: A Basic Paper Prepared for the Secretariat of the United Nations Conference on the Human Environment" (mimeographed August 1971). The paper, designed as a contribution to the U.N. Conference agenda item regarding "the international organizational implications of action proposals", was the product of an international environmental workshop held in Aspen, Colorado, 20 June - 6 August 1971, under the auspices of IIEA and The Aspen Institute for Humanistic Studies.

[11]Principal illustrations are the Maltese 1967 proposal for a seabed regime, initially styled as "draft treaty", or the U.S. proposal for an International Seabed Resource Authority contained in a Draft U.N. Convention on the International Seabed Area and presented in the form of a working paper to the U.N. Seabed Committee in 1970. For the U.S. proposal *see* 9 *ILM* 1046 (1970).

[12]Wooster, "The Ocean and Man," 221 *Scientific American*, Sept. 1969, at 218.

[13]UNESCO, *supra* note 2, at 3-4. The inclination to make social action correspond to a given state of scientific facts is reflected in another statement of the Conference: "There being a wholeness in nature, as shown by ecosystems, there must be consideration of the entire systems of nature because limited single-purpose actions are no longer tolerable". *Id.* at 6. The report was prepared by Professor V. Kovda and associates (USSR) and included comments and additions by Professor F. Smith (USA), Professor F.E. Eckardt (Denmark), Dr. M. Hadley (U.K.), Dr. E. Bernard (Belgium) and the Secretariats of UNESCO and FAO.

[14]Kask, "Tuna — A World Resource" viii-ix, May 1969 (Occasional Paper No. 2, Law of the Sea Institute, Univ. of R.I.). *See also* Kask, "Marine Science Commission Recommendations on International Fisheries Organizations" in *Proceedings: Fourth Annual Conference of the Law of the Sea Institute* (Univ. of R.I.: 1969).

[16]U Thant, "The United Nations: The Crisis of Authority," address by the Secretary Genral reported in U.N. Press Release SC/SM/1323 (1970).

[17]Cheever, "International Organizations for Marine Science: An Eclectic Model," in *Proceedings, supra* note 14, at 378.

[18]Gardner, "Can the U.N. Lead the Environmental Parade?" 64 *A.J.I.L.* 212 (Proceedings, 64th Annual Meeting, 1970).

[19]R. Falk, "Toward Equilibrium in the World Order System," *id.* at 217-218.

[20]*See* ECOSOC Res. 1112(XL) (7 March 1966) and G.A. Res. 2172(XXI) (6 December 1966).

[21]Statement by Mr. Varchaver, U.N. Doc. A/C.1/PV.1527 at 5-6 (1967).

[22]5 SCOR no. 1, at 6-7 (1969).

[23]G.A. Res. 2750 C (XXV) (17 December 1970).

[24]G.A. Res. 2581 (XXIV) (December 15, 1969).

[25]Schachter and Serwer, "Marine Pollution Problems and Remedies," 65 *A.J.I.L.* 99 (1971).

[26]IATTC membership grew from its bilateral (United States, Costa Rica) beginnings in 1949 by the additions of Panama, Ecuador (left again 1969), Mexico, Canada, and Japan. Since the IATTC research budget was based on the utilization of tropical tunas in the repective member countries, the United States dominated it some years with its share given at 100 percent. The financial problems of IATTC started at a time when its scientific research indicated the need for conservation of yellowfin tuna in 1961 and later. One of the Annual Reports issued by IATTC noted then that the level of required research was "quite beyond the present financial means of the Commission". (Annual Report of 1962 at 4). In 1963-64, drastic reductions of research effort were financially necessary, and severe curtailments followed in later years. In 1968, when the United States decided to provide only about 50 percent of the funds requested by the IATTC scientific staff, the Annual Report (1967) stated at 12:

> The inevitable result of this action was that for the fourth consecutive year all effective research at sea had to be eliminated precisely at a point in the history of the fishery when large-scale tagging experiments and other costly research at sea, required to verify theoretical studies, assume great and immediate importance, since the Commission's recommendations on regulation of yellow fin are affecting the livelihood of many individuals in many countries.

[27]When in 1964-65 the International Whaling Commission was discussing with FAO the possibility that FAO would assist in whole stock assessments, FAO indicated its willingness to work with IWC only if IWC adopted scientific advice offered and acted on it. Referring to the practice of IWC countries, a FAO spokesman told one of the IWC meetings that the FAO Director-General had "indicated that this collaboration could not be expected if the Commission permitted the results of the scientific studies to be used merely for the organization of the more efficient destruction of the resource for which it was responsible". See IWC, *Sixteenth Report of the Commission* 818 (1965).

[28]This is not to say that the national political systems, even in advanced societies, do have the experience and the requisite skills to deal on their level with problems and challenges posed by new technologies. See Sayre & Smith, esp. at 34, "Government, Technology, and Social Problems," Institute for the Study of Science in Human Affairs (Columbia University: 1969).

[29]This process of interest mobilization has been analyzed in 2 Slouka, *Scientific Knowledge and International Policy* (forthcoming, 1971-72).

[30]The U.N. Seabed Committee itself has grown from 35 members in 1966 to 42 in 1969 and at present stands at 86 with all other member states invited to participate as observers and be heard on specific points. See G.A. Res. 2750 C (XXV) (December 17, 1970).

[31]A member of a national mission to the United Nations formulated the perspective of some states rather well during a recent interview with this author: "At this time we are quite active in the seabeds because it gives us better leverage in other areas. We are strong in the seabeds issue; we don't think too much of it, not for the present anyway, and therefore we are flexible and can support now this proposal and now that, depending on how we can best secure the support of others in those policy fields where we have less flexibility."

[32]For a discussion of the political aspects of the economic theory of public goods, *see* Mitchell, "The Shape of Political Theory to Come: From Political Sociology to Political Economy," S.M. Lipset, ed., *Politics and the Social Sciences* (1969).

[33]For two illustrative treatments of the application of the public goods theory to problems of international organization *see* Olson, Jr., and R. Zeckhauser, "An Economic Theory of Alliances," 48 *The Review of Economics and Statistics*, no. 3, 266-279 (1966) and Ruggie, "The Theory of Public Goods, Science and Development Planning, and Consequences" (paper presented at the 66th Annual Meeting of the American Political Science Association, Los Angeles, 1970).

234

[34]*E.g.*, Ruggie, *id.* at 40.

[35]For instance, in the case of the continental shelf the onset of the policy process may be put at the time when the need for the new policy was internationally articulated in the 1945 Truman Proclamation and reacted to by other states, or it can be placed in 1949-50 when the U.N. International Law Commission began its work on the law of the sea. The time-spans involved in the 1958 law of the sea policy process have been analyzed in some detail in Slouka, *supra* note 29.

[36]Herrington, "The Future of the Geneva Convention on Fishing and the Conservation of the Living Resources of the Sea," in *Proceedings: Second Annual Conference of the Law of the Sea Institute* at 62 (Univ. of R.I.: 1967).

[37]Based on measurements given in U.S. Department of State, Bureau of Intelligence and Research, "Sovereignty of the Sea," in *Geographic Bulletin*, no. 3, 16-20 (1965).

[38]A few days after the U.S. ratification of the Convention on the Continental Shelf, in May 1961, the Assistant Solicitor of the U.S. Department of the Interior advised that leasing of submarine acreage was possible without regard to the depth of the superjacent water, that there was no seaward limit to the applicability of the Outer Continental Shelf Lands Act, and that "it is possible to hold that with technological progress the act may be applied to areas at greater and greater depth." The unpublished departmental memorandum is analyzed in Z. Slouka, *International Custom and the Continental Shelf*, at 108-109 (1968).

[39]D. Kay, "The Impact of African States on the United Nations," 23 *Int'l Organ.* 46-47 (1969).

[40]J.M. Buchanan and G. Tulloch, *The Calculus of Consent* (Ann Arbor: Univ. of Michigan Press, 1962); *see esp.* pp. 95-115; also reprinted in *Economic Theories of International Politics* 455-471 (B. Russett, ed. 1968).

[41]Russett, *id.*, at 451-52.

[42]R. Dahl and C. Lindblom, *Politics, Economics, and Welfare* (1953). *Also see* Lindblom, "The Science of 'Muddling Through'", 19 *Public Administration Review*, 79-88 (1959). A useful comparative analysis of several related theories is Hirschman and Lindblom, "Economic Development, Research and Development, Policy Making: Some Converging Views," 7 *Behavioral Science*, April 1962, at 211-222; reprinted in Russett ed. *supra* note 40, at 473-89.

[43]Most of the agreements concluded prior to 1967 and reached by Netherlands, Federal Republic of Germany, United Kingdom, Norway, Finland, USSR, Denmark, in various combinations, can be found in U.N. Secretariat, "Survey of Existing International Agreements concerning the Sea-Bed and the Ocean Floor ... ," Doc. A/AC.135/10/Rev.1 (12 August 1968). Further agreements concluded between Italy-Yugoslavia, German Democratic Republic-Poland-USSR, Iran-Saudi Arabia, Indonesia-Malaysia, and Poland-USSR, are 7-9 *ILM*.

While some, such as the USSR-Poland and USSR-Finland agreements basically only implemented rather than modified or deviated from the 1958 Convention, each reflected some particular need not served by the Convention; in the case of the Soviet Union it may have been nothing more than the desire, generally characteristic of Soviet policy, to rely on specific, explicit and precise agreements rather than on more general ones. More than half of the parties to the particular agreements were not bound by the 1958 Convention at the time they concluded the agreements.

[44]*See*, for instance, the 1970 Lima Declaration and resolutions resulting from a Latin American meeting on aspects of the law of the sea, in 10 *ILM* 207 (1971).

[45]Cf., TAN above.

[46]D.W. Bowett, *The Law of the Sea* 24, 60 (1967).

[47]Schachter and Serwer, *supra* note 25, at 86.

[48]*Id.* at 111.

[49]Ruggie, *supra* note 33, at 37.

[50]Gardner, *supra* note 18, at 211.

[51]Falk, *supra* note 19, at 223.

[52]Organization for Economic Cooperation and Development and European Nuclear Energy Agency, "Radioactive Waste Disposal Operation into the Atlantic 1967," OECD Sept. 1968.

[53]The OECD-ENEA disposal is mentioned here solely for illustrative purposes; I do not have sufficient information to criticize the operation as ecologically unsound or dangerous. Possibly the operation was thoroughly responsible in terms of the available knowledge and other alternatives. In general, radioactive waste disposal is probably better planned and controlled than the disposal of any other wastes.

[54]Schachter and Serwer, *supra* note 25, at 111.

[55]9 *ILM* 806 (1970) for the Presidential statement; *id.*, at 1046 for the working paper.

[56]*Id.* at 808.

THE IMCO EXPERIENCE

by *Thomas A. Mensah**

Introduction

The Inter-Governmental Maritime Consultative Organization came into being in 1959 in accordance with the terms of the Convention on the Inter-Governmental Maritime Consultative Organization adopted by the United Nations Maritime Conference held in Geneva in 1948.[1] One of the purposes of the Organization, which is a specialized agency of the United Nations, is to facilitate co-operation among governments in technical matters of all kinds affecting shipping engaged in international trade with particular reference to the encouragement and adoption of the "highest practicable standards of maritime safety and efficiency of navigation."[2]

At an early stage in the life of the Organization, it was recognized that one of the many technical matters affecting shipping, and indeed arising from shipping is the problem of pollution from the operation of ships. In particular it was recognized that pollution of the sea by ship-borne oil had to be controlled and regulated not only as part of the regulation of the technical operations and practices of shipping but also as a major part of IMCO's concern with and work toward the promotion of the highest practicable standards in matters concerning maritime safety. As the only U.N. organization dealing with technical matters affecting shipping, IMCO had a special responsibility to the other users of the marine environment and to coastal States generally to reduce to the minimum possible level the pollution of the seas from ships.

IMCO's concern with the problem of marine pollution began tentatively and in stages. At its inception, it took over the depositary functions in respect of the International Convention for the Prevention of Pollution of the Sea by Oil.[3] This Convention had been concluded in 1954 during the period between the adoption of the IMCO Convention, the coming into force of the Convention and the consequent establishment of IMCO — and the depositary functions had been assigned to the Government of the United Kingdom as an interim measure.

This Convention aimed at prevention of pollution of the sea arising from deliberate discharges of oil, principally oily wastes from ships into the sea.

From this modest beginning, IMCO's involvement and activities in connection with the prevention of marine pollution became greater. As

*The author is Head of the Legal Division, Inter-governmental Maritime Consultative Organization. The views expressed are the personal views of the author and do not represent the views of the Organization or the Secratariat.

the problems to be dealt with broadened and became more complex in consequence, IMCO has had to devise a new approach, including a new institutional framework, to deal with the problem. It has become increasingly necessary to relate the efforts of IMCO not only to the efforts of other agencies and bodies (within and outside of the U.N. system) with varying degrees of interest in the preservation of the marine environment, but also to the efforts aimed at the problems of the environment as a whole.

I. IMCO ACTIVITIES IN RELATION TO THE PREVENTION OF MARINE POLLUTION: A SUMMARY

IMCO's concern with marine pollution was in the beginning confined to the deliberate discharge of oil from ships into the sea; such discharges are made as part of the routine tank cleaning and ballasting operations of tankers. This was the subject of the 1954 Convention for the Prevention of Pollution of the Sea by Oil whose administration IMCO took over in 1959. In 1962 INCO convened a diplomatic conference mandated to review the effects of the 1954 Convention and adopt such amendments as were felt necessary. The Conference adopted a number of far-ranging amendments to the 1954 Convention. The most important of these amendments provided for the extension of the Convention's application to ships of lesser gross tonnage and for the extension of the zones (of the sea) in which discharge of oil from ships was prohibited. This process of amendment and strengthening of the Convention has continued apace. Further amendments were adopted in 1969. These together with other amendments which were adopted by the Assembly of IMCO in October 1971 will, when adopted, considerably reduce the overall total quantity of oil discharged into the sea and achieve significant progress towards the ultimate goal of completely eliminating oil discharges.

Meanwhile the "Torrey Canyon" disaster of 1967 emphasized in a very dramatic way the increasing risk of serious oil pollution resulting from accidents to ships, particularly tankers. This accident brought home to he international community the need for speedy and effective action to deal with the threat of massive pollution of the sea by oil tankers and the rapid and almost revolutionary increases in tank sizes. At this point it became abundantly clear that IMCO's traditional and basic concern with the safety of ships at sea was of great importance and relevance to the prevention of pollution of the sea. Consequently the eighteen point program adopted by the IMCO Council in wake of the "Torrey Canyon" accident included, as principal and vital ingredients, measures designed to prevent the occurrence of accidents as well as practical

238

measures designed to promote rapid and efficient action to deal with accidents if and when they do occur. The former measures included more stringent requirements for the construction, equipment and manning of ships carrying oil with the aim of limiting the possibility of collisons or strandings or the escape of the cargo, the establishment of routing schemes and traffic separation schemes in congested areas of the sea to avoid collisions and the establishment of prohibited areas for ships of certain sizes. The measures to deal with spillages included studies with regard to improved methods of dealing with spillages of oil at sea and on coasts including in particular the development of new agents for removing oil from the sea and/or coastlines; the development of new chemical and other devices for protecting coastal areas from pollution (e.g. the construction and use of booms and emulsifiers) and studies into the effect of the various chemicals etc. on marine life and the ecological balance of the sea. The measures also included recommendations to improve national and regional co-operation in dealing with pollution, to introduce effective systems for reporting significant spillages of oil and to improve the detection of violations of the Conventions prohibiting the discharge of oil into the sea.

In addition to these and other measures, all essentially technical in nature, the Council of IMCO included in the program of action consideration of legal questions. This was the first time IMCO had included purely legal questions in the list of subjects to be considered by and within its bodies. To ensure that these legal questions would be given the thorough and expert consideration that they would obviously require, the Council established, first on an *ad hoc* and later on a more permanent basis, a Legal Committee in which participation is open to legal experts from every Member State of the Organization. The first mandate work program of the Legal Committee related almost exclusively to questions which had arisen directly from the "Torrey Canyon" accident. As the Committee progressed in its consideration of these issues, it became apparent that its scope of activity would have to be extended further afield to include, *inter alia*, legal problems relating to marine pollution generally.

The "Torrey Canyon" accident involved pollution by oil. Consequently, the reaction within IMCO was, at first, confined solely to the problems created by marine pollution by oil. It soon became clear however that no effective scheme for preventing marine pollution could be evolved if attention were paid solely to pollution caused by oil. IMCO has, therefore, directed its attention in both the technical and legal fields to the problems of marine pollution arising from shipborne cargoes other-than oil, even to pollution (including pollution of the atmosphere) arising from the use of the marine environment by ships and other devices, and to pollution arising from the exploration of the oceans and the ocean floor and exploitation of the resources of the marine area. Indeed the

Organization is in the process of planning for a Conference in 1973 whose purpose will be to prepare a suitable international agreement (or agreements) for placing restraints on the contamination of the sea, land and air by ships, vessels and other equipment operating in the marine environment. One of the suggested specific objectives of the Conference is the achievement, by 1975 if possible but certainly by the end of the decade, of the complete elimination of the wilful and intentional pollution of the sea by oil and other noxious substances and the minimization of accidental spills.

II. INSTITUTIONAL FRAMEWORK OF IMCO'S WORK

In its work in relation to marine pollution, and indeed in all other aspects of its involvement with problems of international shipping, IMCO operates through a "consultative" machinery. This machinery enables experts, representing governments, private industry and commerce, as well as international governmental and non-governmental organizations, to exchange views and experiences on a variety of subjects and to arrive at solutions for problems of common concern. Because the discussions involve such wide participation and take reasonable account of (or at least do not disregard completely) the views and interests of any of the interested parties, the solutions and arrangements which finally emerge from them are generally acceptable to the majority. This consultative approach would appear, from the record so far, to have worked particularly well, at least in regard to international regulations and control of marine pollution. Indeed, for a number of reasons, this consultative approach appears to be the only approach with any realistic possibility of success.

In the first place, the seas and oceans bind the countries and continents of the world with such unbroken and multi-directional links that it is often difficult or impossible to localize within the confines of a single State the effects of marine pollution incidents or tendencies. To be successful control and regulation of marine pollution must be regarded not as a national, but rather as in most cases as a regional or sub-regional problem. Hence, the measures and schemes designed to deal with this type of pollution must, if they are to be really effective and sufficiently comprehensive, be devised with the active co-operation and participation of all interested States.

In the second place, it is a fact (perhaps to be deplored but nonetheless a fact) that in the preponderant majority of cases, regimes for preventing pollution of the sea can only be enforced, if at all, by States. There is not now, and there is not likely to be in the near future, any other method; there is no international body with jurisdiction to enforce measures to prevent pollution on the high seas — let alone in the territorial seas of States. Nor is there any power or competence in States to enforce such measures or schemes against any but their own ships. Under the circumstances, it would seem not only desirable but imperative, if the required and realizable minimum uniformity of enforcement is to be achieved, that such schemes be based on the widest measure of agreement among States and that the international legislative and regulatory activity be in the form of the search for, and articulation of, the highest possible standards which the interested States (or the majority of them) are willing to accept and to promote. This exercise can, in my view, only work well and on a continuing basis, if it is based four-square on consultation, information and accommodation rather than on legislative fiat — regardless whether such fiat is based on majority vote or on so-called "objective facts and criteria".

In IMCO these considerations have been found to be compelling. As a result, the consultative approach has been used at every turn. True, this has its drawbacks. One main disadvantage has been, and is, that even when after long consultation and hard bargaining a scheme or arrangement is finally agreed upon there is no guarantee that some State will not, for some reason, fail to play its part. And when this happens there is no real sanction against such a defaulting State. This is admittedly true and could detract considerably from the success of an important scheme and, possibly, even nullify it altogether. However, it is worthwhile noting that in a large number of cases most States find it in their interest, either because they deem it necessary that the schemes be implemented effectively or because they do not relish the possibility of being branded as international delinquents, to make serious efforts to comply with their international undertakings. The case of a State deliberately failing to take action at the State level in clear and acknowledged violation of its international undertakings is the rare exception rather than the rule. This applies not only to these schemes which are embodied in formal international treaties or similar instruments but also to those arrangements which have the nature of recommendations or non-legal understandings between interested States. An example of such an arrangement is the International Regulations for the Prevention of Collisions at Sea, 1960.[4] Although it is not a treaty and does not as such impose any legal obligation on the States which have accepted it, almost all the States which are "parties" to it have in fact taken appropriate and necessary action at the state level to implement and enforce them. And, of course, we ought to take serious note of the sad but hard fact that the scope of international coercive action against defaulting States is, in any case, very limited.

In addition to the consultative approach, IMCO's work in relation to marine pollution makes use of a number of institutional arrangements which are designed to ensure that all possible interests are taken fully into account and all possible aspects are explored adequately.

In order to ensure that all possible interests are taken fully into account, a scheme of special relationship has been developed with a large number of international bodies — some representing governments and others representing specialized industrial and commercial concerns. The relationship with inter-governmental organizations is usually produced by means of formal agreements of co-operation or less formal working arrangements. In the case of non-governmental bodies, the method of liaison is usually through the grant by IMCO of consultative status to the body concerned. But, irrespective of the particular method used in each case, all organizations who have been accorded this "special relationship" with IMCO are entitled to attend meetings of various IMCO bodies, to participate without vote in the discussion of matters of importance to them, contribute information and make suggestions on methods of approach as well as on solutions and generally to assist the respective IMCO organs and bodies by furnishing them with information (whether of an expert factual character or of the state of thinking and attitudes within given disciplines, industries or commercial circle). In many cases the success or failure of schemes or arrangements agreed upon among Governments may depend in significant measure on the extent to which they take such facts, interests or even attitudes into account. In the case of some of the bodies in special relationship, their participation is not merely advisory and useful but in fact substantive and indispensable. Thus, for example, in the preparation of traffic separation schemes (designed to regulate shipping traffic in areas of high shipping density in order to avoid collisions, strandings, etc. and consequential pollution especially where tankers are concerned), the initative for schemes and some actual details of some of the schemes originated from some of the organizations in consultative status, chiefly the International Chamber of Shipping whose members have special knowledge on the requirements of safe navigation and a very high stake in the safety of life, ships and cargoes at sea. Similarly, in their work on civil liability for oil pollution damage, the legal bodies of IMCO relied not only on the advice and assistance of the Comité Maritime International (CMI), the international association of national maritime law associations, but actually based their work on a scheme first produced by the CMI. In the preparations leading to the establishment of an international compensation for oil pollution damage, the legal bodies of IMCO have again relied on the expert know-how and have taken full advantage of the resources of the Oil Companies International Marine Forum, an association of the major oil companies of the world. Accepting advice from and relying on the expertise of specialized bodies is a major and now an established part of the institutional arrangement within IMCO. It has worked well mainly because even though these bodies, especially the industrial and commercial concerns among them, are profit-making bodies and hence presumably generally interested financially in the schemes and measures being discussed, they are all international organizations in which the competing (sometimes even conflicting) interests of component national bodies have first been harmonized and accommodated. The result is that it is very rare, if ever, that one finds their advice or proposals wholly unacceptable to the majority of governments in the respective IMCO organs and bodies.

Another aspect of the special relationship arrangement in IMCO's institutional framework is of course the close collaboration between the organs and bodies of IMCO and the United Nations including the various U.N. subsidiary organs and bodies and the specialized agencies and the International Atomic Energy Agency (IAEA). This particular aspect of IMCO's collaboration is founded on two main considerations. The first is the recognition of the essential unity of the United Nations effort in the prevention of pollution and in the achievement of the other purposes for which the U.N. and the specialized agencies were created. Collaboration with the Organizations within the United Nations system is, therefore, part of the "way of life" of IMCO — as it is of the other specialized agencies. Another reason for the close and intensive collaboration between IMCO and many of the specialized agencies of the U.N. is the recognition of the fact that pollution of the seas does not result solely from activities in the marine environment but also from activities which take place in other sectors of the environment, from land and from the atmosphere. This recognition leads to the conclusion that any program designed to regulate and control marine pollution must also have some regard to activities in other sectors which may have polluting effects on the seas. The need for collaboration with other organizations is even more compelling in view of the fact that IMCO, while it is the only U.N. Specialized Agency concerned exclusively with maritime matters, it is not the only such agency which deals with maritime matters. Other agencies are concerned with activities in the sea and the effects of such activities on the various uses of the sea; these organizations are deeply interested in the effects which the pollution control measures adopted in IMCO may have on their interests. Similarly, IMCO is interested in the effects of other activities on the marine environment and, in particular, on the effectiveness of the measures and arrangements which are adopted under their auspices. All these reasons have led to the closest possible co-operation between the work of IMCO and the work of these other organizations. This co-operation and collaboration has been on two levels: the regular institutional level and the *ad hoc* level. The regular level provides for participation by these agencies in IMCO's deliberations (and vice-versa) and the exchange of information and documentation. The *ad hoc* level involves closer co-operation, including the co-sponsoring and establishment of new institutional arrangements, in relation to subjects of common concern. In the matter

243

of marine pollution one of the most important of these institutional arrangements is the establishment of the Group of Experts on the Scientific Aspects of Marine Pollution (GESAMP). This is an interdisciplinary group co-sponsored by IMCO along with five other agencies: FAO, UNESOC, WHO, WMO and IAEA. The Group is composed of a slate of members who are all experts appointed in their individual capacity but not, it must be added, without reference to their nationality since this is a Group which is, in the last analysis, responsible to and financially dependent on the member States of the sponsoring organizations. The functions of the Group are *inter alia* to advise the sponsoring organizations on specific aspects of marine pollution and to advise member States of the Organizations which may request help with particular problems through one of the sponsoring organizations. The Group reports to the sponsoring organizations which in turn make the reports available to their member Governments. In addition each Organization may, on the basis of these reports and other information and material available to it, make such recommendations or take such appropriate action as it may deem necessary. One of the most important contributions made recently by GESAMP to the marine pollution control program has been the establishment of a list of possible pollutants other than oil with an indication of their various polluting potentialities. The results of this study are going to form the basis of a great part of IMCO's work and the work of other organizations in relation to pollution of the sea by agents other than oil.

Other arrangements — of an even more *ad hoc* character — include arrangements whereby IMCO and one or several organizations give joint consideration to subjects of mutual interest. In many instances provision has been made for special, joint bodies, comprised of governmental representatives from the various organizations, to discuss and produce solutions on particular questions. Where the solutions have to be submitted to diplomatic conferences, the practice has now developed whereby the interested organizations co-sponsor the required diplomatic conference.

The purpose of these co-operative arrangements with organizations, both within and without the U.N. system, is to ensure that as much expertise as possible is brought to bear on the consideration of the various questions relating to marine pollution. It is unrealistic to expect that international discussion of any subject, particularly one with such economic, social and hence political implications as marine pollution, can be completely devoid of politics but it is also appreciated that the less political the atmosphere in which these discussions are held, the better are the chances of arriving at practical, effective and generally acceptable solutions. Even when the questions involved are purely technical or purely legal — as they hardly ever are — the fact remains that any schemes or measures aimed at regulating pollution of the seas arising from a variety of commercial and state activities must take account of the politically acceptable, the scientifically possible, the technically feasible and the commercially tolerable. The purpose and achievement of the consultative method has been to enable the Organization to discover the limits to which different political, commercial and other national and disciplinary interests will go and, to the extent compatible with the objectives in hand, to respect these limits. In spite of the fact that this has produced schemes and measures which are generally weaker than what is needed or desired, this approach has helped to produce a wide measure of international agreement not only in the objectives of governments as expressed in international treaties and similar agreements, but even in the content of various legislative and related measures adopted at the national level by various States. Even in the areas of minimal achievement, the consultative approach has not failed to produce agreement on what is needed or imperative. Progress has been balked only as regards agreement on what is to be done. But the ascertainment of the remedy is a useful, not to say indispensalbe, beginning in the quest for the cure.

III. INTERNAL INSTITUTIONAL ARRANGEMENT

Within the context of the consultative framework, the internal institutional arrangement for dealing with the problem of marine pollution has followed the pattern used in relation to other aspects of IMCO's work. This proceeds on the assumption that while it is legitimate and even useful to view the problem of pollution as a single issue requiring comprehensive treatment, the realities of the situation make it impossible to devise such a comprehensive treatment; therefore, the several aspects of the problem have to be given separate consideration before a more integrated solution can be attempted. Experience in IMCO has not only shown that this is a useful and practical approach but has, perhaps, also demonstrated that no other approach would have or could have worked as well. Thus, in IMCO the question of marine pollution is considered in its various aspects within a number of bodies.

A. *Maritime Safety Committee*[5]

The chief operative body of the Organization is seized with the technical aspects of the problem. Within the jurisdiction of the Maritime Safety Committee the question of marine pollution is dealt with in various sub-committees. The most important of these is the Sub-Committee on Marine Pollution, which deals with all aspects of marine pollution including the consideration of the causes of pollution and the various

245

ways in which pollution of the sea can occur; the various types of pollutants and their polluting potentialities; the practical and other arrangements for preventing and controlling pollution and mitigating the effects of pollution, including scientific methods of fighting pollution; the international methods including treaties, agreements, and recommendations for effective control and means of enforcing and improving such treaties; and the gathering and dissemination of information on all aspects of the question. This Sub-Committee is IMCO's main unit of liaison with the GESAMP.

Other Sub-Committees of the Maritime Safety Committee also deal with the different aspects of the question of marine pollution. For example, the Sub-Committee on Safety of Navigation deals with, *inter alia*, the procedures, techniques and equipment for preventing accidents. To the extent that the reduction of accidents involving tanker collisions and strandings, for example, leads to a reduction in the incidents of discharge of cargoes into the sea, the work of that Sub-Committee is particularly relevant to the task of pollution prevention. Other Sub-Committees deal with the construction of ships (the establishment of standards for construction of different types of ships), the use of radio-communications for navigation and the treatment of various cargoes. Each of these sub-committees is concerned with some aspect of marine pollution. Since the reports of all these sub-committees eventually go to the Maritime Safety Committee and are discussed in that Committee, the necessary co-ordination is assured. We have the advantages of separate treatment without the disadvantages of over compartmentalization. To ensure the widest participation, most of these sub-committees are open to States which are not members of the Maritime Safety Committee itself.

B. *Legal Committee*

The Legal Committee was created in response to the situation created by the "Torrey Canyon" accident of 1967 and has since become the principal medium of the Organization's legal work. This Committee is also open to participation by all member States of IMCO. Its main responsibility is to devise the legal framework in which the procedures and measures deemed necessary or desirable may be enjoined, where appropriate, on States; it also formulates internationally uniform principles and procedures to ensure that, to the greatest extent possible, the same procedures and measures are used to deal with the same problems, irrespective of the State involved or the parties concerned. The purpose of such uniformity is, of course, to ensure that there are no undesirable incentives or disincentives for various parties at different times and in different places to disregard the requirements of internationally agreed measures.

Again, it has at all times been recognized that an attempt to place the legal solutions and various technical measures into separate water-tight

246

compartments would not only be undesirable but also unworkable. Therefore, in addition to the internal arrangements by which the various Committees keep each other informed of their work, a process facilitated by a unified Secretatiat, the necessary co-ordination is provided by the fact that the reports, recommendations, etc., of all bodies, technical as well as legal, go to the Council of the Organization and from that body to the IMCO Assembly, which is the sovereign governing body consisting of all Members of the Organization. Thus, the principle that marine pollution must be considered as a whole is fully respected in the IMCO framework — although this does not, and has not, detracted from the validity and practical necessity of first considering the problem in its separate aspects before an attempt is made to discover the underlying unity and, where possible, to devise a comprehensive solution, procedural or institutional. This approach has worked well in IMCO. The IMCO experience and methodology cannot but be of significance to the problem of the human environment as a whole. Any differences that may arise — and there are bound to be many — must be of degree rather than of principle.

IV. LEGAL FRAMEWORK

As has been indicated earlier, IMCO's work on marine pollution has consisted mainly in providing the forum and expert services for inter-governmental discussion and adoption of the most practicable measures to prevent or reduce the causes of pollution — including machinery for ensuring that the agreed measures are adopted and enforced by individual States. In almost all cases the necessary measures require a degree of international acceptance and adoption to be effective; in the absence of an international authority to enforce, or even to oversee enforcement by States, reliance has been placed less on legal restraint and more on informed recommendations whose authority stems from the fact that they have been adopted after due deliberation and on the basis of the best available information and expertise.

However, some use has been made of legal restraints. Since its inception in 1959, IMCO has been responsible for the adoption of three international conventions dealing with some aspects of marine pollution. And I do not include in this number the various instruments and agreements designed to improve general safety at sea which, in a direct way, are also part of the general program to save the seas from pollution. The IMCO agreements on marine pollution have followed a general pattern and have utilized a number of legal techniques of control whose development has been dictated by the requirements of circumstances as well as by the realities of the international political situation.

The most important of these techniques consists in the States coming

247

to agreement as to what measures are required to deal with a particular problem. They then agree to adopt these measures and each undertakes at the national level to enforce them to the full. In some cases they go to the extent of agreeing, even if only in outline, on the measures of enforcement which each State undertakes to adopt. The States also agree to inform each other of the measures they take to implement the agreement, including action taken against those who contravene these measures. Provision is generally made for information to be made available by States to IMCO for further dissemination to other members. This latter measure is presumably to ensure that States take their obligations seriously, since any failure to do so could attract publicity detrimental to the state concerned. It may be said that mere publicity cannot be a very strong sanction. One has to bear in mind, however, that between States which have voluntarily agreed to adopt certain measures, this kind of adverse publicity may be a greater deterrent than is readily apparent. In any case, there may be no other sanction.

The next technique used is to direct some of the enforcement measures against the person whose act or forbearance might lead to pollution of the sea. Again one must take account of the "facts of life" in the international situation. Two of these "facts" are the politico-legal principles of the "freedom of the high seas" and the "exclusive jurisdiction of States over ships flying their flags while on the high seas." These two principles make it unrealistic to consider legal regimes whose enforcement can meaningfully go beyond the control of individual flag States. All States have, so far, been unwilling to agree to relax any of these rules in order to grant any really effective measure of jurisdiction over their ships on the high seas either to other States or even to a world body.

Faced with this legal and political barrier IMCO bodies have generally restricted enforcement measures to action which States may take within their territorial waters. One typical technique in this area is for the States to agree to adopt certain required measures and to implement each within its jurisdiction. By way of sanction they agree to two further procedures:

First, each of the Contracting States may take "enforcement" action against the ships of other Contracting States for infringements of the agreed measures when such ships are within the ports or territorial waters of the Contracting States. Such enforcement action may even involve action relating to infringements which may have occurred while the ship was on the high seas. For example, under the 1954/62 Oil Pollution Convention a Contracting State may examine the Oil Record Book of a ship which enters its ports and ascertain whether the ship has or has not violated the prohibitions of the Convention relating to the discharge of oil into the sea. This inspection may reveal a violation which occurred while the ship concerned was on the high seas. The only drawback is that the inspecting State can only ascertain the occurrence of a violation; it can-

248

not take any action against the ship. This is still reserved for the flag State. However, the conventions generally provide for the "inspecting State" to report the alleged infringements to the flag State, which is then obliged to take action against the offending ship and to report the action taken both to the "reporting State" and to IMCO for the information of other member States and Contracting States of the relevant agreement.

Second, an even stricter enforcement procedure is the agreement by the States that where a ship is in violation of the agreed measures, such a ship may be excluded from the ports and territorial waters of other Contracting States. In this way a really effective sanction is granted to the non-flag State since it can hit the ship where it hurts most. Since ships depend for profit exclusively on the ability to enter ports of other states to load and unload cargo, a sanction which excludes ships from ports can be expected to evoke some response from their owners.

A new and more drastic variant of this sanction is the granting to the coastal States the power to take "preventive" measures outside its territorial seas in order to prevent, control or eliminate pollution to its coasts and coastal waters where such pollution or threatened pollution may in fact arise from beyond territorial jurisdiction of the State concerned. This new sanction, adopted for the first time in the 1969 Convention of Rights of Coastal States to Intervene in Casualties on the High Seas Causing Oil Pollution (the IMCO "Public Law" Convention),[6] appears to blaze a new and hopeful trail in the development of truly effective measures at the international level to combat oil pollution damage. Whether its full promise can be realized soon enough and over a wide-enough field is yet unknown. All that can be said is that it is a far cry from the full rigors of the "freedom of the high seas" principle and is an indication of the extent to which the international community is willing to go in its fight against pollution of the sea, as well as providing a revealing testimony of the flexibility of the legal responses which are possible in this area.

In recent years a new approach to the problem of marine pollution control has emerged within IMCO. This draws attention to the problem of reparation and compensation for pollution damage suffered. The rationale of this approach has been that, regardless of what preventive measures are taken, it can be assumed that some pollution incidents will occur and that someone will suffer damage as a result of such incidents. Therefore, it has been held that a program to control and regulate marine pollution should, to be complete, include a scheme for repairing damage and paying compensation. No one has, of course, assumed that providing for compensation to victims is the best way to prevent damage, but it has been recognized that at least in some cases a clear enough imposition of responsibility for damage may provide additional incentives on the actor to avoid the damage. This is particularly true when the responsibility is absolute or near absolute and involves heavy financial liabilities as well as important disabilities. For example, under the 1969 Convention on Civil Liability for Oil Pollution Damage (the IMCO "Private Law" Convention)[7] the owner of a tanker which is involved in an accident resulting in oil pollution damage is deemed to be liable for the damage caused. This liability is strict with very few exceptions and involves payment by the shipowner of compensation over and above the normal shipowner's liability. Moreover, the Convention requires each tanker owner in Contracting States to maintain insurance covering the full limit of their possible liability for damage; Contracting States may, in some cases, deny ships which do not carry such insurance the right to enter or leave their ports or off-shore terminals. The possibility of such exclusion makes it unlikely that any shipowner would refuse to take the required insurance; and the fact that the accident record of a ship can have an impact on the cost of insurance may not be an entirely impotent incentive to the shipowner to be extra-cautious in his management and running of the ship, in order to reduce the possibility of accidents and consequential pollution of the sea.

This emphasis on compensation and insurance will be carried even further when, at the end of 1971, a convention is adopted to establish an International Compensation Fund for Oil Pollution Damage.[8] The Convention will establish a fund, contributed by the major oil companies of the world, to provide a form of insurance for all Contracting States in respect of pollution damage occurring within their territories. The fund is also expected to provide assistance and financing to States to combat pollution incidents and, possibly, to engage in anti-pollution activities, including scientific research and regional co-operation.

It can thus be seen that, in spite of very serious legal and political obstacles, considerable progress has been made in IMCO to evolve a system, by legal means, of dealing with the problem of marine pollution. Much of the IMCO effort, it must be admitted, has been in the technical field; but the legal method has been a useful, and, in some cases, indispensable supplement to the technical effort. The indications are that this is likely to be the case for quite some time.

While the legal responses have been progressive and sometimes very bold and imaginative, more remains to be done if a really effective system of control and regulation of marine pollution is to be developed. In particular, it would appear that an even more radical departure from the traditional notions of "freedom of the high seas" and "flag State jurisdiction" will have to be accepted by all States. For example, it may very well become necessary for States to empower coastal States to take really effective enforcement action against any ship which is in or enters their coastal jurisdiction in respect of any international anti-pollution measures, irrespective of the time and place where such a ship may have violated the measures in question. States may even go futher and agree that ships which pollute the sea may be treated in the same way as pirate ships

250

are treated under present international law, i.e., that even on the high seas, they should be considered as being within the jurisdiction of all States and not merely the jurisdiction of their flag States. It may be that the problems of pollution have reached the point where "polluters" of the sea may be likened to pirates. But whether or not the community of States is prepared to go to such a length, and if so, how soon, it appears to me that the experience of IMCO, both in regard to the institutional machinery and procedures which may feasibly be used and the kind of legal and other responses which are necessary and practicable in the fight against marine pollution, will be of undoubted relevance to, and possibly of use in, the efforts to deal with the pollution of the human environment as a whole.

NOTES

[1] Convention of the Intergovernmental Maritime Consultative Organization 9 UST 621 TIAS 4044, 289 UNTS 48 (1959); amended 17 UST 1523, TIAS 6109 (1962) [hereinafter cited as "Convention of the IMCO"].

[2] *Id.*, art. 1, para. (a).

[3] 12 UST 2989, TIAS 4900, 327 UNTS 3 (1954).

[4] 16 UST 794, TIAS 5813 (1960).

[5] *See* Convention of the IMCO, *supra* note 1, at arts. 28-32.

[6] 8 *ILM* 466 (1969).

[7] 8 *ILM* 453 (1969).

[8] Proposed Convention on the Establishment of an International Compensation Fund for Oil Pollution Damage, discussed at a diplomatic conference beginning on November 29, 1971.

THE POTENTIAL OF REGIONAL ORGANIZATIONS IN MANAGING MAN'S ENVIRONMENT

by *Robert E. Stein**

I GENERAL BACKGROUND

It has become commonplace to talk about our global environmental crises, the fragile nature of Spaceship Earth, the effects of man upon our endangered planet. While properly calling attention to the state of man's environment, and while urging increased global action to meet the environmental crises which we all face, many writers ignore the valuable work that is presently being done by international organizations and the potential increased role for actual environmental management by a class of the organizations which can generally be called "regional". The purpose of this paper is to examine the role of regional organizations in the solution of international environmental management problems.

A. *Scope of Environmental Problems.*

It is the view of many governments, and many individuals, that a great proportion of environmental problems can be dealt with — and dealt with most effectively — on the national or sub-national level. In this they are correct. But while actual management of most environmental problems can be effectively dealt with — if there is both a political will and effective application of adequate technology — on a national or sub-national level, there is still often a need for international cooperation. In many instances, technology, although available, is unknown to the governments and industry groups which desperately need it. Thus, there is a need for international exchanges of information and technology as well as training programs to enable a broader range of states to cope with essentially domestic environmental problems. The political will to actually recognize and face up to environmental threats is often lacking although there is a great deal of well meaning verbiage which points our need to do something about the environmental crisis. In developing countries, environmental problems are often considered subsidiary to development rather than a method of obtaining more efficient economic development. In developed countries government and industry

*The author is a Fellow at the Woodrow Wilson International Center for Scholars, Washington, D.C., on leave from the Office of the Legal Adviser, the U.S. Department of State.

may be at odds as the need for regulation or the manner of evaluating or assessing the costs of pollution control. Assuming that governments, industry, and individuals within each country are doing all they can to meet various environmental problems head-on with adequate political, economic and technical resources, there still remain a number of problems which cannot be solved solely through national means.

A river basin may lie entirely within the borders of one particular state making feasible and practicable state regualtion of that river basin. On the other hand, the river or its tributaries may extend along the border of two or more states or run from one state to another. In this situation, it is recognizably necessary to ;have the various states within or along whose borders the river flows deal together with this common problem The prevailing currents of air may deposit sulfur dioxide or particulates within the borders of a particular state, or because of the currents, the air flow may transcend state borders and be deposited up to several hundred miles away. If the latter is the case, it makes eminently good sense to have those states concerned deal with the problem. Oceans and noise and emissions from aircraft also need regulation from a broader scope. Moreover, when states engage in activities within or outside their borders which run the risk of having a harmful environmental effect, those other states which are potentially affected should be notified of the activity in advance and have the opportunity to comment upon it.

The effects just discussed are physical. Other effects requiring international cooperation are not. The trade and economic implications of environmental improvement need to be discussed and harmonized internationally to reduce inequities that might result from one state's imposing strict pollution control policies while a competitor state does not.

It can be concluded from these examples that national solutions for some types of environmental problems may be inadequate and, even more seriously, ineffective. At the same time, it is evident that there exists a resistance on the part of many governments to seek broader international solutions.

B. *Principle of Inclusion of States with Direct Interest.*

It is the basic thesis of this paper that those states directly concerned with an environmental problem should most often be the states to deal with it. The first step taken by states concerned must be to identify those problems that they wish to consider together: those for which more information is needed, as well as those which cannot be dealt with effectively by a single state and in which solutions taken by a single state will be inadequate and ineffective. The next step is to identify the geographic extent of the problem so that the most effective means of coping with the situation will be to organize around those states which have a direct interest in it, even though the states may not be geographically contiguous. This can be categorized as the principle of inclusion of states with direct interest.

This principle is analogous to the principle of proportionality which can be traced back to the Caroline affair.[1] The case for the principle of inclusion of states with direct interest was well put by Robertson who, after describing the lack of success of the international community through the United Nations due to "the heterogeneous character of their civilizations [which] produced irreconcilable differences of policy," continued that:

the natural corollary to this state of affairs was that more homogeneous, and therefore more restricted, groups of states might succeed where the larger groups had failed. As the idea of universalism waned, therefore, that of regionalism developed; the comparative failure of the former gave the latter its opportunity.[2]

Although the United Nations Charter recognized a role for regional organizations in Chapter VIII, the definition of the role has largely been limited to peace and security functions.[3]

The purpose of a regional approach in the field of environmental management is to recognize that there are problems and interests which are larger than national and in which national actors can participate, yet which are not global in scope. It might properly be asked whether there can be an intermediate stage between national concerns and those of a global nature. One could say that in the environmental arena even the longest journey begins with a single step, and that there is an intermediate stage which might expand some interests so that states might be willing to work together towards a common end.

Regionalism is an oft neglected phase of environmental management which would enable states sharing common interests and affinity to develop social and legal structures to an extent that they would not be willing to do on a global basis, where states not directly sharing the same concerns would be involved.[4] Additionally, a group of weaker, or developing nations, which individually might be unable to make their views felt in the larger international community, might successfully band together to deal with their common problems and reduce the danger of big power interference.[5]

At the same time as a regional organization might move foreign policy in international relations beyond the dicision-making of a single state and may create a central organization to deal with environmental affairs, it might also serve to polarize larger groups and cement vested interests in certain groups of states making ultimate global integration more difficult.[6] In this sense, it might be argued that the single step approach, mentioned above, is not very effective for crossing a wide ditch and that the jump to a global system from the nation state is necessary.

The agenda for the 1972 U.N. Conference on the Human Environment recognizes that a role can be played by regional organizations. The section of the agenda concerned with the international organizational implications of action proposals includes an item on "particular organizational requirements for meeting needs at regional levels.[7] Moreover, there is increasing recognition that even if a specific environmental problem is global in nature, the solutions to it need not be.[8]

It is clear that there are some problems which, because of their nature, encompass the interests of the global community of states. A good example of this is the broad range of questions encompassed in the term pollution of the seas. All states have an interest in the amelioration of a condition which sends oil slicks up on the shores of the United States, Europe and Latin America, and through which the fish that exist all over the world are found with increasing quantities of toxic substances in their bodies. Yet, the ships that ply the sea lanes, and intentionally or accidentally discharge oil and other hazardous materials into the oceans, fly the flag and are owned by nationals of a particular state. Drilling for oil is another potential pollution source, and discharges of effluent into the ocean or a river emptying into it contribute greatly to the increasing amounts of harmful waste.

There are areas of the high seas where a good case can be made for regulation and control by those states bordering the seas. Recognizing this, the North Sea states[9] agreed in 1969 to cooperate in dealing with pollution of the North Sea by oil,[10] principally by informing one another of the presence of oil slicks or of a casualty likely to cause oil pollution of the sea[11] and calling for the assistance of other contracting states, principally those which seem likely to be affected by the floating oil.[12] However, wastes are also discharged into the sea and tributary rivers in sewage (*e.g.*, nutrients, bacteria and organic loading), from industry, and in the form of pesticides, and oils and detergents.[13] It would appear that agreement could be reached among the same states to deal in a cooperative way with these problems, either through carrying out on a regional level the drafting of standards and policies or developing harmonized legislation, which would be adopted within the individual states.

For this purpose, the North Sea states met in London on June 11, 1971, to consider the problems of the conservation of the living resources of the sea, and the prevention of pollution "whether from inflowing rivers, pipelines and outflows, aerial pathways or from ships."[14] The representatives recognized the urgency of their reaching agreement "as rapidly as possible towards concerted measures to protect the North Sea and other seas from pollution."[15] Some of the urgency is dissipated by the view of the U.K. that the North Sea is not in a polluted state because of the sea's capacity to dilute and purify the wastes.[16]

256

The same cannot, however, be said for the Baltic, where the hydrographical conditions are characterized by the waters of the deep basins being considered stagnant, with an increasing oxygen deficit, phosphorous loading and salinity.[17] Although the area is considered by many to be ripe for regional treatment, there are political problems which must still be overcome. The German Democratic Republic borders on the sea but other states including the West German Federal Republic do not recognize or wish to have formal diplomatic dealings with the GDR, and have thus prevented any formal intergovernmental cooperation. The International Council for the Exploration of the Sea (ICES) which is a non-governmental organization of experts has included information presented to it by oceanographers from the GDR.[18]

If the Stockholm Conference succeeds in concluding an ocean dumping convention, the terms are likely to be flexible enough to permit regional and national requirements that do not fall beneath the minimums established in the agreement.[19]

One of the General Principles stated at the November, 1971 Session of the Intergovernmental Working Group on Marine Pollution which is focusing on those problems as part of the Stockholm Conference preparatory process was that:

States should join together regionally to concert their policies and adopt in common measures to prevent pollution of the areas which for geographical or ecological reasons, form a natural entity and an integrated whole.[20]

C. *The Term Regional Organizations..*

It is very difficult to define exactly what is meant by a regional organization. Among the criteria usually given are geographic proximity, common institutions, common purpose or purposes, and independence of other organizations. For the purposes of this paper, no concise and inclusive definition will be sought. There will be no necessity for an organization to control all or even many of the relations between the various states. In this sense, a regional organization may be either single purpose in nature or multi-purpose. There will also be no necessity for the organization to include states only with geographic contiguity. Such a definition would rule out the OECD and the Economic Commission for Europe. The use of the term will include organizations and commissions of a bilateral nature in addition to those including more than two states. (Organizations of a global nature — such as those of the U.N. and the organization of the U.N. family which operate centrally are not included.) What will be meant in this paper by a regional organization is a body through which two or more states cooperate in the study and/or management of an environmental problem or set of problems, although it may well be that environmental problems form only a small portion of

257

the group's activity. This organization may be an off-shoot of a larger body or may be completely independent. It may be permanent in nature or established for a specific task or tasks. The organization could be one in which only some measure of authority or responsibility is given by the members, or one in which there is a transfer of elements of sovereignty. In fact, the only apparent limitation that this paper puts upon regional organizations is that they are inter-governmental in nature. This is not to underestimate or disregard the contribution that has and is being made by a number of non-governmental organizations which have actively been working and are continuing to work for better environmental quality throughout the world. This is especially true at the scientific and technical level in which both governments and international organizations are dependent on these groups for their expertise and analyses.[21] If, at some future time, one or more of these organizations is involved in a joint effort with a regional organization of an inter-governmental nature (as has been the case with some UNESCO and FAO activities in the past), that joint effort would be included within the term 'regional organization' as used by this paper.

II. THE PRESENT ROLE OF REGIONAL ORGANIZATIONS

Many international organizations of a governmental nature — both global and regional — have been working on selected aspects of environmental problems for many years. The recent excitement, enthusiasm and even perceived need for environmental control has forced many of them to reorganize and rename some of their efforts to attract the attention of this new constituency, as well as the continued support of the member governments.

In examining the role of various existing regional organizations working with environmental problems, there are three major areas of functions which will be considered that they can perform. These functions are: (a) study, (b) catalyst, and (c) management. The present work of some organizations falls into several of these categories, and it is recognized that individual activities may also fit several categories. As used in this section, the functions attempt to be descriptive although their use as normative categories may also be appropriate. Since the management function is the focus of this paper, an extended analysis is given to specific organizations which have been created to carry out management activities.

A. *Study.*

A favored occupation of international organizations is studying specific

258

problems put to the organization by its members or initiated by the secretariat of the organization itself. The OECD, Council of Europe, NATO, CCMS and the ECE engage in such studies. They may merely be to provide exchanges of information among the member states, such as a compilation of the national organizations of each state dealing with environment[22] or a collection of monographs of each state's activities in the field.[23] These reports inform the membership of new techniques and approaches, or help the organization develop its own data or information which might result in action by governments.

In carrying out the studies, regional organizations use several different approaches. First, they might rely on the expertise of members of the secretariat of the organization and draft secretariat reports which would then be presented to the members in the course of meetings either of the committe charged with environment or a parent body. Second, the organization might hire outside consultants — experts in specific fields — to prepare the reports for the secretariat. Third, they might utilize experts drawn from the individual member states who serve in their capacities as experts but who, in fact, often represent the interests and views of the specific governments. It is in this last case that the recommendations of the organization, which are approved by experts from the various countries concerned, stand the best chance of ultimate acceptance by the governments.

This latter point is significant since in the case of many organizations such as the Council of Europe, OECD, or the Regional Economic Commissions, once the study has been completed and recommendations made to governments, the organization is virtually powerless to obtain its enaction into the national law of various states, or accepted as the basis for an international agreement on the subject. It is, perhaps, for this reason that secretariats usually take the view that the actual drafting of a report requiring the agreement of experts from member states constitutes a significant step on the road toward ultimate acceptance by the states of the views contained within the report. However, unless the organizations can go further to secure the implementation of their conclusions, a gap between the idea and the reality will remain.

The great majority of regional organizations, especially in Europe, believes that they each have a special function or constituency which distinguishes their role from that of other organizations, and thus justifies their separate existence. The OECD, consisting of the industrialized countries of the Western World with over two-thirds of the world's trade and a high standard of living, is a unique body for dealing with the economic implications of environmental problems as they affect a market economy system.[24] NATO's CCMS seeks to take advantage of the spirit of cooperation and high level attention which is given to NATO matters by member governments.[25] The U.N.'s Economic Commission for Europe (ECE) finds its special role in the East-West nature of its membership, including all member states of the U.N. or specialized agencies within the European region.[26] The Common Market seeks to take advantage of the degree of cooperation, harmonization and amalgamation among the members of the European Communities.[27] The Council for Mutual Economic Assistance (CMEA) relies on the similar nature of the political and economic systems of its members to ensure cooperation.[28] The Council of Europe attempts to take advantage of the close relationship among legislators and parliamentarians of its wide range of member countries,[29] many of which utilize Council documents in securing legislation at home. The OAS and the OAU seek to represent the interests of the countries of their regions. The U.N.'s three Economic Commissions for regions other than Europe (Africa, Latin America, and Asia and the Far East) seek to exploit their ability to represent regional interests within the context of the U.N. Family.

Information exchange is an important result of studies carried out by these regional organizations. In this way, environmental problems which are both national and international can be aired and techniques and solutions which have been successfully applied by one state can be made known and available to another. The organization can itself develop a range of suggested techniques to be applied in specific environmental circumstances. This, for example, is the aim of the OECD sector groups on air managment, water management, pesticides and urban problems.[30] It is one of the reasons for the pilot study approach taken by the NATO CCMS in such areas as air pollution in which three individual cities — St. Louis, Frankfurt, and Ankara — are being studied by development of air pollution models and techniques for management of urban air pollution problems.[31] Similarly, the Economic Commission for Europe has held seminars on a variety of subjects including river basin management, the desulphurization of fuels and combustion gases, and the protection of ground and surface waters against pollution by oil and oil products.[32]

Included in some of these last ECE documents are recommendations for establishing international standards or international agreements governing the uses of specific areas, such as river basins.

The formulation of recommendations for action by governments comprises another function of these regional organizations. Again, the main problem faced by regional organizations is translating these recommendations into specific action or convincing member governments to accept them.[33] In areas other than the environment, the ECE has been successful in establishing regulations for such technical projects as transport of perishable foodstuffs and vehicle safety. It is too early to determine whether they can be this successful in the environmental sector.

In the late 1970 the ECE adopted a work program stressing action-oriented projects. The program was to be adopted by the ECE Conference on Problems Relating to the Environment planned for Prague in May 1971. Conference results would be assigned to the newly created group of Senior Environmental Advisers. However, because of Eastern Bloc insistence on inviting the East German Democratic Republic as a full participant at the Conference[34] and western rejection of this view the conference was relabeled a "symposium" "with the sole purpose of providing an opportunity for an exchange of views on selected problems in this field."[35] Whether the ECE will be able to meet its potential in this field by sponsoring an active environmental program and utilize its unique role as an organization of developed countries bridging the gap between East and West remains to be seen. The organization is entirely dependent on the good will and initiative of its member states; although some experts attending the Prague Symposium evinced willingness to cooperate, the political constraints on the Symposium made this difficult. The Symposium will, however, be of value to the 1972 Stockholm Conference both in terms of the wealth of documentation on the environmental probelems of developed countries and the political pitfalls of a supposedly non-political topic.[36]

While the ECE has been deeply involved, the other three U.N. Regional Economic Commissions, for Africa (ECA), Latin America (ECLA) and Asia and the Far East (ECAFE), have been far less concerned with environmental problems. In his effort to develop interest among the developing countries, the Secretary-General of the Stockholm Conference has attended regularly scheduled meetings of the Councils of the three organizations and made his pitch to the representatives about the plans for the 1972 Conference. Additionally, a seminar was held in the fall of 1971 by each of the three Regional Commissions which was devoted to the subject of development and environment. A fourth seminar in the series was held by the U.N. Economic Office in Beirut.[37]

There are several relevant questions which should be asked. First, what is the interest of the states from these regions in environmental problems? This is a subject which has and will continue to create controversy and discussion. Two of the three regional organizations passed resolutions which indicated their awareness of the problems, as well as recommending that member states take necessary measures to assist in the preparations for the Conference and the regional seminars preceding it.[38] The second and more relevant question is whether these regional organizations are the proper ones for dealing with regional environmental problems, or for co-ordinating environmental problems in the regions concerned. U.N. population programs are carried out through the Regional Economic Commissions. With respect to the ECA, one commentator has written that "given the political power of functional organizations and the apparent intractability of African political rivalries, the future of regionalism in Africa, and therefore of ECA, is not promising".[39] The strength of the Secretary-General and the use of ECA to co-ordinate and channel development activities such as those of the UNDP may make this body more effective than ECLA and ECAFE, even though ECAFE does have a history of activity in the area of water resources development, including the Mekong River Basin. It is to be noted that although neither the ECA nor the ECLA resolution on the human environment or the ECAFE report contained any expression of interest in developing a future work program on the environment by the regional commission, the reports of the Regional Seminars did forsee a role — albeit a vague one — for these Commissions.

With a view towards changing its orientation from research toward "action", the OECD Council in a resolution of July 24, 1970, terminated the mandate of the Committee on Reserach-Co-operation and established an Environment Committee.[40] The purposes of the committee were to investigate the problems of preserving or improving man's environment and to review members' actions or proposed actions with particular reference to their trade and economic implications; to propose solutions for environmental problems taking into account all relevant factors including cost effectiveness; and to insure that the results of environmental investment would be effectively utilized in the organization's work on economic policy and social development.

With this in mind, the OECD Environment Committee meeting in March of 1971 set out three new programs: one is concerned with international economic implications of environmental policy; another program calls for *ad hoc* studies and sector groups including studies on pollution by the pulp and paper industry, an air management sector group, and an urban environment sector group which is considering the impact of the motor vehicle;[41] finally, a consultative process was established for the early notification of the environmental control measures which would significantly affect international activity. This procedure would give OECD members an opportunity to understand the technical basis for the measures so they can take corrective measures themselves or adopt similar standards. It enables a "confrontation" mechanism to be called into play by the OECD Secretariat or a member country when either believes a measure will adversely affect it.[42]

B. *Catalyst.*

Regional organizations also serve as a catalyst, either to the member governments themselves or to other organizations involved in environmental work. This was one of the major purposes of the U.S. initiative to set up a Committee on the Challenges of Modern Society (CCMS) within NATO. CCMS was begrudgingly foisted upon the NATO alliance by the U.S. which regarded it "as a matter of the highest importance"[43] It was designed to take advantage of NATO's experience in technology transfer and the attention and response the alliance gets from high political officials in member states.[44] One of the benefits of CCMS, according to Daniel P. Moynihan, who as White House Counselor also served as U.S. Representative, will:

come from common undertakings, agreements to act in concert with respect to this or that difficulty or opportunity as such present themselves. This has been the great feat of the Alliance with respect to matters of defense and political consultation. It can become a not less important feature of our response to the common peril of a threatened and threatening environment.[45]

Using a pilot study approach led by one or two countries, with the others as "co-pilots" in specific areas,[46] CCMS has been successful — in fact, more successful than far many other regional organizations. Admittedly, the great majority of action has resulted from U.S. initiatives and U.S. arm-twisting to achieve this success. Yet, it remains that the high level attention given to NATO actions has borne fruit.

A good example is the CCMS experience with the practice of ships intentionally discharging oil and oily wastes into the oceans. On May 20, 1970, President Nixon sent a message to Congress concerning the problem of the threat of oil pollution.[47] This was followed by a Study on Ocean Dumping, transmitted to the Congress on October 7, 1970.[48] The subject was then considered at a special CCMS Oil Spills Conference in Brussels from November 2-6. Secretary of Transportation Volpe, delivering the U.S. position, proposed that "NATO nations resolve to achieve — by mid-decade but not later than 1980 — a complete halt to all intentional discharge of oil and oily wastes into the oceans by tankers and other vessels."[49] In describing how the NATO Conference would help achieve this goal, Secretary Volpe articulated the catalyst function:

We view this conference as a gathering where recommendations for action may be agreed upon which in large part can be individually and collectively implemented elsewhere.[50]

A resolution of the Conference, adopted on November 6, accepted and approved the U.S. proposal and urged the convening of a special session of the IMCO Assembly in 1971 for the "preparation and effective implementation of such measures in a treaty to be drafted and adopted in 1973 at the International Conference on Marine Pollution."[51] Within a month, this resolution was "endorsed" by the North Atlantic Council meeting in Ministerial Session.[52]

The next step took place at the March 1971 meeting of the IMCO Maritime Safety Committee which after discussion and amendment approved the holding of a Conference to draft an agreement governing the international discharge of oil and oily wastes and noxious substances other than oil into the oceans by tankers and other vessels.[53] The Soviet Union added the phrase "noxious substances other than oil" pursuant to their long-held view that radioactive wastes not be disposed of at sea.[54] More significant than the amendment is the fact that non-NATO states, including the Soviet Union, were willing to accept an agreement having its origin in a NATO CCMS activity.

The Council of Europe also attempts to act as a catalyst in its Ministerial declarations by recommending the enaction of legislation in member countries and through the "raising of the level of consciousness" on the environment, which was one of the principle purposes of the 1970 Conservation Year.

A second aspect of catalytic activity is through education and training. The purpose is to develop expertise in a needed field among a broader range of individuals who can either serve their own country or an international organization. Here the regional organizations have been behind the global institutions in developing programs. As examples of the work of some of the global institutions, the IAEA has a well developed program for training nuclear inspectors. Although the program goes through the Agency, it is actually carried out by one or more of the members. Thus, the U.S. Atomic Energy Commission holds programs for inspectors at its Argonne Laboratory in Illinois. WHO has devoted upwards of 10% of its project expenditures to education and training.[55] WHO trains sanitary engineers, medical hygienists, specialists in public health, epidemiology of environmental health, and in part operates through regional affiliates such as the Pan American Health Organization.[56] Fellowships are offered for advanced research by some of the regional organizations, but only NATO has earmarked a specific number for environmental studies.

C. Environmental Management.

The third category of functions which have been performed by regional organizations with respect to environmental problems are those of management. Included in this category are planning functions, such as the development or use of the resources of an area; actual standard setting and enforcement; the drafting of effluent charges which apply internationally; other avenues of enforcement such as policing along the boundaries and questions of the settlement of the disputes of environmental nature. The organizations which thus far have engaged in or have the potential for this kind of function have been different from those discussed above. They are usually organizations centering around an individual river basin or charged with environmental problems that may arise between the borders of two or more states. They are a good example of the application of the principle of inclusion of those nations with direct interest. There are too many of these organizations to describe, or even list in detail. There are some, however, which because of the enormity of the problems they deal with should be discussed. The three organizations which will be treated deal with the Rhine River, the

Danube River, the border between the United States and Canada which includes the Great Lakes system, the St. Lawrence River and the Columbia River system.

1. *The Rhine River.*

The Rhine River, from Basel to its mouth at Rotterdam, is polluted.[57] Of the four riparian states, Switzerland, the Federal Republic of Germany, France and The Netherlands, The Netherlands as the lower riparian state is most concerned. Upstream poisoning can render the entire water supply drawn from the Rhine useless in The Netherlands. The Rhine has reached its heavily pollutied state while it has been subject to regulation by two Commissions. The first, the Central Commission for the Navigation of the Rhine, was established as a result of the Congress of Vienna in 1815. The Central Commission's present statute dates from the Convention of Mannheim which was signed on October 17, 1868. The members of the Commission at this time are Belgium, France, the Federal Republic of Germany, Netherlands, Switzerland and the United Kingdom. The United States, which was a member after World War II pursuant to its responsibility for Germany, no longer considers itself an active member. The limitation of the Central Commission in dealing with environmental problems on the Rhine River is that its concern is solely navigation: only if the cause of pollution on the river stems from navigation, would it fall within the competence of the Commission. If, as is the case in the Rhine, waste salts from the Alsatian region in France, industiral pollution around Basel in Switzerland, and German industry in the various tributaries to the Rhine comprise the great majority of the pollution, this commission is without responsibility or competence.

As concern with Rhine pollution grew, it did not seem likely that the Central Commission would be wiling to expand its functions to include those of land-based pollution on the river. This was in part due to historic reasons. The Central Commission includes states solely interested in the navigation of the river while only the riparian states — Switzerland, Germany, France and The Netherlands — are concerned with its pollution. Of those four, as indicated above, The Netherlands is predictably the most concerned. Belgium, a member of the Central Commission which is not a riparian state, is concerned with pollution only insofar as pollution at the mouth of the Rhine might affect the port of Antwerp. Thus, in 1963, at the primary urging of The Netherlands, the second Rhine Commission, the International Commission for the Protection of the Rhine against Pollution, came into being with Switzerland, the Federal Republic of Germany, France, The Netherlands and Luxembourg as parties.[58] However, despite the hopes for cleaning up the Rhine as a result of the formation of this new body, little has been done.

It is clear that it is not the Commission which has the primary responsibility for water pollution problems on the Rhine, but the national authorities who carry out this responsibility, each for its own territory in accordance with its own legislation.[59] The Commission is composed of up to four delegates from each party and experts designated by them.[60] Decisions are taken by unanimous vote with each delegation casting one vote. Abstention of one delegate is not an obstacle to unanimity.[61]

Under Article 2 of the Convention, the Commission prepares and carries out research to determine the nature, quantity and origin of the pollution of the Rhine and analyzes the results of the research. It can also propose to the governments measures susceptible of protecting the Rhine against pollution. It is entrusted with working out details of future arrangements between the signatory governments concerning the protection of the waters of the Rhine. The Commission is competent to act in all other such matters as the signatory governments may by agreement refer to it. Among the areas of research engaged in by the Commission is a solution for the elimination of residual salts ffrom the French potash mines in Alsace, the problem of the discharge of cooling water from thermal power stations and problems resulting from the emissions of radioactive substances and bilge water into the river.[62]

The problem with the Commission, as noted above, is that its independent power is nil. Even with power, it is not clear that they would effectively exercise it. Further, its Statute requires a unanimous vote of the delegation being present in order to take any action.[63] Thus, when millions of fish died in the Rhine in June 1969 as a result of a pesticide spill, it was extremely difficult for the Commission to establish the causes (which have still not been definitively established) and to seek action against the plant discharging the pesticide.[64] As a result of this accident, however, which, in addition to the fish kill, caused severe danger to the drinking water supply in The Netherlands, cooperation has increased. In the view of The Netherlands, dead fish are too late a warning that there is a poison problem in the Rhine River, and they have suggested that there is a serious need for an automatic measuring and alarm equipment system which would signal pollutants or poisons. They regretted that such equipment is not yet available.[65] One group of experts has proposed that each riparian state contribute six percent of its GNP to Rhine cleanup. The response has not been great.[66]

The Commission for the Protection of the Rhine against Pollution was designed to centralize consideration of pollution questions on the Rhine River. However, the Central Commission for the Navigation of the Rhine still retains functions dealing with pollution insofar as it results from navigation. The Central Commission, composed of one representative from each state, votes by a plurality.[67] There is also a secretariat. The Commission has its own enforcement and dispute settlement machinery in the Rhine River Police who are national police of the riparian states who co-ordinate their activities along the river. There is also a court system which can apply criminal sanctions for violations of the regulations concerning navigation of the Rhine.[68]

Thus, if there is an accident such as a collision between two vessels causing pollution on the river, the Rhine River Police would notify interested parties of the accident who could then take the necessary clean-up and preventive action to prevent pollution of the shoreline. The case would then be presented to the Rhine Navigation Court which would have criminal jurisdiction to investigate and judge the contravention to regulations relating to navigation.[69] There is appeal to the Central Commission itself or to a higher court of the country in which the judgment has been given.[70] Civil damages may also be brought on the basis of the criminal action, either in the Rhine Navigation Courts or in the courts of the state when the damage is clearly a result of navigation. The Rhine Court can deal both with criminal and civil damages. The key to the jurisdiction of these courts is that damage must be caused by a ship while on voyage and the damage must relate to navigation. Thus, for example, if there were a fish kill as a result of the accident, any damage or loss of livelihood would be actionable only in a state court and not as a result of the jurisdiction of the Rhine Court.

Recognizing that hazardous materials were carried and transported along the Rhine and as a result of the endosulphan spill into the river from land-based sources, the Central Commission has drawn up regulations for the transport of dangerous materials on the Rhine.[71] These regulations and their technical annexes fix the conditions under which dangerous materials can be transported on the Rhine. The annexes list certain materials which because of the hazard cannot be transported on the river. The regulations, in Article 4, also contain contingency plans for action in the event of emergency by the riparian states, and that there will be a coordination of contingency plans to take care of accidents.[72]

Thus, it appears that the older Central Commission for the Navigation of the Rhine, which has narrowly construed its function to include only navigation, can, because of its stronger Secretariat and its history of authority, play a more vital role than can the newer Pollution Prevention Commission, which is largely advisory in nature and does not contain effective machinery for regulating pollution problems. Faced with a serious problem, the four riparian states were not sufficiently willing to internationalize the management functions because their interests were different and the impetus for the new commission was largely the idea of one state.

2. The Danube.

The Danube River flowing from West Germany to the Black Sea poses different kinds of problems and a different range of interests than does the Rhine. The Congress of Paris in 1856 had declared the river to be an international waterway and provided for a regime including the participation of non-riparian states.[73] In this it is similar to the Rhine. On August 18, 1948, a new convention regarding the regime of navigation on the Danube was signed in Belgrade.[74] The original parties to the convention were the USSR, Bulgaria, Hungary, Romania, the Ukrainian SSR, Czechoslovakia and Yugoslavia. Following independence in 1955 Austria declared that the Convention was not applicable to it, but it later acceded in 1965. The Federal Republic of Germany is not a member of the Danube Commission.[75] The Commission is composed of one representative of each state[76] with a Secretariat from member states.[77] The convention also established special river administrations for the Iron Gates area — between Romania and Yugoslavia — and the lower Danube between the Black Sea and Braila in Romania.[78] Although the primary function of the Danube Commission, like that of the Rhine Commission, is navigation, it has also engaged in coordinative hydrologic services, has worked with problems of flood control, and sponsored hydro-electric planning. The Convention also considers questions of sanitation as well as those of navigation and river inspection,[79] but a narrow reading of the Convention given by many governments ties these interests to the primary interest of navigation. In fact, the sole activity concerning pollution *per se* engaged in by the Commission was a decision of the 19th session in 1961 concerning the disposition of petroleum wastes from boats.[80] This decision forbids boats, either while en route or stationed in port, to put petroleum wastes or other petroleum products in any form into the water. Such wastes or other products are to be placed in stationary or floating containers to be provided by the riparian states. However, the Commission only *recommended* that the Danubian states place sufficient containers in their ports to receive the wastes. Their authority was limited to regulation of navigation and could not extend to shore based facilities. The Commission also *recommended* that the states periodically inform the Commission as to the status of installation in Danubian ports of facilities for receipt of wastes and other petroleum products. At its most recent session in 1971, reports were received from Austria, Bulgaria, Hungary, Czechoslovakia, the USSR and the Federal Republic of Germany concerning the efforts they had made.[81] No reponse was received from Romania and Yugoslavia. Of those states reporting, the size and number of the receptacles seemed inadequate.

With respect to the possibility of international cooperation on the Danube dealing more specifically with pollution problems, there is a great difference in the views of the riparian states. There is general agreement that the Danube is polluted in all of its reaches.[82] Hungary is of the view that:

it is a great problem to keep pollution away from places and areas where the water is abstracted. The difficulty lies in the fact that no international agreement exists. Oil pollution is a special menace and is considerable at present only on the Danube where it appears in small but constant quantities. It is created by oil refineries and improper handling of oil transporting vessels. The purification techniques are imperfect at present.[83]

Hungary is especially concerned since 96% of its water supply comes from abroad, and much of it is in need of treatment. Austria, as the upper riparian state, is one of the major contributors to the pollution of water flowing into Hungary. There are at present no waste treatment facilities in the capital city of Vienna or in Linz. For this reason, Austria is very chary of submitting the question of Danube pollution to an international body. They would rather first put their own house in order before internationalizing the problem. At this time, however, it appears as though waste treatment facilities will not be installed in Vienna and Linz until after 1980. The other state which is most opposed to truly internationalizing questions of Danube pollution is the Soviet Union. Basing their position on the concept of sovereignty and sovereign equality, they consider that international solutions consist only of coordination of national policies.[84] This is what is done presently on the Danube in which basically the riparian states coordinate with one another within their own reach of the river rather than meeting as a collegial body to consider the problems of the Danube as a whole.

Another potential problem of Danube pollution stems from the construction between Romania and Yugoslavia of the Iron Gates hydropower and navigation project.[85] In Yugoslavia where the Tisza, Drava and Sava Rivers empty into the Danube, the river increases in speed from about 2,000 cubic meters per second to over 5,000 cubic meters per second. The rapids at the Iron Gates area between Romania and Yugoslavia have long impeded navigation, and the development of a dam and locks will flood the rapids and increase the ability of ships to navigate the channel. It will also provide considerable hydroelectric power to the two countries. This development is considered by the two countries to be "an extraordinary example of international cooperation both in the hydro-energetics and the sphere of the Danube navigation."[86] However, what is not discussed is the effect that the dam will have on the ability of the Danube, especially in the rapidity of its flow, to cleanse itself of pollutants poured into it. There is also the possibility that siltation will build up on the upstream side of the dam, narrowing the channel and making it more shallow.

Since the elements of sovereignty are so closely involved in the creation of any international body with supervisory and decision making powers, there seems little likelihood at the present that the Danube Commission will expand its role to meet the needs of the Danube states in taking charge of pollution problems. It has been proposed that the U.N.'s Economic Commission for Europe study the problem of pollution of the Danube, the river system being one involving both eastern and western states, all of whom are members of the ECE. Although its

269

task would not be easy, studying the problem might lead to the creation of a new organization to deal specifically with Danube pollution (both air and water) or increase of the functions of the present Commission. The success of these changes would be dependent on the Danubian states to recognize their very real interest in preserving this valuable resource. The degree of recognition varies considerably along the river. Moreover, a super river basin problem will soon become even more real when plans are completed for the joining of the Rhine and the Danube. This may be sufficient to cause the two river basin groupings to consider their problems together.

3. *The International Joint Commission.*

The International Joint Commission (IJC) between the United States and Canada was established by treaty in 1909.[87] The IJC differs from the Rhine and Danube Commissions in that its jurisdiction is not confined to a particular basin or to problems dealing with navigation. The Commission has jurisdiction to prevent disputes regarding the use of the boundary waters as well as jurisdiction to settle other questions or matters of difference between the two states concerning the interests of either in relation to the other along the common frontier between the U.S. and Canada. In addition, the level of boundary waters or structures such as dams cannot be materially altered without the Commission's consent.

As distinguished from the Rhine and Danube Commissions, pollution has been an important area of concern from the very beginning of the IJC's existence. Article 4, paragraph 2, of the Boundary Waters Treaty states that:

It is further agreed that the waters herein defined as boundary waters and waters flowing across the boundary shall not be polluted on either side to the injury of health or property on the other.

There is little doubt that both the spirit and letter of this provision have not been complied with. However, no standards, guidelines or objectives were established to guide the United States and Canada in pursuit of this article. Consequently, the two states have made much greater use of Articl IX of the Boundary Waters Treaty which enables the governments to refer matters to the Commission for its "examination and report."[88] As early as 1918, the IJC concluded in a report dealing with pollution of the boundary waters that pollution was "very intense along the shores of the Detroit and Niagara Rivers" and that "conditions exist which imperil the health and welfare of the citizens of both countries in direct contravention of the treaty."[89] In fact, the IJC was asked by the governments to draft a convention or reciprocal legislation which would give the IJC ample jurisdiction to regulate and prohibit the pollution of boundary waters, but the Commission Draft of October 1920

270

was never negotiated to a successful conclusion.[90] The provisions of that draft agreement are modest, though many years ahead of their time. The Commission was given authority to investigate any alleged violation of Article IV of the Boundary Waters Treaty and was to report on its inquiry. On the basis of the Commission's findings of fact which "shall be final and conclusive", the parties are required to take such proceedings as are necessary to prevent a continuation of the breach.[91] The Commission was also given authority to define classes of vessels "in which apparatus for the disinfection of the sewage, bilge water or ballast discharged therefrom should be installed to prevent the pollution of waters," and the parties agreed not to grant licenses for such vessels as did not meet IJC requirements.[92] Finally, the parties agreed to enact or recommend legislation to their legislatures for full enforcement of the convention.[93]

Had the Commission's foresight been rewarded, and the agreement signed and ratified, the Great Lakes would very likely not be in the heavily polluted state that they now are. The number of instances in which the IJC subsequently considered various pollution problems are too many to be recounted here.[94] Suffice it to say, in addition to questions of water pollution, the Commission has dealt with questions of air pollution, the effects of raising or lowering levels of various boundary waters, and a question of aesthetic pollution involving the enhancement of natural beauty of the American Falls at Niagara Falls, New York[95]

The most recent report of the IJC dealing with the question of pollution of the lower Great Lakes and the St. Lawrence River is worthy of more detailed discussion because of its future institutional impact. On October 7, 1964, by identical letters to the two sections of the IJC, the U.S. and Canadian governments requested the Commission to inquire into and report on three questions: (1) Are the waters of Lake Erie, Lake Ontario and the international section of the St. Lawrence River polluted; (2) if yes, to what extent, by what causes, and where; (3) and if the pollution of the character referred to is taking place, "what remedial measures would, in its judgment, be most practicable from the economic, sanitary and other point of view and what would be the probable cost thereof."[96] This not insubstantial task was added to on March 21, 1969, when, after the Santa Barbara oil pollution incident, the governments requested the Commission to make a special report within the context of the existing reference on the adequacy of existing safety requirements applicable to underwater drilling in production operations in Lake Erie to prevent oil escaping into the lake, known methods of confining and cleaning up the spill, existing contingency plans and their implementation dealing with such spills.[97]

The procedure followed by the International Joint Commission in reaching its conclusions some six years after the initial request was officially made by the governments was typical, though larger in scope than its earlier references. For technical guidance, the Commission appointed Technical Boards composed of senior officials of the federal, state and provincial governments who served in their professional rather than official capacities. In this instance, one Board dealt with the problems of Lake Erie, and a second with Lake Ontario and the International Section of the St. Lawrence. The Boards were directed to review and make use of existing information and data and also to execute the necessary investigations and studies to advise the Commission on the specific questions set out in the reference.

Two interim reports were submitted to the Commission by the Boards before its final detailed summary report was submitted in September 1969. The Board also submitted a separate report dealing with the question of the possibility of oil pollution from drilling in Lake Erie.[98] Following receipt of the Board's report, public hearings on the problem were held on both sides of the border. It was clear that the Commission would find that the waters in question were being seriously polluted on both sides of the boundary to the detriment of both countries and to an extent which is causing injury to health and property on the other side of the boundary.[99] The Commission also recommended both general and specific water quality objectives to be adopted by both the U.S. and Canadian governments as a matter of urgency and urged the immediate reduction in the phosphorus content in detergents.[100] The Commission also concluded, with respect to potential oil drilling in Lake Erie, that safety requirements where they existed and if effectively supervised and enforced are adequate, although current methods of dealing with a major oil spill are primitive and inadequate.[101] The Commission further noted that although the U.S. had a contingency plan for the Lake Erie region, Canada did not, and furthermore, there was no formal plan for international cooperation on oil spills.[102] Therefore, they stressed the need for international contingency planning to cope with major spills of hazardous or radioactive materials.[103]

The Commission also concluded that:

The governments of Canada and the United States specifically confer upon this Commission the authority, responsibility and means for coordination, surveillance, monitoring, implementation, reporting, making recommendations to governments ... and other such duties related to preservation and improvement of the quality of the boundary waters of the Great Lakes-St. Lawrence system as may be agreed by the said governments; the Commission to be authorized to establish, in consultation with the governments, an international board or boards to assist it in carrying out these duties and to delegate to said board or boards such suthority and responsibility as the Commission may deem appropriate.[104]

On June 10, 1971, the Foreign Minister of Canada and the Chairman of the U.S. Council on Environmental Quality met in Washington to discuss problems of pollution in the Great Lakes. Their communique included the following statements:

They agreed that the U.S. and Canadian Governments should conclude, before the end of the year, an agreement on water quality control. The contents of this agreement have been generally agreed during extensive discussion among the governments concerned over the past months. The proposed agreement would establish Common Water Quality Objectives based upon the recommendations of the International Joint Commission for the boundary waters of the Great Lakes System and would commit the Governments to the development of compatible water quality standards and to the implementation of programs and other measures designed to attain these objectives. Under the proposed agreement the Governments concerned would exchange commitments to carry out a variety of pollution control programs within agreed time periods, including: (a) construction of treatment facilities for municipal and industrial wastes and animal husbandry operations, (b) reduction of phosphorus discharges, (c) elimination of mercury and other toxic heavy metals from discharges, (d) control of thermal pollution, (e) control of pollution from radioactive wastes, (f) control of pollution from pesticides, and (g) development of controls for pollution from combined sewer overflows.

They agreed further that the Governments should assign additional responsibility and authority to the International Joint Commission to assist the Governments in their efforts to restore and protect Great Lakes water quality. The Commission would be given a greater role in surveillance of water quality in the Great Lakes, monitoring of the effectiveness of governmental programs to achieve the common water quality objectives, making recommendations for legislation and programs, and coordinating activities to achieve improved water quality in the Great Lakes (including spot checks of water quality in the boundary waters).

With respect to the institutional arrangements which will be required by the International Joint Commission to carry out these new responsibilities, the Ministers and representatives supported the establishment of a Board (or Boards) under the Commission, to assist in the implementation of the agreement. It was agreed that the Board (or Boards) should provide for a balanced membership from Canada and the United States which would be appointed by the International Joint Commission after consultation with the Governments concerned. Sub-Boards could be created to deal with specific functional responsibilities and specific geographical areas within the Great Lakes basin.

It was agreed that it would be necessary to provide the International Joint Commission with additional staff and other resources in order to enable it to carry out its expanded functions. The appointments to the staff would be the responsibility of the International Joint Commission, although the Governments concerned would be consulted. Ministers and representatives believed that the establishment of an office in the Great Lakes area for the performance of the new functions of the International Joint Commission should be considered.[105]

The Ministers noted, however, that the programs recommeded by the IJC would still be implemented through federal, state and provincial government programs. The Ministers also announced that the governments were proceeding with the development of the joint contingency plan for coordinated response to pollution incidents involving oil spills and spills of other hazardous materials and the extension of new references to the IJC broadening their responsibility to Lakes Superior and Huron and requesting them to extend their surveillance of water quality to those two lakes. Finally, in what may be the most significant step, the Ministers stated:

Ministers and representatives envisaged that the process of intergovernmental cooperation employed in designing the proposed agreement on Great Lakes water quality could be applied to the solution of other common environmental problems, for example, air pollution. In this connection, they noted that the International Joint Commission was studying the problems of air pollution in the area of Detroit-Windsor and Port Huron-Sarnia.[106]

Recognition was given by both governments to the fact that there were trade-offs between air and water pollution which might have to be dealt with at the same time rather than separately by different boards or agencies of individual governments. Although the governments in this instance did not commit themselves to any future course of action, this remains a significant finding and hope for the future integration of environmental problems in a central international commission.[107]

Although the IJC has had a long history of involvement in pollution matters, it is only now "coming into its own". The impetus was the realization by both states that the problem was extremely serious, and that it could not be effectively met by individual action. There remains, however, a significant element of unwillingness to place too much responsibility in an international body, to the diminution of national means of regulation.

III. THE FUTURE OF REGIONAL ORGANIZATIONS

A. *The Need for Co-ordination.*

A large number of regional organizations have been carrying out at considerable effort to themselves and cost to their memeber states an examination of a range of subjects which has enabled them to engage in a great number of functions designed to improve and enhance the environmental quality of the area in which they operate. Despite assurances to the contrary, there is an enormous need for coordination of the work of the various regional as well as global organizations to avoid needless duplication in their work. It is recognized that the word co-ordination can mean different things to different people or groups. It can merely connote an awareness of what others are doing; it might indicate formal aspects of co-operation or official "linkages" among organizations; or it could lead to a clearing-house type of operation with a central organ directing priorities among organizations and channeling funds to programs of its choosing. At this time, none of these types exists to a sufficient degree. This co-ordination must be carried out at three levels: nationally, regionally, and globally.

There is first a need for each state to decide what its environmental priorities are domestically and internationally and where, in what manner, and at what cost it will encourage international activity in search of solutions to various environmental problems. At the present time, it

274

seems obvious that the majority of states have not yet co-ordinated their own activities. This does not necessarily have to await a domestic reorganization, but rather requires strong leadership from the Foreign Office or another central body within each government which will oversee international activities. At the present time, this lack of co-ordination is manifested in two separate ways. First, if a state decides that a certain environmental problem needs to be studied internationally, it may instruct its delegates to each and every organization which has even a tangential interest in that problem to urge that organization to study the problem. This results, or can result, in needless duplication of effort. There is also validity to the view that competition among organizations does have value and that programs should be discussed in several organizations. At the other extreme, it is often the case that a state will send different representatives to different organizations who are unfamiliar or unconcerned with centrally directed policy. Therefore, it is not strange that IMCO has been viewed as espousing the interests of the transportation industry, FAO that of the agriculture lobby, and IAEA that of the atomic energy interests.

This disparity is less true of the regional organizations although it is clear that there is a good deal of jockeying among those who attend the various organizations to give pre-eminence at home to the organization they attend. One result of this is a confusion on the part of the secretariats of various organizations which believe that they are espousing the will of their members and at times find it difficult to understand why the views of their membership which is identical or very similar to that of another organization appear to have objectives which may conflict with those of other organizations. It is clear that expertise is needed in the various specialized agencies, as well as in specialized regional organizations. Yet, it is important for each member to have a rationalized policy. There are at least some organizations, however, who view their role as representing a global interest and attempt to fulfill that mission, irrespective of the views of the membership.

On a global level, co-ordination has been attempted. The specialized agencies of the United Nations have an Administrative Coordinating Committee (ACC) which has established a functional group to co-ordinate environmental problems. This has had only limited success, but there is at least a structure and a history bringing together representatives from the various organizations who meet to discuss common problems.

The ACC, however, does not extend beyond the U.N. family and, in fact, some of the organizations which consider their mission global in nature do not see the reason to co-ordinate their activities with those organizations which are "narrower" in scope. GESAMP, a group of experts dealing with the scientific aspects of marine pollution, has been only slightly more successful in co-ordinating their activity.[108]

The regional organizations, even those in Europe, do not have an effective way of co-ordinating their activities. The regional branches of the various specialized agencies, or the Regional Economic Commissions, can co-ordinate through ECOSOC or the parent specialized agency, but in the case of the regional commissions, they do not appear to do this.

Regional organizations utilize three main types of co-ordination: first, there is the invitation of representatives from one organization to attend the meetings, conferences and seminars of the other. This is often done on a formalized basis by means of "relationship agreement". With respect to at least one organization, NATO, there is an inhibition on the part of some organizations which have member states that are "neutral" and which believe that attending a NATO meeting, or inviting a representative from NATO, would in some way impair their neutrality. Second, there are exchanges between the secretariats of various organizations. This is usually done on an "old boy" informal basis by a secretariat member who knows a counterpart in a different organizations. The third method is through officials from member states who, by attending various regional organizations as representatives, are able to bring to several organizations a co-ordinated view of plans and programs. This last mode of co-ordination is, fortunately, on the increase.

What is needed is a reactivation of an institution which at one time served the interests of many organizations in Europe. A consultative committee of Secretaries-General consisting of the senior officer of the Council of Europe, OECD, ECE, ELDO, ESRO, EEC and EFTA met at six to eight-month intervals at the Secretary-General level. They now meet only once a year at a much lower level making more difficult the avoidance of duplication and the co-ordination of actual policies. Such meetings could be carried out in various regions of the world besides Europe, where regional organizations of an environmental bent have flourished more than in the other areas.

Perhaps an additional problem of organizations which have environmental concerns as only one of their activities, is to integrate these concerns into the more traditional concerns of the organization. Thus, the ECE water and energy sectors, for example, may not co-ordinate their activities with the Environment Committee. In trying to overcome the same problem the OAS has attempted to integrate environmental concerns in its existing Housing and Urban Planning and Regional Development divisions.[109] It is very important that any co-ordinating mechanism, established as a result of the Stockholm Conference, provide for co-ordination with regional organizations as well. The idea has been suggested that the Secretariat could remain in continuous consultation with all organizations and could put them in touch with one another by serving as a "switchboard". This makes a great deal of sense. If, as has been suggested, the co-ordination should take place through a subsidiary organ of ECOSOC,[110] regional organizations could be included under

Article 71 of the Charter.[111] This, however, is not a satisfactory solution.

Finally, new means must be found for co-ordination between inter-governmental organizations — regional and global — and the host of non-governmental organizations whose research and data gathering is so necessary to the intergovernmental organizations' efforts. This type of linkage will hopefully result from the efforts of the U.N. Conference on the Environment, possibly through the type of mechanism described by Abram Chayes in his paper on institutions.[112]

B. *The Relationship of Regional Organizations to Global Organizations.*

Much of what has been said in this paper has purposely ignored the role of global international organizations dealing with environmental problems. This is because the principal role to be played in the near future by such organizations, be they intergovernmental or non-governmental, will be that of continuing research into various environmental problems; co-ordinating the activities of the various organizations and of member states; providing valuable services for information exchange, technological assistance, education and training; and serving a management function in those common areas of the world in which all states have a genuine direct interest in assuring that environmental degradation is not increased.[113] If there are to be regional institutions charged with collecting and disseminating information about specific environmental problems within a particular area or researching regional or specific problems, these should be co-ordinated under the umbrella of one global organization since, although a problem may be regional in nature, it might be similar to a problem which exists in another region. Such is the case with eutrophication of lakes,[114] the use and effect of persistent pesticides,[115] the threat of schistosomiasis resulting from the construction of dams, and the sanitary and health problems of urban environments. Management activities present more of a challenge. In those areas in which there are both regional and global interests — such as the pollution of the sea — more attention should be paid to the interaction of standards to assure that they will not be inconsistent. Thus, for example, if as a result of the efforts of the North Sea states to limit dumping of wastes, certain criteria and standards are developed, they should be able to mesh with a convention on the same subject that may result from the Stockholm Conference.[116] The rationalization of standards and policies should also be pursued since the interests of a particular regional organizations might be antithetical to the interests of another region to the global community as a whole.

It is by no means clear how developing countries view the advantages of utilizing regional organizations. If they are dissatisfied with the rule making and law making of the more traditional developed states, as is the case articulated by some states in the Asian-African Legal Development Committee with respect to the rules governing river basins,[117] or if they otherwise seek to develop organizations with those states sharing similar interests, regional organizations could be advantageous. On the other hand, if their principal goal is to obtain capital for their development, be it by environmentally sound or unsound methods, then a global organization might enable them to make their weight felt, by sheer numbers, and thus enable them to capitalize on the greater interest shown by developed countries in environment by insisting that their views are written into resolutions or programs. Thus, the developing countries might well turn to UNCTAD for enaction of their interests with respect to environmental control and development. However, it is also possible for global organizations such as the World Bank or the UNDP to channel their funds through a regional body which might better respond to the needs of the particular region. This is already being done with population and other programs as well as by WHO and FAO, through their regional offices.

C. *The Potential of Regional Organizations.*

The remaining questions concern the future. What sort of roles can regional organizations play in the future in a world which will give more than lip service to meeting environmental problems, yet is beset by internal and international disagreement as to the extent of the problem and its relative importance in relationship to other priority areas such as growth and economic development? The answer to this question depends, in part, on the kind of (rather than the specific) regional organization concerned, the functions given to it, and the area of the world in which it is located. In viewing the potential role, the discussion of functions in terms of study, catalyst, and management will be followed.[118]

1. *Study* — Those organizations which have performed studies for their member states will undoubtedly continue to do so in the future, although there hopefully will be more co-ordination. The sectoral approach adopted by some organizations[119] seems particularly suited to environmental problems. This would encompass both the physical problems and the economic trade and cost problems. Research, both on an individual and group basis, could proceed regionally to consider land use of a specific type of area (e.g., plains, forests) on a biome basis, including those states with a direct interest in the problem. It could include governmental and private efforts harnessed together in a joint venture with funding from a mix of national and international sources.[120]

One of the most significant environmental problems which is in need of study throughout the world is that of the environemntal effects of energy pr●duction. In the United States this is already a major issue which is recognized as in need of serious study.[121] Could not a regional organization consider not only questions of energy needs of its area, but also questions of environmental effects of the use of different forms of energy production and consumption, the ability of long-range transmission of power to reduce some of the harmful environmental effects, and how each region can best deal with the problem?[122]

A priority area for study would be an analysis by either a global organization or a regional organization of the specific problem sheds[123] within a region or regions which would be susceptible of management on a basis of including those states with a direct inerest in the problem. In this context it is important to reiterate that the region is determined by the limits of the problem rather than geographic proximity.

Regional organizations could also establish or sponsor institutes to assist in the training and education of individuals in countries within their region in the skills necessary for better environmental management. This is a key function which has only marginally been explored but which could find sponsorship in the four U.N. Regional Economic Commissions, or the OAS and OAU, within the regional offices of WHO, FAO, or UNESCO for specific functions. Moreover, the channeling of funds from lending agencies to any of these regional groups will help assure a wider than national base for training individuals from several countries.

2. *Catalyst* — Regional organizations can act as catalysts in two separate directions. First, they can influence national legislatures to act more expeditiously. Mention has already been made of the work of the Council of Europe and NATO in this regard. A regional group established or charged by governments to deal with a specific problem may make easier the acceptance by those governments of stringent standards or objectives. This may increasingly be the experience of such bodies as the International Joint Commission. Working outwards, regional organizations can increasingly be used to prod global organizations to action. Groups with similar interests may find it easier to agree, if they are not constantly engaging in disputing claims of states with completely different interests. An end to posturing could only help to enhance the potential for international cooperation and action on an environmental level. This hopefully will be one of the results of the co-ordinating body discussed above.

3. *Management* — For the immediate future, states will continue to be the primary level of government at which environmental protection is practiced. However, with a developing awareness of the actual scope of particular environmental problems there will be an increasing amount of responsibility given to international institutions. The first steps will be small and tentative. They might involve co-ordinated planning of the development of an area such as a river basin or a forest or plains area. An

early step certainly will be an evaluation of the studies mentioned above which identifies the parameters of problem areas and, perhaps, even surveys the environmental problems. Thereafter, those states sharing a particular problem should meet to determine what functions if any they believe can be carried out in common,[124] in addition to those activities which they wish to be carried out in parallel.[125]

Are a host of brand new organizations needed to carry out these new environmental management functions? Not necessarily. There are many existing organizations which because of their technical nature are largely overlooked which might be utilized and, given increased political support, might be considerably more effective. Some of those have been described above;[126] there are similar organizations which, because of their lack of history, are not fettered by the original purposes for which they were established.[127] Commissions are already in existence charged with the development of the Indus River Basin,[128] the Mekong River Basin,[129] the River Plata Basin,[130] the Niger River Basin,[131] the Lake Chad Basin[132] and Lake Constance.[133]

What follows is a discussion of management functions which might be carried out by regional organizations.

Notification. The OECD program for early notification of programs which might have an impact on the environment, with the right of states to consult if they object to the program, could be emulated by other organizations, especially those just mentioned, which are charged with jurisdiction over a particular area or with a particular problem.

Planning. Almost all of the organizations just mentioned above were principally established to develop the regions, utilizing the potential hydroelectric power of the river basin as a key to economic development. An integral part of good planning or development — rather than something set in opposition to it — is sound environmental planning and development. This would include writing in procedures for notification of planned projects, regional consideration of resource and land use, regional site planning for industies and municipalities and use of expert advisors to consider alternatives. It would also include planning to avoid overtaxing the auto-purification capacity of a river, consideration of air pollution problems, in advance, dealing with disposal of solid waste, planning to avoid problems stemming from soil erosion, irrigation and dam construction. The OAS input into the planning of the Rio Plata River Basin Project is attempting to include some of these factors.[134]

Planning could also assist in the development of institutions and trained individuals, working within each country or for the regional body. Without such institutions to effectively implement the goals, plans, and standards, the entire process will be largely ineffective and futile.[135]

Monitoring. An organization charged with responsibility for a particular problem shed, be it river basin or air shed, or both, should effectively be able ot monitor the area under its jurisdiction for compliance with any existing environmental quality standards. The monitoring could be carried out by individuals drawn from the various national bodies presently charged with monitoring, seconded to the international or joint body. This would not involve much of an increased effort on the part of each stae since such monitoring presently takes place or, if the problem exists, will be instituted as required. The experience of the WMO in utilizing national elements for weather monitoring through the World Weather Watch may be helpful. The new authority to be given to the U.S.-Canadian IJC for the Great Lakes area is also in point. Such monitoring could be used for monitoring air currents, fresh water, and even ocean areas such as the North Sea in which a defined region may be circumscribed.

Additionally, continual monitoring should also serve as an early warning device to protect states from environmental dangers which they might not otherwise have knowledge of. This can be done through early warning systems such as proposed by the Netherlands on the Rhine or constatnt surveillance as is proposed for the Great Lakes by the U.S.-Canadian International Joint Commission. Requiring instant reporting of a spill, a dump, a misturned valve on an outfall pipe, or a faulty stack either through domestic legislation or international agreement with stiff penalties for failure to do so, can form part of an early warning system.

Another outgrowth of monitoring should be the capacity to analyze and evaluate the data against established standards, or to find facts which might serve as the basis for enforcement action within a specific country. This was raised in the draft U.S.-Canadian agreement of 1920 in which the findings of fact of the Commission were considered final and conclusive.[136]

Contingency Plans. Another function which might be carried out by regional organizations is the development of plans to cope with environmental dangers once they occur. This could take the form of co-ordinated contingency plans such as exist on the Great Lakes, the plans of the IAEA for nuclear accidents, or a system utilizing national means as exists on the Rhine. What is most important is that a mechanism be established to set the process in motion and that it be in existence before an accident occurs.

Regulation. Additionally, organizations could, either on their own or with the assistance of an organization of broader scope, draft objectives, standards or effluent charges which would effectively limit the amount of effluent permitted to be put into water or air, restrict manufacture, use, transport or dumping of certain hazardous substances, prohibit certain uses of the land which might adversely affect others in the problem shed area through erosion or runoff, regulate noise levels from moveable sources, and attempt to avoid some of the inequitable economic effects of one state's pursuing a vigorous environmental policy

281

while a neighbor does not. One organization which has perhaps the greatest potential in this respect is the European Communities. The basic principles and structure of the Communities, consisting of a group — very likely an increasing group — of states directly interested in the establishment of an integrated set of economies with strong central institutions, lend themselves to the development of harmonized environmental policies, binding directives, and common standards in a range of areas dealing with water, air, solid wastes disposal, agriculture, mining industry and nuclear energy.[137] There are other "Common Markets" in the world, such as in Central America, and it remains to be seen whether they can meet the challenge facing them.

Dispute Settlement. There are mechanisms for the settlement of environmental disputes which might be worked out on a regional level. A global center for the settlement of environmental disputes — with a wide range of choices including mediation, conciliation, negotiation, arbitration, or judicial settlement, and a device for the enforcement of foreign judgments — could operate through regional centers. It should be noted that the *Trail Smelter Arbitration*,[138] the primary example cited for the peaceful settlement of an environmental dispute, stemmed from a reference of the U.S.-Canadian International Joint Commission.[139] In addition to holding Canada responsible for damage to interests and property in the United States, the Tribunal also established a continuing regime and required the development of a system to monitor it.[140] The binding directives of the Council of the European Communities are enforceable in the Court of Justice of the Communities, making even more effective that system of regulation.[141]

The last two management functions of international means of regulation and dispute settlement may be further in the future than others. As the final report of the Study on Critical Environmental Problems stated:

Given the fact that the shift in values and the distribution of priorities between first-order effects and the side effects of technology is of recent origin and has been under way for only a brief period even in the United States, given also the uncertainty of much existing knowledge concerning key pollutants and their effects, and bearing in mind the complexity of international arrangements, it is not at all surprising nor should it be discouraging that the record of international regulatory measures affecting pollution should be rudimentary.[142]

Despite the logic of this reasoning, it leaves out the vital necessity for this situation to change and to change fast. As one author put it in a different context, but one that articulately expresses the state in which the U.S. and the world finds itself with respect to environmental management:

Our difficulty is that as a nation of short-term pragmatists accustomed to dealing with the future only when it has become the present, we find it hard to regard future trends as serious realities. We have not achieved the capacity to treat as real and urgent — as demanding action today — problems which appear in critical dimension only at some future date. Yet failure to achieve this new habit of mind is likely to prove fatal.[143]

Despite the multitudes of efforts being directed towards the need for new international organizations or the restructuring of old ones to deal with international environmental problems, the first group that needs to be reoriented and enlightened is the state itself. We appear to be reaching this point but we have not yet gotten there. It has been the view of this paper that once that stage is reached, the next step is to establish a working relationship which will extend as far as the problem extends. If the problem is global, a good case can be made for global institutions. But if a viable division can be made, and it certainly can for a number of areas causing and capable of causing our most serious environmental problems, then regional organizations should be utilized for effective environmental management.

NOTES

[1]2 Moore, *Digest of International Law*, 409 (1903). *See also* Brownlie, *International Law and the Use of Force by States* (1963) who states at 434 that self defense must be confined to measures reasonably necessary for repelling the danger; McDougal and Feliciano, *Law and Minimum World Public Order* (1961) who considers the doctrine of proportionality in terms of an "economy in coercion" at 218, 241-44.

[2]R.H. Robertson, *The Law of International Institutions in Europe* 5 (1961).

[3]For discussion of this relationship, *see* Frey-Wouters, "The Prospects for Regionalism in World Affairs," in *The Future of the International Legal Order* 461 at 531 (R. Falk and C. Black, eds., 1969).

[4]Frey-Wouters, *supra* at 545 where the author states that:
Evidence so far points against the conclusion that continued regional integration will take place at the expense of greater worldwide integration. An increase in the institutional and behavioral ties that join states across regions can be observed. Many states associate with several regional communities and can help prevent the emergence of sharp conflicts between them. Behavioral ties across regions result in shifting political alignments of the major regions on different issues. Despite many problems and disagreements, there is a slow, but continuing progression toward the integration of the entire global system.
See also W. Friedmann, *The Changing Structure of International Law* 62-3 (1964); E. Plischke, "International Integration: Purpose, Progress and Prospects," in *Systems of Integrating the International Community* at 21-22 (Plischke, ed., 1964).

[5]Friedmann, *supra* at 321; Frey-Wouters, *supra* at 465, 551.

[6]R. Falk, *This Endangered Planet* 334-40 (1971).

[7]Report of the Preparatory Committee for the United Nations Conference on the Human Environment, second sess. 8-19 Feb. 1971, U.N. Doc. A/Conf. 48/PC.9, para. 20, Agenda Item 6.

[8]*See* C. Wilson, ed., *Man's Impact on the Global Environment: Assessment and Recommendations for Action.* (Hereinafter SCEP Report) (1970). The report states:
It should be noted that the existence of a global problem does not necessarily imply the necessity for a global solution. The sources of pollution are activities of man that can often be effectively controlled and regulated where they occur. Most corrective action will probably have to be taken at the national, regional, and local levels. In research and monitoring programs, however, the potential for international cooperation is high. Effective cooperation now might increase the likelihood of smooth international relations should a global problem ever demand strict international regulation or control of pollution producing activities. (at 6-7.)

In the working group discussion, the following pollution problems (some recognized as less than global) lend themselves to regional study and solution: thermal pollution, which will cause heat islands in urban and surrounding areas (at 96); monitoring and cleanup of the oceans oily waste (2.1 million metric tons of oil are introduced into the oceans annually.) (at 138-40). They recommend that the institutional structures for defining, monitoring, and maintaining water quality standards over large areas be improved ... to reduce the multiplicity of authorities. With respect to the study of monitoring the working group concludes that for SST problems of water vapor of the lower stratosphere (55,000-70,000 ft.): "The area coverage is global, but with special emphasis on areas where it is proposed that the SST should fly" (at 212). Additionally, monitoring by radar is needed of optical scattering in the lower stratosphere, again with emphasis on the region in which heavy traffic is planned. With respect to oil spills they recommend "more intensive investigation of local spills and effects" (at 214). They also recommend monitoring nutrients on a local basis (at 216).

In the summer of 1971 an international group of scientists, under the sponsorship of the Massachusetts Institute of Technology, met in Stockholm for a Study of Man's Impact on Climate (SMIC). The Summary of major conclusions and recommendations of the study also alludes to the regional nature of some problems such as the inadvertent change in albedo of arctic ice over the next four decades (at 16), and the regional effects from heat release resulting from energy conversion (at 17).

[9]Belgium, Denmark, France, Federal Republic of Germany, Netherlands, Norway, Sweden, United Kingdom.

[10]Agreement of June 9, 1969 for Cooperation Dealing with Pollution of the North Sea by Oil, entered into force, August 9, 1969, 9 *I.L.M.* 359 (1970).

[11]*Id.* at art. 5.

[12]Art. 7.

[13]*See* Internatinal Council for the Exploration of the Sea (ICES) Cooperative Research Report, Series A., No. 13, Report of the ICES Working Group on Pollution of the North Sea. (1969).

[14]Communique issued by the meeting of the North Sea States on 11 June 1971, reproduced in the report of the Intergovernmental Working Group on Marine Pollution, U.N. Doc. A/Conf. 48/PC/IWGMP. I/CP.5 (1971).

[15]*Ibid.*

[16]*See* the U.K. White Paper, *The Protection of the Environment, The Fight Against Pollution,* Cmn. 4373 (1970).

[17]ICES, Cooperative Research Report No. 15, Report of the ICES Working Group on Pollution of the Baltic Sea 13-16, 48 (1970).

[18]*Id.* at 3-4.

[19]*See* report of the First Session of the Intergovernmental Working Group on Marine Pollution, U.N. Doc. A/Conf. 48/IWGMP. I/5 (1971). The draft convention, attached as Annex V, relies exclusively on national means for regulating dumping: (Art. 1) and states that the agreement does not prevent a Party's establishing criteria stricter than those in the agreement (art. III(d)).

[20]U.N. Doc. A/Conf. 48/IWGMP. II/5 (1971). The revised draft articles continue to rely on national means for regulation. The draft excludes dumping from outfalls, which the author views as a serious omission. The regional approach has been brought to a successful if compromised conclusion in the Convention on the Control of Marine Pollution by Dumping from Ships and Aircraft. The text was made final in Paris on December 7, 1971. The Convention applies to the states and waters of the Northeast Atlantic.

[21]A prime example is the SCEP report, *supra* note 8, A World Environmental Research Institute established by the International Council of Scientific Unions (ICSU) through its newly created Scientific Committee on the Protection of the Environment (SCOPE) is a possible result of the Stockholm Conference's search for a continuing body to carry out the much needed unbiased assessment, research and analysis of environmental problems. This is discussed in Chayes, "International Institutions for the Environment," in this volume.

[22]*See* Note by OECD Secretariat on National Arrangements. ENV (70) 20, 5 Nov. 1970.

[23]Both the Council of Europe and the ECE have requested such reports. Similarly, Country reports are being submitted for the Stockholm Conference.

[24]Speech by G. Eldin, "The Need for International Cooperation and Coordination in Environmental Policy," before a meeting of the Atlantic Institute, January 6, 1971.

[25]Moynihan, Address to the North Atlantic Assembly, October 21, 1969, "The NATO Committee on the Challenges of Modern Society: Response to a Common Environmental Peril," 61 *Dep't. State Bull.* 416 (1969).

[26]Speech by J. Stanovnik, Executive Secretary of ECE, to the ECE Symposium ECE/ ENV/4.

[27]H. Angelo, "Protection of the Human Environment — First Steps towards Regional Cooperation in Europe," 5 *Int'l Lawyer* 511, 516 (1971).

[28]*See* I. Hock, "Organization and Legal Aspects of Water Pollution Control" in *A Challenge to Social Scientists*, Proceedings of ISSC International Symposium on Environmental Disruption 211, 216 (1970); Information on Activities of Council for Mutual Economic Assistance (CMEA) Relative to Environment. Submitted to ECE Symposium ENV/Conf./H.4.

[29]Through the Consultative Assembly.

[30]*See generally*, OECD and the Environment in The OECD Observer 19 (No. 53 1971); OECD ENV (71) 11, 1 June 1971.

[31]Huntley, *Man's Environment and the Atlantic Alliance* 22 (1971).

[32]ECE Report of Seminar on River Basin Management, June 1970 U.N. Pub.ST/ECE/ WATER/3. (1971); Report of Working Party on Air Pollution Problems U.N. Doc. E/ECE/ AIR POLL/4, Feb. 1971; and Report of the Committee on Water Pollution Problems U.N. Doc. E/ECE/WATER/7, 19 February 1970.

[33]For an account of Council of Europe Air Pollution activities, *see* Adinolfi, "First Steps Towards European Cooperation in Reducing Air Pollution Activities of the Council of Europe" 33 *Law and Contemp. Prob.* 421 (1968). The meeting discussed in this Article lead to a Ministerial Resolution on Air Pollution in frontier areas Res. (71) 5 26 March 1971. The Consultative Assembly of the Council of Europe on May 12, 1969, adopted Recommendation 555 recommending that a group of governmental experts prepare "as rapidly as possible" a European Convention on the Protection of Fresh Water Against Pollution. The Convention has been drafted in preliminary form by the Council of Europe Secretariat, but governmental approval, though expected by the Secretariat, has not yet been obtained.

[34]This should have been expected by the West since it has been a traditional part of ECE foreplay. *See* J. Siotis, "ECE in the Emerging European System" 561 *Int'l Conc.* 49-53 (1967). The author states that "ECE is one of the few multilateral, intergovernmental bodies in which the lack of participation of East Germany remains a handicap." at 51.

[35]U.N. Doc. ECE/ENV/SYM/Room Doc. No. 1.

[36]The stage for a similar conflict over invitations for Stockholm appears to be brewing, with traditional lines being taken. On June 13, 1971, a Washington *Star* editorial stated that delegations at Stockholm should not be accepted "according to the rigid standards of traditional diplomacy, but solely on the basis of interest" and that consequently "participation by East Germany and the People's Republic of China should be actively solicited by United Nations' members, including the United States." Responding for the Administration, Russell Train, Chairman of the CEQ, stated that while he agreed with the editorial that "questions such as the status of East Germany should not be permitted to interfere

with real international collaboration for environmental improvement ... we should not permit our very real concern for environmental quality to be used by others as a lever to gain political ends which are unrelated to environmental needs and whose proper disposition should be through normal international political channels." Both the Editorial and the response are quoted in the Congressional Record for July 1, 1971 at H 6319-20.

[31]*See* the reports of the 4 regional seminars on Development and Environment: ECAFE, U.N. Doc. E/CN.11/999, Aug. 30, 1971; ECA, E/CN.14/532; ECLA, ST/ECLA/Conf.40/ L.5, Sept. 11, 1971; UNESOB, ESOB/DE/11 Corr 1, Oct. 15, 1971.

[38]ECA Resolution 224(X) of February 13, 1971, and ECLA Res. The ECAFE conference included a paragraph in its Report of the 27th Session to ECOSOC (32.), but did not adopt a resolution.

[39]J. Magee, "ECA and the Paradox of African Cooperation," 580 *Int'l Conc.* 63-4 (1970).

[40]OECD Council Doc. C(70)135.

[41]*See,* OECD and the Environment, *supra* note 30. For a discussion of the work of the Ad Hoc Group on the Impact of the Automobile on the Environment. See Orski, in OECD Observer, *supra* note 30 at 31.

[42]For a discussion of this program, see OECD *Observer* 10 (No. 52 1971). The program began operation on May 26, 1971, for an initial period of two years.

[43]Moynihan, *supra* note 25. *See also* Hartley, "Challenges to the Environment: Some International Implications" XIV *Orbis* 490 (1970); Huntley, *Man's Environment and the Atlantic Alliance supra* note 31.

[44]Moynihan, *supra* note 25 at 419.

[45]*Ibid.*

[46]At the April 1971 meeting, the following eight items were on the agenda: coastal water pollution; disaster assistance; air pollution (both as affects several chosen cities, St. Louis, Frankfurt, and Ankara, and a low emission vehicle study); inland water pollution; road safety; environment and regional planning; work satisfaction in a technological era; and scientific knowledge and decision manking. Reports have been issued on Coastal Water Pollution and low emission vehicles.

[47]*See* 62 *Dep't. State Bull.* 754 (1970).

[48]*See* the CEQ Report to the President: *Ocean Dumping: A National Policy,* U.S. GPO (1970).

[49]Volpe, Statement of November 2, 1970, 63 *Dep't. State Bull.* 666, 668 (1970).

[50]*Id.* at 666.

[51]*Id.* at 669.

[52]For text of Final Communique, see 64 *Dep't. State Bull.* 2 (1971). The endorsement appears at para. 18.

[53]IMCO Res. (MSC XXIII/19 Annex X); IMCO Council Doc. CXXVI/4/Add. 1, May 7, 1971.

[54]*See* W. Butler, *The Soviet Union and the Law of the Sea* (1971), who in quoting a Soviet jurist states that: "Soviet jurists have, in this same connection, criticized the United

States and other countries for disposing of radioactive wastes from peaceful uses of a-tomic energy at sea in special containers: 'In the USSR special methods and devices have been worked out to reprocess and bury radioactive wastes under the earth ... But capitalist countries do not wish to use this safe but expensive method.'", at 187.

[55]G. Mangone, *International Health Programs: Bilateral and Multilateral Aid* 70 (1970).

[56]WHO has six regional offices for Africa (Brazzaville, Congo); Americas (PAHO, U.S.); Eastern Mediterranean (UAR); Europe (Denmark); South East Asia (India); and Western Pacific (Philippines). For a plea for increased training porgrams, *see* Basu, "International Cooperation: A Plea to Control the Pollution Problem" 286, 290 in "A Challenge to Social Scientists," *supra* note 28.

[57]*See generally*, Wolfrom, "La Pollution des eaux du Rhin," 10 *Ann. Francais de droit Int'l* 737 (1964). Kiss and Lambrechts, "La lutte contre la pollution de l'eau en Europe Occidentale," 15 *Ann. Francais* 718 (1969). For the Statute, *see* Peaslee, Constitutions of International Organizations, 157.

[58]The Convention entered into force on May 1, 1965.

[59]Letter of June 24, 1971 to author from L.J. Huizenga, Secretary of the Commission.

[60]Art. 3.

[61]Art. 6.

[62]Letter, *supra* note 59.

[63]Convention, art. 6(2).

[64]It is presumed that the kill was caused by endosulfan discharged by a chemical industry in Frankfurt.

[65]Country Monograph of The Netherlands submitted to the ECE Conference on Man's Environment. ENV/CONF./B9 at 6 (1971). *See also* Council of Europe Resolution (69) 26, adopted by the Council of Ministers on June 25, 1969, calling upon "all governments of member States to increase their efforts to reduce water pollution, to ensure that rational use of water supplies and to intensify their cooperation within the Council of Europe with a view to agreeing on common action in this field."

[66]*See The Washington Post*, November 4, 1970, at 2, col. 1.

[67]CCNR Convention, art. 46b.

[68]CCNR Convention, art. 32-39.

[69]*Id.*, art. 34(1). According to Art. 35, the Rhine Court in the district where the contravention takes place has jurisdiction.

[70]*Id.*, arts. 37, 45(c).

[71]*Reglement pour le Transport de Matieres Dangereuses sur le Rhin* (ADNR) (1971).

[72]*Id.*, art. 4.

[73]*See generally* S. Gorove, *Law and Politics of the Danube* (1964), and Stainov, "Les Aspects Juridiques de la lutte International contre la pollution du Danube" 72 *Rev. Gen. de Droit Int'l Pub.* 97 (1968).

[74]Convention Regarding the Regime of Navigation of the Danube (Hereinafter Danube

288

Convention) U.N.T.S. 197 (1949).

[75]The Federal Republic of Germany, however, is known to be interested in membership, and has observed Commission meetings. *See* Ely and Wolman, ch. 9 *Administration in The Law of International Drainage Basins,* 126 (Garretson, Hayton, and Olmstead, eds., 1967).

[76]Danube Convention, art. 5.

[77]*Id.,* art. 9.

[78]*Id.,* arts. 20, 22.

[79]*Ids.,* arts. 17 and 26.

[80]Decision of the 19th session "concernant le projet de dispositions au sujet de la lutte contre la pollution des eaux du Danube par les dechets de produits petroliers provenant des bateaux" CD/SES19/28 at 345, 386 (1961).

[81]Information relative to the above cited decision 29th session CD/SES29/8 (1971).

[82]Stainov, *supra* note 73 at 100.

[83]Hungarian Country Monograph for the ECE Conference on Man's Environment ENV/CONF/B 6 at 6-7 (1971).

[84]USSR Monograph on Government Policies and Strategies, for the ECE Conference ENV/CONF./F. 2 at para. 69 (1971). However, a Soviet jurist, J.J. Baskin has taken the view that the individual efforts of each government are insufficient. Baskin, "Questions de droit International relatives a la Pollution des eaux," 73 *Rev. Gen. de Droit Int'l Pub.* 421, 422 (1969).

[85]*See* Ely and Wolman, *supra* note 75 at 217. The agreement was signed in 1955, but actual construction did not get underway until 1964. The system of locks, dams, hydroelectric plants is expected to be operational by the end of 1971.

[86]D. Cuckovic, in Dierdap, *Hydroenergetical and Navigational System* 3 (Export Press, Belgrade). The IJC has 3 U.S. and 3 Canadian Commissioners who do not serve full-time and a small staff for each section. Hence, the Commission relies heavily on technical experts drawn from each country.

[87]Treaty Between the United States and Great Britain relating to Boundary Waters and Questions Arising Between the United States and Canada (1909). U.S.T. No. 548 (Hereinafter Boundary Waters Treaty).

[88]Art. IX states in part that:
The High Contracting Parties further agree that any other questions or matters of difference arising between them involving the rights, obligations, or interests of either in relation to the other or to the inhabitants of the other, along the common frontier between the United States and the Dominion of Canada, shall be referred from time to time to the International Joint Commission for examination and report, whenever either the Government of the United States or the Government of the Dominion of Canada shall request that such questions or matters of difference be so referred.

The International Joint Commission is authorized in each case so referred to examine into and report upon the facts and circumstances of the particular questions and matters referred, together with such conclusions and recommendations as may be appropriate, subject, however, to any restrictions or exceptions which may be imposed with respect thereto by the terms of the reference.

[89]Quoted in the IJC Report on Pollution of Lake Erie, Lake Ontario and the International Sections of the St. Lawrence River at 2-3 (1970). (Hereinafter IJC Pollution Report). *See also* 3 Whiteman, *Digest of Int'l Law* 828 (1964) (Hereinafter Whiteman).

[90]3 Whiteman at 829.

[91]Draft of October 15, 1920, Art. III, on file with U.S. Section, IJC, Docket 4.

[92]*Id.*, art. V.

[93]*Id.*, art. VI.

[94]For a survey of the various Dockets from 1912 to 1964, *see* 3 Whiteman 826-71. *See also* Bloomfield and Fitzgerald. *Boundary Water Problem of Canada and the U.S.* (1958) and Chacko, *The International Joint Commission* (1932).

[95]Docket No. 86. The American Falls.

[96]*See* Dep't. State Press Release No. 441, October 8, 1964.

[97]*See* IJC Pollution Report, Appendix at 163.

[98]*See* Report of the International Lake Erie Water Pollution Board to the International Joint Commission on Potential Oil Pollution Incidents from Oil and Gas Well Activities in Lake Erie: Their Prevention and Control. (1969).

[99]IJC Pollution Report at 136.

[100]*Id.* at 137. It should be noted that the September 1969 Report of the International Lake Erie, Ontario and St. Lawrence Water Pollution Boards to the IJC raised the eutrophication problem in Lake Erie, and identified phosphates as the controlling factor. It was this international report which served as the basis for hearings dealing with phosphates in detergents which resulted in Canadian legislation requiring the elimination of phosphates and various states and municipalities doing the same. For report on the House of Representatives hearings, *see New York Times*, December 15, 1969, at 53, col. 4, stating that Congressman Reuss, who conducted the hearings gave credit to the Board's report for "nudging" the phosphate question. However, U.S. Government officials recently concluded that phosphates are less harmful than the substitutes now available and represent an environmental price we must pay for clean clothes. *N.Y. Times*, Sept. 16, 1971, at 1, col. 3.

[101]IJC Pollution Report at 139.

[102]*Id.* at 149. Both general and specific water quality objectives were recommended. *See id.* at 144-48.

[103]Recommendation No. 21, *Id.* at 155.

[104]*Id.* at 156.

[105]Dep't. State Press Release No. 129, June 10, 1971, paras. 5, 9-11.

[106]*Id.* at para. 18.

[107]See also Joint Air Pollution Study of St. Clair-Detroit River Areas for International Joint Commission, January 1971. At its Spring 1971 semi-annual meeting, the IJC asked other of its Boards dealing with water pollution to initiate liaison with the International Air Pollution Advisory Board in order to insure that control measures of one type of pollution would not nullify control measures of the other.

[108]GESAMP is composed of representatives from IMCO, FAO, UNESCO, WMO, WHO, and the IAEA.

[109]The OAS and The Pan American Health Union (PAHU) held a Technical Seminar on Urban Development and Environmental Change in November, 1971.

[110]Speech by Senator E. Muskie on May 20, 1971, on Conference on International Organization and the Human Environment.

[111]In this capacity, however, they would not participate, but just observe. This limitation may make other alternatives, such as a special office under the Secretary General more appealing.

[112]Chayes, "International Institutions for the Environment," *supra* note 21, at 10.

[113]*See generally* Chayes, *id.*, note 112, SCEP Report, *supra* note 8, at 248-49. On Common Areas, *see* Schachter and Serwer, "Marine Pollution Problems and Remedies" 65 *A.J.I.L.* 84 (1971). *See also* 1969 IMCO Convention on Marine Pollution.

[114]*See* IJC Report on Pollution of Lake Erie, *supra* note 89, at 35. OECD, *Eutrophication in Large Lakes and Impoundments* (1970).

[115]WHO, after examining over 1,400 compounds as pesticides, has selected 5 which pass ecological tests and have recommended only 2, malathion and propoxur, as replacements for DDT. WHO said that DDT should continue to be used in malaria operations until a cheap substitute is found. *New York Times*, July 9, 1971, at 20, col. 2.

[116]At the present time there is no conflict, since the draft convention relies on national legislation. *See* Annex V of the Report of the Intergovernmental Working Group, *supra* note 19. A conflict might result from a discrepancy in a future listing of substances for which dumping was prohibited.

[117]*See* Report of the 9th Session, 55 ff (1967) criticizing the Helsinki rules of the Int'l Law Ass'n. "It can be safely predicted that modern technology and the changed conditions existing in Asia and Africa have rendered international rules regarding rivers mostly otiose, inapplicable and infructuous. Hence the urgent need for the development of such law so as to reflect an Afro-Asian view point."

[118]I recognize that other classifications of functions are equally, if not more apposite than those selected here. One such classification can be found in Skolnikoff, *The International Imperatives of Technology* (1971), who considers functions in terms of General Assistance; Regulation; Operation; and Settlement of Disputes. However, in the immortal words of Bill Klem 'I call 'em as I see 'em."

[119]OECD and ECE have used this approach.

[120]The Man in the Biosphere Program of UNESCO is an attempt at this type of joint venture.

[121]Energy Message to the Congress of President Nixon, June 4, 1971. The President stated that all industrial societies face two challenges: "One, to find new sources of energy to fuel the economy; and two, to find sources of energy that will not pollute the environment."

[122]A portion of this has been done by the IAEA, *see* Environmental Aspects of Nuclear Power Stations. Proceedings of a Symposium, New York, August 10-14, 1970. IAEA STI/PUB/261 (1971). The Economic Commission for Latin America (ECLA) has completed a study of energy needs of that region. *See* 15 Economic Bull. for Latin America No. 2 at 3 (1970). The study does not include environmental considerations.

[123]The term is used by S. Stein in "Environmental Control and Different Levels of Government" in *A Challenge to Social Scientists, supra* note 28, at 249, who states that the governing area should not necessarily be co-extensive with political boundaries but should be equal to the area relevant to the problem.

[124]This category could include various aspects of planning, and operation, in addition to aspects of regulation, such as monetary, standard setting, fact finding and dispute settlement.

[125]Two of the functions referred to above, standard setting and dispute settlement, plus enforcement of standards may initially be carried out nationally in parallel with other states.

[126]The Danube and Rhine Commissions and the International Joint Commission.

[127]Such as the Rhine and the Danube.

[128]*See* Indus Waters Treaty of 19 September 1960 between India, Pakistan and the Internaitonal Bank for Reconstruction and Development, esp. Art. VIII 419 U.N.T.S. 125 (1962).

[129]Agreement of December 29, 1954, between Cambodia, Laos, and Vietnam.

[130]Agreement of April 23, 1969, between Argentina, Brazil, Bolivia, Paraguay, and Uruguay 8 *I.L.M.* 905, September 1969. The OAS has contributed to the Plata River Basin program through an inventory and analysis of basic natural resource information needed for planning and development of the basin. The studies, which are multinational are directed more towards the goal of development than towards purely scientific studies. Such cooperation is viewed by the OAS not as an altruistic gesture, but as "an essential precondition for general progress."

[131]Agreement of 25 November 1964 betwen Cameroon, Ivory Coast, Dahomey, Guinea, Upper Volta, Mali, Niger, Nigeria and Chad concerning the Niger River Commission 587 UNTS 19 (1967).

[132]Convention and Statute relating to Chad Basin between Cameroon, Chad, Niger, and Nigeria. Ft. Lamy, May 22, 1964. The Lake Chad Basin Commission, with the assistance of the FAO, is preparing an Agreement on Water Utilization and Conservation. See FAO Doc. AGL:SF/REG/79, 27 April 1971.

[133]Convention on the Regulation of Water Abstractions from the Lake of Constance below FRG, Austria and Switzerland, 25 November 1967.

[134]*See* note 129 above.

[135]*See* Kasdan, "Third World War — Environment versus Development" 26 *Record of the Ass'n of the Bar of the City of N.Y.* 454 (1971).

[136]*See* Treaty cited *supra* note 91, at Art. III.

[137]*See* Treaty of Rome of 25 March 1951, 298 U.N.T.S. 11; Angelo, *supra* note 26, at 521. *See also Premiere Communication de la Commission sur la Politique de la Communaute en Matiere d'Environnement*, SEC (71) 2616 final 22 July 1971.

[138]3 U.N.R.I.A.A. 1905 (1941).

[139]Docket No. 25, discussed in 3 Whiteman 840. The IJC under Article X of the Boundary Waters Treaty can itself sit as an Arbitral Tribunal, but it has never exercised this power.

[140]*See* R. Stein, Comments, Proceedings, Am. Soc'y. Int'l L. 64 *A.J.I.L.* 224 (1970).

[141]*See* Angelo, *supra* note 27, at 523. If the Declaration on the Human Environment being prepared for the Stockholm Conference contains a statement as to the individual's "right" to a decent environment, an interesting question will arise as to the enforceability of this right in national courts or the European Court on Human Rights.

[142]SCEP Report, *supra* note 19, at 248-49.

[143]T. Hoopes, in "The Persistence of Illusion: The Soviet Economic Drive and American National Interest," Yale Rev. Sp. 1960, at 325. Quoted in Acheson, *Present at the Creation* 16 (1969).

CONTROLLING GREAT LAKES POLLUTION: A STUDY IN UNITED STATES-CANADIAN ENVIRONMENTAL CO-OPERATION

by *Richard B. Bilder*[*]

On June 10, 1971, the United States and Canada issued a Joint Communique announcing their intention to conclude, before the end of the year, a broad-ranging agreement designed to protect and enhance water quality in the Great Lakes and to bring the problem of Great Lakes pollution under substantial control by 1975.[1] The proposed Great Lakes Water Quality Agreement would establish common water quality objectives, commit the two governments to the development of compatible national water quality standards to meet these objectives, and provide for the carrying out of a wide variety of joint and separate pollution control programs and related measures. A major role in overseeing the joint program would be assigned to the International Joint Commission, United States and Canada, a bilateral international commission created by the Boundary Waters Treaty of 1909 between the United States and the United Kingdom. In announcing the two governments' "agreement to agree," Mitchell Sharp, Canada's Secretary of State for External Affairs, noted that the proposed agreement will be the "most far reaching ever signed by two governments in the environmental field."[2] Russell Train, Chairman of the United States Council on Environmental Quality described the proposed agreement as "an historic first" and added that its provisions will be "unprecedented in scope" and provide a model for similar international agreements in other parts of the world.[3]

The proposed Great Lakes Water Quality Agreement would have obvious importance for U.S.-Canadian relations and the efforts of the two governments to deal with the increasingly urgent problems of Great Lakes pollution. But, as the Ministers' statements suggest, it might also have a broader significance. For the two governments' announcement comes at a time of emerging global concern with environmental issues and possible international approaches to their solution[4] — a concern symbolized in the forthcoming United Nations Conference on the Human Environment which will convene in Stockholm, Sweden in June 1972.[5] The Stockholm Conference will have the tasks of focusing the attention of governments and public opinion on the importance and urgency of prob-

[*]The author is Professor of Law at the University of Wisconsin Law School.

A version of this paper has been published separately in the January, 1972 issue of the *Michigan Law Review.*

The author expresses his appreciation to the University of Wisconsin Sea Grant Program, which has facilitated his study of international environmental problems.

lems of the human environment and of identifying those aspects of environmental and pollution problems appropriate for international co-operation and agreement. It will also consider various action proposals for the creation of international institutions and other cooperative measures. Yet, in considering these questions and possibly attempting to forge such cooperative arrangements, the Conference will have little guidance from the past. Precedents for international cooperation and regulation in the environmental area have thus far been sparse and relevant international law is relatively undeveloped.[6] This dearth of experience will increase the difficulties the Conference may encounter in developing practical programs for effective international action and securing their acceptance by governments.

In this context, a study of the proposed Great Lakes Water Quality Agreement, and, more particularly, of the long history of developing U.S.-Canadian co-operation which preceded it, may be of use. First, this U.S.-Canadian experience offers guidance as to some of the specific problems which programs for international environmental co-operation may face — questions of framework and approach; institutional organization, functions and authority; determining objectives; apportioning burdens; co-ordination; and implementation. Second, at a time when international discussion has focused principally on global approaches to the solution of environmental problems, it calls attention to the important, if less dramatic, contribution that can be made by more limited bilateral and regional cooperative arrangements; indeed, it is arguable that such bilateral and regional arrangements will ultimately prove the most significant forms of international environmental cooperation.[8] Finally, this experience may serve to suggest that the concept of international environmental cooperation has limitations as well as potentialities, and thus to provide a more realistic basis for the work of the Stockholm Conference.

I. BACKGROUND

U.S. - Canadian cooperation regarding Great Lakes pollution problems has developed within a special geographical, economic, legal and political context. A brief description of this setting may suggest the significance of these pollution problems and some of the reasons for the particular form this cooperation has taken.[9]

The 5000 mile long U.S.-Canadian common boundary is one of the longest in the world. It extends for about 3500 miles from Passamaquoddy Bay on the Atlantic to the Fuca Straits of Vancouver on the Pacific, and, with respect to the Alaskan - Canadian boundary, for another 1500 miles from the Pacific to the Arctic Ocean. About 2000 miles of this boundary is water, passing along rivers such as the St. Croix, St. John and the St. Lawrence, through Lake Ontario, the Niagara River, Lake Erie, the Detroit River, Lake St. Clair, the St. Clair River, Lake Huron, the St. Mary's River and Lake Superior, and on to Rainy Lake and Lake of the Woods. In addition, a number of rivers, such as the Red, the Columbia and the Yukon flow across the U.S. - Canadian boundary.

The most important of these so-called boundary waters, the Great Lakes, constitute the largest fresh water system in the world, representing about a quarter of the world's total fresh water supply.[10] Of the total Great Lakes water area of 95,000 square miles, about two-thirds is within U.S. jurisdiction, and one-third in Canadian jurisdiction. Of the total Great Lakes drainage basin area of some 300,000 square miles, about 59 percent is in the U.S. and 41 percent in Canada. Eight states of the United States — Illinois, Indiana, Michigan, Minnesota, New York, Ohio, Pennsylvania, and Wisconsin — border on the Great Lakes, and a number of others have close economic links with the region. In Canada, only the Province of Ontario borders on the Lakes, though the Province of Quebec also has considerable concern with Great Lakes problems.

The Great Lakes basin is richly endowed with natural resources — lakes and rivers, agricultural lands, timber resources, minerals, fuels, electric power potential, fish, and superb wildlife and recreation areas. These extensive resources, coupled with the possibility of low cost transportation, have contributed to the development of major industrial complexes and large metropolitan areas around the rim of the Lakes — for example, Toronto, Hamilton, Port Huron and Windsor in Canada; and Duluth-Superior, Milwaukee, Chicago, Gary, Detroit, Toledo, Cleveland, Erie, Buffalo and Rochester in the U.S. In 1966 some thirty million people lived on or near the Great Lakes, comprising about one out of every three Canadians and one out of every eight Americans.[11] All indications are that this Great Lakes population is rapidly expanding; projections for the year 2000 suggest the emergency of a Great Lakes Megalopolis with a population approaching 60 million people.[12]

The immense importance of the Great Lakes region to the two countries is indicated by the fact that the region accounts for over one-half of the Canadian gross national product and about one-fifth of the U.S. gross national product; for example, about 50 percent of U.S. steel production and much of its automotive production is concentrated about the Lakes. With the development of the St. Lawrence Seaway, the Great Lakes have now become part of a major international waterway stretching for over 2300 miles from the Atlantic Ocean to Duluth, Minnesota; each year over 600 foreign vessels utilize the Great Lakes system, in addition to a domestic U.S.-Canadian fleet of another 600 vessels and well over 300,000 pleasure craft.[13]

In view of the length of this common boundary and the substantial clustering of people and industry along certain portions of it, it is not surprising that problems of boundary waters and transboundary pollution have assumed a growing importance in U.S.-Canadian relations. This has been particularly the case with respect to the Great Lakes. While concern of the two governments with boundary pollution problems dates back at least to the early years of the twentieth century, these problems assumed a new dimension and importance as a result of rapid industrial and population development during and after World War II.

It is now widely recognized that, at a time when water demand problems have become more pressing and complex, the quality of the Great Lakes is rapidly deteriorating.[14] Recent studies have confirmed that Lake Erie, and particularly its western basin, is in advanced state of eutrophication, largely as a result of excessive enrichment by nutrients, especially phosphorus; indeed, Lake Erie has become a prime example of the consequences of environmental neglect.[15] Accelerated eutrophication is occurring in Lake Ontario, and the other Lakes are considered seriously threatened.[16] A number of industries, such as fishing and recreation, have already been affected, and there is growing concern that future industrial and urban development may be impeded. The sources of pollution include waste disposal from municipalities and industries, agricultural runoff, dredging, sedimentation, and waste from commercial and pleasure craft.[17] The consequences of such pollution on the water of the Lakes include eutrophication, oxygen depletion, biological changes, organic contamination from substances such as DDT and PCB, accumulation of solids and accumulation of oil and of toxic materials such as mercury in trace amounts.[18] While pollution occurs on both sides of the border, the bulk of the problem appears to originate from the larger concentrations of population and industry on U.S. side.[19]

As these dangers have become more widely perceived, public concern on both sides of the border has mushroomed, and the problem of control of Great Lakes pollution has now achieved a leading place on both governments' agendas. A measure of government recognition of the seriousness of this problem is the recent statement by Mitchell Sharp, Canada's Secretary of State for External Affairs, made at the recent Joint Ministerial Meeting, that pollution of the Great Lakes had reached the point where "two of the richest societies on earth are knowingly and wantonly poisoning this unique resource, and by extension, each other."[20] A variety of national and international measures to cope with this situation is now being undertaken. But it has become increasingly clear that effective solutions will involve major governmental commitments, years of intensive effort, and very substantial costs.

In view of the federal character of both countries' governments, efforts to control pollution in the Great Lakes raise particularly complex jurisdictional questions. The waters of the Lakes are not "high seas" for international purposes; each nation treats the Lakes' waters on its side of the international boundary as its own "internal waters." U.S. law regards each of the eight riparian states as owning, in its respective public capacity, the Lake waters and beds adjacent to its coast, out to the international boundary, and also as having certain broad regulatory powers in their adjacent waters, at least in the absence of federal assertions of authority.[21] The same principles appear to be applicable in Canada, with respect to the waters and beds in the Province of Ontario, the only Great Lakes riparian province.[22] In each country, however, the federal government retains substantial regulatory powers with respect to matters affecting the Lakes, though the situation as regards the division of power between the respective federal and the state or provincial governments appears to differ somewhat as between the two countries. In the case of the U.S., there is little question but that the U.S. Federal government has broad constitutional authority, under the commerce power and other constitutional grants to regulate and control virtually any activities contributing directly or indirectly to Great Lakes pollution; should the U.S. Federal government choose to exercise such authority, any state and local government interference with such regulation will be considered unconstitutional and invalid.[23] Moreover, the U.S. federal treaty power may constitute and additional source of Congressional authority in this respect.[24] With respect to Canada, however, it is less clear that federal powers are so broad. Respectable arguments have been made that, under relevant provisions of the British North America Act, provincial authority over most aspects of water pollution affecting the Great Lakes is constitutionally protected from federal intrusion, and that Canadian federal authority in this field, even when exercised pursuant to treaty, is inherently limited.[25]

In any event, whatever the theoretical reach of U.S. and Canadian federal powers, in practice the regulation of water pollution in each country has remained largely in state, provincial and local hands. It is only recently that the respective federal governments have begun to exercise their regulatory authority in any substantial way, and the burden of regulation is still primarily non-federal in character.[26] As a result, the law governing Great Lakes pollution continues to be a complex hodge-podge of proliferating and occasionally inconsistent laws, regulations and ordinances, issued separately by the two federal governments and their various agencies, the eight riparian states of the United States, the Province of Ontario, and the hundreds of cities, towns, and other local jurisdictions that exercise relevant authority. This jurisdictional complexity has been a major obstacle in efforts at the coordinated handling of over-all Great Lakes' problems.[27]

Finally, it is worth noting that U.S.-Canadian efforts to deal with Great Lakes' pollution problems are but one aspect of broader relations between the two countries, which have a unique and special character. On the one hand, U.S.-Canadian relations have been remarkably amicable; the two countries have been at peace since 1814, the U.S.-Canadian border has been demilitarized since 1817,[28] and the two nations have long been linked by strong cultural and economic bonds. Moreover, the two governments have developed a strong tradition of formal and informal peaceful adjustment of their disagreements and disputes, relying heavily in their relations on such formal legal techniques as international agreement, the establishment of joint institutions, and arbitration;[29] for example, there are presently some 200 bilateral agreements in force between the two countries, as well as numerous lower-level and less formal arrangements.[30] On the other hand, U.S.-Canadian relations have also been marked by certain strong and continuing differences. In particular, Canada has manifested a persistent, strongly felt, and understandable fear of political, economic and cultural domination by its more populous and powerful neighbor to the South, and Canadian nationalists have frequently responded with resentment to any U.S. policies which appeared to exploit superior American power or wealth at Canada's expense.[31] Where issues of this nature have arisen, U.S.-Canadian relations have on occasion proved sensitive and delicate.

In recent years, the problem of Great Lakes' pollution appears, to some extent, to have become such a sensitive issue between the two countries.[32] The Great Lakes are regarded by Canada as crucial to its future. Not only does a very substantial part of Canada's population and industry cluster on the Lakes, but Canada, in addition, is currently experiencing a broad reawakening of national pride in its natural environment, and the government has been militant in efforts to protect the Canadian environment from harm by external interests.[33] Moreover, since much of Great Lakes' pollution stems from the giant urban and industrial concentrations on the American side of the border, the situation, in Canadian eyes, calls for the most urgent and far-reaching measures by the U.S. in order to prevent irreversible harm to Canadian environment and economic development interests. Canada, however, in view of its lesser contribution to the problem, should assume somewhat less of this burden. To the U.S., on the other hand, with only a relatively small proportion of its population and industry centered on the Lakes, the problem of Great Lakes pollution, while important, is only one among a great many that press with equal urgency for its limited resources and funds. Moreover, the U.S. would, of course, prefer that Canada share with it the costs and burdens of remedial action to the fullest extent possible. These differences in view have only rarely publicly surfaced and, hoepfully, they have been at least temporarily resolved by the proposed Great Lakes Water Quality Agreement. Nevertheless, should current efforts to resolve these Great Lakes pollution problems prove ineffective, significant foreign relations issues could re-emerge.

U.S.-Canadian cooperation regarding boundary waters pollution is closely linked to the provisions of a unique treaty — the Boundary Waters Treaty of 1909 — and to the developing responsibilities of a unique institution — the International Joint Commission. Consequently, the provisions of the Treaty, the nature of the Commission and its procedures, and the history of the Commission's increasing activity with respect to pollution, all merit examination in some detail.[34]

A. *The Boundary Waters Treaty*

The basic framework for U.S.-Canadian cooperation respecting boundary waters problems is the U.S.-U.K. Boundary Waters Treaty of 1909,[35] which established the International Joint Commission between the United States and Canada (hereafter referred to as the "Commission" or "IJC"). The treaty, which developed out of earlier *ad hoc* efforts to deal with boundary waters questions,[36] was designed primarily to protect the levels and navigability of the Great Lakes and other boundary waters against unilateral diversion or obstruction, but it has provided the basis for an increasing involvement by the Commission in pollution and other problems as well. The Treaty's structure and more important provisions may be summarized as follows:

While the Treaty is usually referred to as the "Boundary Waters Treaty," its full title — "Treaty... Relating to Boundary Waters, and Questions Arising Between the United States and Canada" — is significant. According to its Preamble, the purpose of the Treaty is:

... to prevent disputes regarding the use of boundary waters, and to settle all questions which are now pending between the United States and the Dominion of Canada involving the rights, obligations or interests of either in relation to the other or to the inhabitants of the other, along their common frontier, and to make provision for the settlement of all such questions as may hereafter arise.

Thus, the potential reach of the Treaty extends beyond boundary waters issues to all boundary questions, and arguably to other questions of common concern as well.

The Treaty establishes an International Joint Commission of the United States and Canada[37] and defines its jurisdiction, authority and procedure.[38] These provisions will be more fully discussed in the following section.

The Treaty makes distinctions among (1) "boundary waters," which are difined as those waters along which the international boundary runs; and (2) "tributary waters," which are defined as the waters flowing into such boundary waters; (3) waters flowing from such boundary waters; and (4) the waters of rivers flowing across the boundary.[39] For example, since the international boundary does not run through Lake Michigan, that lake is considered a tributary water rather than a boundary water.

The rights and obligations of the countries under the Treaty differ as among these various categories of waters. Thus, the Treaty provides that navigation of all boundary waters shall be free and open to the inhabitants and vessels of each country without discrimination; this same right shall apply to the waters.[40] On the other hand, the Treaty provides that each country retains exclusive jurisdiction and control over the use and diversion of all waters on its own side of the boundary which in their natural channels would flow across the boundary or into boundary waters.[41] However, if through interference with or diversion of such waters injury is caused on the other side of the boundary, any injured party is entitled to the same legal remedies as if such injury took place in the country where such diversion or interference occurs.[42] Moreover, neither party surrenders rights it may have to object to interference with or diversion of waters on the other side of the boundary which would have the effect of materially injuring navigation interests on its own side of the boundary.[43]

A principal purpose of the Treaty is the regulation of certain uses, obstructions or diversion of the boundary waters, and the Commission is given broad powers in in this respect, stated again with reference to particular categories of waters. Unless otherwise provided by special agreement, the Commission's approval is required for any uses, obstructions or diversions of boundary waters on either side of the boundary which affect the natural level or flow of boundary waters on the other side of the boundary.[44] Moreover, the Commission's approval is required for the construction or maintenance of any remedial or protective works or dams or other obstructions in waters flowing from boundary waters or in waters at a lower level than the boundary in rivers flowing across the boundary, the effect of which is to raise the natural level of waters on the other side of the boundary.[45] In passing upon such cases, the Commission is to be guided by certain rules and principles.[46] One of these is that the parties shall have, each on its own side of the boundary, equal and similar rights in the use of the boundary waters.[47] Another is that an order of precedence is established among various uses of the waters, namely: (1) uses for domestic and sanitary purposes, (2) uses for navigation, and (3) uses for power and navigation purposes. No use shall be permitted by the Commission which tends materially to conflict with or restrain a preferred use.[48]

Article IV of the Treaty includes a provision that "... boundary waters, or water flowing across the boundary, shall not be polluted on either side to the injury of health or property on the other."[49] Neither the term "pollution" nor the term "injury" are defined, and the Treaty is silent with respect to any procedures for enforcement of this obligation.

The Treaty sets forth special provisions regarding the Niagara River[50] and the St. Mary and Milk Rivers.[51]

Finally, the Treaty established broad and flexible provisions concerning the handling of disputes and other questions between the governments. Article IX authorizes the Commission to render advisory reports to the governments at their request. It provides that: "Any other questions or matters of difference" arising between the two countries "involving the rights, obligations or interests of either in relation to the other or to the inhabitants of the other, along the common frontier... shall be referred from time to time to the International Joint Commission for examination and report," whenever either government requests such reference. The Commission is authorized in each case so referred to examine into and report upon the facts and circumstances of the particular questions referred, together with such conclusions and recommendations as may be appropriate, subject, however, to any restrictions which may be imposed by the terms of the reference. However, such reports of the Commission shall not be regarded as decisions of the questions or matters submitted either on the facts or the law, and shall in no way have the character of an arbitral award. Procedures are set forth governing such advisory references.

In addition, Article X provides detailed procedures under which such questions or matters of difference may be referred to the Commission, by the consent of the two governments, for a binding arbitral decision or finding. However, to date the provisions of Article X have never been utilized.[52]

B. *The International Joint Commission and Its Procedures*

The provisions of the Boundary Waters Treaty are implemented principally through the activities of the International Joint Commission. The Commission consists of six members, three (including a chairman of that nation's section) from each country.[53] U.S. Commissioners are appointed by and serve at the pleasure of the President; Canadian Commissioners are appointed by order-in-council of the Canadian government and serve at the pleasure of that government.[54] Each of the two national sections has appointed a permanent secretary; the two national secretaries act as joint secretaries at Commission meetings.[55] Otherwise the Commission maintains an exceptionally small staff, typically drawing on personnel of agencies of their respective governments, as need has arisen, for the performance of specific tasks. Permanent IJC offices are maintained in Washington and Ottawa,[56] but meetings and public hearings are held wherever convenient,[57] the Canadian chairmen presiding at meetings in Canada and the U.S. Chairman presiding at meetings in the U.S.[58] Under its rules the Commission is required to meet at least semiannually,[59] but in practice, especially in recent years, it has met much more frequently. Decisions of the Commission are made by a majority of the Commissioners, irrespective of their nationality, with provision for separate dissenting reports.[60] The IJC's various activities are governed by published Rules of Procedure.[61]

Broadly speaking, the IJC's responsibilities fall into three broad categories. First, under Articles II, IV, and VIII, it exercises the essentially regulatory or licensing function of passing upon applications for approval of works that affect water levels or flows in the boundary water; no individual or corporation can erect a mill or dam upon a boundary water or certain other waters without securing the Commission's prior approval. Second, under Article IX of the Treaty, the IJC performs investigative, recommendatory and certain administrative functions with respect to specific questions or matters the governments refer to it. Third, under Article X of the Treaty, the IJC may exercise judicial functions respecting any questions or disputes which the two governments may specifically refer to it for binding decision, though it has not as yet been called upon to exercise this authority.

The Commission's regulatory responsibilities with respect to approval of various works affecting water levels or flows are brought before it by what are termed "applications" filed by the persons or corporate bodies concerned.[62] Such applications have ranged from simple log booms on the Rainy River to major hydroelectric developments on the St. Lawrence. The applicant has the burden of furnishing all necessary information and data, and other persons interested may intervene in support of or opposition to the application. The Commission usually holds public hearings on the application, frequently in both countries. The Commission then issues its order which is final. If it wishes, the Commission may make its approval conditional upon the construction of remedial or protective works to compensate so far as possible for the particular use or diversion proposed, and may also require suitable and adequate provision for protection against injury of any interests on either side of the boundary. In some cases, where the IJC has approved an application for works only upon specified conditions, it has appointed an International Board of Control to exercise continuing supervision and ensure compliance with such conditions.[63]

The Commission's responsibilities under Article IX of the Treaty, with respect to requests by the two governments for investigation and recommendation as to specific problems, are performed pursuant to what are termed "references." Only the national governments can initiate such investigations; the Commission has no inherent powers of inquiry, except such as may be granted by the governments by reference or otherwise. Moreover, while the Treaty suggests that a single government may make such a reference, in practice all such references have been made by the joint or concurrent requests of both.[65] Under

Article IX, the subject of a reference is not restricted to boundary waters or even closely related problems, but can embrace "any other questions or matters of difference" arising between the two countries "involving the rights, obligations or interests of either in relation to the other or to the inhabitants of the other, along the common frontier." References have in fact been made on an extremely wide range of subjects,[66] including regulation of the level of the Great Lakes,[67] preservation of the American Falls at Niagara,[68] the water resources of the Columbia River region,[69] the tidal power potential of Passamaquoddy Bay,[70] and a considerable number and variety of water and air pollution problems.[71] Some of these references have been of outstanding significance: The 1944 Columbia River reference laid the basis for the negotiation of the landmark Columbia River Treaty of 1961 between the two countries;[72] the 1964 Great Lakes water levels reference, which is still continuing, involves the most extensive hydrological survey ever attempted;[73] and the 1964 Lake Erie-Lake Ontario-International St. Lawrence Pollution Reference involved what is probably the most extensive, detailed and scientifically sophisticated study of a major water environment yet undertaken, and, as we shall see, has led to current negotiation of the Great Lakes Water Qaulity Agreement.

A "reference" is normally initiated by identical letters from each government to the IJC specifically setting out the subject matter for investigation and the action requested.[74] The letters typically authorize the Commission, in conducting its investigation, to utilize the services of specially qualified personnel of the technical agencies of the two countries, acting in an expert rather than a representative capacity, and also to draw upon such information and technical data as these agencies may possess.[75]

Upon receipt of the reference, the Commission has occasionally held an initial round of public hearings to broadly acquaint itself with the problem. Moreover, where appropriate, it has frequently carried out the investigative phase of its assignment through appointment of an International Technical Advisory Board, which will include personnel from federal, state and provincial, or other official departments or agencies of the two governments with particular responsibilities and expertise concerning the subject matter of the reference.[76] The Technical Board organizes and carries out the necessary technical work and field studies, drawing as necessary upon the facilities of relevant agencies of the two governments and consulting with interested and knowledgeable persons. Progress reports may be submitted to the Commission as appropriate. Upon completion of its work, the Board files its formal report and recommendations with the Commission.

Upon receipt of the Board's report, the Commission normally publishes and distributes it to interested persons and organizations in both countries. It will then usually schedule public hearings, typically in each country in the particular areas concerned, at which interested persons may, under informal procedures, present evidence or comment on the Board's findings and recommendations. Then, drawing upon the Board's report, material presented at the hearings, and other information and advice received, the Commission prepares and submits its own report and recommendations to the two governments. In contrast with "applications," the Commission's recommendations respecting "references" are not binding, and either government is free to accept or reject them. In practice, the governments have generally formally "accepted" the recommendations,[77] though such acceptance does not necessarily imply that further governmental action has been taken respecting them.

While the IJC's role respecting "references" has typically ended with the submission of its report, the Commission has, in recent years, on occasion recommended that the governments authorize it to appoint an International Advisory Board to maintain continuing surveillance respecting compliance with objectives recommended in the Commission's Report. The governments have in several instances complied with this recommendation, and five such Advisory Boards are presently operating.[78] In addition to the regular activities of the Advisory Boards, the IJC has recently experimented with the technique of calling public international meetings to inquire into the progress being made with respect to recommendations accepted by the governments.[79] These developments have involved the Commission in a continuing, though very limited, administrative role.

Since the IJC commenced operations in 1912, it has dealt with 92 applications and references.[80] During this period of almost sixty years, there has been a gradual but steady shift in the burden of the Commission's work from applications to references: During the period 1912 to 1944, the Commission dealt with 39 applications and 11 references; in the period since 1944, it has handled 19 applications and 23 references.[81] Moreover, many of these recent applications have been comparatively minor in importance, whereas a number of the recent references have involved issues of major significance. The fact that "references" now comprise the major work of the Commission reflects the increased willingness and desire of the two governments to employ the IJC for a widening range of common problems and tasks, far transcending the limited role originally envisioned for the Commission in 1909. It also demonstrates the remarkable adaptability of the Treaty, which, through this change of emphasis in the nature of the Commission's work, has assumed a growing importance in U.S.-Canadian relations.

C. *The Commission's Activities Regarding Pollution*

Our particular concern, of course, is the IJC's work regarding problems of boundary waters pollution and, in particular, pollution of the Great

Lakes. It will be recalled that, while Article IV of the Boundary Waters Treaty provides that boundary and transboundary waters shall not be polluted on either side of the boundary to the injury of health or property on the other, it does not confer any specific power on the IJC in this respect or provide any other procedures for implementing this obligation. Nevertheless, the IJC has been gradually entrusted with a growing role concerning pollution problems through a series of references under Article IX, and pollution has now become one of the Commission's principal concerns. To date, the IJC has dealt with ten references relating to pollution, eight of which have been received since the Second World War.[82] A summary of these pollution references will indicate their character.

It is interesting to note that one of the first of the two governments' references to the IJC under Article IX of the Treaty, made only shortly after the Commission was constituted, was a 1912 request that it investigate and report upon "the causes, extent, location and remedies of pollution of boundary waters" on one side of the boundary which extended to and affected the boundary waters on the other side."[83] The request was apparently related to recurrent outbreaks of typhoid fever in various of the Great Lakes and connecting waters communities and the Commission's subsequent investigation was essentially a bacteriological study of this region. The Commission submitted a comprehensive report in September, 1918, finding that, while the Great Lakes beyond the coastal waters and mouths of tributary rivers were pure, the shore waters and rivers mouths themselves were in various states of serious pollution, to an extent which rendered the water in an unpurified state unfit for drinking purposes.[84] The survey disclosed "a situation along the frontier which is generally chaotic, everywhere perilous, and in some cases disgraceful."[85] Pollution was "very intense along the shores of the Detroit and Niagara Rivers" and "conditions exist which imperil the health and welfare of the citizens of both countries in direst contravention of the Treaty."[86] To deal with this situation, the IJC recommended that the two governments confer on the Commission jurisdiction to regulate and prohibit such transboundary pollution. The governments accepted the report and requested the IJC to prepare reciprocal legislation or a draft convention for this purpose.

The IJC submitted such a draft convention in October, 1920.[87] In view of the current proposal for the Great Lakes Water Quality Agreement, some history of this early effort may be of interest. In transmitting the draft convention, the IJC stated that:

The Commission is firmly of the view that the method best adapted to avoid the ends which the Treaty is designed to correct is to take proper steps to prevent dangerous pollution crossing the boundary line rather than wait until it is manifest that such pollution has actually physically crossed, to the injury of health or property on the other side, and that to this end the convention should clothe the commission with authority and power, subject to all proper limitation and restrictions, to make such orders rules and regulations as may be proper and necessary to maintain boundary waters in as healthful a condition as practicable in view of conditions already created, and should contain proper provisions for the enforcement of such orders, rules and regulations.[88]

Under the draft convention, the Commission would have been given authority to investigate any alleged violation of Article IV of the Boundary Waters Treaty and to report to the governments on its inquiry. On the basis of the Commission's findings of fact, which "shall be final and conclusive," the governments would be obligated to take such proceedings as might be necessary to prevent a continuation of the breach. The Commission was also given authority to define classes of vessels "in which apparatus for the disinfection of the sewage, bilge water or ballast discharged therefrom should be installed to prevent the pollution of waters," and the parties agreed not to grant licenses for such vessels as failed to meet IJC requirements. Finally, the parties would have agreed to enact or recommend legislation to their legislatures for full enforcement of the Convention. The draft convention was discussed by the governments but they were unable to reach agreement and negotiations terminated in 1929.[89] Apparently, one obstacle was U.S. objection to the provision that the Commission's findings of fact as to the existence of pollution and its injurious nature would be final.[90] Canada attempted to reopen the negotiations in 1942, but the U.S. State Department took the position that the time was not propitious.[91] Many years were to pass before the governments were again to consider an expansion of the IJC's formal authority, and even then in much less sweeping terms than proposed in the Commission's 1920 draft.

The IJC's activities regarding pollution in the inter-war years were limited. The Commission did, however, play a role in the famous *Trail Smelter* arbitration, a landmark case of continuing importance in the field of developing pollution law. In 1928 a reference was filed by the U.S. and concurred in by Canada concerning: the extent to which property in the state of Washington had been damaged by fumes drifting from a smelter located at Trail, British Columbia; the amount of indemnity to compensate for past damage caused by such fumes; the probable effects in the state of Washington of future operations of the smelter; and the method of providing indemnity for any future damages; together with the Commission's recommendations.[92] In its report of February 28, 1931, the IJC recommended payment of $350,000 to cover damages sustained in the state of Washington resulting from the operation of the Trail Smelter up to the end of 1931.[93] The two governments decided to entrust the remaining aspects of this problem to a special tribunal, and, under the terms of a Convention signed April 15, 1935, established an *ad hoc* arbitral tribunal to determine, *inter alia*, whether further damage had been caused in the state of Washington by the Trail Smelter subsequent to January 1, 1932, and, if so, the amount of that damage.[94] In its decision reported to the two governments on April 16, 1938, the arbitral tribunal concluded that such damage had been caused between January, 1932 and October 1, 1937, and that an indemnity of $78,000 with interest should be paid.[95] In its final decision reported March 11, 1941, the Tribunal concluded that no further damage had occurred since 1937, but recommended a "prescribed regime to avoid future damage."[96] In the course of its opinion, the Tribunal made what is still the broadest judicial suggestion of international liability for transnational pollution.

... under principles of international law, as well as the law of the U.S., no state has the right to use or permit the use of its territory in such a manner as to cause injury by fumes in or to the territory of another or the property or persons therein, when the case is of serious consequence and the injury is established by clear and convincing evidence.[97]

Following World War II, the problem of pollution of boundary waters, as well as other transboundary pollution problems, began to assume increasing importance to the two countries. In view of the provisions of Article IV of the Boundary Waters Treaty and the expertise and patterns of U.S.-Canadian cooperation already developed by the IJC, it is not surprising that the two governments turned increasingly to the Commission in an effort to deal with these problems.

In 1946 the two governments requested that the IJC investigate problems arising from pollution in the St. Clair River, Lake St. Clair, the Detroit River, and the St. Mary's River — the so-called "Connecting Channels" Reference.[98] A further reference was submitted in 1948 to include the Niagara River as well,[99] the two references being administered as one. The Commission's 312-page report on the Connecting Channels Reference, submitted on October 11, 1950, constituted a major advance in international pollution control experience, in terms of both its technical comprehensiveness and the nature of its recommendations.[100] The report disclosed serious pollution in the various connecting channels, resulting principally from the discharge of domestic sewage and industrial wastes, which the Commission suggested required urgent action. As an approach to dealing with the problem the Commission recommended adoption by the two governments of a number of specific "Objectives for Boundary Water Quality Control;" in essence, these objectives are technical criteria which should be met in order to maintain the waters in a satisfactory condition. The idea of recommending technical water quality objectives was a major innovation which the Commission has continued to follow in its other pollution references since that time. The objectives were the first of their kind on an international basis and anticipated national action in both countries;[101] this concept was ultimately embodied in the U.S. Federal Water Quality Act of 1965 some fifteen years later. The Commission also recommended appointment of two Advisory Boards on Control of Pollution — one for the Superior-Huron-Erie section connecting channels, and the other for the Erie-Ontario section connecting channels. The Boards were to assist the Commission in maintaining continuing surveillance of the connecting channels in terms of compliance with the recommended objectives, notifying those responsible for objectionable pollution, and, in the absence of corrective measures being taken, making appropriate recommendations to authorities having jurisdiction. Again, it has now become standard practice of the Commission to recommend that an Advisory Board be established to maintain continuing surveillance on developments with respect to a particular reference. The Connecting Channels Report was approved by the governments and the two Boards established, and they have since functioned continuously. A program of periodic conferences with interested persons was also commenced to assist in promoting compliance, and this also has continued.

In 1949 the IJC was asked to investigate the contribution made by vessels in the Detroit River to atmospheric pollution in the Detroit-Windsor area.[102] The Commission established a Technical Board on Atmospheric Pollution to conduct the investigations. The IJC's Report, issued May 31, 1960, found serious air pollution on both sides of the river causing health and economic injuries.[103] The Commission concluded, however, that the major source of atmospheric pollution was industrial and transportation activities in the land areas, and that fumes from vessels contributed only a minimal amount to this pollution. It recommended adoption by the governments of certain regulations for the emission of smoke from vessels and concluded, as to other sources, that there was existing adequate legal and administrative authority in each country to enforce proper controls on emission of wastes into the atmosphere. On January 30, 1961, the governments authorized the IJC to continue its surveillance program pending transmittal of the views of the governments concerning the report. An Advisory Board has been established and its work continues.

On June 10, 1955, the two governments submitted a reference to the IJC requesting it to investigate and study redevelopment of the St. Croix River Basin, looking to improvement of the use, conservation, and regulation of the waters of the Basin.[104] While the reference did not expressly refer to pollution, the Commission dealt with that subject extensively. The Commission established the International St. Croix River Engineering Board to conduct the investigation. In 1957 the Engineering Board completed a preliminary report, and on October 13, 1959 the Commission reported to the two governments on the regulation and pollution of the waters of the basin.[105] The Report recommended, *inter alia,* that the "Objectives for Boundary Waters Quality Control" which were set forth in Commission's Report on the Pollution of Boundary Waters, dated October 11, 1950 (the "Connecting Channels" Report) be adopted by the governments of Canada, the U.S., New Brunswick and Maine as the criteria to be met in maintaining the basin waters in satisfactory condition, that those responsible for existing or potential pollution put into effect remedial measures necessary to meet these "Objectives", and that it be authorized to establish and maintain continuing supervision over boundary waters pollution in the Basin through a technical advisory Board. In April 1960 the Commission received a supplementary report from the Engineering Board concerning pollution, which was transmitted on to the two governments. On October 2, 1961, the Governments announced that they had approved the recommendations of the Commission, with an exception not here pertinent. The Advisory Board was established and is presently operating.

In May, 1959, the two governments submitted a reference to the IJC with respect to pollution of Rainy River and the Lake of the Woods.[106] The Commission established a Technical Board on Water Pollution, Rainy River and Lake of the Woods, which submitted a comprehensive report to the Commission on April 4, 1963. The Commission issued its Report in February, 1965 concluding that the waters of the Rainy River were being seriously polluted, primarily from the discharge of wastes of pulp and paper industries, but that the water quality of Lake of the Woods appeared satisfactory.[107] It recommended adoption by the concerned state and provincial governments of specified water quality objectives for the Rainy River; that appropriate authorities require the industries and municipalities concerned to initiate, at the earliest possible date and pursuant to a definite time schedule, construction of pollution abatement facilities; and that the Commission be authorized to establish and maintain continuing supervision over the waters of the Rainy River in relation to pollution. The Report was accepted by the governments and a Supervisory Board established.

In October, 1964, in the only pollution reference respecting a river which was not a boundary water, the two governments also requested the IJC to investigate pollution of the Red River.[108] The Commission created the International Red River Pollution Board to undertake the necessary technical investigations and studies, and the Board submitted a two-volume report in October 1967. In the Commission's final report submitted in April 1968,[109] it concluded that, during the survey period, the River waters crossing the boundary were not polluted to an extent that caused injury to health or property in Canada, and such injury was unlikely to occur if standards established pursuant to legislation in Minnesota and North Dakota were adhered to in those states. It further concluded that, to ensure maintenance of satisfactory water quality conditions at the boundary, there was need for adoption of mutually acceptable water quality objectives for the Red River at the international boundary and for continuous supervision to attain compliance with such objectives. Accordingly, the IJC recommended general and specific water quality objectives for the area and that it be authorized to establish an International Board to maintain such continuing supervision. These recommendations were accepted and the Board established.

Also, in October, 1964, in one of the most significant and broad-ranging post-war pollution references, the two governments requested

310

that the IJC inquire into the extent, causes and location of pollution of Lake Erie, Lake Ontario and the international section of the St. Lawrence River — the so-called Lower Great Lakes Pollution Reference.[110] The Commission established two international technical advisory boards — the International Lake Erie Water Pollution Board and the International Lake Ontario-St. Lawrence Water Pollution Board — to conduct the technical investigations. The Boards' investigation was the most extensive water pollution study to be undertaken anywhere to date, involving the concerted efforts of twelve agencies of the two national governments, the States of New York, Pennsylvania, Ohio, Michigan, and the Province of Ontario; the work of several hundred scientific, engineering and technical experts from a variety of disciplines; and a multi-million dollar cost.[111] During the period 1964-70, the Boards submitted 10 semiannual progress reports and two interim reports to the IJC. The IJC itself made three interim reports to the two governments. In September, 1969, the two technical advisory boards submitted to the Commission a comprehensive three-volume 800-page joint final report on the subject of the reference, containing detailed technical findings and a wide variety of recommendations.[112] During the period December 1969-February 1970, the IJC held six hearings on this report in eight U.S. and Canadian cities. On January 14, 1971, the IJC issued its own 174-page final report to the two governments, signed on December 9, 1970, adopting most of the Board's recommendations.[113] These recommendations were to play a crucial role in the proposal and negotiation of the Great Lakes Water Quality Agreement and deserve fuller description for a moment in order to complete the summary of certain other pollution matters dealt with by the Commission during the period 1964-70 prior to issuance of the Lower Lakes Report.

On September 23, 1966, the governments expanded upon the 1949 Detroit River air pollution reference by requesting the IJC to ascertain whether the air in the vicinity of Port Huron, Michigan-Sarnia, Ontario, and Detroit, Michigan-Windsor, Ontario is being polluted on either side of the boundary to an extent that is detrimental to the public health, safety or general welfare of citizens or property on the other side of the boundary.[114] If this question is answered in the affirmative, the Commission is to indicate the sources and extent of the air pollution and to recommend to governments the most practical preventive or remedial measures. This reference also authorizes the IJC to call to the attention of the governments any air pollution situation along the entire boundary meriting concern.[115] The Commission assigned this study to its existing International St. Clair, Detroit Air Pollution Board.

On February 4, 1971, the Board submitted a comprehensive 250-page report to he Commission.[116] The report concludes that the transboundary flow of air pollutants produce pollution levels that are in excess of the air quality standards established in Ontario and about to be established in Michigan. In the Detroit-Windsor area far more sulfur oxides and particulate matter are being transported from the United States into Canada than are carried in the opposite direction. In the Sarnia-Port Huron area the contribution of sulfur oxides and particulate matter from each country to transboundary air pollution is approximately equal; however, odors which have long been a source of complaints by residents in the Port Huron area were considered in the Board report to be a mixture caused by petroleum refining and petroleum-related organic chemical manufacturing in Sarnia. The report recommends that the responsible control agencies in both countries accelerate abatement programs to bring all sources of air pollution into compliance; that both countries and their respective air pollution control agencies establish uniform air quality standards as soon as possible; and that the governments of Canada, the United States, the State of Michigan and the Province of Ontario co-operate to control transboundary air pollution from existing sources and to prevent creation of new sources of transboundary air pollution. A final report on this reference is reportedly in preparation.

Following the Santa Barbara Channel oil pollution incident off the coast of California in the winter of 1969, the two governments become concerned with the situation in Lake Erie, where some oil and gas exploration has been carried on in the Canadian waters since 1913. In March 1969 the governments requested the IJC, within the framework of its existing study of Lower Lakes pollution, and as a matter of urgency, to investigate and make a special report on the adequacy of existing safety requirements applicable to underwater drilling and production operations so as to prevent oil spilling into Lake Erie, on the adequacy of known methods of clearing up any major oil spill that may occur from any source and on the adequacy of existing contingency plans in both countries for dealing with such oil spills.[117] The Commission instructed its existing International Lake Erie Water Pollution Board to carry out the technical investigation. Five months later the Board issued a 163-page report[118] concluding that the current regulations of Ontario, New York and Pennsylvania pertaining to oil and gas exploration and production are adequate, and if effectively enforced will provide satisfactory protection for the water resources of the Lake. It further found that while oil and gas exploration and development is a potential source of oil pollution in Lake Erie, other potential sources possibly pose a greater threat. It pointed out that the daily discharge of oil to the Detroit and St. Clair Rivers exceeds the peak daily flow that escaped from the well off Santa Barbara, California, and that possibly the greatest threat to the water resources of the lake is the significant amount of oil carried in ships for their own use, on the average 1000 tons per vessel, as well as the oil and other hazardous cargoes carried by some ships. The Board carefully examined technical aspects of containment and clean-up of

312

major oil spills, and existing contingency plans in both countries, and emphasized the urgent need for international co-ordination and co-operation to deal effectively with a major oil spill. It recommended an accelerated and expanded concerted program on containment and clean-up of oil spills, development of more complete national contingency plans and a co-ordinated international contingency plan, the temporary limitation of drilling and production in certain parts of Lake Erie pending development of such programs, the exclusion from the Great Lakes of ships and masters likely to present an unreasonable risk of oil pollutions, and provisions to alert appropriate officials when hazardous materials are in transit in Lake waters. The Commission held public hearings on the Board's Report in December 1969. On May 21, 1970 the IJC submitted to the two governments its third interim report on the progress of its Lower Lakes study entitled "Special Report on Potential Oil Pollution, Eutrophication, and pollution from Watercraft," which, *inter alia*, adopted most of the conclusions of the Board with respect to the oil pollution question.[119] The Commission's interim conclusions were subsequently confirmed in its January 1971 final Report on the Lower Great Lakes Reference.[120]

This survey may be concluded by returning to a fuller description of the IJC's Report on the Lower Great Lakes Pollution Reference, signed in December 1970, but issued in January of 1971. Briefly stated, the questions posed to he Commission in the Reference were:

1. Were the boundary waters of Lake Erie, Lake Ontario, and the International Section of the St. Lawrence River being polluted on either side to an extent injurious to health or property on the other side?

2. If so, to what extent, by what causes, and in what localities was such pollution taking place?

3. What remedial measures would be the most practical from economic, sanitary, and other points of view, and what would the probable cost of these measures be?[121]

The IJC's Report is extremely comprehensive. It contains an extensive discussion, based on the Joint Board's technical studies, of all aspects of the Lower Great Lakes pollution problems; a number of specific conclusions; a listing of both General and Specific Proposed Water Quality Objectives, and 22 specific recommendations for action by the two governments and responsible jurisdictions in both countries. The Commission's answers to the questions presented in the Reference are, in summary, as follows:[122]

In answer to the first question, the Commission found that the waters of the Lower Great Lakes are being seriously polluted on both sides of the boundary to the detriment of both countries. While it is difficult to establish positively that the concentration of a particular pollutant on one side of the boundary is due to a specific source on the other side,

313

there is no doubt that contaminants originating in one country do move across the boundary and degrade the quality of water in the other country to an extent which is causing injury to health and property on the other side of the boundary.

In answer to the second question, the Commission found that water pollution extends throughout the lower lakes; that the principal causes are wastes discharged to the boundary waters and tributaries by municipal and industries; and that pollution is taking place in all jurisdictions sharing the boundary waters. It found that Lake Erie, particularly its western basin, is in an advanced state of eutrophication or aging, and that accelerated eutrophication is occuring in Lake Ontario. A controlling factor in this process is discharge of phosphorus from the use of detergents and other municipal and industrial wastes.

Finally, in answer to the third question, and as a result of its previous answers, the Commission found that urgent measures are required, and it recommended that both Canada and the United States adopt specific water quality objectives, as set out in the Report, and enter into agreement on a wide range of programs, measures and schedules to achieve them. The Report lists specific remedial actions to be taken on an urgent basis, including the immediate reduction of the phosphorus content in detergents and the prompt implementation of a vigorous program to treat municipal and industrial waste and to reduce phosphorus inputs into these waters. Estimated cost in terms of 1968 dollars for municipal and industrial treatment facilities in Canada is $211 million and the cost in the U.S. is estimated at $1,373 million. The Commission recommends that, until it is in a position to recommend Quality Objectives for Lake Huron and Lake Superior, the States of Michigan, Wisconsin, Minnesota, and the Province of Ontario recognize the Objectives recommended for the Lower Lakes as the initial basis for the establishment of their water pollution control programs for the upper Lakes.

The Commission Report, however, is not limited to technical evaluations and recommendations. It also deals extensively with the surveillance, monitoring and implementation arrangements required to achieve the recommended remedial measures,[123] and, to this end, concludes by recommending a substantial expansion of its own authority and jurisdiction. Recommendation 20 is that the two governments extend, at the earliest practicable date, the existing Lower Lakes Reference so as to authorize the Commission to investigate pollution in the remaining boundary waters of the Great Lakes system and the waters tributary thereto.[124] Recommendation 22, the final recommendation is more far reaching; the Commission recommends that:

The Governments of Canada and the United States specifically confer upon this Commission the authority, responsibility, and means for co-ordination, surveillance, monitoring, implementation, reporting, making recommendations to governments, all as outlined in Chapter XIII of this report [which contains a detailed discussion of needs respecting surveillance, monitoring and implementation], and other duties related to preservation and improvement of the quality of the Great Lakes-St. Lawrence System as may be agreed by the said governments; the Commission to be authorized to establish, in consultation with the governments, an international board or boards to assist it in carrying out those duties and to delegate to said board or boards such authority and responsibility as the Commission may deem appropriate.[125]

D. *The Proposed Great Lakes Water Quality Agreement*

The completion in September 1969 of the two Lower Lake Technical Boards' intensive study of lower Great Lakes pollution, and the joint Boards' strong conclusions and recommendations to the IJC concerning the continued grave deterioration of water quality in many areas of the Lakes, coincided with a surge of public anxiety over environmental problems in both the U.S. and Canada, public demands in both countries for government action to deal with these problems, and strong international pressures by the Canadian government upon the U.S. government urging the adoption of more effective measures to cope with Great Lakes pollution. Influenced no doubt by all of these factors, President Nixon charged the U.S. Council on Evironmental Quality to work with Canada on this matter.

On June 23, 1970 the two governments convened a high level ministerial meeting in Ottawa to discuss common Great Lakes pollution problems.[126] The Canadian delegation was led by Mitchell Sharp, Secretary of State for External Affairs, and the U.S. delegation was led by Russell Train, Chairman of the Council on Environmental Quality. Both delegations included state and provincial as well as federal officials and representatives. At the conclusion of this initial meeting, the Ministers expressed deep concern about the critical situation in the Great Lakes, noted the determination of the governments to take decisive action, and agreed on a number of specific remedial measures.[127] The Ministers further agreed to the establishment of a joint Working Group, composed of representatives of federal, state and provincial agencies having responsibilities in the field of water quality, to consider various aspects of the problems of Great Lakes pollution, possible common water quality objectives, and such implementing programs as either government might wish to propose. The Working Group was charged to report back to the Ministerial Conference, which would be reconvened subsequent to the IJC's issuance of its final report on the Lower Great Lakes Reference.

The Working Group divided into ten subgroups, each dealing with particular aspects of the Great Lakes problem. The reports of the subgroups were presented to the full Working Group in February and March 1971, and the final report of the Working Group was approved by the full group in April 1971 and presented to the Ministerial Meeting in June 1971. The central recommendation of the Working Group Report was that the U.S. and Canada enter into a comprehensive new agreement on Great Lakes water quality control, and that the agreement should include adoption of common water quality objectives for the Great Lakes, programs for a-chieving these objectives, and an expansion of the IJC's authority to permit it to effectively monitor these efforts.

On June 10, 1971 the Ministerial Conference reconvened in Washington to review the Working Group's report. The result of that meeting was broad acceptance of the Working Group's major recommendations, including its proposal for a new agreement on Great Lakes water quality control. A joint communique was issued at the conclusion of that meeting committing the two governments to conclude such an agreement before the end of 1971.[128]

As this article goes to press, the details of the proposed Great Lakes Water Quality Agreement are still in process of negotiation by the two governments. However, the general character and coverage of the proposed Agreement and associated arrangements are spelled out at some length in the Joint Communique, and at least some of the probable details may be surmised from the recommendations in the IJC's Lower Great Lakes Report and other sources.[129]

The Agreement will be a formal and binding international agreement, which will, however, reportedly be entered into by the U.S. as an executive agreement rather than as a treaty ratified pursuant to formal U.S. Constitutional processes.[130] It will presumably first establish certain broad General Objectives for water quality throughout the Boundary Waters of the Great Lakes System. These will probably conform closely to the General Objectives stated in the IJC's Report, and will include, for example, such objectives as keeping the waters free from substances in concentrations that are toxic or harmful to human, animal or aquatic life; free from nutrients in concentrations that create nuisance growths of aquatic weeds or algae; and free from other substances, floating debris or materials in amounts sufficient to be deleterious or objectionable.[131]

To achieve these General Objectives, the parties will agree to adopt specific Common Water Quality Objectives,[132] perhaps with associated Target Loadings and Target Dates, applicable to specific areas. These Specific Water Quality Objectives will again most likely be essentially the same as those recommended by the IJC in its Report; these suggest specific technical criteria for the quality of the receiving waters as to microbiology, dissolved oxygen, total dissolved solids, temperature, taste and oder, pH, iron, phosphorus and radioactivity, and, as required, toxic materials, oils, and heavy metals.[133] Presumably there will be some arrangement under which these objectives, loadings and dates may be supplemented or modified from time to time under agreed procedures without necessity for revising the Agreement as a whole.

To meet these Specific Objectives, each party will undertake to establish, through its own legal procedures, a broad range of national Water Quality Standards for the Boundary Waters of the Great Lakes System;

316

these standards will have to be compatible with the Common Water Quality Objectives set forth in the Agreement, and, of course, may hopefully exceed them.[134]

As further measures to achieve the Common Water Quality Objectives, the two governments will exchange commitments to carry out a variety of pollution control programs within agreed time periods, or as rapidly as feasible, including:[135]

(a) construction of treatment facilities for municipal and industrial wastes and animal husbandry operations;

(b) reduction of phosphorus discharges from municipal and industrial sources;

(c) elimination of mercury and other toxic metals from discharges;

(d) control of thermal pollution;

(e) control of pollution from radioactive wastes;

(f) control of pollution from pesticides, herbicides and other organic contaminants; and

(g) development of controls for pollution from combined sewer overflows.

The two governments will also agree to effective and compatible regulations for: (a) ship design and construction to prevent fuel and cargo loss, (b) control of vessel waste discharges, (c) disposition of polluted dredge spoils, and (d) preventing discharges of oil and hazardous pollution substances from on-and-off shore facilities and transportation by land.[136] The Agreement will also provide for a joint investigation by the two governments for the purpose of agreeing upon measures respecting new navigation equipment, establishing traffic lanes on the Lakes, and the manning and operation of vessels.[137] The Communique also announces that, without waiting for the negotiation of the Agreement, the governments are proceeding immediately with certain additional measures, including a joint contingency plan for a co-ordinated response to pollution incidents involving spills of oil and hazardous materials on the Great Lakes.[138]

The Communique expresses the two governments' agreement that they should assign additional responsibilities and authority to the IJC to assist them in their efforts to restore and protect Great Lakes Water Quality, and gives considerable emphasis to the enhanced role envisioned for the Commission.[139] More specifically, the Commission will be given a greater role in collecting, analyzing and disseminating relevant data and information; surveillance of water quality in the Great Lakes System; monitoring of the effectiveness of governmental programs to achieve the common water quality objectives; co-ordinating activities to improve water quality; tendering advice and assistance; and recommending legislation and programs.[140] Arrangements will be established within the IJC for the co-ordination of water quality research. Presumably the IJC will render regular reports on progress made under the Agreement. The Communique also states that the governments intend to extend new References to the IJC: (a) requesting the Commission to conduct an investigation of water quality in Lake Superior and Lake Huron, and (b) requesting the Commission to extend its surveillance of water quality to Lakes Huron and Superior.[141] A separate reference may provide for a study by the IJC of pollution from agriculture, forestry and other land source pollution.

The Communique also addresses the question of IJC institutional arrangements to carry out these new responsibilities.[142] The two governments agreed that it will be necessary to provide the Commission additional staff and resources; such new appointments in staff will be the Commission's responsibility, although the governments will be consulted. The establishment of an IJC office in the Great Lakes area is suggested. The Ministers further suggest establishment of a special Board under the Commission to assist in the implementing of the Agreement; it is suggested that sub-Boards might be created to deal with specific functional responsibilities and specific geographical areas within the Great Lakes basin. This Pollution Advisory Board should have a balanced binational membership. The Communique makes clear, however, that the two governments do not intend to grant the Commission any specific enforcement authority. While the Commission is to aid the governments by providing an independent overview and other assistance, the various agencies of the federal, state and provincial governments will continue to implement the programs and measures required to achieve the water quality objectives.[143]

In the Joint Communique, each of the two governments addressed themselves briefly to certain domestic measures which they were already undertaking to meet these problems, and various related points.[144] The U.S. representatives reviewed the extensive U.S. federal programs directed towards remedying Great Lakes pollution which were underway. The Canadian ministers indicated the desirability of a 1975 deadline for completion of certain of the proposed Lower Great Lakes programs, particularly those directed to the reduction of phosphorus inputs. They also noted that implementation of many of the Canadian commitments under the proposed agreement will be the joint responsibility of the Canadian federal government and the government of Ontario; and that the apportionment of responsibility among the Canadian government, the government of Ontario and the municipalities concerned for the financing of the required accelerated program of improvements to municipal sewage treatment facilities in the Lower Lakes area will be the subject of a detailed agreement to be negotiated between the Canadian Government and the government of Ontario.

Both groups of ministers expressed in the Communique their optimism

318

as to the future. But, in a significant note of caution, they added that: "In designing the agreement, it was accepted that programs and other measures established to meet urgent problems would in no way affect the rights of each country to the use of its Great Lakes waters."[145] In an interesting conclusion to the substantive part of the Communique, the ministers noted that the process of intergovernmental co-operation employed in designing the proposed Great Lakes agreement might be applied to the solution of other common environmental problems — for example, air pollution.[146] Finally, the Communique makes no mention of any special procedures for dispute-settlement in the event of claims of non-compliance with proposed Agreement. Presumably, such claims will be dealt with under the dispute-settlement provisions of the Boundary Waters Treaty.

III. SOME ASPECTS OF U.S.-CANADIAN EXPERIENCE

While every international environmental arrangement is necessarily unique, there are certain problems many will have in common. These include the initial decision that a particular environmental problem or set of problems is an appropriate subject for international co-operative or other measures, determining the broad form such measures should take; structuring required institutions; determining objectives; apportioning burdens; establishing co-ordination; and providing for implementation. It may be useful to take a closer look at how the U.S. and Canada have dealt with these problems.

A. *The Need for International Co-operation*

A threshold stage of any arrangements for international environmental co-operation is a recognition by governments that the particular problems involved are appropriate matters for international treatment. With a few exceptions,[147] pollution and other environmental problems were long regarded as of primarily national rather than international concern. It is only within the last few years that this perspective has undergone substantial change and the propriety of broader international involvement in environmental issues has become more widely accepted. Nevertheless, states are still inclined to think of such questions as primarily national in character and, unless they see some national interest which can be pursued through international environmental co-operation, will have little inclination to participate. Thus, with respect to each proposal for international environmental measures, it is useful to ask why such measures are needed and what they can add to alternative approaches based on national action alone.[148] There are at least three types of situations

319

where such international treatment seem suggested.

First, the clearest case for international co-operation is where a particular environmental problem both produces significant potentially harmful international effects and is of such a nature, or manifested in such an environment, that measures to effectively deal with it inherently require some type of joint or co-ordinated international action. The most typical of such cases is where several countries share a river, a lake or an enclosed sea, or where all nations in common share an environment such as the high seas or outer space beyond the reach of any single national jurisdiction. Clearly, pollution problems cannot in these situations be adequately assessed or controlled except through common or joint action by all of the states contributing to the problem or sharing control of the relevant environments, and over time, a broad consensus has developed as to the desirability of international treatment of many of these issues.[149] In the broadest sense, perhaps all environmental problems are of this character in terms of their ultimate effect on the total global environment. Of course, different types of measures may be appropriate to different cases: some situations may suggest only limited programs of exchange or information and data, co-ordinated or joint monitoring or surveillance, or, as in the case of recent U.S.-Canadian co-operation, the setting of minimum common objectives; other situations may call for more far-reaching techniques of international or supra-national regulation or enforcement.

Second, international measures may be useful where a state fails for some reason to adequately control what is primarily its own national environmental problem, with consequent significant spill-over effects of some type damaging other countries. The passage of fumes from a smelter across an international boundary, as in the *Trail Smelter* arbitration,[150] is an example of this type of situation. The type of international measures suggested may vary with the case. Thus, a state may simply be unaware of the international impact of its environmental policies, in which case international measures may alert it to the problem. Or a state may be indifferent as to the international environmental consequences of its actions, in which case some type of international persuasion or pressure may be required to induce it to change its attitude. A state may be concerned that in taking national measures to control pollution, it will be put at a competitive economic or military disadvantage vis-a-vis other states with similar problems which do not take such action; this is illustrated by the current widespread concern regarding the impact of differential national environmental quality programs costs on international trade and investment.[151] Problems of this nature might be met by international measures requiring similar levels of national action by all, or at least most, of the states concerned.[152] A state may simply not have the financial resources, or scientific or technical expertise necessary to develop and maintain required pollution control programs; measures of international financial and technical assistance can help to fill such a gap.

Finally, even in cases where the international impact of particular environmental problems is minimal and where the national governments are prepared to take necessary action to control them, if the problems are ones common to various countries, there may be substantial mutual gains to governments from a sharing and exchange of relevant scientific data, institutional experience and technology.

The problem of pollution of the internationally-shared environment of the Great Lakes and other U.S.-Canadian boundary waters is one in which both countries have an obvious common concern and the solution of which can clearly be advanced by their international co-operation. Indeed, it is perhaps the most typical such situation. A major accomplishment of the Boundary Water Treaty of 1909 was its early recognition of this fact, at a time when most other countries with similar problems still regarded such problems as entirely each of such country's separate business. By including in the Treaty the provision of Article IV prohibiting pollution, the U.S. and Canada not only recognized this common concern but established a broad international jurisdictional basis for their subsequent common treatment of such problems. Indeed, pollution references under Article IX of the Treaty have traditionally contained language directing the IJC to conduct its investigations "with reference to the principles contained" in Article IV, and it can be assumed that the Preamble to the new Agreement will contain some similar reference.

However, while Article IV provides a broad jurisdictional basis for further cooperative efforts by the U.S. and Canada to implement its prohibition of pollution, it does not in itself require such action. And it is interesting to note that, despite the two countries' broad acceptance of the principle of such international concern in Article IV, they have in practice continued to exercise a careful control over the extent to which specific boundary waters environmental problems are in fact dealt with on an international basis.

The technique by which the two governments make a particular boundary waters pollution problem the subject or international treatment between them is submission of a joint reference concerning the problem to the Commission under Article IX of the Treaty.[153] While unilateral Article IX references are theoretically possible,[154] neither government has sought to make such a unilateral reference and all references have in fact been jointly agreed to. The suggestion and initiative for particular pollution references may come from various sources — concerned agencies of the Federal, State or provincial governments of either country, complaints by affected groups or individuals, or information brought to the attention of the governments by the Commission itself. The governments have not, as yet, seen fit broadly to authorize the Commission to institute investigations on its own motion, though on occasion, as in the case of the "watching brief" given the Commission under the

Air Pollution reference, the governments have in effect conferred certain limited investigatory powers.[155]

If one of the governments considers a proposed reference too sensitive, it will simply refuse to agree to its submission. In any event, the terms of the reference will be carefully negotiated. Moreover, the Commission's jurisdiction, and thus the scope of international co-operation, is limited by the terms of reference. Thus, the reference procedure permits each country to retain a veto over the Commission's investigation and consequently the international handling of particular problems, and such vetoes have occasionally been exercised.[156] Ax previously discussed, the history of U.S.-Canadian Great Lakes co-operation is in effect a history of the various references from time to time agreed to by the two governments.

The proposed Great Lakes Water Quality Agreement, and its related arrangements, will presumably serve to bring the entire range of Great Lakes' problems into the sphere of the IJC's concern and at least limited joint and common action by the two countries. But the two government's caution and reluctance to abandon the prerogatives of sovereignty remain evident. The new agreement will probably provide little in the way of effective international enforcement procedures and the Commission's role in this respect continues to be carefully restricted.

B. *The Role of Legal Prohibitions and Remedies.*

One way of attempting to prevent transnational pollution is simply to prohibit it by international law, with resort by an injured state to the usual processes of international claim and adjudication. One interesting aspect of U.S.-Canadian experience is that, while this technique was expressly available to each country, it has been employed by the two governments only on one occasion — the *Trail Smelter* case, which dealt with air rather than water pollution.[157] Instead, the two countries have chosen to deal with their joint or common pollution problems through the establishment of on-going institutional arrangements and co-operative techniques of investigation and assessment, or, more recently, under the proposed Agreement, through the establishment of broad co-operative programs and agreed minimum water quality objectives.

The Boundary Waters Treaty of 1909 contains a specific prohibition on transnational pollution. The relevant provision of Article IV states that:

It is further agreed that the waters herein defined as boundary waters and water flowing across the boundary shall not be polluted on either side of the boundary to the injury of health or property on the other.

This provision was an early and still significant precedent in international environmental law. Indeed, there is considerable question whether, even today, customary international law has progressed to the point where transnational water pollution is clearly prohibited.[158] And while provisions in treaties relating to water pollution have become more numerous, they vary widely in content, context and application.[159]

The Treaty is silent as to specific procedures to be followed in the event of either country claiming a violation of Article IV and seeking traditional international legal remedies. However, since Aritcle IX permits either government to refer "any questions or matters of difference arising between them" to the IJC for examination and an advisory report, each country may, at least in theory, unilaterally compel an advisory opinion on its claim that the other has violated Article IV. Article X goes further by providing procedures under which both governments, by common consent, may submit questions or differences to the Commission for a binding decision; however, this procedure cannot be unilaterally invoked. Since the Treaty predates the establishment of either the Permanent Court of International Justice or its successor International Court of Juste, there is, of course, no reference in the Treaty to the submission of disputes to those bodies. However, international pollution disputes under the Treaty would presumably, at least between the years 1946 and 1970, arguably have been within the compulsory jurisdiction of the International Court of Justice under the terms of both the U.S. and Canadian acceptances, as effective during that period, of the International Court's jurisdiction under the "optional clause" of the Court's statute, and either country could consequently have sought to invoke the Court's jurisdiction.[160] While the U.S. "Connally" reservation might have been invoked by the U.S. to attempt to defeat the Court's jurisdiction over any such claim brought by Canada, or invoked on the basis of reciprocity by Canada with respect to a claim brought by the U.S., the propriety of the reservation's use in a case so clearly involving international treaty as well as customary rights would at least have been open to serious question.[161] Thus while the Treaty's dispute-settlement procedures leave something to be desired, traditional international claims procedures for Treaty violation would appear to have been available to the U.S. and Canada with respect to Great Lakes pollution problems, at least in principle, for over sixty years. Moreover, pollution problems between the two countries have been recurrent and of growing urgency and significance in this period, and Canada has not been remiss in charges that the U.S. bears the major responsibility. Nevertheless, the provisions of Article IV have never been invoked by either government as the basis of a formal specific international claim.

This is not to suggest that Article IV has not had an important influence in the handling of U.S.-Canadian pollution problems. As previously indicated, it has traditionally been invoked as an additional jurisdictional basis for pollution references to the IJC under Article IX of the Treaty; typically, each such reference directs the Commission to conduct its

323

investigation "with reference to the principles contained in Article IV," and the first question typically asked by the governments in each pollution reference is, in effect, whether the situation in question reveals a general violation of Article IV.[162] But, with a few exceptions such as the *Trail Smelter* reference, the terms of such references have usually been broad rather than specific, with their thrust clearly towards technical assessment and the recommendation of on-going and future-directed proposals rather than the determination of legal responsibility and specific remedies for past treaty violation.

Various explanations have been suggested for this failure of the U.S. and Canada to use traditional legal techniques as a method of dealing with boundary waters pollution problems:[163]

First, any specific claim by one government that the other is in violation of Article IV would probably encounter both legal and evidentiary difficulties. The scope of the prohibition is unclear; the terms "pollution" and "injury" are undefined, and their interpretation would raise difficult issues of policy. Moreover, evidentiary issues abound. It may be relatively easy for one country to show broadly the existence of specific injury from pollution on its side. But to establish the necessary casual link between the two will usually be extremely difficult. Absent exceptional situations, such as a massive oil spill or possibly a significant discharge of particularly toxic heavy metals or chemicals, the pollution of a large body of water such as a lake typically occurs through gradual and cumulative processes, arising from a variety of sources on both sides, whose effluents and other inputs into the lake's waters slowly mix under the influence of complex hydrological factors. In general, the most that can be said with confidence is that mutual transboundary pollution in its broadest sense, occurs. Thus, in the IJC's Report on the Lower Great Lakes reference the Commission concluded:

It is difficult to establish positively that the concentration of a particular pollutant on one side of the boundary in the lakes is due to a specific source on the other side. However ... there is no doubt that contaminants originating in one country do move across the boundary and degrade the quality of the water in the other country.[164]

Second, a binding decision granting traditional international legal remedies may be not only difficult and cumbersome to obtain, but ultimately of little practical help. Article X permits such a binding decision only with both government's consent, which the other party may refuse to give. While it has been suggested that the International Court of Justice might arguably have had compulsory jurisdiction over such matters during most of the post-World War II period, this question is not free from doubt. Even if resort to an international tribunal is possible, the process of adjudication is likely to be expensive and time-consuming. Moreover, in view ot the rudimentary state of international pollution law, the outcome will necessarily be uncertain. Finally, the impact of pollution is most typically an accumulation of small and often subtle harms, affecting large numbers of people, and money damages may be hard to calculate and ineffective as a solution. The injunctive powers of international tribunals are limited, and, in any event, injunctions appropriate to the complexities of large scale Great Lakes pollution would be difficult to fashion or administer.

Third, each country has been well aware of its own contributions to boundary waters pollution and of its consequent own potential exposure to complaints under Article IV. A resort to formal claims by one country might have invited a retaliatory submission of counterclaims by the other, with considerable risk to both and little gain to either.

Finally, governments have traditionally been reluctant to entrust their own significant national concerns to the unpredictable and inflexible outcomes of international adjudicative processes, and have in general preferred the less risky technique of negotiated settlement of their mutual differences.

In view of these considerations, it is not surprising that the two governments have chosen not to adopt liability-based approaches to Great Lakes pollution problems and have tended instead to use the technique of advisory references to the Commission under Article IX of the Treaty. In effect, the Article IX technique offers each country significant advantages at little risk. It permits the two countries to explore the possibilities of useful international co-operation while retaining full control over the most significant decisions and policy. Moreover, it reflects their judgment that the most sensible way of dealing with such complex, continuing, technical and politically sensitive problems is through flexible and on-going programs which take account of a multiplicity of factors and the necessity for a compromise and balancing of interests, rather than through legal techniques base on rigid rules and adjudication of past liability.[165]

C. *Institutional Structure.*

International environmental co-operation can, of course, be implemented through a variety of formal or informal institutional arrangements.[166] The U.S. and Canada, of course, have employed principally the technique of the binational commission,[167] thus far with considerable success.

As previously indicated, the IJC is composed of six members, three of whom are nationals of each country, selected by their respective governments. The commissioners need not be technical experts; while they have in general tended to be well-qualified, political factors have on occasion influenced appointments and they have varied in background.[168] During recent years at least, only the Chairman of the U.S. section has received a regular salary; other members for some time received only expenses and are presently being paid on a "when working" bais. Up to the present, the Commission's permanent staff has been very small, consisting principally of permanent Secretaries for each of the two national sections, who together act as the Commission's administrators. While the Canadian section has long included an attorney and engineer on its staff, the U.S. section has not; this situation is in process of being somewhat changed by additions of an attorney and an environmental expert ot the U.S. section's staff. The Commission has typically operated on an extremely limited budget.[169] The recent Joint Communique raises a possibility that the Commission's situation with respect to both staffing and budget may improve.

An important characteristic of the IJC has been its tradition of independence and impartiality, somewhat akin to an international civil service tradition. The Commission has long prided itself on the fact that, despite its binational structure, it has consistently put aside national loyalties and operated in an essentially apolitical manner. It has seen its task primarily as one of reaching reasoned judgments on the basis of scientific investigation, technological data and impartial assessment. The strength of this tradition is suggested in a recent article by the two then Joint Chairmen:

The concept of the treaty negotiators was that solutions to problems in which the two countries had differing — even opposing — interests should be sought, not by the usual bilateral negotiation, but in the joint deliberations of a permanent tribunal composed equally of Canadians and Americans. In other words, the Commissioners were to act, not as separate national delegations under instruction from their respective governments, but as a single body seeking common solutions in the joint interest.[170]

The fact that the Commission has divided along national lines or failed to reach agreement in only three of the cases and references it has dealt with is often cited in Commissioner's writings as evidence of the effectiveness of this commitment to impartiality and a search for the common interest.[171]

Another significant characteristic of the Commission has been its use of the technique of appointing special joint technical and advisory boards. As indicated, these are composed of various experts drawn from knowledgeable federal, state and provincial agencies of the two governments, who serve in an expert rather than a representative capacity. A Joint Board is given the task of carrying out the necessary investigations and making preliminary recommendations on the reference in question, and the Commission in most cases bases its own Report largely on that of the Board. The governments in their references to the IJC have frequently specifically authorized the use of this technique.[172] Through the use of such Boards, the Commission, while retaining its nominally small staff, has been able to mobilize and deploy a substantial task-force of highly trained experts, whose collective services might not otherwise be available on a permanent basis. There is apparently an international civil service type of tradition associated with these Boards as well as with the Commission itself.

A third important feature of the Commission has been its flexibility and capacity to effectively respond to the varied tasks the governments have assigned it. Over the years, the Commission dealt successfully with a remarkable variety of references involving a wide array of problems and disciplines. This flexibility is, of course, in large part, a reflection of the breadth of the reference procedures of Article IX itself. But it may also reflect both the adaptability of the joint technical board technique and the Commission's own spirit.

Nevertheless, while the IJC's performance as an international institution generally merits high marks, and it has achieved considerable respect and credibility, a note of caution may be in order before this experience is generalized. In particular, it may be worth reflecting whether the Commission's independence and impartiality are necessarily inherent in its structure, or may instead be related to other factors which may not persist. Thus, it is arguable that the Commission has been left relatively free from political pressures by the two governments principally because, until recently, they have had only limited interest in its work and have consequently had little reason to exert such pressures. From the U.S. governmental perspective, at least, the Commission has been relatively obscure; its work has for the most part been regarded as of minor political significance; its functions have been largely limited to scientific and technical investigations concerning which government officials would presumably not wish to, and probably could not, influence results; and it has, in general, had little occasion or tendency to ruffle important feathers. Moreover, the governments have been in a position to readily protect their national interests against adverse Commission action through means other than attempts at direct influence on their national sections. They have consistently retained careful control and veto powers over the submission and terms of references to the Commission, and are, in any event, free to reject, or to "accept" and ignore, its advice.

It is possible that with the growing political importance of the problems with which the IJC deals, with increasing governmental concern over these issues, and with the Commission's growing responsibilities, the two governments may in the future prove less inclined to respect its traditional independence. There may consequently be at least some pressures towards its politicization. The recent appointment of Mr. Christian Herter, Jr., already at the time Director of the Office of Environmental Affairs and Special Assistant to the U.S. Secretary of State in the U.S. government, to serve simultaneously as Chairman of the U.S. section, could herald such a trend, though that appointment was reportedly based more on budgetary than on policy considerations.

Attempts to bring governmental political influence to bear on the

Commission's purely scientific and technical investigations and recommendations would, of course, have a disastrous effect on the Commission's usefulness and credibility. But there are also arguments that at least limited politicization of the national sections in other respects would be less threatening, perhaps even enhancing rather than diminishing the Commission's usefulness. Thus the governments might be more prepared to give enhanced regulatory or enforcement powers to a more "political" Commission, in which they could trust their national sections to better reflect and protect their respective interests, than to an "independent" Commission, whose actions they could neither predict nor control. A "political" Commission might also better reflect the real problems and differences between the countries, and furnish a continuing forum for negotiation of these differences. Moreover, each national section of a more "political" Commission would presumably have more direct access to and influence with the respective national agencies on whose decisions the real solutions of Great Lakes pollution problems ultimately depend.

D. *Determining Objectives.*

A basic issue in any pollution control program is deciding how to define "pollution" — what types of man-made changes in the environment should be regarded as unacceptable and made the targets for corrective action.[173] Clearly, it is neither possible nor desirable to prevent every kind of human impact on the environment. Human activity inevitably produces waste as a by-product, and the capacity of the national environment to receive, assimilate and recycle such wastes is one of its most significant resource characteristics. Thus, the term "pollution" is essentially a pejorative term typically applied, not to all waste discharges into the environment, but only to those particular types or level of wastes in particular receiving environments which, due to their adverse impact on matters of human concern, suggest a need for social action. Scientists, engineers, economists, social planners and politicians might each define pollution differently. Pollution control thus involves determining the kinds and levels of wastes that merit attention, assessing the costs and benefits of alternative ways of dealing with particular wastes, deciding on priorities, planning balanced programs, deploying and implementing effective measures of control, and monitoring progress made with a view to possible readjustment of programs.

There is increasing recognition that many of these tasks involve essentially policy or value judgments rather than purely scientific or technical assessment.[174] The role of science in this process is, of course, vital. Scientists alone can alert societies to the existence of environmental threats and provide data relevant to rational decisions — in particular, the amounts, sources and pathways of various pollutants, and their po-

328

tential consequences in terms of the specific degrees of risk to particular interests that may result from exposure to particular types and levels of pollutants under varying circumstances. Similarly, engineers perform an essential role in defining technological possibilities and options for control. But questions as to goals, priorities, and the weights a society should properly give to the costs, risks and benefits of alternative courses of action in varying circumstances — choices as to what we really want and what we are willing to pay to get it — are ones which science and technology can rarely answer, though we may, if we wish, let scientists or engineers make for us the policy decisions necessarily involved.

The Boundary Waters Treaty does not define pollution,[175] and the difficulties of formulating a simple, sufficiently broad, generally applicable and operationally useful definition are apparent.[176] The Commission, however, has in effect provided a way of defining pollution, applicable to varying circumstances, through its technique of recommending common water quality objectives.[177] Since the water quality objectives recommended in the Lower Great Lakes Report will reportedly in substance be incorporated in the proposed Great Lakes Water Quality Agreement, the Commission's approach may be briefly described.

The Lower Great Lakes Report defines common water quality objectives as desirable levels of quality to be attained in the receiving waters, taking into account the scientific requirements or criteria for a whole spectrum of water uses: supplies for municipal, industrial and agricultural purposes, recreation, aesthetic enjoyment and the propagation of aquatic and wild life.[178] The Report recommends both "General Objectives" and "Specific Objectives." The "General Objectives" are the goals of an effective pollution control program stated in very broad terms.[179] The "Specific Objectives" are the desirable levels of water quality, stated for the most part in terms of specific scientific indices setting forth maximum permissible levels and concentrations of the pollutant in the waters, considered necessary to achieve the general objectives. These objectives are to apply to all jurisdictions sharing the waters of the Lower Great Lakes, at all times and places, and are particularly applicable to inshore waters. Specific objectives are recommended for microbiology (coliform group), dissolved oxygen, total dissolved solids, temperature, taste and odor, ph. iron, phosphorus, and radioactivity; when required, appropriate specific objectives will be established for water quality parameters including but not restricted to toxic wastes, oils and heavy metals.[180]

The Report contemplates that these objectives will be implemented by each government through appropriate national, state or provincial action. Thus, the specific objectives are intended both as the minimum basis for formulating provincial and state water quality standards and as parameters against which the effectiveness of such programs can be measured.[181] Presumably such governmental authorities will establish

329

compatible ambient water quality standards for the lakes with at least as stringent maximum permissible levels for each relevant pollutant; establish, as needed, effluent, discharge or emission standards setting the maximum acceptable release of a particular pollutant from a given source to the water under specified circumstances; establish as appropriate, technological standards or codes of practices; and take other action to ensure that the objectives are achieved. The Commission stresses that the important criterion of compliance is not the degree of treatment of wastes but the amount of wastes left in the effluent, and from the standpoint of a broad pollution control program, the total amount of contaminants discharged by all sources within the jurisdiction.[182]

The Lower Great Lakes Report gives special emphasis to the problems of phosphorus wastes as a critical factor in Lower Lake pollution. It points out that, of the nutrients involved in eutrophication of Lake Erie and Lake Ontario, phosphorus is the only one that is both growth-limiting in the Lakes and controllable effectively by man with present tehcnology.[183] The Commission takes the position that the reduction of phosphorus input into the waters will significantly delay further eutrophication and will allow the recovery of the Lakes to begin through natural processes.[184] It indicates that the recommended Specific Objective for phosphorus[185] can be achieved if all phosphorus is eliminated from detergents, plus a 95 percent removal of the predicted 1968 load of phosphorus at municipal and industrial waste plants.[186] The Commission's reasons for emphasizing a reduction in phosphorus in detergents are: (1) if a replacement for detergent phosphorus can be developed rapidly, a significant reduction of phosphorus inputs can be achieved prior to completion of phosphorus removal facilities at sewage treatement plants; (2) the effect would be to reduce phosphorus input from small communities, cottages and individual homes where the installation of phosphorus removal facilities would be very costly; and (3) it is estimated that treatment costs for phosphorus removed at sewage treatment plants would be reduced considerably by removing phosphorus from detergents.[187] The government of Canada has already taken steps to limit the phosphorus content of detergents to 20 percent by weight expressed as phosphorus pentoxide, effective 1 August 1970, and has announced a further reduction to 5 percent by December 1, 1972, and some of the Lake states and local authorities have adopted or introduced legislation to limit the phophorus content of detergents.[188]

The Commission's concept of establishing specific water quality objectives is a significant contribution to pollution control techniques, which is being widely copied.[189] It focuses on the matter of principal international concern — the quality of the receiving waters — while leaving to each jurisdiction wide flexibility as to the choice of the means which in terms of local circumstances and conditions, are best suited to achieving those objectives. It embodies an approach to problems of

330

international pollution in terms of continuing regulation and control to attain goals, rather than in terms of rights, duties and legal liability for past actions. It provides concrete scientific criteria against which performance and compliance can be measured. Finally, it permits ready revision and adjustment of objectives in the light of new information or other current considerations.

The process by which the Commission arrives at its recommendations of specific objectives is not entirely clear. Presumably, the Commission will typically accept the specific objectives suggested by its Technical Boards. Since the Boards include members from the principal federal, state and provincial standard-setting and implementing agencies, it is not surprising that the recommended international objectives in general tend to be compatable with and not to exceed already established state and provincial standards. In some cases, however, the recommended international objectives will require a tightening of particular state or provincial standards. Despite the policy component in all such decisions, the process of establishing objectives has apparently been treated as a matter of purely scientific and technical judgment, though some internal negotiation may occur. If, however, the Commission were ever to consider recommending specific objectives considerably more stringent that those then applicable in the various states and provinces, it is conceivable that substantial policy issues might emerge. This would, of course, cast the Commission in a new and more difficult role.

A final issue is posed by the U.S. government's September 15, 1971 announcement, through Surgeon General Jesse L. Steinfeld, advising housewives to continue using phosphorus detergents.[190] The basis for the government's shift of policy is its judgment that some phosphate substitutes are highly caustic and may constitute a health hazard. EPA Administrator William A. Ruckelhaus stated, in connection with the Surgeon General's announcement, that the government would increase its financial assistance for the removal of phosphates at sewage treatment plants, as an alternative to the banning of phosphate detergents.[191] The new U.S. government position could raise doubts as to the ability of the U.S. effectively to achieve the Commission's recommended phosphorus objectives by the proposed Agreement's 1975 target date. First, it is questionable whether, if the use of phosphate-based detergents continues to be permitted, it will be technically possible through more intensive sewage treatment techniques alone to reduce phosphate loadings into the Lakes to the extent recommended by the Commission. Second, such additional techniques will presumably involve substantial additional costs, making such programs politically more vulnerable. In view of the pivotal role of phosphorus in the solution of the Great Lakes' pollution problems, Canada's particular concern over high U.S. phosphorus loadings,[192] and Ontario's own legislation committing it to the banning of phosphate detergents, the recent U.S. action could conceiv-

331

ably raise new difficulties for the negotiators of the proposed Great Lakes Water Quality Agreement.

E. *Apportioning Burdens*

Another major potential issue of international environmental co-operation is how the burden of international pollution control measures is to be shared or apportioned among the various governments contributing to the relevant pollution problem. This question arises most clearly in situations involving pollution by several riparian states of a confined and complex mixing environment such as the Great Lakes or enclosed or semi-enclosed seas such as the Baltic, Mediterranean, Black, Carribbean, or North Seas.

A first step in any process of apportionment is presumably agreement on broad water quality objectives, from which at least broad estimates of the maximum total amount or loading of each pollutant which can be permitted to be discharged into the total basin environment in order to attain or maintain that level of water quality can be derived. Once this total basin-wide maximum amount for permissible waste discharges into the total environment is determined, the pie might then be divided or apportioned among the contributing states according to various bases or formulas.[193] The possible apportionment formulas might include division in equal shares; in proportion to relative total populations; in proportion to relative total gross national products; in proportion to relative basin populations; in proportion to relative basin GNPs; in proportion to the relative proportion of basin to total populations; in proportion to the relative proportion of basin to total GNPs; in direct proportion to relative past waste discharges or contributions to total existing pollution; in inverse proportion to relative past waste discharges or contribution to total existing pollution; and so forth. Alternatively, a total overall basin-wide quota of the necessary or desired amounts of total reductions in waste discharges could be determined, and this pie of necessary cutbacks apportioned on one or another of the above bases. Finally, the burden of pollution control could be indirectly apportioned through the establishment of uniform specific quality, discharge or technological standards. Clearly, different rules will effect various states differently.

With respect to the U.S., Canada and the problem of Great Lakes pollution, this issue might have been posed in considerable complexity; for example, while the U.S. has both greater total and Great Lakes population and GNP than Canada, and in general contributes more wastes to the Lakes than Canada, the Canadian Great Lakes population and GNP is of considerably greater relative importance to that country than in the case of the U.S. On the other hand, about two-thirds of the Great Lakes water area is in the U.S. and only one-third in Canada. In practice, however, the differences between the two countries in this respect have been

332

primarily shaped less by abstract theories of apportionment than by differing interpretations of the express provisions of the Boundary Water Treaty.

The Canadian position is reportedly based primarily on Article VIII of the Treaty, which *inter alia,* provides: "The High Contracting Parties shall have, each on its own side of the boundary, equal and similar rights in the use of the waters hereinbefore defined as boundary waters." The Canadian view is apparently that "use of the waters" in this provision includes their use as a receiver of wastes, and that Canada is consequently entitled to an equal right to, or share in, the use of the Lake's capacity to assimilate polluted effluent. Since the U.S. has already discharged wastes into U.S. waters in amounts far in excess of the wastes Canada has discharged into Canadian waters, Canada argues that it is in principle entitled to continue discharging wastes into its waters until such discharges reach the amount of the U.S. level of discharges into U.S. waters. Put otherwise, if the IJC standards are to be met and Great Lakes pollution prevented, the U.S. must restrict its discharges to a level not to exceed fifty percent of the total loading the Lakes can receive without exceeding the IJC's water quality objectives. Carried to the extreme, this position would place virtually the entire burden of the reduction of waste discharges and of effective Great Lakes pollution control on the U.S. In practice, however, Canada apparently does recognize some obligation to reduce its discharges in order to help prevent pollution.

The U.S., on the other hand, reportedly rejects this Canadian position and takes the view that the broad prohibition on pollution in Article IV of the Treaty is controlling. It argues that use of the Great Lakes water as a receptor for waste effluents is not one of the uses protected by Article VIII, that Article VIII is by its terms concerned only with establishing rules and principles solely for the specific purpose of governing the Commission in passing upon applications for the use or obstruction or diversion of the waters;[194] and that the "equal and similar rights" language relied upon by the Canadians consequently has no relevance to broader questions of pollution. In the U.S. view, the Treaty provision in fact relevant is the paragraph of Article IV providing that: "It is further agreed that the waters herein defined as boundary waters and waters flowing across the boundary shall not be polluted on either side to the injury of health or property on the other." Under this provision, neither country has a "right" to pollute the boundary waters and consequently there is no question as to the division of any such "rights" to pollute. Instead, the two countries have equal obligations to take measures to limit and control harmful discharges which the Commission has indicated emanate from both of their territories, even if these in fact come principally from the U.S. shore. The important consideration is not how much waste each country has in the past contributed to the Lakes, but the fact that the Lakes, for whatever reason and due to whoever's fault, are *now* in a con-

333

dition of threatened danger. Faced with such a situation each nation has, under Article IV, an equal obligation to act to correct it.

Neither country appears to have carried its position to the logical extremes the above arguments suggest, and these differences have in effect largely been by-passed and accommodated in the relevant arrangements. Thus, in practice, Ontario has imposed strict water quality and discharge standards and other pollution controls, and the U.S. is apparently willing to concede that control of the situation on the U.S. shore will require substantially greater expenditures — perhaps as much as six times greater — than those Canada must assume. Moreover, it would seem that the IJC's recommended specific objectives, if incorporated in the proposed agreement, will, in practice, impose a substantially heavier burden on the U.S. than on Canada. Since the objectives apply uniformly and to inshore waters, and since the U.S. in general, contributes more waste to the lakes, the U.S. will presumably have to take more stringent measures of control than Canada in order to maintain the same inshore water quality. The proposed Agreement may thus, in effect, settle this issue. However, neither government has formally abandoned its position. This is made clear by the fact that, in the Joint Communique announcing the proposed Agreement the Ministers were careful to note that:

In designing the agreement, it was accepted that programs and other measures established to meet urgent problems would in no way affect the rights of each country in the use of its Great Lakes waters.[195]

Thus, the question of apportionment remains one which in principle could prove very troublesome and on occasion rearise.

F. Co-ordination

One of the more complex and confusing aspects of Great Lakes pollution problems is the diversity of jurisdictions and multiplicity of official and unofficial agencies and institutions involved. A brief survey may indicate the dimensions of the problem.[196]

Eleven separate major governmental jurisdictions border on the Great Lakes. These are the U.S. and Canada (in their national governmental capacity), eight states of the U.S. (Illinois, Indiana, Michigan, Minnesota, New York, Ohio, Pennsylvania and Wisconsin), and the Canadian province of Ontario.[197] Each of these jurisdictions has its own laws, agencies, policies, programs, and enforcement techniques concerned with or bearing upon Great Lakes pollution problems. In addition, several hundred municipalities and local communties, each with its own ordinances and practices, border both sides of the Lakes. Making sense of the complex governmental situation respecting Great Lakes pollution problems in any one of these jurisdictions can be difficult; when they are considered together, the problem is immense.

334

In the U.S., there are at least nine federal agencies which are heavily involved in problems of Great Lakes pollution. These include the Departments of State,[198] Agriculture,[199] Interior,[200] Commerce,[201] Defense,[202] Transportation,[203] and Health, Education and Welfare;[204] the Council on Environmental Quality;[205] and the Environmental Protection Agency.[206] Other agencies such as the Department of Housing and Urban Development, the Atomic Energy Commission, Federal Power Commission, National Council on Marine Resources and Engineering Development, National Science Foundation, and Water Resources Council also have strong interests in this area.[207] The Federal Inter-Agency Committee on Great Lakes Research has in its membership all U.S. agencies with an active interest in the Lakes. A considerable number of Congressional committees are also concerned with various aspects of Great Lakes pollution, and may on occasion seek to exercise competing jurisdiction over relevant legislation.[208] In addition, each of the states bordering the Great Lakes has at least one, and frequently several, state agencies concerned with Great Lakes pollution problems.[209]

Two U.S. federal-state commissions and one interstate commission have a major involvement in Great Lakes problems. The Great Lakes Basin Commission, established under the authority of the Water Resources Planning Act of 1965,[210] is composed of representatives of the eight Great Lakes states, a number of concerned Federal agencies, and the Great Lakes (Compact) Commission. Operating with extensive federal financial assistance, this important commission has responsibility for improved comprehensive planning of the water and related resources in the U.S. portion of the Great Lakes, and is designed to be the effective coordinating agent for the federal, state, and local agencies and non-governmental entities having planning responsibilities in these fields.[211] The Upper Great Lakes Regional Commission, created by the Secretary of Commerce under the Public Works and Economic Development Act of 1965,[212] is composed of a federal member appointed by the President, and members from the states of Michigan, Minnesota and Wisconsin. It has the task of identifying economic problems and potentials of the Upper Lakes and recommending public investment to stimulate the lagging economy of the region. The performance of these responsibitities necessarily involves the Regional Commission in consideration of Upper Lakes pollution problems.[213] The Great Lakes Commission is established by the Great Lakes Basin Compact, an interstate agreement among the eight Great Lakes states consented to by Congress in 1968,[214] which designates the Commission as a joint state instrumentality on Great Lakes water resources development, programs, and problems.[215] It serves as a clearing house for information, a council for joint consideration of common and regional Great Lakes problems, and an instrument for co-ordinating state views, plans, recommendations, programs and policies.[216]

In Canada, the recently created Department of the Environment now exercises principal responsibility for Great Lakes pollution problems.[217] Other Canadian federal agencies with concerns in this area are the Departments of External Affairs; Energy; Mines and Resources; Natural Health and Welfare; Public Works; and Transport.[218] Additional research responsibilities are carried out by the Canada Centre for Inland Water, the Fisheries Research Board of Canada, and the Great Lakes Working Group of the Canadian Committee on Oceanography.[219] In the Province of Ontario, the Ontario Water Resources Commission has primary responsibility for Great Lakes pollution problems and the Department of Lands and Forests and the Hydro-Electric Power Commission of Ontario are also heavily involved.[220]

Several U.S.-Canadian international institutes other than the International Joint Commission are actively engaged in co-operation on Great Lakes problems. The Great Lakes Fishery Commission is a formal intergovernmental international organization established by the Great Lakes Fisheries Convention of 1955; it is primarily a research organization but has also administered an extensive program of sea lamprey control.[221] The Great Lakes Study Group, an informal international organization including representatives of Canadian and U.S. agencies and institutions engaged in research and investigations related to the development and utilization of Great Lakes resources is intended to facilitate the exchange of information and provide informal co-ordination including the sponsorship of a data repository.[222] Other international co-operative institutions include the St. Lawrence Seaway Commission, the International Association for Great Lakes Research, the Co-ordinating Committee on Great Lakes Basic Hydraulic and Hydrologic Data, and the International Field Year for the Lakes.[223] A number of private scientific, professional, research and industry associations, as well as universities and colleges in all of the Great Lakes states and Ontario, are also active with respect to Great Lakes problems.[224]

With so many jurisdictions concerned with controlling Great Lakes pollution and a remarkable number of agencies and institutions engaged in studying these problems, the chances of interference, overlap and duplication are obvious.[225] However, while various institutions within each country attempt to co-ordinate national approaches to Great Lakes problems, there is as yet no formal machinery for such co-ordination at the international level.

The IJC played an important informal role in this respect, particularly through the operation of its joint technical boards. Since the members of these boards are drawn from a variety of federal state and provincial agencies,[226] the boards serve to bring responsible officials at the U.S. and Canadian federal, state and provincial levels into continuing face-to-face contract, in a context which facilitates the free flow of information and views among them. Presumably, some informal co-ordination results. Indeed, the Boards have in large part been able to perform their tasks

336

largely through collecting and assessing relevant work already done by the various official agencies and other institutions in both countries; typically, relatively little new research has been required.[227]

Nevertheless, the IJC's role has remained informal, and the recent Ministerial Conference was apparently the first effort at a concerted and sustained high-level official discussion and exchange of views on Great Lakes pollution problems. In the IJC's Lower Lakes Report, which formed a basis for the Ministers' discussions, the Commission noted that:

> In order to achieve effective pollution control and acceptable water quality in these boundary waters, the policies and laws of the several jurisdictions concerned must have a common goal and the programmes to achieve that goal need to be coordinated with the programmes of the other jurisdictions involved in the Lakes. Otherwise, efforts put forth in one jurisdiction may be frustrated either by inaction or by inconsistent action in another jurisdiction. Water quality surveillance and monitoring to assess the effectiveness of control measures undertaken or the need for additional measures also need to be coordinated with similar activities in the other jurisdictions if meaningful results are to be obtained. A high degree of cooperation and a free exchange of relevant data and information among all jurisdictions concerned are essential elements of an effective programme to achieve and maintain a satifactory water quality in these boundary waters.[228]

With the conclusion of the Great Lakes Water Quality Agreement and the Commission's strengthened mandate to promote co-ordination, some more formal arrangements for co-ordination might be considered. One likely mechanism for such co-ordination might be the Joint Great Lakes Pollution Advisory Board suggested by the Ministers, to operate under the Commission but to include responsible officials from all concerned planning research and operating agencies. Alternatively, institutions other than the IJC might be used for this purpose. Thus, co-ordination might be sought with respect to planning through some type of "internationalized" Great Lakes Basin Commission; with respect to research through an expanded Great Lakes Study Group; and in the area of actual policy-making, regulation and implementation through the two governments' establishment of a new high-level Joint U.S.-Canadian Inter-Agency Committee on Great Lakes Pollution, in effect continuing on a permanent basis the work of the Ministerial Conference.

In pursuing the goal of co-ordination, some caution may be called for. Co-ordination is clearly desirable in certain areas. Obviously, there is little point in different jurisdictions or groups working at cross-purposes. As the Commission suggests, co-ordination may also be essential to the operation of an effective monitoring and surveillance program. Moreover, a free exchange of data and information, perhaps with centralized storage and retrieval capabilities, cannot fail to provide mutual benefits. Finally, co-ordination may serve the function of identifying and filling gaps in research or action programs. On the other hand, co-ordination has its own costs and may even prove dysfunctional to the extent it results in inflexible determinations of priorities, the stifling of competitive research, or an unwillingness to experiment with new approaches. Some overlapping, duplication, inefficiency, and even a testing of inconsistent techniques may be unavoidable in constructive attempts to solve a problem as complex as that of Great Lakes pollution.

G. *Implementation*

A major problem of international co-operation in the environmental, as in other fields, is that of implementation. U.S.-Canadian experience supports this judgment.

The IJC has no direct authority to either implement or enforce its recommendations. These recommendations come to the governments by way of the Commission's formal reports, and are typically distributed to concerned agencies within each government for comments. In the absence of strong objection from within either government, they are normally routinely "approved." However, there is no obligation upon either government to actually implement the Commission's recommendations, even if approved, and their subsequent impact is hard to determine.

Until recently there was apparently no established procedure within the U.S. government for either feeding recommendations into regular policy-making channels or ensuring that they were carried out. Traditionally, the State Department, through the Assistant Secretary of State for European Affairs (who has responsibility for Canadian matters), has carried primary U.S. governmental authority for working with the Commission and taking action on its recommendations. However, the State Department has little expertise or interest in the technical aspects of pollution problems, has only limited channels of regular communication with agencies that do, and has typically treated IJC matters as of comparatively limited importance appropriately handled at relatively low official levels. The Council on Environmental Quality now shares implementing responsibility on certain IJC recommendations concerning environmental matters and the Council may provide a more interested, technically qualified, and effective U.S. governmental constituency for the IJC. Canada has traditionally put more emphasis on the Commission and its work and has apparently accorded its recommendations more status and attention.

In practice, the Commission's influence may be somewhat greater than suggested above, though the means by which this influence is exerted are principally informal. First, the Commission's Reports are significant technical studies which undoubtedly come to the attention of many relevant policy-making officials, and, through their high quality, may influence official decisions. This is, of course, the major purpose of the governments' references and the Commission's work. Second, the Reports reflect the work of the Joint Technical Boards, which are themselves composed of influential officials from a variety of concerned agencies of each government. Since these government officials are largely responsible for the Commission's recommendations, they will presumably carry-over

338

these findings and judgments into their work and recommendations within their own operating agencies. Third, the wide publication of the IJC's Reports, and also of the Interim Reports the Commission has adopted the practice of issuing, may exert some public pressures on officials to take recommended actions, though the extent or impact of such pressures are hard to gauge. As a related technique, the Commission has recently instituted the practice of convening public meetings to acquaint the public with relevant problems and the Commission's recommendations regarding them.[229] To a very limited extent, the Commission has commuicated with concerned officials, calling their attention to the lack of progress made or to particular problems or polluters. On occasion, as where the Commission called broad public attention to the contribution of phosphorus-based detergents to Great Lakes eutrophication, it has, through these various means, clearly has some effect on public policy; the recent statements by the U.S. Surgeon General and the administration of the Environmental Protection Agency suggesting that housewives should continue to use phosphate based detergents rather than their possibly more hazardous substitutes, however, indicates that this particular impact may prove short-lived.[231]

Since implementation of the Commission's recommendations rests with the various national, state and provincial governments themselves, a brief look at the current situation in this respect may be of interest. Broadly speaking, there are considerable differences between these various jurisdictions as to the type and extent of relevant legislation and programs, the level of financing, the strictness of water quality standards and other control measures and the procedures and practical level of enforcement.[232]

As previously indicated, while the U.S. federal government has in recent years assumed a growing role in water pollution control programs, primary authority for establishing and enforcing regulations and standards remains in the states.[233] The Council on Environmental Quality has noted that, while remarkable progress has occurred with respect to the scope of both U.S. federal and state legislation programs in the last five years, standards remain in many respects inadequate and compliance and enforcement leave much to be desired.[234] Nevertheless, the federal government appears to have adequate authority under existing legislation to implement both the Commission's recommendations respecting Great Lakes pollution and the provisions of the proposed Agreement. The federal government also clearly has constitutional authority to enact such further legislation in this respect as may be necessary.[235]

The principal U.S. federal legislation in the water pollution area is the Federal Water Pollution Control Act of 1956, as amended.[236] The 1965 amendments of the Act require the states to establish water quality standards for their interstate waters, which state standards can then be approved as federal standards by the Environmental Protection Agency

(EPA).[237] The states retain primary responsibility both for drawing up and for enforcing these standards. If the states fail to set such standards, the EPA may set standards and enforce them.[238] The standards of all of the states are now "approved," though many of them have serious deficiencies.[239] The Act also provides certain enforcement mechanisms for abatement of interstate water pollution by the federal government, but the procedures are limited and cumbersome.[240] It is interesting to note that Section 10(d) (2) of the Act specifically provides that a foreign state affected by interstate pollution may participate in the Act's enforcement conference procedures; this participation is only on the basis of reciprocity,[241] however, and Canada has never sought to utilize this procedure.[242]

In addition to authority exercised under the Water Pollution Control Act, the federal government has recently initiated an important program under the authority of the Refuse Act of 1899,[243] making permits mandatory for all industrial discharges into navigable waters of the U.S.[244] Other federal legislation provides for federal control of water pollution in various special contexts (such as oil pollution and pollution from vessels), authorizes extensive federal financial and technical assistance to state and local water pollution control programs, and supports federal efforts in the field of research and development, monitoring and surveillance.[245] The Administration is presently seeking broader authority in this area, including authority to require states, with federal approval, to set specific effluent discharge requirements, and it is also seeking Congressional approval of legislation providing six billion dollars of federal funds to support a twelve billion dollar total national program; a significant amount of these funds will be directed toward the Great Lakes.[246] As this article is written, even further reaching legislation is under consideration by Congress.[247]

Each of the Great Lake states of the U.S. has its own water control legislation, programs and agencies, which differ substantially in breadth and effectiveness.[248] In general, during the last several years there has been a tendency towards rationalization of pollution control administration and a strengthening of such legislation.[249] The states seem clearly to have legal authority to enact legislation and standards implementing the Commission's recommended objectives if they so desire. It is interesting to note that the Great Lakes states have enthusiastically backed the concept of an international Great Lakes Water Quality Agreement and of a strengthened IJC,[250] perhaps at least partly in the hope that "internationalizing" the problem may increase the likelihood of more extensive federal funding.

The Canadian federal government has also recently legislated extensively in the area of water pollution, though primary responsibility in this regard remains in the Province of Ontario. As previously indicated, there is apparently some question among Canadian constitutional experts as to the permissible reach of Canadian federal power with respect to the broad regulation of Great Lakes pollution, even pursuant to treaty; it has been argued that provincial authority may be, for the most part, paramount in this field.[251] These doubts buttress the likelihood that the Province of Ontario will carry the major burden of implementing the IJC's recommendations and the provisions of the proposed agreement. The Joint Communique indicates that the Canadian Government contemplates that a federal-provincial agreement will be entered into for this purpose.[252]

The major Canadian federal legislation in this area is the Canada Waters Act of 1970.[253] The Act provides a framework for federal-provincial planning and co-operation. Among other things, it provides for the creation of joint water quality management agencies for waters designated by the federal and provincial governments. These agencies would be empowered by regulation to set water quality standards and to implement programs to achieve these standards. With regard to international waters and boundary waters, it is provided that if provincial co-operation cannot be achieved, the federal government itself may designate the waters, establish the agencies and standards, and carry out implementation of the programs.[254] Other federal legislation is applicable to particular aspects of Great Lakes pollution problems.[255]

The responsibilities of the Province of Ontario respecting Great Lakes pollution are exercised principally under the provision of the Ontario Waters Resources Commission Act.[256] The Act establishes the Ontario Water Resources Commission and gives it broad jurisdiction over Provincial water management. The Act generally prohibits any pollution which might impair the quality of the water in the Province and empowers the Commission to seek injunctions against and to prohibit such activities. In addition, the Commission is authorized to construct treatment facilities for municipalities, investigate water pollution and its causes, and to make regulations prescribing standards of water quality, operating standards for sewage works, and rules for discharges of wastes from boats. In general, the Ontario Water Resources Commission has adopted strict standards and broad programs, compatible with those recommended by the IJC, and is enforcing them vigorously.

The proposed Great Lakes Water Quality Agreement is in effect a formal endorsement of the Commission's recommendations in its Report on the Lower Lakes reference, lifting these recommendations to the level of international obligation. As such, the probabilities of compliance by the governments will be greatly enhanced. Nevertheless, the Communique makes clear that the Commission will not be vested with any new powers in the area of enforcement. The Communique states that:

While the International Joint Commission would aid the Governments by providing an independent overview and other assistance, the various agencies of the Federal, State and

341

Provincial Governments would continue to implement the programs and measures required to achieve the water quality objectives.[257]

However, the Commission's prestige and informal influence on both governments and polluting municipalities and enterprises will presumably increase.

IV. PROSPECTS AND PROBLEMS

To attempt any detailed assessment of the proposed Great Lakes Water Quality Agreement at this time, before its negotiation is even completed, would clearly be premature. However, some comments might be ventured regarding both the Agreement's general significance and the longer-term prospects for U.S.-Canadian Great Lakes cooperation.

The proposed Agreement would constitute a major accomplishment. It represents a significant advance in U.S.-Canadian efforts to control Great Lakes pollution and an important addition to broader global experience in international environmental co-operation. The Agreement expressly recognizes the problem of Great Lakes pollution as a major and independent subject of U.S.-Canadian concern, rather than as an adjunct of other water problems, and reflects firm national commitments by both governments to take urgent and effective measures to solve this problem. It emphasizes the fact that these governmental commitments are a matter of international as well as national obligation, provides technical criteria by which the extent of each government's complicance can be determined, and thus buttresses the pressures within each country for adoption of meaningful pollution control programs. Moreover, it reflects a more comprehensive, integrated and "basin-wide" approach to Great Lakes pollution problems than has previously been taken. Finally, the Agreement serves to considerably strengthen the IJC's international institutional role by recognizing the Commission as primary intergovernmental agent, co-ordinator and overseer for all Great Lakes pollution control programs. It can be expected that the IJC's effectiveness with respect to its monitoring, surveillance and co-ordinating activities will increase; that its recommendations will carry added weight; and that, through such devices as regular public reports, it will be in a position to exert a growing pressure for effective government action.

Yet, without discounting the considerable achievement the Agreement represents, it must still be asked whether this step goes far enough — whether even the new Agreement is likely to prove a sufficient answer to the complex and pressing problems of Great Lakes pollution. The IJC has conducted a number of Great Lakes pollution studies in the last twenty-five years, and the two governments already have instituted a number of separate and joint Great Lakes pollution control programs. But, despite those measures, the process of Great Lakes deterioration has continued and indeed seems to grow worse. And, in substance, the new Agreement is simply "more of the same," representing only a relatively limited departure from the past. The Agreement's concept and structure is still primarily binational co-operation rather than international regulation; the choice of specific standards and techniques for meeting the international water quality objectives remains firmly in each government's discretion; and procedure for inducing international compliance are weak. Existing IJC powers are strengthened, but the role of the Commission and the scope of co-operation continue to be limited to monitoring, surveillance and co-ordination, and the key functions of implementation, enforcement and funding are solely in each government's hands. Presumably, each government will continue to be free to ignore Commission recommendations, and to check any Commission activities which prove embarrassing to government policies.

There have been many suggestions that something more — some different, more innovative, and far-reaching approach — is needed[258] The range of possibilities is obviously broad. Some of these might simply expand the IJC's authority, while essentially retaining the existing Treaty framework. For example, the IJC could be given at least limited powers to establish pollution standards, to approve or license particular waste disposal facilities, and to initiate complaints of non-compliance before the courts or agencies of either country. Other more far-reaching possibilities might involve abandoning the present framework of limited co-operation and establishing in its place a supranational Great Lakes Authority, exercising direct and comprehensive investigating, planning, regulatory and enforcement powers over all aspects of Great Lakes environmental problems. Conceivably, the Authority might administer and allocate a substantial pollution-control fund, financed by mandatory contributions from the two government, or through special taxes or effluent charges on polluting enterprises. It might even enforce its rules through a special international tribunal. International and federal experience suggests a number of models for such broader experiments in Great Lakes regulation, such as the European Coal and Steel Community,[259] the American Tennessee Valley Authority[260] and the Delaware River Basin Commission.[261] Such proposals for granting the IJC broad regulatory powers, or for establishing some type of supranational Great Lakes agency, would, raise interesting legal and constitutional problems for each government.[262]

There is much to the argument that effective solutions to Great

Lakes pollution problems may ultimately require some more broad-ranging international approach than the present structure and authority of the Commission under the Boundary Waters Treaty, or even under the proposed new Great Lakes Water Quality Agreement permits. Great Lakes pollution is but one aspect of a total Great Lakes Basin ecological and social system and cannot be dissociated from the complex and inter-related web of physical, hydrologic, geographic, demographic, economic, cultural and political factors which together define and comprise that system. For example, approaches in terms of separate programs aimed at individually controlling "water pollution," "air pollution," or "land use management," make little sense when measures taken in one area inevitably affect the others. The establishment of a supranational Great Lakes Authority would permit a rational, comprehensive, integrated and co-ordinated approach to these problems, in accord with modern concepts of "problem-shed" management; would eliminate the recurrent and perplexing problems of jurisdictional conflict, duplication, and lack of co-ordination which trouble present international efforts; and it would encourage effective decision-making in a sufficiently large context to permit a fuller analysis and balancing of policy alternatives and trade-offs and the determination of optimal solutions.[263]

Nevertheless, while the concept of a supranational Great Lakes Authority has considerable intellectual and dramatic appeal, it seems unlikely to be achieved in the near future. Indeed, there is much to suggest that the proposed Agreement represents the practical limits which U.S.-Canadian co-operation can at present hope to reach, and that attempts to go further in the direction of international or supranational regulation might be unrealistic, unnecessary, and even potentially harmful.

First, neither the United States or Canada seem presently interested in such broad regulatory schemes. There are many reasons for this attitude. Important differences remain between the governments as to their respective share of responsiblity for Great Lakes problems and the burdens each should properly assume. The economic stakes of pollution control and the balance of internal political pressures acting upon the governments are still uncertain.[264] Finally, the potential costs involved in such programs are extremely high.[265] In this context, neither government appears prepared to relinquish control over relevant decisions affecting significant national interests or to reduce its broad options to respond flexibly to developing situations. Thus, the relatively limited reach of the proposed Great Lakes Water Quality Agreement may reflect not a lack of imagination — both governments have been well aware of such broader possibilities at least since the tabling of the Commission's draft Convention in 1920 — but only political realism.

344

Second, any considerable expansion of the IJC's regulatory power, or, *a fortiori*, the creation of a new Authority, would probably require either development of a new treaty or substantial amendment of the existing Boundary Waters Treaty. Any such negotiation would be complex, difficult and time-consuming, with no guarantee as to results. In contrast, the proposed Agreement retains and exploits the remarkable flexibility of the present Treaty and has been comparatively easy to achieve. Moreover, it builds on established traditions and experience which have in the past proved relatively successful. In this respect, there seems wisdom in the adage "let well enough alone."

Finally the proposed Agreement appears in accord with the present level of real needs and co-operative possibilities as between the two governments. It commits the governments to new levels of co-operation in areas where the immediate pay-offs from such co-operation seem highest and the risks to the governments lowest — monitoring, surveillance, technical recommendation, and coordination. Moreover, the Agreement is relatively open-ended, and it does not preclude the taking of more far-reaching measures should further experience so suggest. Indeed, the Commission will presumably now be in a position to give sustained and expert study to suggestions for further institutional change, and, if it considers them desirable, to recommend them to the governments.

As to the directions of future development of U.S.-Canadian Great Lakes cooperation, certain broad trends seem possible. First, as the IJC's responsibilities grow in importance and it begins to deal with issues more central to government concern, the Commission may become more political in character. Each of the governments will now follow its work more closely and may appoint Commissioners who will reflect or be more responsive to their government's attitudes and policies. Second, there may well be an increasing movement towards treating the Great Lakes on a regional basis as a single research planning, co-ordinating, and management unit. This tendency is already noticeable in the trend towards Basin-wide references, the probable appointment of a single continuing Pollution Advisory Board for all of the Lakes, and in beginning efforts to co-ordinate the work of the Commission's separate water and air pollution boards.[266] In this connection, U.S.-Canadian Great Lakes co-operation may expand into the field of long-range planning.[267] Third, the Commission, with a strengthened staff and the additional prestige of its new status and responsibilities under the new Agreement, may exhibit more aggressiveness than in the past, in terms of both the strength of its reports and recommendations and efforts to cultivate a binational public constituency. Finally, if the Agreement proves relatively successful, the two governments may be prepared to further buttress and perhaps gradually to increase the Commission's authority.

Such expansion of the Commission's powers and procedures might take various directions.[268] Thus, it might include authority for the Commission to itself initiate investigations, or at least formally petition the governments for particular references; broader Commission authority respecting issuance of subpoenas and the holding of public hearings; or perhaps authority for informal Commission investigation, on its own initiative, of local problems of immediate concern, without the necessity for invoking cumbersome and time-consuming reference procedures. The Commission might be given greater power to formally initiate, and perhaps participate in, proceedings against polluters in the national courts and agencies of the two countries. Formal channels of communication between the Commission and national policy-making and enforcement authorities in each country might be given some role as a forum for "preventative diplomacy" respecting environmental problems, perhaps through the institution, under Commission auspices, of "confrontation" procedures under which either of the two governments could require the other to consult regarding proposed environmental measures which may significantly affect it.[269]

Each government now has the capability — technical, economic and legal — to do what is required to control Great Lakes pollution. Thus, the success or failure of efforts to control Great Lakes pollution will depend, ultimately, not on what the new Agreement says or what the IJC does, but on what the two governments themselves choose to do — the extent to which they are prepared to adopt the necessary national legislation and standards, to implement these programs through effective judicial and administrative enforcement, and to provide the substantial funds required. What the governments choose to do will, in turn, depend largely on shifting public attitudes and the eventual outcome of the clash of complex competing policial and economic forces now operating upon relevant governmental environmental policies in each country.

In this respect, it may be unrealistic to project more than moderate optimism. There are signs, at least in the United States, that the present wave of public environmental concern may be diminishing, and that politicians may be perceiving the "environmental issue" as having less practical political impact than previously assumed. Enthusiasm for stringent pollution controls has lessened as it has become increasingly evident to both the public and politicians that effective pollution control will be inconvenient, costly, slow to produce results, and possibly work hardship to particular industries and communities. Countervailing pressures by special interests affected by possible control programs are growing, and under these pressures, government attitudes are becoming increasingly ambivalent.[270] If these pressures increase, the course of least resistance for government policy-makers may be programs and levels of funding which give the appearance rather than the reality of effective action.

The IJC's role in the working out of these economic and political conflicts will be inherently limited. However, its influence will continue to be felt in at least two ways. First, the governments, in making their policies and decisions in this area, will inevitably have to take into account the relevant scientific data and technical assessments as to the facts of Great Lakes pollution supplied by the Commission, and they will hopefully make sounder decisions because of the availability of this data. Second, by making these facts public, the Commission will exert a continuing public pressure on the governments to live up to their professed commitments and to adopt policies reasonably related to the realities of Great Lakes pollution problems and long-run public needs. The Commission's performance of these functions will in itself represent a substantial contribution, amply justifying continued U.S.-Canadian cooperation.

V. SOME TENTATIVE LESSONS

The co-operative arrangements which the U.S. and Canada have developed in their efforts to control Great Lakes pollution reflect a particular historical, geographic and political context, and any attempt at generalization involves risks. Nevertheless, this experience is one of the few examples we have of relatively complex system of international environmental co-operation and we should try to derive what lessons we can. These lessons might include the following:

First, large-scale environmental problems, such as that of Great Lakes pollution, are extremely difficult to solve. Despite the long history of U.S.-Canadian co-operation in this area, the Lakes are continuing to deteriorate. The roots of such problems often lie in social forces and attitudes which defy control — exploitative attitudes towards the environment, economic expansion, population increase, and technological change. Our knowledge of the specific causes and effects of environmental deterioration, scientific, technical, economic, sociological and other; of the multitude of factors and complex interactions involved; of the optimal technical and institutional means for remedy; and of the time scales such remedies may require, remains limited, imprecise and uncertain.[271] The costs of effectively coping with environmental deterioration may be substantial. Finally, alternative patterns of solution may alter existing social and economic patterns in different ways, and various groups may consequently have high stakes in the approach chosen. Where environmental issues engage such strongly competing interests, they may transcend science and technology and become deeply involved in the political process.[272]

347

Second, many environmental problems are largely localized, with their causes and effects occurring principally within a single nation, or, at most, geographically contiguous nations. Such problems must necessarily be handled on a primarily national basis, with international measures playing, at most, only a supplementary role. Moreover, even where international measures can appropriately play a useful role, limited bilateral or regional arrangements may often prove more suitable than global approaches. The U.S. and Canada have consistently regarded the problem of Great Lakes pollution as primarily a matter for solution by national action, with international measures supplementing, buttressing and co-ordinating rather than replacing country programs. And, it is difficult to see how direct involvement by other nations in the problem of Great Lakes pollution could substantially contribute to its solution.

Third, governments will be reluctant to subject their flexibility and freedom of action regarding relevant environmental policies to international constraints. Consequently, they will enter into international environmental programs only where they are persuaded that these programs offer substantial practical benefits unobtainable by national action alone, or where these programs involve only minimal obligations. The reasons for this have been noted, including the high potential costs of pollution control programs, the uncertainty of their national impact, and their consequent political sensitivity. Canada and the U.S. share a deep concern for Great Lakes pollution problems, have co-operated in this area for almost sixty years, and now concede the urgent need for common and joint solutions; moreover, the two countries share common traditions and have relatively close political, economic and cultural ties. Despite the strength of the factors favoring co-operation, neither government seems yet prepared to delegate substantial powers to the IJC or to otherwise limit its national freedom of action in significant ways.

Fourth, since even concerned countries can be expected to be reluctant to accept international environmental constraints, it follows that the price of including relatively unconcerned countries in an environmental arrangement may be one so watered-down as to have little content; the commitments will be reduced to the "lowest common denominator" of the least interested potential party. This again suggests that, in many contexts, bilateral and regional environmental programs, involving only countries with a direct and urgent concern with the problem, may prove more politically attainable, far-reaching and effective than broader global programs, which include nations with only marginal interests. Moreover, neighboring or regional states may be more likely to share common values, congenial legal systems, and traditions of co-operation, and these factors will also buttress the chances for successful environmental co-operation.

348

Fifth, the possibilities for successful international co-operation with respect to particular environmental problems may be enhanced by a formal acknowledgement of the international character of such problems and of the propriety of their international treatment. While the provision prohibiting pollution in the U.S.-Canadian Boundary Waters Treaty has had little direct application, it has facilitated the subsequent development of international environmental co-operation through the IJC.

Sixth, in attempting to deal with international environmental problems, governments may often prefer loose co-operative arrangements to techniques of formal legal prohibition. As previously noted, governments will, for a variety of reasons, be reluctant to submit to rigid rules or formal constraints. Moreover, specific environmental prohibitions will be difficult to agree upon, evidence of violation may be hard to establish, and legal remedies may prove cumbersome and incapable of dealing effectively with broad-scale, complex, and multi-faceted environmental problems changing over time. Again, the fact that neither the U.S. nor Canada has sought to utilize the Boundary Waters Treaty's provisions formally banning pollution, and the two governments resort instead to the more flexible techniques involved in IJC references, strongly suggests this tendency.

Seventh, if formal treaty arrangements and institutions are established for environmental co-operation, there are strong arguments for making these arrangements relatively flexible and open-ended, with a capacity to expand and adapt as problems and needs clarify and the parties gain confidence in their co-operative activities. The point is not that the parties need abdicate control over the growth of the authority and activities of such institutions, but that they should plan to permit such growth through relatively informal procedures rather than through the difficult, cumbersome and time-consuming process of formal amendment. The development of U.S.-Canadian environmental co-operation was clearly facilitated by the fact that the IJC was an institution already "in place," capable of such expanded and innovative use as the two governments wished to make of it.

Eighth, U.S.-Canadian experience demonstrates that international environmental co-operation can yield useful dividends at relatively low costs and with limited political risks. While Great Lakes problems are still a long way from solution, the IJC has clearly performed a valuable function in developing governmental and public awareness of Great Lakes pollution problems, providing scientific and technical information relevant to rational policy choice, suggesting the nature of the remedies required and furnishing a means through which national programs could be better co-ordinated. It has also shown that even partial programs may be worth pursuing.

Ninth, some of these functions potentially involved in international environmental co-operation such as monitoring, surveillance, and the presentation of technical objectives and options, seem best performed by institutions acting in a relatively expert and apolitical capacity. The IJC's reputation as an expert impartial body has probably made the U.S. and Canadian governments more willing to use it and given its reports more credibility. The Commission's technique of using joint technical boards, composed of officials drawn from agencies of the participating governments, serving in an expert rather than represen- tative capacity, is particularly suggestive as a method of deploying substantial expertise on relevant international problems without incur- ring the problems of large permanent international staffs and budgets. However, where international co-operative institutions begin to take on policy-oriented tasks, such as co-ordination program recommenda- tion, implementation and enforcement, the possibility and usefulness of a wholly apolitical orientation may become more questionable.

Tenth, even limited patterns of international environmental co-opera- tion may produce possibly useful secondary effects. The IJC's pol- lution studies have helped to create public pressures for effective gov- ernment action in both countries, and the proposed new Agreement will buttress arguments for greater commitment of government re- sources to this area. Moreover, the work of the Commission's various expert Boards has resulted in continuing contacts and interaction be- tween federal, state and provincial officials concerned with Great Lakes pollution, and has thus helped to establish important informal channels of communication, co-ordination and influence respecting information, policies and programs.

Finally, the problem of pollution of the Great Lakes has much in common with similar pollution problems in many other large lakes and enclosed and semi-enclosed seas in other parts of the world; as well as in some of the major international river.[273] Collectively, such internationally-shared lake, enclosed sea, and river problems comprise a significant segment of the problems which are likely to be broadly recognized within the next few years as clearly requiring international treatment. International initiatives to promote the exchange of ex- perience in this area, perhaps through periodic international meetings of concerned officials or through the establishment of a small inter- national Secretariat to facilitate such exchanges of information on a continuing basis, might be useful and appropriate.

NOTES

[1]U.S.-Canadian Joint Communique issued by the Joint U.S.-Canada Ministerial Meeting on Great Lakes Pollution, Washington, D.C., June 10, 1971, published in 64 *Dept. St. Bull.* 828-831 (June 28, 1971) (hereafter cited as "Joint Communique"). As this article is written there are indications that negotiation of the proposed agreement is delayed and, in all likelihood, will not be fully completed and signed until possibly the spring of 1972.

[2]*N.Y. Times,* June 11, 1971, at 11, col. 1-3.

[3]*Ibid.*

[4]The recent literature in this area is vast. *See e.g.,* C. Wilson (Ed.) *Man's Impact on the Global Environment. A Report on the Study of Critical Environmental Problems (SCEP)* (1970); R. Falk, *This Endangered Planet* (1971); Ritchie-Calder, "Mortgaging the Old Homestead," 48 *Foreign Affairs* 207 (1970); Wolman, "Pollution as an International Issue," 47 *id.* 164 (1968). And *see,* as here particularly relevant, *e.g.,* the various papers in this volume; Schachter and Serwer, "Marine Pollution, Problems and Remedies," 65 *A.J.I.L.* 84 (1971); and Proceedings of a Symposium held in Vancouver, Canada, Sept. 1970, on "The International Legal Aspects of Pollution," 21 *U. Toronto L. J.* No. 2 (1971).

[5]*See* U.N. General Assembly Res. 2398 (XXIII) of 3 December 1968; 2581 (XXIV) of 15 December 1969; and 2567 (XXV) of 14 December 1970. *Cf.* The Report of U.N. Secretary General to the 47th Session of the Economic and Social Council on "Problems of the Human Environment," U.N. Doc. E/4667 (1969), and The Reports of the Preparatory Committee for the U.N. Conference on the Human Environment for its three working sessions held in N.Y. in November, 1970, Geneva in Feb., 1971, and N.Y. in September, 1971 (U.N. Docs. A/CONF. 48/PC.1, 11 and 111).

[6]*See* references cited in note 4 *supra. Cf.* notes 147, 158 and 159 *infra.* However, international activities in the environmental area are rapidly proliferating, and more than a score of U.N. organs and agencies and other international organizations are presently engaged in environmental programs. *See generally Environmental Activities of International Organizations,* A Report prepared for the use of the Senate Committee on Commerce, March 17, 1971; *Environmental Quality-1970,* the First Annual Report of the Council on Environmental Quality (Aug. 1971), at 200-206 (hereafter cited as "CEQ 1970 Report"); *Environmental Quality-1971,* the Second Annual Report of the Council on Environmental Quality (Aug. 1971) (hereafter cited as "CEQ 1971 Report"), at 29-31; and the various papers in this volume. These activities of international organizations include the World Meteorological Organization's (WMO) World Weather Watch; the World Health Organization's (WHO) work on fresh water supplies and sewage disposal; the Food and Agricultural Organization's (FAO) broad concerns with resource management; the International Labour Organization's (ILO) regulation of the environment of the work place; the U.N. Educational, Scientific and Cultural Organizations (UNESCO) Intergovernmental OceanographicCommission (IOC) and its Man and the Biosphere Program (MAB); the Intergovernmental Maritime Consultative Organization's (IMCO) activities in the field of marine pollution; the International Civil Aviation Organization's (ICAO) work on air and noise pollution connected with civil air transport; and the International Atomic Energy Agency's (IAEA) surveillance of radioactive substances in the environment. The Environment Committee of the Organization for Economic Co-operation and Development (OECD) is conducting significant work on the international economic effects of member countries' environmental policies. The North Atlantic Treaty Organization's (NATO) Committee on Challenges of Modern Society (CCMS) is studying special problems of industrialized societies. The Economic Commission for Europe (ECE), which is serving as a valuable forum for information exchange between Eastern and Western European nations on pollution control, held an important symposium on this subject at Prague, Czechoslovakia in May 1971, and has established a permanent body of Senior Environmental Advisers to the Commission. In 1969, the International Council of Scientific Unions (ICSU) established a Special Committee on

351

Problems of the Environment (SCOPE) which is co-ordinating global research on a number of environmental problems.

[7]While this study deals primarily with U.S.-Canadian co-operation with respect to problems of pollution of the Great Lakes and other boundary waters, the two countries have also developed co-operative arrangements with respect to other aspects of environmental problems. The work of the International Joint Commission respecting boundary air pollution problems, which is briefly mentioned in this article, is more fully discussed in Note, "International Air Pollution — U.S. and Canada — A Joint Approach," 10 *Ariz. L. Rev.*138 (Summer 1968). The 1916 Convention for the Protection of Migratory Birds in the United States and Canada, 39 Stat. 1702; TS 628; 111 Redmond 2645 (1923), which was involved in the famous case of *Missouri v. Holland*, 252 U.S. 416 (1920), is still in force. On June 1, 1971, the U.S. National Aeronautics and Space Administration announced that the U.S. and Canada had agreed on a joint program to use satellites and aircraft in surveying the natural environment; the joint program will advance remote sensing technology through monitoring of air, water, land, forest and crop conditions, the mapping of ice movements and ocean currents in Canadian and U.S. waters, and the mapping of geologic, hydrologic, vegetation and soil phenomena. *N.Y. Times*, June 2, 1971, at 7, col. 1. The U.S. is also in the process of developing bilateral relations on environmental problems with Mexico, Japan and other countries. *See CEQ 1971 Report*, at 30.

[8]*See, generally, e.g.* Stein, "The Potential of Regional Organizations in Managing Man's Environment" in this volume, and, more broadly, Frey-Wouters, "The Prospects for Regionalism in World Affairs" in *The Future of the International Legal Order* (R. Falk and C. Black, eds., 1969) at 461.

The agenda for the 1972 U.N. Conference on the Human Environment, in its section concerned with the international organizational implications of action proposals, includes an item on "particular organizational requirements for meeting needs at regional levels." Rpt. to the Prep. Comm. for the U.N. Conf. on the Human Environment, second session, 8-19 Feb. 1971, U.N. Doc. A/CONF. 48/PC.9, (1971) para. 20, Agenda Item 6. The Secretary General of the U.N. Conference on the Human Environment, Mr. Maurice Strong, has suggested as among the principles which might guide the decision of governments on organizational questions:

"(g) In the establishment of any additional or new machinery it is essential to provide strong capability at the regional level."

As quoted in Rpt. to the Prep. Comm. for the U.N. Conf. on the Human Environment, third session, 13-24 September 1971, U.N. Doc. A/CONF. 48/PC.11 (1971) at 56.

See also Man's Impact on the Global Environment (C. Wilson, ed.), *supra* note 4, at 6, which comments:

"It should be noted that the existence of a global problem does not necessarily imply the necessity for a global solution. The sources of pollution are activities of man that can often be effectively controlled and regulated where they occur. Most corrective action will probably have to be taken at the national, regional or local levels;"

and Schacter and Serwer, "Marine Pollution Problems and Remedies," 65 *A.J.I.L.* 99, at 111 (1971), who note:

"... there has come to be a greater recognition of the need for regional pollution control organs since it is apparent that, although pollution is a global problem, it is not uniformly global. Regional arrangements in the Baltic, the North Sea, Mediterranean, Carribean and perhaps the Arctic are now underway, and it is likely that these organs will have a decisive part to play in achieving day-to-day practical controls."

[9]The factual information in this section is drawn or collated principally from the following sources: International Joint Commission, United States and Canada, Report on *Pollution of Lake Erie, Lake Ontario and the International Section of the St. Lawrence River* (1970) (hereafter cited as "IJC Lower Lakes Report"); Piper, *The International Law of the Great Lakes* (1967); *Great Lakes Institutions: A Survey of Institutions Concerned with the Water*

and Related Resources in the Great Lakes Basin, published by the Great Lakes Basin Commission and the Great Lakes Panel of the Committee on Multiple Use of the Coastal Zone, National Council on Marine Resources and Engineering Development (June 1969) (hereafter cited as "Great Lakes Institutions"), at 1-2, 7, 12; MacNish and Lawhead, "History of the Development of the Great Lakes and Present Problems," in *Proceedings of the Great Lakes Water Resources Conference,* June 24-26, 1968, Toronto, Canada (Engineering Inst. of Canada and Amer. Soc. Civ. Engrs.); and Great Lakes Basin Commission, *Commentator,* Vol. 1, No. 9 (March 1971).

[10]This excludes the Antarctic ice-cap. Lake Baikal in the Soviet Union is apparently larger in volume than any of the Great Lakes.

[11]IJC *Lower Lakes Report,* at 17.

[12]MacNish and Lawhead, *supra* note 9, at 19.

[13]In 1966, a total of about 246 million net tons of cargo moved in ships on the Great Lakes. Of this, about 185 million net tons were domestic, within either the U.S. or Canada; 47 million net tons moved between the two countries; and 14 million net tons were overseas traffic. In terms of ton miles, over 40 per cent of all traffic on U.S. waterways moved on the Great Lakes. In its 9 months open season, the St. Lawrence Seaway carries more traffic than the Panama and Suez Canals combined when operating a full year. *Id.* at 25.

[14]The IJC *Lower Lakes Report* (1970) represents the most current and comprehensive discussion of the problem of pollution in the Lower Lakes, and this discussion is broadly applicable to many aspects of the Upper Lakes as well. For good summaries of sources, processes, effects and costs of water pollution and water pollution control programs more generally, *see, e.g., Environmental Quality-1970,* First Annual Report of the Council on Environmental Quality (Aug. 1970), ch. 4; A.V. Kneese and B.T. Bower, *Managing Water Qaulity: Economics, Technology, Institutions* (1968); and *Water Pollution Control and Abatement* (T.L. Willich and N. W. Hines, eds., 1967).

[15]*See, e.g., IJC Lower Lakes Report,* Conclusion 9, at 140-41. For comprehensive discussions of Lake Erie problems, U.S. Dept. of Interior, Federal Water Pollution Control Authority, *Lake Erie Report: A Plan for Water Pollution Control* (Aug. 1968), and Reitze, "Wastes, Water and Wishful Thinking: The Battle of Lake Erie," 20 *Case Western Law Rev.* 5 (1968).

[16]*See* IJC *Lower Lakes Report,* Conclusion 9 at 140-41. And *see also* U.S. Dept. of Interior and N.Y. State Dept. of Health, *Water Pollution Problems and Improvement Needs: Lake Ontario and St. Lawrence River Basins* (June 1968).

[17]*Id.,* ch. IX, at 72-83.

[18]*Id.,* ch. X, at 84-107. On the mercury pollution problem, which in April 1970 resulted in Canada's banning fishing on its side of the St. Clair River and Detroit River and Lake St. Clair, and in partial bans by Ohio in Lake Erie, *see e.g., Time* magazine, May 4, 1970, at 85 and *Wall St. J.,* Apr. 28, 1970, at 1, col. 1. This situation gave rise to the case of *Ohio v. Wyandotte Chemicals Corp.,* 401 U.S. 493 (1971) discussed in note 165, *infra.*

[19]As to the Lower Lakes, *see id.,* Table 2, at 80 and Table 3, at 82. This is particularly true as to phosphorus inputs into Lake Erie. In 1967, the input of total phosphorus from U.S. municipal sources into Lake Erie was 35.7 million pounds, of which 25 million pounds came from detergents; whereas the input of total phosphorus from Canadian municipal sources into Lake Erie was 2.5 million pounds, of which 1.3 million pounds came from detergents. As to Lake Ontario, the U.S. municipal input of phosphorus is 7.7 million pounds, of which 5.4 million came from detergents, and the Canadian municipal input 7.0 million pounds, of which 3.5 million came from detergents. *Id.,* at 83.

[20]N.Y. Times, *Supra* note 2.

[21]*See, e.g.,* Piper, *The International Law of the Great Lakes* (1967), at 19. The principle of state ownership of the Lake beds is affirmed in the Submerged Lands Act of 1953, 67 Stat. 29 *See also Illinois Central R.R. v. Illinois,* 146 U.S. 387 (1892); *Hilt v. Weber,* 252 Mich. 198, 200; 233 N.W. 159, 191 (1930). The Supreme Court has recognized the vital interest of the states in the control of water resources and has specifically conceded the power of the states to exercise control over navigable water for the interests of their citizens until Congress in some way asserts a superior power. *U.S. v. Rio Grande Dam and Irrigation Co.,* 174 U.S. 690, 703 (1899).

[22]Piper, *id.* at 19.

[23]Congress has power to regulate all navigable waters under the Commerce Clause, U.S. Const., Art. 1, Sec. 8, Cl. 3, and navigability is broadly defined. *See, e.g., Gibbons v. Ogden,* 22 U.S. (9 Wheat) 1 (1824) and *Pollardis Lessee v. Hagan,* 3 How. 212 (1845), and, with respect to pollution, *U.S. v. Republic Steel Corp.,* 362 U.S. 482 (1960). *See* Hines, "Nor Any Drop to Drink: Public Regulation of Water Quality. Part III: The Federal Effort," 52 *Iowa L. Rev.* 799 (Apr. 1967), who suggests that; "It seems relatively clear that constitutionally Congress could preempt the entire field of water quality control, if it so elected," (at 800). *See, generally, e.g.,* Edelman, "Federal Air and Water Control: The Application of the Commerce Power," 33 *Geo. Wash. L.Rev.* 1067 (1964-65) and 1 Schwartz, *The Powers of Government* 218-19 (1963); 2 *Waters and Water Rights,* (R.E. Clark, ed., 1967) ch. 7, and H. Ellis, J.H. Beuscher, C.D. Howard, J.P. DeBraal, *Water Use Law and Administration Wisconsin* (Dept. of Law, Univ. Extension, Univ. of Wisconsin 1970), ch. 17.

[24]Treaties made by the President by and with the advice and consent of the Senate are, together with the federal Constitution and laws, the supreme law of the land. U.S. Const., Art. VI. A treaty dealing with Great Lakes pollution problems would appear a clearly legitimate subject of U.S. foreign policy concern. *See, e.g. Missouri v. Holland,* 252 U.S. 416 (1920), and generally, American Law Institute, *Restatement, The Foreign Relations Law of the United States* (1965), Sec. 121. The interests of the nation are more important than those of any state, and the federal government may act to prevent a state from interfering with a national treaty obligation. *Sanitary District of Chicago v. U.S.,* 266 U.S. 405, 425-26 (1925); cf. *Missouri v. Holland, supra,* and *First Iowa Hydro, Elec. Corp. v. Federal Power Comm'm.,* 328 U.S. 152, 171 (1946). Treaty obligations of the U.S. may give the federal government an additional basis for authorizing improvements on international waterways. *Arizona v. California,* 283 U.S. 423, 457-58 (1931). However, in view of the broad expanse of the Article 1 commerce clause and other powers of Congress, it may be questioned whether the exercise of the treaty power with respect to Great Lakes problems would in practice constitute any significant addition to existing Congressional authority. *See, e.g.,* Henkin, "The Treaty Makers and the Law Makers; The Law of the Land and Foreign Relations," 107 *U. Pa. L. Rev.* 903 (1959).

[25]*See* Landis, "Legal Control in Canada of Pollution in the Great Lakes Drainage Basin," *Proceedings of the Great Lakes Resources Conference* (Toronto 1968), *supra* note 9, at 158-200; Landis, "Legal Control of Pollution in the Great Lakes Basin," 48 *Can. Bar Rev.* 66 (1970), especially at 96-106. And *see* Gibson, "The Constitutional Context of Canadian Water Planning," 7 *Alta. L. Rev.* 71 (1969); Note, "An Opionion on the Constitutional Validity of the Proposed Canada Water Act," 28 *Fac. Law Rev.* 74 (1970).

[26]*See* discussion in text at notes 232-257.

[27]*Id.*

[28]The Rush-Bagot Agreement of 1817, U.S.T.S. 110 1/2; 8 Stat. 231; 1 Malloy, *Treaties, etc.* 628 (1910). See generally on U.S.-Canadian disarmament arrangement Piper, *supra,* ch. 7, and 3 Whiteman, *Digest of International Law* 741-52 (1964). More generally, on international boundary arrangements and the Permanent Boundary Commission established by the Boundary Treaty of Feb. 24, 1925, U.S.T.S. 720, 44 Stat. 2102; IV Trenwith, *Treaties, etc.* 3988 (1938), *see* Piper, *supra,* ch. 2.

354

[29]*See*, generally, D. Deener, *Canada-U.S. Treaty Relations* (1963), and Piper, *id.*

[30]U.S. Dept. of State, *Treaties in Force* (1970), at 30-42.

[31]*See*, generally, *e.g. Neighbors Taken for Granted* (L. Merchant, ed. 1966) (particularly Introduction and chs. VII and VIII); The American Assembly, *The United States and Canada* (Columb. Univ. 1964) (particularly ch. 6); and the various proceedings of the recent series of annual *Seminars on Canadian-American Relations* held at the University of Windsor. Cf. Lynch, "Canada's New Anti-Americanism," *Wall St. J.*, Nov. 12, 1971, at 12.

[32]Certain aspects of this issue, in particular the questions of apportionment and detergents, are more fully discussed in sections 11 (d) and (e) *infra*.

[33]I have described this Canadian concern in another context also involving some element of U.S.-Canadian policy conflict in Bilder, "The Canadian Arctic Waters Pollution Prevention Act: New Stresses on the Law of the Sea," 69 *Michigan L. Rev.* 1 (1970). It is relevant that Canada chose as its project for exploration in connection with the North Atlantic Treaty Organization's (NATO) program on "Challenges of Modern Society" the subject of control of pollution in inland waters, with particular reference to the Great Lakes.

[34]The literature on the Boundary Waters Treaty and the International Joint Commission is surprisingly extensive, if relatively inaccessible. Bloomfield and Fitzgerald, *Boundary Waters Problems of the United States and Canada* (The International Joint Commission 1912-1958, Toronto 1958) is an extremely useful concise study, containing a history of the Commission and a summary of its dockets through 1958, and also appendices setting forth the Treaty, Rules of Procedure, national implementing legislation, membership on the Commission 1911-58, related treaties, lists of boundary waters and waters crossing the boundary, a selected bibliography, and maps showing the location of the various references and applications. *See, also*, for an earlier study, Chacko, *The International Joint Commission Between the United States and the Dominion of Canada* (1932). The Commission is also described and its dockets summarized through the early 1960's in 3 Whiteman, *Digest of Intl. Law* (1964), at 826-71. *See, also*, Piper, *supra* at 72 *et seq.*

Various IJC Commissioners have also written excellent brief descriptions of the Commission and its work. I have drawn particulary on Welsh, "Role of the International Joint Commission," *Proc. 12th Conf. Great Lakes Resources 1969* (Intl. Assoc. Great Lakes Research); Welsh, "The International Joint Commission," *Dept. St. Bull.* 311 (Sept. 23, 1968); Welsh and Heeney, "The International Joint Commission-United States and Canada," Paper P/247 presented at the Intl. Conf. on Water for Peace, May 23-31, 1967, Washington, D.C., reprinted in 5 *Intl. Conf. On Water for Peace* 104-109 (1967); and Ross, "The International Joint Commission," Address at the International Symposium on Legal Aspects of Pollution, University of Manitoba, March 7, 1970. *See also*, Heeney, "Diplomacy with a Difference: The International Joint Commission," *INCO*[International Nickel Co.] *Magazine* (Oct. 1960); Kyte, "Organization and Work of the International Joint Commission" (pamphlet issued Ottawa 1937); Weber, "Activities of the International Joint Commission, United States and Canada," 31 *Sewage and Industrial Waste*, 71 (Jan. 1959); and Weber, "Functions of the International Joint Commission," *J. of the Power Division, Proc. of Amer. Soc. Civil Engrs.* (Nov. 1968), at 177.

For scholarly discussion, *see* the excellent recent articles by Jordan, "Recent Developments in International Environmental Pollution Control," 15 *McGill L.J.* 279 (June 1969) and by Ericksen-Brown, "Legal Implications of Boundary Waters Pollution," 17 *Buffalo L. Rev.* (Fall 1967). *See also*, Note, "International Air Pollution — U.S. and Canada — A Joint Approach," 10 *Arizona L. Rev.* 138 (Summer 1968); Waite, "The International Joint Commission — Its Practice and Impact on Land Use," 13 *Buffalo L. Rev.* 93 (Fall 1963); Adams, "Water Pollution Control in the Great Lakes Region," 37 *U. of Detroit L. J.* 96 (1959-60); and Griffin, "A History of the Canadian-United States Boundary Waters Treaty of 1909," 37 *U. of Detroit L.J.* 76 (1959).

[35]Treaty Between the United States and Great Britain Relating to Boundary Waters

and Questions Arising Between the United States and Canada, signed Jan. 11, 1909, proclaimed May 13, 1910, U.S.T.S. 548, 36 STAT. 2448, 111 Redmond, *Treaties, etc.* 2607 (1923) (hereafter cited as "Treaty"). The Treaty was signed by Great Britain on behalf of Canada, which did not acquire full powers in treaty-making until 1923. However, the Treaty has been implemented completely by Canada. *See* Piper, *supra* at 5-6.

[36]The history of the Treaty is summarized in Bloomfield and Fitzgerald, *supra* note 34, at 2-14; Piper, *supra* at 72 *et seq.*; and in articles by Griffin, Kyte and Heeney (in *INCO Magazine*), *supra* note 34. Briefly the Treaty grew out of the work of an Ad Hoc Temporary International Waterways Commission created by concurrent legislation of the U.S. and Canada in 1903 for the purpose of investigating and reporting upon the condition and uses of the boundary waters and making recommendations for navigational improvements and regulations. The temporary group, and particularly its Chairman, George Gibbons, an Ontario lawyer, became convinced that effective development of the boundary water resources required some prior agreement on principles and a permanent body to apply them. Gibbons went to Washington in 1907 to explore possibilities. U.S. Secretary of State Elihu Root was at first unenthusiastic but was finally won over. The International Waterways Commission was discontinued after the 1909 Treaty entered into force.

[37]Treaty, art. VII.

[38]Treaty, arts. III, IV, VI, VIII, IX, X, XII.

[39]Treaty, Preliminary Article.

[40]Treaty, art. I.

[41]Treaty, art. II, first para.

[42]*Ibid.*

[43]Treaty, art. II, second para.

[44]Treaty, art. III, first para.

[45]Treaty, art. IV, first para.

[46]Treaty, art. VIII, first para.

[47]Treaty, art. VIII, second para.

[48]Treaty, art. VIII, third para.

[49]Treaty, art. IV, second para.

[50]Treaty, art. V. Certain of these provisions have been terminated and a special regime established by the Convention Concerning the Uses of the Waters of the Niagara River, signed Feb. 27, 1950, T.I.A.S. 210, 1 U.S.T. 694, 132 U.N.T.S. 223.

[51]Treaty, art. VI. Other special regimes have also been established by subsequent agreement. *See, e.g.,* Treaty between the U.S. and Great Britain in Respect of Canada concerning the Regulation of the Level of the Lake of the Woods, signed Feb. 25, 1925, U.S.T.S. 721, 44 Stat. 2108; IV Trenwith, *Treaties, etc.* 3993 (1938); and Convention between the U.S. and Canada on Emergency Regulation of the Level of Rainy Lake and of other Boundary Waters in the Rainy Lake Watershed, signed Sept. 15, 1938, T.S. 967; 54 Stat. 1800; 203 L.N.T.S. 207.

[52]*See, e.g.,* Whiteman, *supra* note 34 at 816.

[53]Treaty, art. VII.

[54]*Ibid.*

[55]Treaty, art. XII, second para. Rules of Procedure of the International Joint Commission (hereafter cited as "Rules"), Rule 4.

[56]Rule 2.

[57]Treaty, art. XII, first para. Rule 5.

[58]Rule 2.

[59]Rule 5(2).

[60]Treaty, art. VIII, final para.

[61]Treaty, art. XII, final para. *The Rules of Procedure,* as revised December 2, 1964, are available from the Commission.

[62]As to application procedures, *see generally* Part II of the *Rules of Procedure* (Rules 12-25).

[63]Fourteen International Boards of Control are presently operating, with respect to Kootenay Lake, St. Lawrence River, Niagara, Rainy Lake, Osoyoos Lake, Skagit River, Columbia River, Souris River, Prairie Portage, Lake Champlain, St. Croix River, Lake Superior, Lake of the Woods, and apportionment of the Waters of the St. Mary and Milk Rivers.

[64]As to Reference Procedures, *see* generally Part III of the *Rules of Procedure* (Rules 26-29).

[65]*See, e.g.,* Waite, *supra* note 34, at 111.

[66]*See, e.g.,* the listing and description of the various dockets, including references, in Bloomfield and Fitzgerald, *supra* note 34, and in 3 Whiteman, *supra* note 34.

[67]IJC Docket No. 82.

[68]IJC Docket No. 86.

[69]IJC Docket No. 51.

[70]IJC Docket No. 60.

[71]*See* Section 11(i) *infra.*

[72]*See, e.g.,* J.V. Krutilla, *The Columbia River Treaty: The Economics of an International River Basin Development* (1967), especially ch. 4.

[73]*See, e.g.,* Piper, "Comment: A Significant Docket for the International Joint Commission," 59 *A.J.I.L.* 593 (1965).

[74]*See, e.g.,* the questions presented in the Lower Lakes Pollution Reference of October 7, 1964, set forth in the text at notes 121-2. For text of Reference in that matter, *see* IJC *Report on Lower Lakes Pollution,* at 161-62.

[75]*See, e.g.,* the language in the Lower Lakes Pollution Reference, *id.* at 162:
In the conduct of its investigation and otherwise in the preformance of its duties under this reference, the Commission may utilize the services of engineers and

357

other specially qualified personnel of the technical agencies of Canada and the United States and will so far as possible make use of information and technical data heretofore acquired or which may become available during the course of the investigation.

[76]Eight International Investigative Boards are currently operating, with respect to the American Falls, St. Clair-Detroit Air Pollution, Lake Ontario-St. Lawrence River Water Pollution, Lake Erie Water Pollution, Great Lakes Levels, St. John River Engineering, Souris-Red Rivers Engineering, and Roseau River Engineering.

[77]For example, the Commission's Report on the 1962 reference on Co-operative Development of the Water Resources of the Pembina River Basin, Docket No. 76, has not yet been accepted.

[78]The International Air Pollution Advisory Board; International Red River Pollution Board; International Rainy River Water Pollution Board; Advisory Board of Control of Water Pollution St. Croix River; and the Advisory Board to the IJC on Control of Pollution of Boundary Waters (Lake Erie-Ontario Section and Lakes Superior-Huron-Erie Section). See, for an example of the work of such boards, the Report prepared by the Laksene-Ontario Advisory Board on *The Niagara River: Pollution Abatement Progress* (Aug. 1971).

[79]See *Welsh and Heney*, supra note 34, at 313. The first such meeting was held in January, 1968 with regard to pollution of the Niagara River. Similar meetings have been held at St. Stephen, New Brunswick regarding pollution of the St. Croix River, in Sault Ste. Marie, Michigan regarding the St. Mary River, and at Windsor, Ont. concerning the St. Clair and Detroit Rivers. See for example, the IJC notice of 28 Oct. 1971 of the convening of a public meeting on December 16, 1971 in Niagara Falls, N.Y., "to inquire into the progress made in the U.S. and Canada since 1967 in the abatement of pollution of the Niagara River from municipal and industrial sources and to ascertain why the Water Quality Objectives for the River are not being met," and also informing the public of the availability of the Advisory Board study on this subject, *supra* note 78.

[80]See IJC Docket Index. The dockets are also listed and described in Bloomfield and Fitzgerald, *supra* note 34, at 65-205 (through Docket No. 72, August 1956) and in 3 Whiteman, *supra* note 34, at 826-72 (through Docket No. 80, March 1964). The latest Docket No. is actually No. 93, an application concerning Cominco Kootenay Lake 1971. The discrepancy is explained by the assigning of Docket No. 50 to the Rainy Lake Investigation under the Protocol, which was technically neither an application nor a reference.

[81]See IJC Docket Index. For a similar breakdown of the docket as of several years ago, *see* Welsh and Heeney, *supra* note 34, at 3, and Welsh (*St. Dept. Bull.*), *supra* note 34, at 312.

[82]These pollution references have the following IJC Docket Numbers and Titles: 4-Pollution of Boundary Waters (1912); 25-Trail Smelter (1928); 54-Pollution of Boundary Waters (1946); 55-Pollution of Boundary Waters from Lake Erie, Lake Ontario-Waters of Niagara River (1948); 61-Smoke Abatement Investigation (1949); 71-St. Croix River (1955); 73-Pollution of Rainy River and Lake of the Woods (1959); 81-Pollution of the Red River of the North (1964); 83-Pollution of the International Section of the St. Lawrence River, Lake Ontario and Lake Erie (1964); 85-Air Pollution (1966). The St. Croix River reference (Docket 71) was not by its terms a pollution reference, but, since the IJC dealt with basin pollution problems in some detail, I have included it in this list and the subsequent discussion.

[83]IJC Docket No. 4.

[84]Report of the IJC on *Pollution of Boundary Waters* (1918).

[85]*Id.* at 51.

[86]*Id.*, as quoted in IJC *Lower Lakes Report*, at 2-3.

[87]Draft of October 15, 1920, on file with U.S. Section under IJC Docket No. 4, described by Stein, *supra* note 8.

[88]*Id.*, as quoted in Ross, *supra* note 34.

[89]*See* 3 Whiteman, *supra* note 34 at 828-29.

[90]*See* Piper, *supra* at 86.

[91]*Ibid.*

[92]IJC Docket No. 25.

[93]*See* 3 Whiteman, *supra* at 789.

[94]Convention of April 15, 1935, U.S.T.S. 893, 49 Stat. 3245, IV Trenwith, *Treaties, etc.* 4009 (1938).

[95]111 *U.N. Rpts. Intl. Arb. Awards* 1905 (1949); 33 *A.J.I.L.* 182 (1939).

[96]3 *U.N. Rpts. Intl. Arb. Awards* 1908 (1949); 35 *A.J.I.L.* 684 (1941).

[97]*Id.* at 1964. Since Canada had accepted liability by the terms of the arbitral agreement, the statement is technically *dicta*. The history of the arbitration is well covered and the decisions analyzed in Read, "The Trail Smelter Dispute," 1 *Can. Yrbk. Intl. L.* 213 (1963).

[98]IJC Docket No. 54.

[99]IJC Docket No. 55.

[100]Report of the IJC on the *Pollution of Boundary Waters* (1950).

[101]IJC *Lower Lakes Report*, at 4.

[102]IJC Docket No. 61.

[103]Report of the IJC on *Pollution of the Atmosphere in the Detroit River Area.*

[104]IJC Docket No. 71.

[105]Report of the IJC on *Development of the Water Resources of the St. Croix River Basin* (7 October 1959).

[106]IJC Docket No. 73.

[107]Report of the IJC on *Pollution of Rainy River and Lake of the Woods* (Feb. 1965).

[108]IJC Docket No. 81.

[109]Report of the IJC on *Pollution of the Red River* (April 1968).

[110]IJC Docket No. 83. *See also* Dept. St. Press Release No. 441, Oct. 8, 1964. The reference is reprinted in full in the IJC *Lower Lakes Report*, Appendix, at 161-62. The Commission's procedures and method of work with respect to this reference, briefly described in the text following, is set out in detail in chs. I, IV and V of the IJC *Lower Lakes Report*.

[111]IJC *Lower Lakes Report*, at 25. The Boards' investigation required nearly 450 man years of work by scientists, engineers and technical experts. The offshore studies involved over 100 cruises on Lake Erie and 200 on Lake Ontario to obtain on a regular basis, water samples and retrieve data at 13,000 stations. The Ontario Water Resources Commission

alone at various times deployed as many as 12 survey vessels to collect data at 50,000 sampling locations. In all, 600,000 samples were analyzed for a number of constituents. *Id.* at 26-7.

[112]Report to the IJC on *Pollution of Lake Erie, Lake Ontario and the International Section of the St. Lawrence River* (Vols. 1-3) (Sept. 1969).

[113]Report of the IJC on *Pollution of Lake Erie, Lake Ontario and the International Section of the St. Lawrence River* (1970). The Report is summarized in *Dept. St. Bull.* 203 (Feb. 15, 1971).

[114]IJC Docket No. 85.

[115]The penultimate paragraph of the reference states:
"The Commission is also requested to take note of air pollution problems in boundary areas other than those referred to in Question 1 [the vicinity of Port Huron-Sarnia and Detroit-Windsor] which may come to its attention from any source. If at any time the Commission considers it appropriate to do so, the Commission is invited to draw such problems to the attention of both governments."

[116]*Joint Air Pollution Study of St. Clair-Detroit River Areas for International Joint Commission, Canada and the United States* (January, 1971).

[117]The text of the request is set forth in the IJC *Lower Lakes Report*, at 163-4. The U.S. letter is reprinted in 60 *Dept. St. Bull.* 296 (April 7, 1969).

[118]Report of the International Lake Erie Water Pollution Board to the IJC on *Potential Oil Pollution Incidents from Oil and Gas Well Activities in Lake Erie: Their Prevention and Control* (Sept. 1969).

[119]The Report is summarized in 62 *Dept. St. Bull.* 807 (June 29, 1970).

[120]IJC *Lower Lakes Report*, ch. VII, at 52-61.

[121]*Id.* at 5. The full reference is reprinted in *id.* at 161-2.

[122]*Id.*, ch. XIV ("Conclusions"), especially at 136-38.

[123]*Id.*, ch. XIII, at 130-35.

[124]*Id.* at 155.

[125]*Id.* at 156.

[126]U.S.-Canadian Joint Communique issued at Washington, D.C., June 23, 1970 (Press Release 129); 63 *Dept. St. Bull.* 36 (July 13, 1970).

[127]*Ibid.* The agreed measures included coordination of national contingency plans for spills of oil and hazardous materials; reduction of inputs of phosphates into the lakes, and achievement of compatible regulations concerning waste disposal by commercial vessels and water craft.

[128]U.S.-Canadian Joint Communique issued at Washington, D.C., June 10, 1971 (Press Release 129); 64 *Dept. St. Bull.* 828 (June 28, 1971). (Hereafter cited as "Joint Communique").

[129]*See, e.g.,* 13 *Ocean Science News*, No. 37 (Sept. 10, 1971). which reports that the heart of the agreement will be contained in nine annexes dealing with water quality objectives, contingency plans, vessel construction, vessel wastes, a navigation study, dredged spoils,

360

onshore and offshore facilities, transportation by land, and co-ordination of research. It also notes that the 1975 target date for implementation of objectives will be set back to 1976, and that, among the differences remaining to be negotiated, are that, while Canada wants a definite financial commitment from the U.S. for the Joint Water Quality Board being set up under the IJC, the U.S. must anticipate variations in funds approved by the House Appropriations Committee, whose Chairman, Rep. John Rooney (D.-N.Y.) has not reacted favorably to IJC funding requests.

[130]The proposed agreement will presumably be an "umbrella-type" arrangement in that it will commit each government to use the legislative and regulatory powers available to it from time to time to take action to control pollution. Thus, the initial U.S. programs will not require additional legislation, but, with enactment of new legislation, the U.S. will be able to expand such programs.

[131]See IJC *Lower Lakes Report* at 116-117. *See* text at note 179 *infra*.

[132]Joint Communique, para. 5.

[133]See *id*. at 118-20, quoted in part in text at note 180 *infra*.

[134]Joint Communique, para. 5.

[135]*Ibid*.

[135]*Id*., para. 7.

[137]*Id*., para. 8.

[138]*Id*., para. 13.

[139]*Id*., para. 9.

[140]The authority contemplated is presumably a reflection of the arrangements for surveillance, monitoring and implementation more fully discussed and suggested in ch. XIII of the IJC *Lower Lakes Report,* at 130-35.

[141]*Id*., para. 13.

[142]*Id*., paras. 10 and 11.

[143]*Id*., para. 12.

[144]*Id*., paras. 13-18.

[145]*Id*., para. 17.

[146]*Id*., para. 18.

[147]See, *e.g.*, the agreements cited in note 149 *infra*.

[148]See, **generally,** the report and papers included in this volume. Russell and Landsberg, "International Environmental Problems — A Taxonomy," 14 *Science* 1307 (No. 172, 1971), and the references in note 4 *supra*.

[149]See, *e.g.*, the various agreements relating to the pollution of international rivers and lakes cited in note 167 *infra*.

The principal convention dealing with pollution of the oceans is the 1954 International Convention for the Prevention of the Pollution of the Sea by Oil (12 U.S.T. 2989, T.I.A.S. 4900, 327 U.N.T.S. 3), as amended in 1962 (17 U.S.T. 1523, T.I.A.S. 6109, 600 U.N.T.S.

332) and 1969 (annexed to IMCO Ass. Res. A.175(VI) (Oct. 21, 1969). *See also* Articles 24 and 25 of the 1958 Geneva Convention on the High Seas (13 U.S.T. 2312, T.I.A.S. 520, 450 U.N.T.S. 82) relating respectively to oil pollution and pollution by radioactive materials and other harmful agents; Article 5(7) of the Geneva Convention on the Continental Shelf (15 U.S.T. 471, T.I.A.S. 5578, 499 U.N.T.S. 311), requiring that a coastal state engaged in exploring or exploiting the resources of the shelf takes appropriate measures for protection of the living resources of the sea from harmful agents; the 1969 Brussels International Convention on Civil Liability for Oil Pollution Damage (reprinted in 64 *A.J.I.L.* 481 (1970)); the 1969 Brussels International Convention Relating to Intervention on the High Seas in Cases of Oil Pollution Casualties (reprinted in 64 *A.J.I.L.* 481 (1970)); and the Agreement for Cooperation in Dealing with Pollution of the North Sea by Oil, June 9, 1969, between the various states bordering on the North Sea, reprinted in 9 *I.L.M.* 359 (1969). During the last several years, the U.N. General Assembly has adopted a number of resolutions dealing with various aspects of marine pollution. *See, generally, e.g.,* Schachter and Serwer, *supra* note 4, and Hardy, "International Control of Marine Pollution," 11 *Natural Resources J.,* 221 (1971).

Both the 1959 Antarctic Treaty (12 U.S.T. 794, T.I.A.S. 4780, 402 U.N.T.S. 71) and the 1967 Treaty on Principles Governing the Activities of States in the Exploration and Use of Outer Space, including the Moon and other Celestial Bodies, (18 U.S.T. 2410, T.I.A.S. 6347) contain provisions directed at protecting these unique environments. The 1963 Treaty Banning Nuclear Weapons Tests in the Atmosphere, in Outer Space and Under Water (14 U.S.T. 1313, T.I.A.S. 5433, 480 U.N.T.S. 43) was also motivated largely by global environmental considerations.

[150]*See* text at notes 92-97 *supra.*

[151]*See, e.g.,* the CEQ Report on *Environmental Quality — 1971,* at 131-33, and G. and U. Curzon, *Hidden Barriers to International Trade* 30-1 (1971). The Organization for Economic Co-operation and Development is currently experimenting with techniques for harmonizing environmental standards, as in its introduction, for an initial period of two years, of a "Procedure for Notification and Consultation on Measures for Control of Substances Affecting Man or his Environment," adopted on May 18, 1971, OECD Doc. C (71), 73/Annex (1971). (As described in Stein, *supra* note 8.)

[152]Compare the analogous concept of mutual limitation in the Treaty Banning Nuclear Weapon Tests in the Atmoshpere, in Outer Space and Under Water, done at Moscow, August 5, 1963, 14 U.S.T. 1313, T.I.A.S. 5433; 480 U.N.T.S. 43. Similar considerations are an important factor in the negotiation of international commodity arrangements. *See, e.g.,* Bilder, "The International Coffee Agreement: A Case History in Negotiation," 28 *L. and Contemp. Probs.* 328 (1963).

[153]The reference procedure is in the text at notes 64 to 81 *supra.*

[154]Article IX provides that questions or matters of differences shall be referred to the IJC for examination and report "whenever *either* the Government of the United States *or* the Government of the Dominion of Canada shall request that such questions or matters of difference be so referred." (emphasis added).

[155]*See* text at note 115.

[156]For example, Canada has reportedly been reluctant to extend a pollution reference to the Commission concerning pollution of the St. John's River.

[157]*See* text at notes 92-97 *supra.*

[158]*See also,* the Comments to chapter 3 (Pollution) of the Helsinki Rules on the Use of the Waters of International Rivers, cited in his note *infra,* Garretson, et al., *supra,* at 791-802; Manner, "Water Pollution in International Law," in *Aspects of Water Pollution Control,* W.H.O. (Public Health Papers), at 53, Nov. 13, 1963; and 3 Whiteman, *supra,*

at 1040-50.

See, generally, e.g., the excellent discussions in Bourne, "International Law and Pollution of International Lakes and Rivers," in "International Legal Aspects of Pollution: Proceedings of a Symposium held in Vancouver on September, 1970," 21 *U. Toronto L.J.* No. 2 (1971), at 21; Jordan, "Recent Developments in International Environmental Pollution Control," 15 *McGill L.J.* 279 at 285-88 (1969); Lester, "River Pollution in International Law," 57 *A.J.I.L.* 828 (1963); and Lester, "Pollution," in *The Law of International Drainage Basins,* (A.H. Garretson, Hayden and Olmstead, eds., 1967). The authors appear to be in broad agreement that relevant international law is sparse, general in terms and often closely related to specific situations and agreements — in the words of one of the authors, "rudimentary" and "embryonic." (Jordan, *supra* at 285).

International agreements having reference to water pollution problems generally do so in differing terms and with respect to special situations, and no clear rule can be adduced from them other than a very general tendency to condemn pollution, a term which is generally undefined. *See,* Lester in Garretson, et al., *supra* at 109. And relevant decisions by international tribunals are few in number and largely *dicta.* Thus, in the *Corfu Channel Case,* (U.K. v. Albania), [1949] *ICJ Rep.* 3, in dealing with the alleged responsibility of the Albanian Government for the mining of an international strait, the Court referred broadly to "Every state's obligation not to allow knowingly its territory to be used for acts contrary to the rights of other states" (at 22). In the *Lake Lanoux Arbitration* between Spain and France, involving the right of France to divert and use certain waters of a transnational river system which flowed eventually into Spain, thereafter returning them to the system unchanged in quantity or quality, the tribunal, while refusing relief to Spain, commented that its decision might have been otherwise if pollution of the waters had been established. The arbitral decision is reported in 53 *A.J.I.L.* 156 (1959), and commented on in Laylin and Bianchi, "The Role of Adjudication on International River Disputes: The Lake Lanoux Case," 53 *id.* at 30 (1959). In the *Trail Smelter* arbitration, *supra* note 94-97, which involved an air pollution dispute between the U.S. and Canada, the tribunal asserted in very broad language the existence of a principle of international responsibility for permitting transnational air pollution of serious consequence (*see* text at note 97 *supra*), but, since Canada had already assumed such responsibility, the tribunal's statement is essentially *dicta.*

A leading recent effort to restate the international legal principles relating to international drainage basins is the "Helsinki Rules on the Uses of the Waters of International Rivers," prepared by the International Law Association's Committee on the Use of the Waters of International Rivers and adopted by the International Law Association in 1966. *See* Report on the Fifty-Second Conference of the International Law Association held at Helsinki, August 14-20, 1966, (London 1967) at 484, also reprinted in Garretson, et al., *supra* at 791-802. Article IV of the Rules provides that "each basin state is entitled, within its territory, to a reasonble and equitable share in the beneficial uses of the waters in an international drainage basin." Article V provides that "what is a reasonable and equitable share within the meaning of Article V is to be determined in the light of all the relevant factors in each particular case." With reference to pollution, the Rules, after defining the term "water pollution" in article IX, provide, in chapter 3; as follows:

Article IX

As used in this Chapter, the term "water pollution" refers to any detrimental change resulting from human conduct in the natural composition, content, or quality of the waters of an international drainage basin.
...

Article X

1. Consistent with the principle of equitable utilization of the waters of an international drainage basin, a State

(a) must prevent any new form of water pollution or any increase in the degree of existing water pollution in an international drainage basin which would cause substantial injury in the territory of a co-basin State, and

(b) should take all reasonable measures to abate existing water pollution in an international drainage basin to such an extent that no substantial damage is caused in the territory of a co-basin State.

2. The rule stated in paragraph 1 of this Article applies to water pollution originating

(a) within the territory of the State, or

(b) outside the territory of the State, if it is caused by the State's conduct.

...

Article XI

1. In the case of violation of the rule stated in paragraph 1(a) of Article X of this Chapter, the State responsible shall be required to cease the wrongful conduct and compensate the injured co-basin State for the injury that has been caused to it.

2. In a case falling under the rule stated in paragraph 1(b) of Article X, if a State fails to take reasonable measures, it shall be required promptly to enter into negotiations with the injured State with a view toward reaching a settlement equitable under the circumstances.

On the law of international drainage basins more generally, *see, e.g., The Law of International Drainage Basins* (A.H. Garretson, et al., ed. 1967), *supra,* which contains a number of excellent monographs and also reprints The ILA's Helsinki Rules; Bourne, "The Development of International Water Resources: The Drainage Basin Approach," 74 *Can. Bar Rev.* 62 (1969); Shapiro-Libai, "Development of International River Basins: Regulation of Riparian Competition," 45 *Ind. L.J.* 20 (1969); Griffin, "The Use of Rules of International Drainage Basins under Customary International Law," 53 *A.J.I.L.* 50 (1959); and 3 Whiteman, *supra,* ch. VII, at 872-1075.

[159]*See, e.g.,* Lester (in Garretson et al.) *supra* at 102-06, Jordan, *supra* at 287-88 and Bourne, *supra* at 28. And, *see, generally,* the compilation in *Legal Problems Relating to the Utilization and Uses of International Rivers,* U.N. Doc. A/5409, and 3 Whiteman, *Digest of International Law,* 1043-45 (1964). Bourne, *supra,* notes that up to 1965 there were some 52 treaties which related to pollution; of these, some 40 were European and 12 were non-European, and only six dealt exclusively with pollution questions, all of these six being European and all being entered into between 1960 and 1965. The agreements establishing permanent international commissions are, of course, of particular interest, and are listed in note 167 *infra. See also* the draft conventions which would establish specific standards cited in fn. 189, *infra.*

[160]The jurisdiction of the International Court generally depends upon specific consent of the parties to the dispute, expressed either in a special agreement or in a dispute settlement provision of a more general international agreement. However, under Article 36 (2) (the so-called "optional clause" of the Statute of the Court (59 Stat. 1055 (1945), T.S. No. 993) the states parties to the Statute may at any time declare that they recognize as compulsory ipso facto and without special agreement, in relation to any other state accepting the same obligation, the jurisdiction of the Court in certain broad classes of legal disputes.

Canada made such a declaration, with certain conditions, with respect to the Permanent Court of International Justice, on Sept. 20, 1929, and this declaration was made applicable to the International Court of Justice, as the Permanent Court's successor, by I.C.J. STAT. art. 36(5). For 1929 Canadian Declaration, *see* [1960-1961] *I.C.J.Y.B.* 198, 217.

The U.S. made a declaration accepting the compulsory jurisdiction of the International Court under the "optional clause" of the Statute of the Court (Art. 36(2) on Aug. 14, 1946, 61 Stat. 1218 (1946), T.I.A.S. No. 1598, reprinted in 15 *Dept. St. Bull.* 452 (1946). The U.S. acceptance, however, includes a "self-judging" reservation added by the much criticized Connally Amendment, by which the U.S. reserved such acceptance concerning "disputes with regard to matters which are essentially within the domestic jurisdiction of the United States of America *as determined by the United States of America*" (emphasis added).

On April 7, 1970, the Canadian representative to the United Nations presented to Secretary General U Thant, a declaration amending Canada's acceptance of the compulsory jurisdiction of the International Court by adding a reservation that Canada retains jurisdiction over:

disputes arising out of or concerning jurisdiction of rights claimed or exercised by Canada in respect of the conservation, management or exploitation of the living resources of the sea, or in respect of the prevention or control of pollution or contamination of the marine environment in marine areas adjacent to the coast of Canada.

See N.Y. Times, April 9, 1970, at 13, col. 5. The full text of the present Canadian declaration is reprinted in 9 *I.L.M.* 598 (1970). It is, of course, an interesting question as to whether pollution control in the Great Lakes was intended to be or can be interpreted as being, embraced within the language "prevention or control of pollution or contamination of the marine environment in marine areas adjacent to the Coast of Canada." If so, since the U.S. acceptance of the "optional clause" is on terms of reciprocity, the U.S. could presumably now invoke the Canadian reservation as a bar to any attempt by Canada to bring it before the Court under the "optional clause."

[161]The reciprocal availability of such a self-judging reservation was sustained by the International Court in the *Case of Certain Norwegian Loans* [1957] ICJ 9. It may be noted that the Dept. of State was subjected to heavy criticism when it invoked the "Connally Reservation" in the *Interhandel* case with respect to the limited issue of its right to sell or otherwise dispose of General Aniline and Film Co. shares after Switzerland had taken that case to the I.C.J. The case was ultimately disposed of on other grounds [1959] *I.C.J. Rep.* 6.

For references to the criticism of this U.S. action on the *Interhandel* case, and on the Connally Amendment problem generally, *see, e.g.*, Bilder, "The Office of the Legal Adviser: The State Department Lawyer and Foreign Affairs, 56 *A.J.I.L.* 633 note 77 (1962).

[162]*See, e.g.*, Question 1 of the Lower Lakes reference, indicated in the text at note 121 *supra.*

[163]*See, e.g.*, Jordan, *supra* at 292-3; Lester, *supra* at 850-53; and Sen. Ericksen-Brown, *supra* at 65-7.

[164]IJC *Lower Lakes Report*, at 70. Ch. VIII of the Report discusses the "Transboundary Movement" of pollutants in detail.

[165]The desirability of handling common pollution problems through co-operative procedures rather than through adjudicative techniques has been stressed by a number of commnetators.

See also Hines, "Nor Any Drop to Drink: Part II: Interstate Arrangements for Pollution Control," 52 *Iowa L. Rev.* 432, 434:

Although it has long been settled that one state may maintain an action against another state to enjoin harmful pollution of shared waters, the states almost never resort to litigation to settle their water quality differences. Instead, where real or potential conflicts appear in the uses to be made of water in a watershed encompassing two or more states, the states involved usually seek to resolve their differences through co-operative arrangements.

While the U.S. Supreme Court has adjudicated pollution controversies between one state and another state or citizens of another state, *see Missouri v. Illinois and the Sanitary District of Chicago*, 180 U.S. 208 (1901), 200 U.S. 496 (1906); *Georgia v. Tennessee Copper Co.*, 206 U.S. 230 (1907); *New York v. New Jersey*, 256 U.S. 296 (1921); *New Jersey v. New York City*, 283 U.S. 473 (1931), it has noted the difficulties involved in such adjudications. A recent illustration is *Ohio v. Wyandotte Chemicals Corp.*, 401 U.S. 493 (1971), in which the State of Ohio filed a motion for leave to file a bill of complaint invoking the Court's original jurisdiction against Wyandotte Chemicals Corp. (incorporated in Michigan), Dow Chemical Co. (incorporated in Delaware) and Dow Chemical Company of Canada, Ltd. (incorporated in Ontairo) to abate an alleged nuisance resulting in the contamination and pollution of Lake Erie from the dumping of mercury into its tributaries. The Court, by an eight to one decision, with only Justice Douglas dissenting, declined to exercise its jurisdiction in this case since the issues were bottomed on local law that the Ohio Courts were competent to consider, several national and international bodies were actively concerned with the pollution problems involved in the case, and the nature of the case requried the resolution of complex, novel, and technical factual questions that the Court felt did not implicate important problems of federal law, which are the primary responsibility of the court. In the course of its opinion, the Court, through Justice Harlan, commented, at 501-05:

> Our reasons for thinking that, as a practical matter, it would be inappropriate for this Court to attempt to adjudicate the issues Ohio seeks to present are several. History reveals that the course of this Court's prior efforts to settle disputes regarding interstate air and water pollution has been anything but smooth." In *Missouri v. Illinois*, 200 U.S. 496, 520-22 (1906), Justice Holmes was at pains to underscore the great difficulty that the Court faced in attempting to pronounce a suitable general rule of law to govern such controversies. The solution finally grasped was to saddle the party seeking relief with an unusually high standard of proof and the Court with the duty of applying only legal principles "which [it] is prepared deliberately to maintain against all considerations on the other side," *id.*, at 521, an accommodation which, in cases of this kind, the Court has found necessary to maintain ever since. *See, e.g., New York v. New Jersey*, 256, U.S. 296, 309 (1921). Justice Clarke's closing plea in *New York v. New Jersey, supra*, at 313, strikingly illustrates the sense of futility that has accompanied this Court's attempts to treat with the complex technical and political matters that inhere in all disputes of the kind at hand:

> We cannot withhold the suggestion, inspired by the consideration of this case, that the grave problem of sewage disposal presented by the large and growing populations living on the shores of New York Bay is one more likely to be wisely solved by co-operative study and by conference and mutual concession on the part of representatives of the States so vitally interested in it than by proceedings in any court however constituted.

> The difficulties that ordinarily beset such cases are severely compounded by the particular setting in which this controversy has reached us. For example, the parties have informed us, without contradiction, that a number of official bodies are already actively involved in regulating the conduct complained of here. [The Court here refers to the involvement of a Michigan circuit court, the Michigan Water Resources Commission, the Ontario Water Resources Commission, the Lake Erie Enforcement Conference, and the International Joint Commission] (at 501-502).

> In view of all this, granting Ohio's motion for leave to file would, in effect, commit this Court's resources to the task of trying to settle a small piece of a much larger problem that many competent adjudicatory and conciliatory bodies are actively grappling with on a more practical basis.

> The nature of the case Ohio brings here is equally disconcerting. It can fairly be said that what is in dispute is not so much the law as the facts. And the fact-finding process we are asked to undertake is, to say the least, formidable...(at 503)

> To sum up, this Court has found even the simplest sort of interstate pollution case an extremely awkward vehicle to manage. And this case is an extraordinarily complex one both because of the novel scientific issues of fact inherent in

it and the multiplicity of governmental agencies already involved. Its successful resolution would require primarily skills of factfinding, conciliation, detailed co-ordination with — and perhaps not infrequent deference to — other adjudicatory bodies, and close supervision of the technical performance of local industries. We have no claim to such expertise or reason to believe that, were we to adjudicate this case, and others like it, we would not have to reduce drastically our attention to those controversies for which this Court is a proper and necessary forum...(at 504-05).

[166]*See,* this volume generally. And *see also* the various arrangements noted in *supra* notes 6 and 149 and *infra* note 167.

[167]A number of international agreements relating to international rivers or lakes establish international commissions to implement certain of their provisions. *See, generally, e.g.,* Ely and Wolman, "Administration," in *The Law of International Drainage Basins* 126 (Garretson, Hayton and Olmstead, eds., 1967) and Stein, "The Potential of Regional Organizations in Managing Man's Environment" in this volume. Stein lists the following agreements as establishing such Commissions: (1) The Convention of Mannheim of Oct. 17, 1868, Central Commission for Navigation of the Rhine (originally created by the Congress of Vienna of 1815), of which the present parties are Belgium, France, the Federal Republic of Germany, the Netherlands, Switzerland and the United Kingdom, as revised by the Convention Relating to the Revision of the 1868 Mannheim Act, adopted Nov. 20, 1963, 11 *European Yrbk.* 175 (1963); (2) The Agreement of April 29, 1963 between Switzerland, the Federal Republic of Germany, France, the Netherlands and Luxembourg establishing the International Commission for the Protection of the Rhine Against Pollution; (3) the Convention Regarding the Regime of Navigation of the Danube, U.N.T.S. 197 (1949); (4) Indus Waters Treaty of September 19, 1960 between India, Pakistan and the International Bank for Reconstruction and Development, 419 U.N.T.S. 125 (1962), reprinted in 55 *A.J.I.L.* 797 (1961); (5) Mekong River Basin Agreement of December 29, 1954 between Cambodia, Laos and Vietnam; (6) River Plata Basin Agreement of April 23, 1969 between Argentina, Brazil, Bolivia, Paraguay and Uruguay, 8 *I.L.M.* 905 (1969); (7) Agreement of November 25, 1964 between Cameroon, Ivory Coast, Dahomey, Guinea, Upper Volta, Mali, Niger, Nigeria and Chad concerning the Niger River Commission, 587 U.N.T.S. 19 (1967); (8) Convention and Statute relating to the Chad Basin between Cameroon, Chad, Niger and Nigeria, signed May 22, 1964; and (9) Convention on the Regulation of Water Abstractions from the Lake of Constance below the Federal Republic of Germany, Austria, and Switzerland, signed November 25, 1967. Yates, "Unilateral and Multilateral Approaches to Environmental Problems," Vancouver Symposium, *supra* note 4, at 15-16, lists as Commissions particularly relevant to pollution control, in addition to the Rhine Commission: (1) The Convention of October 27, 1960 between Baden, Wurtemburg, Bavaria, Austria and Switzerland establishing the Commission for the Protection of the Waters of Lake Constance; (2) The Convention of 16 November 1962 between Switzerland and France establishing the Commission for the Protection of Lake Leman; and the Convention of 1 July 1962 between France and the Federal Republic of Germany establishing the Commission of the Saar and Moselle. *See* further on the Danube Commission and its quite limited pollution responsibilities. Stanov, "Les Aspects Juridique de la Lutte Internationale contres la pollution du Danube," 72 *Rev. Gen. de Droit Int'l Pub.* 97 (1968), and on the broader responsibilities of the new Rhine Pollution Commission, Kiss and Lambrechts, "La Lutte Contre la pollution de l'eau en Europe Occidentale," 15 *Ann. Francais de Droit Int'l.* 718 (1969).

[168] The present membership of the Commission is as follows: *U.S. Section* — Christian A. Herter, Jr. (Chairman), Eugene W. Weber, and Charles R. Ross; *Canadian Section* — Louis J. Robichaud (Chairman), A.D. Scott, and Bernard Beaupre. I am informed by the U.S. Section staff that the Commissioner's backgrounds are as follows: *U.S. Section* — Chairman Herter is an attorney and presently a high official in the U.S. State Department; Commissioner Weber is an engineer who was for many years Chief of Civilian Planning with the U.S. Army Corps of Engineers; Commissioner Ross is an attorney and formerly a member of the Federal Power Commission; *Canadian Section* — Chairman Robichaud

is an attorney and formerly Premier of New Brunswick; Commissioner Scott is a professor of economics at the University of British Columbia; Commissioner Beaupre is an engineer with long experience in the water field.

[169]For Fiscal Year 1972, the total U.S. budget for the U.S. Section of the IJC is approximately $549,000. Of this amount, $138,000 is allocated to the Environmental Protection Agency for its work on pollution references, $221,000 to the Geological Survey for hydrologic data-gathering, and the balance of $190,000 is available for U.S. section staff and administrative expenses (Information supplied by IJC, U.S. Section).

[170]Welsh and Heeney, *supra* note 34, at 3.

[171]*See, e.g.*, Heeney, *supra* note 34, at 4, and Welsh (1969 Proceedings), *supra* note 34, at 4. The U.S. Section has identified one of the cases to me as the Belly Water Rivers Investigation (Docket No. 57), a reference, in which each Section of the Commission reported separately to their own government and a Joint Report was not filed.

[172]*See supra* note 75.

[173]On the special problems of international standard-setting in the area of pollution, *see, e.g.,* "International Environmental Regulation: A UNITAR Study" (prepared by D. Serwer in consultation with O. Schachter).

[174]*See, e.g.,* J.C. Davies, *The Politics of Pollution* 17-21 (1970).

[175]*See* Treaty, article IV. In practice, however, the Commission has frequently been prepared in its reports on various references to conclude that transboundary pollution was occurring to the detriment of both countries. Note also the statement in the Commission's 1918 Report on Pollution of Bumardy Waters (as quoted by Erickson-Brown, *supra* note 34) that:

> The Commission regards the word 'injury' when used in the reference or treaty as having a special significance — one somewhat akin to the term 'injuria' in jurisprudence. It does not mean harm or damage but harm or damage which is in excess of the amount of harm or damage which the sufferer, in view of all the circumstances of the case, and of all the coexistence rights ... and of the paramount importance of human health and life, should reasonably be called upon to bear.

[176]*But see,* for examples of such definitions, the definition adopted in article IX of the "Helsinki Rules on the Uses of the Waters of International Rivers," *Int'l Law Assoc.,* Report of the Fifty-Second Conference, Helsinki, at 477 (1966):

> Article IX. As used in the chapter, the term "water pollution" refers to any detrimental change resulting from human conduct in the natural composition, content or quality of the waters of an international drainage basin.

Compare the Canada Waters Act, Stats. Can. 1969-70, c. 72, which defines "waste" as:
> ... any substance that, if added to any waters, would degrade or alter or form part of a process of degradation or alteration of the quality of those waters to an extent that is detrimental to their use by man or by any animal, fish or plant that is useful to man, and includes any water that contains a substance in such quantity or concentration, or that has been so treated, processed or changed, by heat or other from a natural state that it would, if added to any waters, degrade or alter or form part of a process of degradation or alteration of the quality of those waters to an extent that is detrimental to their use by man or by any animal, fish or plant that is useful to man.

The definition of "waste" in the Canadian Arctic Waters Pollution Prevention Act, 18-19 Eliz. 2, ch. 47, section 2(h) (Can. 1970) is similar.

Compare also the definition suggested by the International Oceanographic Commission and accepted by the Joint IMCO/FAO/WMO Group of Experts on the Scientific Aspects of Marine Pollution (GESAMP), which defines marine pollution as:

Introduction by man, directly or indirectly, of substances or energy into the marine environment (including estuaries) resulting in such deleterious effects as harm to living resources, hazard to human health, hindrance to marine activities including fishing, impairment of quality for use as sea water and reduction of amenities.
Comprehensive Outline of the Scope of the Long-Term and Expanded Progamme of Oceanic Research, U.N. Doc. A/7750, pt. 1, at 3 (Nov. 10, 1969).

[177]As indicated in the text at supra note 98, this technique was first used in the Commission's Report in the 1950 "Connecting Channels" Reference. The proposed water quality objectives for the Lower Lakes are discussed in ch. XII of the *Lower Lakes Report* and set forth as proposals in ch. XIV of the Report.

[178]*IJC Lower Lakes Report*, at 113.

[179]The proposed "General Objectives," set forth at 144-45 of the *IJC Lower Lakes Report*, and described therein as the "five freedoms" of a pollution control program, are:
The receiving waters of Lake Erie, Lake Ontario, the International Section of the St. Lawrence River and the Connecting Channels of the Great Lakes at all places and at all times should be:
(a) free from substances attributable to municipal, industrial or other discharges that will settle to form putrescent or otherwise objectionable sludge deposits, or that will adversely affect aquatic life or water.
(b) free from floating debris, oil, scum and other floating materials attributable to municipal, industrial or other discharges in amounts sufficient to be unsightly or deleterious.
(c) free from materials attributable to municipal, industrial or other discharges producing colour, odour, or other conditions in such a degree as to create a nuisance.
(d) free from substances attributable to municipal, industrial or other discharges in concentrations that are toxic or harmful to human, animal or aquatic life.
(e) free from nutrients derived from municipal, industrial and agricultural sources in concentrations that create nuisance growths of aquatic weeds and algae."

[180]*Id.* at 145-8. Examples of the Specific Objectives are:
(a) *Microbiology (Coliform Group)* — The geometric mean of not less than five samples taken over not more than a 30-day period shall not exceed 1,000/100 ml. total coliforms, nor 200/100 fecal coliforms in local waters. Waters used for body contact recreation activities should be free from bacteria, fungi, or viruses that may produce enteric disorders, or eye, ear, nose, throat and skin infections.
(b) *Dissolved Oxygen* — In the Connecting Channels and in the upper waters of the Lakes not less than 6.0 mg./l at any time; in the hypolimetic waters not less than the concentrations necessary for the support of fish life, particularly cold water species. (at 145-146)
Contrast the objective for:
"(d) *Temperature* — No change which would adversely affect any local or general use of these waters." (at 146)

[181]*Id.* at 114-15.

[182]*Id.* at 115-16.

[183]*Id.* at 141.

[184]*Id.* at 123-5.

[185]The recommended phosphosphorus objective is as follows:
Phosphorus — Concentrations limited to the extent necessary to prevent nuisance growths of algae, weeds and slimes which are or may become injurious to any beneficial water use. (Meeting this objective will require that the phosphorus loading to

Lake Erie be limited to 0.39 g/m²/yr. and the phosphorus loading to Lake Ontario be limited to 0.17 g/m²/yr." *Id*, at 147.

[186]*Id*. at 125. The major source of phosphorus is municipal sewage. In the U.S. 70 percent of the phosphorus in sewage originates from detergents, most of the remainder from human excreta. In Canada, approximately 50 percent originates from each sewage source. Apart from municipal sewage the other significant sources of phosphorus are agricultural runoff and some industrial wastes. *Id*. at 141. The research results from "Project Hypo," a joint U.S.-Canadian project carried on in Lake Erie in the summer of 1970 to obtain more precise data on Lake nutrients, suggests that the 98 percent removal goal may have to be attained by 1975 rather than 1986 if eutrophication of the Lake is to be effectively reversed.

[187]*Id*. at 125.

[188]*See* Joint Communique, para. 6, and *infra* note 226. Compare the European Agreement on the Restriction of the Use of Certain Detergents in Washing and Cleaning Products, adopted by the Council of Europe on Sept. 16, 1968, 16 *European Yearbook* 335 (1968), and already implemented by several member states, establishing an 80 percent biodegradability level.

[189]*See* text of note 101. *See also, e.g.*, the 1971 Draft European Convention on the Protection of Freshwater Against Pollution, prepared by the Council of Europe, which now envisages the establishment of "minimum water quality standards," Rpt. of the First Meeting (Feb. 1971) of the Expert Commission on a Draft European Convention on the Protection of Freshwater Against Pollution; and the 1971 Draft Agreement on Water Conservation and Utilization in the Lake Chad Basin (prepared by FAO and the Lake Chad Basin Commission) which provides standards for water-abstraction and pollution control. (*See* FAO Doc. AGL: SF/REG/79 [1971].)

[190]*See N.Y. Times*, Sept. 16, 1971, at 1, col. 2. For further comments and developments following the announcement, *see id.*, Sept. 16, 1971, at 37, col. 2; *id.*, Sept. 17, 1971 at 1, col. 4 and at 20, col. 1; *id.*, Sept. 18, 1971, at 58, col. 1; *id.*, Sept. 19, 1971, at 52, col. 3; *id.*, Sept. 22, 1971, at 46, col. 1 (Ed.); and *id.*, Sept. 24, 1971, at 40, col. 3."

[191]*Id., See also* the October 27, 1971 statement by CEQ Chairman Russell E. Train, before the House Government Operations Sub-Committee on Conservation and Natural Resources, that the elimination of phosphates would not eliminate eutrophication, that the principal strategy in controlling eutrophication will be provision of adequate waste treatment, and that, given the present state of knowledge, there is no one answer as to which discharges of phosphorus should be controlled to limit accelerate eutrophication and the possible problems with currently available substitutes for phosphates: *see* 2 *Environ. Reptr.* 763, No. 26 (1917).

[192]*See e.g.*, the comment in a paper by the Canadian Minister of Energy, Mines and Resources, Greene, "Policy on the Environment" in the Univ. of Toronto Symposium, *supra*, 69 at 74, that:

Even between nations that do not have disparate levels of economic development, agreement is difficult to achieve. The record of cooperation between Canada and its closest friend and neighbor, the USA, is anything but bright, notwithstanding the excellent investigatory work of the International Joint Commission. It is now clearly established on the basis of independent expert evidence that the Great Lakes water system will not be cleaned up until the USA takes the tough decision to ban phosphates from detergents. This it seems reluctant to do. I feel that the only way to achieve real progress in the clearing up of our international boundary waters would be to equip the IJC with the authority to enforce its ruling with regard to pollution of international boundary waters.

[193]*See, e.g.*, the interesting paper by A. Sparring on "Pollution Control as a Problem of International Politics: Models for a Baltic Convention," prepared for the 21st Pugwash

370

Conference on Science and World Affairs on "Problems of World Security and Development," Sinaia, Romania, 26-31 August, 1971.

[194]Article VIII provides more fully, in relevant part:
This International Joint Commission shall have jurisdiction over and shall pass upon all cases involving the use or obstruction or diversion of the waters with respect to which under Articles III and IV of this Treaty the approval of this Commission is required, and in passing upon such cases the Commission shall be governed by the following rules or principles which are adopted by the High Contracting Parties for this purpose.

The High Contracting Parties shall have, each on its own side of the boundary, equal and similar rights in the use of the waters hereinbefore defined as boundary waters.

...
The requirement for an equal division may in the discretion of the Commission be suspended in cases of temporary diversions along boundary waters at points where such equal division cannot be made advantageous by an account of local conditions, and where such diversion does not diminish elsewhere the amount available for use on the other side.

[195]Joint Communique, para. 17.

[196]See, generally, the useful pamphlet *Great Lakes Institutions: A Survey of Institutions Concerned with Water and Related Resources of the Great Lakes Basin,* published by the Great Lakes Basin Commission and the Great Lakes Panel of the Committee on Multiple Use of the Coastal Zone, National Council on Marine Resources and Engineering Development (June 1969).

[197]While the Province of Quebec is not a Great Lakes riparian, it was represented in the Ministerial Conference's Joint Working Group and may be represented on a Great Lakes Pollution Advisory Board.

[198]Principally, the Bureau of European Affairs, which has responsibility for relations with Canada.

[199]Principally, the Soil Conservation Service, Forest Service, Agricultural Research Service, and Economic Research Service.

[200]Principally, the Bureau of Commercial Fisheries, Bureau of Outdoor Recreation, Bureau of Sport Fisheries and Wildlife, U.S. Geological Survey and National Park Service.

[201]Principally, the National Oceanic and Atmospheric Administration (NOAA), Economic Development Administration, and Maritime Administration. NOAA, established in 1970, consolidates the major Federal oceanic and atmospheric research and monitoring programs. Both the Weather Bureau and the Coast and Geodetic Survey now operate within NOAA.

[202]Principally, The Army Corps of Engineers, Dept. of Navy (concerned with ship pollution control), and Office of Naval Research.

[203]Principally, the U.S. Coast Guard (which is concerned with ship sanitation and oil spills) and St. Lawrence Seaway Development Corporation.

[204]Principally, the Public Health Service.

[205]The Council on Environmental Quality (CEQ) was established January 1, 1970 by the National Environmental Policy Act of 1969, P.L. 91-190. The Act charges the Council with assisting the President in preparing an annual environmental quality report and making recommendations to him on national policies for improving environmental quality; empowers the Council to analyze conditions and trends in the quality of the environment and to

conduct investigations relating to the environment; and gives the Council responsibility for appraising the effect of Federal programs and activities in environmental quality.

[206]The Environmental Protection Agency (EPA) was officially established on December 2, 1970. It consolidated into one agency the major federal programs dealing with air pollution, water pollution, solid waste disposal, pesticides regulation and environmental radiation. Its offices specifically concerned with Great Lakes pollution are the Office of International Affairs, the Office of Waters Programs under the Assistant Administrator for Media Programs, and the Assistant Administrator for Research and Monitoring. The Great Lakes is a primary responsibility of the EPA's Region V regional office.

[207]See Great Lakes Institutions, supra at 22-4. On March 25, 1971, President Nixon sent to Congress legislation to create a Department of Natural Resources which would include, inter alia, an Administrator for Water Resources. S. 1431, H.R. 6959, 92nd Cong., 1st Sess. (1971). See Environmental Quality — 1971 (CRQ), at 6-7.

[208]The Senate and House Committees on Public Works have been particularly concerned with water pollution problems. Both the Senate and House have recently passed joint resolutions to create a Joint Committee on the Environment. S.J. Res. 17, 92nd Cong., 1st Sess. (1971); H.J. Res. 3, 92nd Cong., 1st Sess. (1971). The Congress has also recently reorganized and expanded existing committees to give more explicit attention to environmental problems See Environmental Quality — 1971 (CEQ), at 8. See generally, J.C. Davies, The Politics of Pollution 65-70 (1970).

[209]See Great Lakes Institutions, supra note 196, at 26-38 (as of June 1969). Some reorganization and consolidation of state agencies has occurred in the last several years. For more recent developments, see the Environmental Reporter (Bureau of National Affairs), a weekly report on national and state legislative and other developments in the environmental field, including water quality.

[210]P.L. 89-80, 79 Stat. 244 (1965).

[211]See, generally, e.g., Great Lakes Institutions, supra at 24-5; The Commission's pamphlet, Great Lakes Basin Commission-What It is-What It Does, and the Commission's Report, Challenges for the Future: An Interim Report on the Great Lakes Basin Framework Study (Aug. 17, 1971). The Commission also issues a monthly newsletter titled the Communicator. The Commission's headquarters are located at Ann Arbor, Michigan.

[212]Public Works and Economic Development Act of 1965, 42 U.S.C. Sec. 3121, et seq. (1965).

[213]See, e.g., Great Lakes Institutions, supra at 25.

[214]Act of July 24, 1968, P.L. 90-419, 82 Stat. 414, containing text. By Artcile 1, Sec. 10 of the Constitution, such compact require Congressional consent.

[215]The Compact was formed in 1955 through ratification of five of the eight states, with Ohio, Pennsylvania and New York ratifying subsequently. The text of the Compact, with notes on its legislative history, is also reprinted in Documents on the Use and Control of the Waters of Interstate and International Streams (1968), House Doc. No. 319, 90th Cong., 2d Sess. (1968), at 177-83

It is interesting to note that article 11(B) of the Compact provides that "The Province of Ontario and the Province of Quebec, or either of them, may become states parties to this compact by taking such action as their laws and the laws of the Government of Canada may prescribe for adherence thereto." In addition, article VI provides that the Commission shall have power to:
    J. With respect to the water resources of the Basin or any portion thereof, recommend agreements between the governments of the U.S. and Canada.
    K. Recommend mutual agreements expressed by concurrent of reciprocal legislation

on the part of Congress and the Parliament of Canada including but not limited to such agreements and mutual arrangements as are provided for by Article XIII of the . . . [Boundary Waters Treaty of 1909]

M. At the request of the United States, or in the event that a Province shall be a party state, at the request of the Government of Canada, assist in the negotiation and formulation of any treaty or other mutual arrangement or agreement between the United States and Canada with reference to the Basin or any portion thereof.

The State Department objected to these provisions when the compact was presented to Congress for its approval on the grounds, *inter alia*, that Provincial participation and the above-cited provisions would involve the Commission in the field of international relations. See Piper, *supra* at 80. The Act of July 24, 1968 consequently limited Congressional consent by providing, that the consent granted does not extend to the above Sections (Sec. 2) and that nothing contained in the Act "shall be construed to establish an international agency or to limit or affect in any way the exercise of the treaty making power or any other power or right of the United States." (Sec.3).

[216]*See, e.g., Great Lakes Institutions, supra* at 25 and the Commission's descriptive pamphlet, *Great Lakes Commission.* Under Art. VII(B) of the Compact, the states agree to consider the recommendations of the Commission with respect to "measures for combatting pollution."

The Commission is financed entirely by state funds and has its headquarters in Ann Arbor, Michigan.

On interstate compacts, generally, *see, e.g.,* Zimmerman and Wendell *The Law and Use of Interstate Compacts* (1961), 3 Clark, *Water and Water Rights* 332-48 (1967), W. Barton, Interstate Compacts in the Political Process (1965) and references in *infra* note 271.

[217]The Department of the Environment was established in 1971, incorporating as components the former Department of Fisheries and Forestry; essentially all of the Water Sector of the Department of Energy, Mines and Resources, including the inland Waters Branch, the Marine Science Branch, The Policy and Planning Branch, and the Canada Centre for Inland Waters; the Canadian Meteorological Service, and the Canadian Wildlife Service, and those units of the Department of National Health and Welfare concerned with public health engineering and air pollution. It will have primary responsibility for support of the IJC. *See, e.g.,* Vol. 1, No. 8 Great Lakes Basin Commission *Communicator* (Feb. 1971).

[218]*See Great Lakes Institutions, supra* at 8-10.

[219]*Id.* at 7-8.

[220]*Id.* at 10-11.

[221]*Id.* at 4-5. The Commission is established by the Convention on Great Lakes Fisheries, signed at Washington, Sept. 10, 1954, entered into force October 11, 1955, 6 U.S.T. 2836; T.I.A.S. 3326; 238 U.N.T.S. 97, as amended April 5, 1966 and May 19, 1967, 18 U.S.T. 1402; T.I.A.S. 6297. *See also* the Great Lakes Fisheries Acto of 1956, P.L. 84-557. The sea lamprey is a species of eel, native to the Atlantic Ocean, which was enabled to enter into the Great Lakes System through the opening of the Welland Canal, multiplied in the absence of its natural biological controls, and has preyed upon and wreaked havoc among certain Great Lakes fish species.

[222]*Id.* at 5.

[223]*Ibid.*

[554]*See* references interspersed in *id.* at 26-40.

[225]*See, e.g.,* the references to these problems in the *IJC Lower Lakes Report,* at 108, 110 and 111. For example, the Commission comments (at 110) that:

> while in some cases the differences among jurisdictions are more apparent than real, in others the differences are such that the laws as applied in the various jurisdictions are incompatible. Obviously, such inconsistency presents serious obstacles to the effective implementation of any concerted programme of pollution control and abatement throughout the Lower Great Lakes.

The Commission cites as an example of such incompatability differing legal requirements for the control of waste discharges from watercraft using the Lakes.

[226]*See, e.g.,* the list of members of the International Lake Erie Water Pollution Board and of the International Lake Ontario-St. Lawrence Water Pollution Board, and of their committees, in IJC *Lower Lakes Report,* Appendix, at 165-7.

[227]For example, in 1960, prior to the Commission's receipt of the Lower Lakes reference from the two governments, Congress had already appropriated funds under the Federal Water Pollution Act of 1956 for a comprehensive study of Great Lakes pollution problems, which was already in progress at the time of the reference, IJC *Lower Lakes Report,* at 8. Additional research for the Lower Lakes study was conducted by the responsible government agencies of the two governments, rather than by the Commission itself. *Id.* at 8-9. And *see supra* note 111.

[228]IJC *Lower Lakes Report* at 111. And *see also id.* at 130-31.

[229]*See supra* note 79.

[230]The Commission's 1969 interim reports on the Lower Lakes pollution reference stressing the role of phosphorus and particularly phosphorus-based detergent in eutrophication of the Lakes, received wide attention and apparently played some part in influencing federal environmental officials at that time to urge consumers to avoid phosphate detergents. In February, 1970, Canada announced plans to ban all phosphates in detergents over a two-year span. *N.Y. Times,* Feb. 20, 1970, at 2, col. 3-5. A number of states and communities, such as Connecticut, Florida, Indiana, Maine, Minnesota and New York State, Dade and Lake Counties in Florida, and Chicago, Detroit and Akron have subsequently passed legislation to regulate the phosphate content of detergents, most of which legislation is to take effect in 1972 or 1973. Many other states and communities are considering phosphates legislation. *Environmental Quality 1971* (CEQ at 44). and *see* Madison (Wis.) *Capital Times,* Sept. 17, 1971, at 6, col. 1-5.

[231]*See* text at *supra,* notes 190 and 191.

[232]*See, e.g.,* the IJC *Lower Lakes Report,* which notes at 108, that:

> As might be expected in such circumstances [of a number of jurisdictions with different laws and administering agencies], the policies and goals and the vigour with which they are pursued in the several jurisdictions are not uniform; and there is considerable variation in the actual laws, their administration and enforcement.

[233]*See* Section 1(b) of the Federal Water Pollution Control Act, as amended, 33 U.S.C. Section 1151(b), note 242 *infra,* which declares that the policy of congress is "to recognize, preserve and protect the primary responsibilities of the States in preventing and controlling water pollution." *See also* Section 10 of that Act which provides that, except where the Attorney General has actually obtained a court order of pollution abatement on behalf of the United States, "State and interstate action to abate pollution of ... navigable waters ... shall not ... be displaced by Federal enforcement action." Section 10(b), 33 USCA Section 1160(b). And *see* further the Environmental Quality Improvement Act of 1970, 84 Stat. 114, 42 U.S.G.A. Section 4371 (Supp. 1971) which, while stating the general policy of Congress in protecting the environment, also states that: "The primary responsibility for implementing this policy rests with state and local governments." 42 U.S.C.A. Section 4371(b) (2) (Supp. 1971). *See, generally,* for an excellent and comprehensive discussion of U.S.

federal and state Water Quality legislation and practice, H. Ellis, J.H. Beuscher, C.D. Howard and J.P. de Braal, 1 *Water Use Law and Administration in Wisconsin* (Dept. of Law, Univ. Extension, Univ. of Wisconsin, 1971) ch. 17, and as of 1966-1967, Hines, "Nor Any Drop to Drink: Public Regulation of Water Quality;" Part 1: State Pollution Control Programs, 52 *Iowa L. Rev.* 186 (1966); *Part II: Interstate Arrangements for Pollution Control, 52 Iowa L. Rev.* 432 (1966); Part III: The Federal Effort, 52 *Iowa L. Rev.* 799 (1967).

[234]*Environmental Quality*-1970, at 44. For several interesting case studies of the problems involved, *see, e.g.*, Reitze, "Wastes, Water and Wishful Thinking: The Battle of Lake Erie," 20 *Case Western L. Rev.* 5 (1968), and, with respect to Lake Michigan, Polikoff, "The Interlake Affair," *The Washington Monthly*, Vol. 3, No. 1 (March 1971), at 7.

[235]*See supra* note 23.

[236]33 USC 466, *et seq.* The Basic Act (Public Law 84-660) approved July 9, 1956, as amended by the Federal Water Pollution Control Act Amendments of 1961 (P.L. 87-88), approved July 20, 1961; by the Water Quality Act of 1965 (P.L. 89-234), approved October 2, 1965; by the Clean Water Restoration Act of 1966 (P.L. 89-753), approved November 3, 1966; and by the Water Quality Improvement Act of 1970 (P.L. 91-224), approved April 3, 1970. The Environmental Protection Agency has taken over the Secretary of Interior's functions under the Act. Exec. Order No. 11548, F.R. Doc. 70-9493 of July 20, 1970.

[237]Federal Water Pollution Control Act, as amended, *supra* Section 10(c) (1).

[238]*Id.* Section 10(c) (2).

[239]*See, e.g., Environmental Quality-1970* (CEQ), at 44.

[240]Federal Water Pollution Control Act, as amended, *supra* Section 10(c) (5), (d), (e), (f) and (g); 33 USC 1160. Two procedures are provided. The first is a three-step procedure consisting of a conference of federal, state and interstate water quality agency representatives; a public hearing; and finally court action. Among the conferences convened under the Act are the four-state Lake Michigan Enforcement Conference, first convened in 1968, focusing on the need to protect Lake Michigan from waste heat discharges, the Lake Superior Enforcement Conference, first convened in 1969, involving *inter alia*, discharges of taconite taling into the Lake from a Reserve Mining Company facility in Minnesota, and the Lake Erie Enforcement Conference, convened in 1970, studying all forms and sources of pollution affecting Lake Erie. The second enforcement procedure calls for notification both to the violator of water quality standards and to interested parties, followed by court action if necessary in cases of non-compliance. EPA issued a violation notice to Reserve Mining Company because of its failure to present an acceptable abatement plan to the Lake Superior enforcement conference. *See Environmental Quality-1971* (CEQ), at 12-14. Senator Muskie is reported as having noted that there has been almost no enforcement under the Act, with only one case reaching the Courts. *N.Y. Times*, Nov. 3, 1971, at 1, col. 1, and (continuation) at 22, col. 3.

[241]Section 10(d) (2), added by Sec. 206 of the Clean Waters Restoration Act of 1966 (P.L. 89-753), provides:
Whenever the Secretary [now the Administrator of the EPA], upon receipt of reports, surveys, or studies from any duly constituted international agency, has reason to believe that any pollution referred to in subsection (a) of this Section which endangers the health or welfare of persons in a foreign country is occurring, and the Secretary of State requests him to abate such pollution, he shall give formal notification thereof to the State water pollution control agency of the State in which such discharge or discharges originate and to the interstate water pollution control agency, if any, and shall call promptly a conference of such agency or agencies, if he believes that such polltuion is occurring in sufficient quantity to warrant such action. The Secretary, through the Secretary of State, shall invite the foreign country which may be adversely affected by the pollution to attend and participate in the conference, and the representative of such country shall, for the purpose of the conference and any further proceeding resulting

from such conference, have all the rights of a State water pollution agency. This paragraph shall apply only to a foreign country which the Secretary determines has given the United States essentially the same rights with respect to the prevention and control of water pollution occurring in that country as is given that country by this paragraph. Nothing in this paragraph shall be construed to modify, amend, repeal or otherwise affect the provisions of the 1909 Boundary Waters Treaty between Canada and the United States or the Water Utilization Treaty of 1944 between Mexico and the United States (59 Stat. 1219) relative to the control and abatement of water pollution in waters covered by those treaties.
Similar provisions are contained in Section 115 of the Clean Air Act, 42 U.S.C. 1857 ff.

[242]Canada does not have reciprocal legislation, and, in any event, may view the language giving it "the rights of a state water pollution agency" as unacceptable in terms of its national dignity.

[243]30 Stat. 1151 (1899), 33 U.S.C. Section 403-404, 406-409, 411-16, 418 (1964). The Act makes it unlawful, without a permit, to:
...throw, discharge or deposit...any refuse matter of any kind or description whatever other than that flowing from streets and sewers and passing therefrom in a liquid state, into any navigable water...or into any tributary of any navigable water. (33 U.S.C. 407).
Knowing violation of the Refuse Act is a misdemeanor, subject to $2500 fine or six months imprisonment. Violators are also subject to Civil suits for injunctive relief. The act was upheld and broadly interpreted by the U.S. Supreme Court in *United States v. Republic Steel Corp.*, 362 U.S. 482 (1960).

[244]On December 23, 1970, the President announced a new program to control water pollution from industrial sources through the permit authority of the Refuse Act. See *N.Y. Times*, at 1, col. 1. The program initiated by the President makes a permit mandatory for all industrial discharges into navigable waters of the U.S. Ex. 0. no. 11574, 3 CFR 188 (1970). For the Corps of Engineers' proposed rules and procedures, *see* 35 *Fed. Reg.* 20005 and 36 *Fed. Reg.* 983. Violators of water quality standards — including standards imposed by the EPA when federal-state or state standards do not apply or are clearly deficient — are ineligible for permits and liable for enforcement proceedings. All dischargers were required to file information on discharges by Oct. 1, 1971. *See Environmental Qualtiy-1971* (CEQ), at 10-12; and, *e.g.* Rodgers, "Industrial Water Pollution and the Refuse Act: A Second Chance for Water Quality," 119 *U.Pa.L.Rev.* 761 (1971).

[245]*See, generally, e.g., Laws of the United States Relating to Water Pollution Control and Environmental Quality*, compiled by the Committee on Public Works, U.S. House of Representatives (Committee Print, 91st Cong., 2d Sess., July, 1970). Much of this other legislation is in the form of amendments to the Federal Water Pollution Control Act — for example, the Water Quality Improvement Act of 1970 (P.L. 91-224, approved April 3, 1970), which embodies comprehensive federal legislation covering the control of vessel wastes. Section 5(f) of the Federal Water Pollution Control Act specifically directs the Secretary of the Interior (now transferred to the Administrator of the EPA) to "conduct research and technical development work, and make studies, with respect to the quality of the waters of the Great Lakes." Section 15 of the Act authorize the Secretary (the EPA), in cooperation with other government agencies, to enter into agreements with state or other public agencies, with the federal government paying up to 75% of the costs:
. . . to carry out one or more projects to demonstrate new methods and techniques and develop preliminary plans for the elimination or control of pollution, within all or any part of the watersheds of the Great Lakes. Such projects shall demonstrate the engineering and economic feasibility and practicality of removal of pollutants and prevention of any polluting matter from entering into the Great Lakes in the future and other abatement and remedial techniques which will contribute to effective and practical methods of water pollution eliminator or control. (Sec. 15(a)).

[246]*See* President Nixon's Message to Congress, 8 Feb. 1971, "Progress for a Better Environment," H.R. Doc. No. 46, 92nd Cong., 1st Sess. (1971), *Environmental Quality-1971* (CEQ), at 284, and Joint Communique, *supra*, para. 16.

[247]On November 2, 1971, the Senate approved 86-0 a far-reaching and comprehensive 180-page bill, "The National Water Quality Standards Act of 1971," sponsored by Senator Muskie and approved by the Senate Public Works Committee, designed to eliminate the discharge of all pollutants into navigable waterways by 1985 and in large measure shifting responsibility for controlling water pollution from the states to the federal government and the Environmental Protection Agency, *N.Y. Times, Nov. 3, 1971*, at 1, col. 1, and at 22, col. 3-4. *N.Y. Times*, Nov. 8, 1971, at 1 col. 4 and at 28, col. 3-5. The bill would *inter alia*, broaden the 1899 Refuse Act by establishing Federal effluent or discharge standards; extending the dumping ban without permit to municipal wastes, industrial waste discharged into sewer systems, outfalls into the ocean and agricultural wastes for livestock over certain numbers on an acre of land; and transferring the permit system from the Army Corps of Engineers to the EPA. The bill would permit the states to administer the permit program, once the EPA approved their programs for achieving Federal effluent standards, but EPA could cancel the states' authority to issue permits if the state did not administer its program in conformity with Federal law. Moreover, EPA could veto any state permit and also take a violator to court if the state failed to act against him. The bill contemplates a two-phase program to achieve the national no-discharge standard. Under Phase One, cities must have secondary treatment plants for sewage under construction by 1974, and industries must be using the "best practicable control technology" by 1976. Under Phase Two, to be in force by 1981, all industries and communities, if they have been unable to achieve the goal of no-discharge at reasonable cost, must be able to demonstrate that they are at least using the "best available technology." The burden of proof is on the cities and industries. The bill would also authorize $14 billion for sewage treatment construction grants for fiscal 1972-5 and increase the percentage of federal sewage treatment plant construction aid. *Ibid.*

[248]*See, e.g., Great Lakes Institutions, supra* at 26-38, listing the various responsible state agencies and their responsibilities as of June 1969; J.C. Davies, *The Politics of Pollution*, at 120-5 (1970); and for a broader and somewhat earlier look at state laws generally, Hines, "Nor Any Drop to Drink," *supra*, Part 1, "State Pollution Control Programs," 52 *Iowa L. Rev.* 186 (1966). I have not attempted to collect the currently effective laws of all the riparian states. But, *e.g.*, for comprehensive studies of the water-control legislation and practice in my own state of Wisconsin, *see* H. Ellis, J.H. Beuscher, C.D. Howard, and J.P. De Broul, *Water-Use Law and Administration in Wisconsin* (Dept. of Law, Univ. Extension, Univ. of Wisconsin 1970), and Carmichael, "Forty Years of Water Pollution Control in Wisconsin: A Case Study," 1967 *Wis. L. Rev.* 350.

[249]*See, e.g.*, the recent Illinois Environmental Protective Act, 1970 Laws of Illinois, House Bill 3788; 1970 Laws of Penn., Act No. 275, eff. January 19, 1971; and New York Environmental Conservation Law, N.Y. State Laws of 1970, ch. 140. And *see, generally, Environmental Qaulity-1970* (CEQ), at 50, and *Environmental Qaulity-1971* (CEQ), at 170-75.

[250]The Environmental Conference of Great Lakes Governors and Premiers, meeting at Mackinac Island, Michigan, August 16-17, 1971, adopted resolutions strongly supporting the proposed Great Lakes Water Quality Agreement. *See N.Y. Times*, Aug. 18, 1971, at 62, col. 1-2. The resolutions commended the proposal to extend the IJC's surveillance responsibilities to Lakes Huron and Superior, (Res. No. 1); supported the establishment of a single IJC water quality board for all of the Great Lakes (Res. No. 2); urged that the new agreement provide the IJC with an independent staff and allied resources (Res. No. 3); and recommended that the role of the IJC be strengthened by authorizing its Water Quality Board to monitor the effectiveness of governmental water pollution control programs, to recommend legislative and program improvements as warranted, to coordinate water quality control activities, and to direct specific recommendations relative to individual waste discharges to appropriate water pollution control agencies and make public its finding and recommendations. (Res. No. 4). Other resolutions recommended that national governments expand current programs to provide financial assistance to aid communities to construct facilities to abate water pollution from combined sewer overflows (Res. No. 6); recommended implementation of a no discharge concept for sewage from vessels in the Great Lakes and the retention of all sewage for discharge at approved on-land treatment facilities (Res. No. 7 and 11); acknowledged the importance of shoreland management policies and control programs; and recommended establishment of a Michigan-

Ontario committee to prepare a proposal for a cooperative program for abatement of transboundary air pollution. (Copy of Resolutions supplied by Office of the Governor of Wisconsin).

[251]*See* references cited in *supra* note 25.

[252]Joint Communique, para. 15.

[253]Canada Waters Act, Stats. Can. 1969-70, c. 52. The Act is briefly described in the IJC *Lower Lakes Report*, at 109.

[254]Canada Waters Act, section 5(2).

[255]*See, e.g.* the Navigable Waters Protection Act, R.S.C. 1952 c. 41; Canada Shipping Act, R.S.C. 1952, c. 29, as amended by 4-5 Eliz II, S.C. 1956, Vol. II c. 34, S.25; Fisheries Act, R.S.C. 1952, c. 119.

[256]Ontario Rev. Stat. c. 281 (1961).

[257]Joint Communique, para. 12.

[258]*See, especially,* Jordan, *supra* note 34, at 300-01, and, more generally, Lyle and Crain, "Development and Use of the Great Lakes: Policy and Institutional Needs," Presentation to the Great Lakes Panel of the National Council on Marine Resources and Engineering Development, Symposium at Ann Arbor, Mich., Oct. 29-30, 1968. *See also* comments in Heeney, (INCO article), *supra* note 34, at 6, and Ross, *supra* note 34, at 8. For a broad survey of relevant problems and experience, *see* A. V. Kneese and B. T. Bower, Managing Water Quality: Economics, Technology and Institutions (1968). Established by a treaty signed at Paris, April 18, 1951, effective July 23, 1952. 26 UNTS 140; 1 *Eur. Y.B.* 359.

[259]*See e.g.,* Lister, *Europe's Coal and Steel Community* (1960), and Mason, *The European Coal and Steel Community* (1955).

[260]*See, e.g.,* D.E. Lilienthal, *TVA: Democracy on the March* (20th Anniv. Ed. 1953); C.H. Pritchett, *The Tennessee Valley Authority: A Study in Public Administration* (1943). Cf. as an example of an early TVA effort in water pollution studies, Scott, *Studies of the Pollution of the Tennessee Valley River System* (1941).

[261]The Delaware River Basin commission is a federal-state agency, established by the Delaware River Basin Compact, 1961, between Delaware, New Jersey, New York, Pennsylvania and the United States of America, consented to by Congress by the Act of September 27, 1961 (72 Stat. 688). The text, together with Congressional conditions and reservations to consent, is set forth in *Documents on the Use and Control of the Waters of Interstate and International Streams, supra* note 15, at 95-127. The Commission reviews all projects that might have a substantial effect on the resources of the Delaware River Basin and, as part of this review, requires that any project affecting water quality must conform to applicable water quality standards. *See, generally,* the Commission's *Annual Reports;* Grad, "Federal State Compact: A New Experiment in Co-operative Federalism," 63 *Columb. L. Rev.* 825 (1963); Kneese and Bower, *Managing Water Quality*, at 274-81 (1963); and Hines, "Nor any Drop to Drink," *supra* 52 *Iowa L. Rev.* 432 at 454-6.

[262]These would involve not only issues of delegation of national and state or provincial powers to an international authority but the differing complexities of U.S. federal-state and Canadian federal-provincial relations. Cf. P. Hay, *Federalism and Supranational Organizations* (1966), ch. 6 ("Supranational Organizations and U.S. Constitutional Law").

[263]*See, e.g.,* Hines, "Nor Any Drop to Drink," *supra*, Part II: "Interstate Arrangements for Pollution Control," 52 *Iowa L. Rev.* 432 (1966), where he comments:
Conditions of water pollution ... frequently assume a configuration that bears little resemblance to the political geography of any of the states affected. Great acumen

378

is not required to realize that little success is likely to accrue to attempts to regulate pollution of interstate waters unless the control effort has a scope of planning and an enforcement authority roughly congruent with the dimensions of the problem. The vesting of regulatory power in some form of supra-state organization seems essential to effective handling of pollution situations, the causes and effects of which overflow state lines.

And *see also* Lyle and Craine, *supra* note 258, at 13.

[264]*See, generally*, J.C. Davies, *The Politics of Pollution* (1970), for an able survey of the political and administrative context of present U.S. efforts to deal with water pollution problems.

[265]*See*, the Commission's finding that the estimated cost for municipal and industrial treatment facilities sufficient to meet its proposed objectives as necessary to reverse pollution of the Lower Lakes is, in terms of 1968 dollars, $211 million for Canada and $1,373 million for the U.S. IJC *Lower Lakes Report*, at 138.

[266]At its Spring 1971 semiannual meeting, the IJC requested its various boards dealing with water pollution to initiate liaison with the International Air Pollution Advisory Board in order to ensure that control measures of one type of pollution would not nullify control measures of another.

[267]*See* the Comments by Chairman Rouse of the Great Lakes Basin Commission to the Council on Environmental Quality, on review of the Advisory Board's Lower Lakes Report, as quoted in the GLBC *Communicator*, Vol. 1, No. 9:
> Effective management of Great Lakes resources requires a comprehensive, coordinated joint effort in both operation and planning on a short- and long-range basis. This approach is not to be confused with the artificial stapling together of a number of independently arrived at, single-purpose plans and operations agreements. Our present problems are largely a result of this approach. Their solution surely does not lie in its continued application.

[268]*See, e.g.*, the suggestions in Jordan, *supra*, at 300-01.

[269]*Compare, e.g.*, the proposal for such "confrontation" procedures at the March 1971 meeting of the Organization for Economic Cooperation and Development's (OECD) Environmental Committee, OECD *Observer* 10 (No. 52, 1971), as discussed by Stein, *supra* note 8. Cf. the Canadian reaction to the recent U.S. "Canniken" underground nuclear test on Amchitka island, Alaska, which occasioned protests by the Canadian Prime Minister, Secretary of State for External Affairs, Minister of the Environment, and Ambassador to the U.S.; the adoption on October 15, 1971 by the Canadian House of Commons, with only one dissenting vote, of a resolution condemning the test; and mass demonstrations in Canada. *See, e.g., Washington Post*, Oct. 28, 1971, at 1, col. 1 at (continuation) A-4, col. 8, *Wall St. J.*, Oct. 28, 1971, at 1, col. 3; *N.Y. Times*, Nov. 3, 1971, at 29, col. 1.

[270]*See, generally*, for a discussion of competing interest groups, J.C. Davies, *The Politics of Pollution* (1970) esp. ch. 4. And *see, e.g.*, for some recent indications, Kenworthy, "Efforts to Place Limits on Environmental Agency," *N.Y. Times*, August 6, 1971, at 33, col. 5-8, and *Wall St. J.*, Sept. 24, 1971, at 1, col. 5 ("Backlash builds against environmental protection moves, with some apparent effect"), reporting, *inter alia*, that the Surgeon General's advice to return to phosphate detergents (*see supra* notes 190 and 191) followed pleas from industry. *See, more generally, N.Y. Times*, Nov. 3, 1971, at 1, col. 1 ("Senate approves Bill to Clean up Waterways by '85") reporting industry opposition and (in continuation, at 22, col. 3) that:
> In what was interpreted by some Democratic Senators as an Administration attempt to undermine support for the legislation, Russell E. Train, Chairman of the Council on Environmental Quality, circulated among Governors and some Senators an estimate that the cost of eliminating all pollutants from industrial and municipal sources would run to $94.5 billion.

379

As floor manager of the bill, Senator Muskie protested that Mr. Train's estimate was an attempt to 'frighten' the people and intimidate the Congress.

And further, Kenworthy, "White House Opens A Drive to Re-Draft Senate's Water Bill," *N.Y. Times*, Nov. 8, 1971, at 1, col. 4, reporting that "The White House has begun an intensive campaign among state governments to get support against the extremely tough water pollution control bill passed by the Senate ..."

[271]*See, e.g.,* IJC *Lower Lakes Report,* at 128-129:

Although available technology can remedy many of the pollution problems, solutions to many other problems cannot be prescribed at this time because the knowledge and understanding of the physical phenomena, chemical interactions and biological activities are woefully inadequate ...

Among the scientific problems of the environment needing the most urgent attention are those concerned with the nutrient requirements for algae growth and more refined determinations of whether and how micronutrients may limit growth; environmentally harmless substitutes for phosphorus in detergents; sediment-water interchange of polluting substances; movement of pesticides and heavy metals through the food chain and their effect on various life forms; more refined estimates of lake chemical budgets, including an assessment of the extent of man-made and natural sources; the impact of pollutants on particular fish populations; better understanding of circulation of lake waters and diffusion of pollutants; development of reliable remote reading or automatic recording instruments for monitoring chemical, biological and physical parameters in the lakes; effects of increased thermal inputs on the heat balance and the ecological balance of near-shore areas; and viral epidemicology.

There is need to find alternative means for reducing the pollution overflows from combined storm and sanitary sewage systems. Further studies are needed not only to develop water quality prediction models but also to incorporate into such models and other studies the sociological and economic aspects of pollution and its control. They would enable authorities to anticipate water pollution control needs and permit rational planning for pollution control.

[272]*See, e.g., id.* at 129, where the IJC notes:

Studies are also necessary to find solutions to legislative, legal and enforcement problems relating to water pollution. Indeed, the solution of some of these complex social problems may weel be as difficult and as time consuming as the solution of some of the scientific and technical problems.

[273]*Supra* note 167. *See, e.g.,* on the problem of Baltic Sea pollution, Sparring, *supra,* note 193, and Tonselius, "The Stagnant Sea," 12 *Environment* 2-11 (July-Aug. 1970); and on the problem of North Sea pollution, *e.g., The Christian Science Monitor,* 24 May 1971. And *see, e.g.,* the recent report that the Soviet leadership, in a decree by the Central Committee, has called for prompt measures to protect the environment of Lake Baikal, the world's largest fresh water lake. *N.Y. Times,* Sept. 25, 1971, at 4, col. 3-6.

Dartmouth Conference, 10

Declaration on the Human Environment, 61, 74-85
Critique of, 83-5
Debate in Preparatory Committee, 81-3
Preamble, 76-7
Rights and responsibilities of states, 75, 78-81, 98
Role of, 85, 86, 101-3
UNGA, 1, 101
see also U.N. Conference on the Human Environment

Developing Countries, 12, 182, 188, 189, 202, 277
Attitudes toward Stockholm conference, 18-9, 50
Attitudes toward U.N., 5, 150
Global monitoring systems, 22
Interdependence of rich and poor countries, 5, 50-1
Need for better resource management, 5, 23
Need for trained personnel, 13, 73-4
Relocation of industries in, 49, 51, 66

Development and Environmental Protection, 5, 22-3, 48-9, 61, 77-8, 86, 146
Cost considerations, 4, 23-4, 49, 50, 66, 80, 199, 200, 203
Environmental considerations in development planning, 7, 64-5, 81-2
by IBRD, 24, 59, 201
by UNDP, 29, 59

Development Assistance Committee, 24

Economic Commission for Europe (U.N.), 257, 276, 279

As East-West forum, 6, 259-61
Prague Symposium, 204, 213, 261
River basin management, 260, 269-70
Studies on environment, 259, 260-1

Economic Implications of Environmental Programs, 6, 47-9, 65-6, 179-80, 183, 191, 194, 221-2
International trade implications, 6, 26, 55, 179-80, 182-3, 188

Ecuador, Santiago Declaration, 107, 113, 226

Energy Needs, 3, 54-5, 71-2, 278
Potential use of the sea, 123-5
Regional planning, 71

European Coal and Steel Community, 303

European Common Market, 260

European Communitites,
Council, 282
Court of Justice, 282
Development of environmental policies, 260, 282

European Nuclear Energy Agency, ocean dumping, 229

Falk, Richard, and international environmental authority, 216, 229

Fisheries,
Conservation zones, 107
Convention on Fisheries and Conservation of the Living Resources of the Sea, 223, 226
International law, 105, 226

383

Nuclear weapons, 67
Protection of wildlife, 57

Indochina, use of herbicides in, 67-8

Indonesia, archipelago claims, 107

Inter-American Tropical Tuna Commission, 214-5, 219

Intergovernmental Maritime Consultative Organization (IMCO), 7, 136-8, 237-52
Assembly, 247
Civil Liability for Oil Pollution Damage (Private Law Convention), 95, 136-8, 142-3, 195-6, 250
Art. 3, 137-8
Art. 7, 137
Compliance with conventions and recommendations, 240-1, 248-9
"Consultative" approach, 240-1, 245, 247
Cooperation with specialized agencies, 243-4
Council, 238, 277
accident prevention program, 238
Legal Sub-Committee, 239, 246-7
International Compensation Fund, resolution on, 118, 250
International Cooperation concerning Pollutants other than Oil, 119, 239
International Regulations for the Prevention of Collisions at Sea, 241
Intervention on the High Seas in Cases of Oil Pollution Damage (Public Law Convention), 94, 117-20, 180, 249

Annex 8, 118
Art. 3, 119
Art. 5, 119-20
Art. 6, 119-20
Marine pollution, conference on (1973), 26, 240, 263-4
Maritime Safety Committee, 245-6, 263
Sub-Committee on Marine Pollution, 245
Sub-Committee on Safety at Sea, 247
Ocean monitoring, 146
Prevention of Pollution of the Sea by Oil, convention on, 237
amendments, 118, 238
lack of effectiveness, 118, 141, 186, 200, 239, 248-9
Relations with other organizations, 238, 240, 242-4, 246
Reparation for pollution damage, 120, 249-50
Secretariat, 247

Intergovernmental Oceanographic Commission, 7, 205
Pollution monitoring, 129, 146
Program for oceanic research, 204-5

Integrated Global Ocean Stations System, 129

INTELSAT, 31

International Atomic Energy Agency (IAEA), 246, 275
Contingency planning for nuclear accidents, 251, 281
Effectiveness of, 18
Monitoring of radioactive materials, 7, 17, 198
Staff, 13
Standard-setting, 188, 200
Training of inspectors, 264

385

Bonn agreement on, 108, 226, 256, 277
draft convention on, 198
Oil pollution, 3, 5, 39, 52, 53, 142, 186
NATO convention on, 39, 52, 98, 115
Other pollutants, 119, 239
Radioactive wastes, 52, 98, 115, 142, 191, 198, 229
see also Intergovernmental Maritime Consultative Organization

Marshall Islands, compensation for U.S. H-bomb tests, 132-33

Mekong River Basin, 262, 280

Mero, John, mining of the sea, 122

Michigan Environmental Protection Act, 146

Military Expenditures, diversion of resources, 47, 67, 86

Moynihan, Daniel, and NATO concern for environment, 263

Multinational Enterprises, problems of liability, 144-5

National Petroleum Council, and continental shelf, 112

Netherlands, Rhine pollution, 265-6, 281

North Atlantic Treaty Organization (NATO),
Agreement on oil spills, 39, 52, 98, 115
Catalytic function, 279
Committee on Challenges to Mod-

ern Society (CCMS), 259, 262-3
Studies on environment, 259-60, 264

North Seas, 227
Bonn agreement on oil pollution, 108, 226, 256, 277
Conservation of resources, 256
Continental shelf case, 112, 118

Nuclear Energy, 71
Convention on Third Party Liability, 71, 134, 135
Art. 9, 142
see also Radioactive Materials

Nuclear Ships,
Convention on Liability of Operators, 135-6, 142
Art. 3, 136

Nuclear Weapons,
Proliferation of, 67
Test Ban Treaty, 53, 105, 107, 191
Testing of, 132-3, 142

Ocean Data Acquisition Systems, 128

Ocean Dumping, *see under* Marine Pollution

Organization for Economic Co-operation and Development, 257
Economic impact of environmental programs, 6, 259, 262
Environmental Committee, 262
Planning and environmental programs, 280
Radioactive wastes, 229

Organization for European Economic Cooperation, 135

388

Use of force, 99-100

Serwer, Daniel,
Control of marine pollution, 227, 229
Information and decision making, 219

Sharp, Mitchell, U.S.-Canadian cooperation, 294, 297, 315

Spain, 132

Specialized Agencies (U.N.), 17, 78, 169, 177
Attitudes of developed and developing countries, 6, 19
Coordination of activities, 19, 29, 65, 175, 273
Environmental programs, 7, 19, 42, 172, 243
Opposition to new environmental agency, 6-8, 27
Relations with national bureaucracies, 7-8, 18-9, 174
Relations with regional organizations, 258, 279
Strengths and weaknesses of, 6, 18-9, 175
see also individual agencies

Stockholm Conference,
see U.N. Conference on the Human Environment

Sweden,
Declaration on Human Environment, 82
Initiative for Stockholm conference, 1

Technology, *see* Science and Technology

Territorial Sea and Contiguous Zones, 241
Canadian claims, 113, 115-6
Creeping jurisdiction, 115-6
Definition of, 109-10
Geneva Convention on, 109, 110
Art. 24, 110
negotiation of, 223
Innocent passage, 109
U.S. claims under Water Quality Act, 110
Zones of special jurisdiction, 107, 110-1

Torrey Canyon Disaster, 122, 126, 136, 238, 239
British claims, 109
IMCO convention, 143
Self-help, 117

Trail Smelter Case, 64, 95-6, 130, 320
International Joint Commission, 307-8, 322, 324
Liability under international law, 130, 131-2, 143, 195
Special regime, 96, 132, 282, 308

Train, Russell, U.S.-Canadian cooperation, 294, 315

Union of Soviet Socialist Republics, 10, 263-4, 269
Danube Commission, 268, 269
Declaration on Human Environment, 80
Innocent passage, 109
Military expenditures, 68
Population growth, 71
Preference for national action on environmental problems, 115

Union Oil Company, and oil spills, 109, 111

391

United Kingdom,
Declaration on Human Environment, 80, 82
North Sea pollution, 256
Torrey Canyon claims, 108-9, 136

United Nations,
African states in, 224
Charter:
Art. 19, 39
Art. 51, 100
Art. 71, 227
Chapt. VIII, 255
peacekeeping, 38-9
use of force, 99-100
Committees:
Administrative Committee on Coordination, 29, 275
Advisory Committee on Science and Technology, 57
Housing, Building and Planning, 55
Natural Resources, 52
Outer Space, 134
Seabeds, 218
Environmental activities, 5-8, 17, 27, 31, 35, 171-2, 209-10, 217-8, 222, 228
Environmental Unit (proposed):
financing of, 12, 20-5, 29, 49
functions, 9, 10, 12-3, 29, 171
relations with other U.N. bodies, 14-5, 20, 29
relations with proposed international research institute, 15-7
staffing, 7, 13, 29-30
Economic and Social Council (ECOSOC), 14-5, 29, 58, 115, 276
General Assembly:
declarations adopted by, 76, 79, 98, 101, 129, 134, 204
formulation of resolutions, 229

392

international law-making capacity, 102-3
proposed environmental committee, 15, 29
Stockholm conference, 1, 15, 16, 20, 21, 48, 101, 218
Peacekeeping, 38-9
Registration of multinational public enterprises, 145
Registration of space satellites, 198
Second Development Decade, 49, 61, 204
Secretary General, 2, 5, 6, 7, 29, 44, 68, 215
see also Regional Economic Commissions; Specialized Agencies

United Nations Conference on the Human Environment,
"Action" proposals, 1, 40, 294-5
Agenda, 2, 61-2, 68-72, 98, 200, 256
Attitude of developing countries, 48-9, 50, 80-2
Declaration on Human Environment, *see that title*
General Assembly and, 1, 15, 16, 20, 21, 48, 101, 218
Participation in conference, 228-9
Participation in preparatory work, 8, 10, 12, 40, 48-9
Preparatory Committee, 14, 218
debate on Declaration, 74, 82-3
decisions on terminology, 206-7
Intergovernmental Working Group on Declaration, 75-80, 98
Intergovernmental Working Group on Marine Pollution, 25-6, 186, 257
Intergovernmental Working Group on Monitoring, 18, 257
Secretary General, 14, 48, 81, 218

393

OTHER TITLES PUBLISHED
BY
OCEANA PUBLICATIONS INC. / A. W. SIJTHOFF
FOR
THE AMERICAN SOCIETY OF INTERNATIONAL LAW

RUBIN, SEYMOUR J., Ed. *Foreign Development Lending: Legal Aspects.* 379-00129-2 352 pp. 1971 $18.20/B

Papers and proceedings of the conference of legal advisers of national and international institutions on legal problems of foreign lending and assistance.

SCHWEBEL, STEPHEN M., Ed. *The Effectiveness of International Decisions.* 379-00462-3 538 pp. 1971 $19.50/B

The papers and proceedings of a conference of official legal advisers on the problem of how decisions of international organizations may be rendered more effective.

LEIVE, DAVID M. *International Telecommunications and International Law: The Regulation of the Radio Spectrum.* 379-00458-5 386 pp. 1970 LC# 74-114161 $16.50/B

The first detailed examination of an increasingly significant but hitherto neglected subject.

MERILLAT, H. C. L., Ed. *Legal Advisers and International Organizations.* 379-00294-9 142 pp. 1966 LC# 66-20029 $4.00/B

A discussion of problems which arise in the practice of legal offices of international organizations.

MERILLAT, H. C. L., Ed. *Legal Advisers and Foreign Affairs.* 379-00223-X 176 pp. 1964 LC# 64-19355 $4.25/B

The actual and potential roles and functions of international legal advisers to governments.

TITLES PUBLISHED
BY
OCEANA PUBLICATIONS INC./A. W. SIJTHOFF
FOR
CARNEGIE ENDOWMENT
FOR INTERNATIONAL PEACE

CARNEGIE CLASSICS OF INTERNATIONAL LAW 379-20001-5
22 vols. (temporarily out-of-print)

The most important treatises on international law from the 15th to the 20th century. Includes works by AYALA, BELLI, BYNKER–SHOEK, GENTILI, GROTIUS, LEGNANO, PUFENDORF, RACHEL, SUÁREZ, TEXTOR, VATTEL, VICTORIA, WHEATON, WOLFF and ZOUCHE.

HUDSON, MANLEY *International Legislation* 379-20110-0 9 vols. (approx.) 750–800 pp. per vol. $50.00/X per vol.—the set—$400.50

A collection of the texts of multipartite international instruments of general interest. Begins with the Covenant of the League of Nations.

HUDSON, MANLEY, ed. *World Court Reports* 397-00428-3
379-00429-1 (Vol. 1); 379-00430-5 (Vol. 2); 379-00431-3 (Vol. 3); 379-00432-1 (Vol. 4) $50 per vol.—the set—$140.00

A collection of the judgments, orders and opinions of the Permanent Court of International Justice. Included are tables, lists and indices.

A REPERTOIRE OF LEAGUE OF NATIONS DOCUMENTS, 1919–1947 379-00371-6 500 pp. $50.00 Victor-Yves Ghebali, Ed.

Table of contents includes: Foreword; Introduction; The Classification System of League of Nations Documents; Survey of the Classification System. Part 1: Institutional Framework of the League; Part 2: The League as an Instrument for the Application of the Peace Treaties; Part 3: The League as an Instrument to Maintain International Peace and Security; Part 4: The League as an Instrument to Promote Functional Cooperation.